Being There

Being There

Culture and Formation in Two Theological Schools

JACKSON W. CARROLL
BARBARA G. WHEELER
DANIEL O. ALESHIRE
PENNY LONG MARLER

New York   Oxford
OXFORD UNIVERSITY PRESS
1997

Oxford University Press

Oxford   New York
Athens   Auckland   Bangkok   Bogota   Bombay   Buenos Aires
Calcutta   Cape Town   Dar es Salaam   Delhi   Florence   Hong Kong
Istanbul   Karachi   Kuala Lumpur   Madras   Madrid   Melbourne
Mexico City   Nairobi   Paris   Singapore   Taipei   Tokyo   Toronto   Warsaw

and associated companies in
Berlin   Ibadan

Copyright © 1997 by Oxford University Press, Inc.

Published by Oxford University Press, Inc.
198 Madison Avenue, New York, New York 10016

Oxford is a registered trademark of Oxford University Press

Library of Congress Cataloging-in-Publication Data
Being there : culture and formation in two theological schools /
Jackson W. Carroll . . . [et al.]
    p.   cm. — (Religion in America series)
ISBN 0-19-511493-0
1. Theological seminaries—United States—Case studies.
2. Theology—Study and teaching—United States—Case studies.
3. Educational sociology—United States—Case studies.
4. Education, Higher—United States—Case studies.   I. Carroll,
Jackson W.   II. Series: Religion in America series (Oxford
University Press)
BV4030.B45   1997
230'.071'173—dc21   96-39062

9 8 7 6 5 4 3 2 1

Printed in the United States of America
on acid-free paper

*We dedicate this book to the students, faculty members,
administrators, and staff of "Evangelical" and "Mainline"
Theological Seminaries. We have disguised your names,
but we do not wish to disguise our deep gratitude
for your gracious hospitality and openness to us and our research.*

Preface

This society is a strong believer in the importance and efficacy of education—even when expectations are often disappointed. It not only looks to its schools to provide knowledge and technical skills essential for contributing to an increasingly complex world but also expects that, somehow, our schools will play a critical role in forming the character of their students. The Greeks called this kind of education *paideia*. How both of these things happen, when they do, is often a mystery—like the proverbial "black box" through which things pass and are changed in the process. This book, as we explain in greater detail in the following chapters, is an effort to peer inside the black box to gain at least a partial answer as to what transpires in the educational process. In particular, it is an effort to understand the critical role of a school's culture in the formation of its students. We interpret this process in large measure by telling stories: stories of the interaction of faculty members, students, and administrators in two Protestant theological seminaries. One school stands in the stream of so-called mainline or liberal Protestantism, and the other reflects Protestantism's evangelical or conservative stream. By telling their stories and then stepping back to reflect on what we have observed and learned, we try to give insights into the ways in which a school not only imparts information but also shapes the beliefs, values, and perspectives of its students. In the course of doing so, given the two schools and their respective heritages, we also provide insight into some of the important dynamics of contemporary American religion—what some have referred to with metaphors such as "culture wars" (Hunter 1991) or "fault lines" (Wuthnow 1988). Although we believe (and argue) that these metaphors overstate the differences that we found in our two schools, our descriptions of their cultures illumine some of the issues and conflicts that currently are being played out in the broader context of American religious life.

This book is the result of almost eight years' collaboration on the part of the four authors. Several institutions have made our work possible. We are especially indebted to the Pew Charitable Trusts and the Spencer Foundation for generous grants in support of this research. We are grateful to Hartford Seminary, where Carroll and Marler worked when the project began; Auburn Theological Seminary (Wheeler); the Association of Theological Schools (Aleshire); Duke University Divinity School (Carroll); and Samford University (Marler).

Elliott Wright melded four different prose styles into what we hope reads like a single work. His editorial expertise as well as assistance in giving aliases to the characters in our story were invaluable. Early in our planning, consultations with Howard S. Becker (on recording and managing ethnographic data) and George Marsden, Grant Wacker, James Davison Hunter, and Garth Rosell (on issues of project design and selection of the schools to be studied) helped to shape our work in important ways. Sheryl Wiggins and Mary Jane Ross of Hartford Seminary's Center for Social and Religious Research, Karen Spierling of Auburn Theological Seminary, Susan Beckerdite of the Association of Theological Schools, and Karen Teague of Duke Divinity School provided significant logistical and clerical support, especially in transcribing hours of tapes of field observations and interviews. Anne Carroll proofread the entire manuscript draft and made many helpful editorial suggestions. Julie Kelsey read sections of the ethnography and offered perceptive comments on style and structure.

Those to whom we are most indebted for making the study possible will necessarily remain anonymous: the students, faculty members, administrators, staff, and governing boards of the two theological schools. For reasons that we explain in the Introduction, we have disguised the names of the two institutions and the individuals whose stories we recount. Yet without their courage in allowing us entrée and full access to the life of their institutions and the gracious hospitality they extended to us, we could not have undertaken the study. Unnamed (or at least disguised) though they are, we nevertheless have tried to show our respect and appreciation by dedicating this book to them. Although they may disagree with some of our interpretations, we have made every effort to repay their trust in us by presenting their stories as honestly and fairly as possible. We personally are indebted to them, and insofar as this book contributes to a fuller understanding of the role of culture in the formation of students, the larger audience of readers of this book also owes them applause for their willingness, as one of the school presidents was fond of putting it, to "go under the microscope."

Contents

Being There

Introduction

Campus buildings at Evangelical Theological Seminary look like those of many
college campuses built in the last fifty years. The library, chapel, cafeteria, administration, and classroom buildings—all of different architectural vintages—are
grouped together, but residence halls are widely separated by drives and lawns on
the school's spacious campus. The terrain is hilly enough that in bad weather
students often drive from their dormitories to the central cluster of buildings.
Though the campus is located in an affluent exburb, a perimeter of dozens of acres
of seminary-owned woodland creates the impression of a rural retreat. The main
building does display a prominent cross, but compared with the neo-Gothic campuses of mainline Protestant seminaries in the same metropolitan area, Evangelical
does not look very ecclesiastical at all.

Standard academic features dominate the interiors of buildings as well. Nothing
marks most of the public spaces as religious. Administrative offices are sparely
decorated, with almost no religious art or artifacts in evidence. Rooms in the older
classroom building are grimly functional: They have tile and plaster walls and
heavy metal chairs with imitation wood writing arms. The new academic center,
by sharp contrast, has upholstered swivel chairs, handsome wood paneling, and
indirect lighting, but like the other public areas, it could serve any kind of academic institution. The function of the chapel is clear from its pews and organ, but
many other features—the absence of a cross, a wall of clear glass, subtle stained
wood on the walls, a media booth at the back, and an elevated stage in front—
make it look more like a small performance hall.

The chapel and the administrative buildings, nestled on a shaded hill above a
rolling lawn, give first notice of Mainline Theological Seminary as the campus is
approached along a wide, tree-lined street. The front of the brick chapel rests on
the crest of the hill. Coming closer, the dominant feature of the structure is a
weathered sculpture, a stone figure suspended midway up the wall. This shaggy-
haired, bearded rendering of Jesus wears a loosely draped robe and sandals. Rain

and sun have darkened the areas running from the inner corners of the eyes down each cheek. His stone face seems to weep.

The main seminary driveway leads into a small parking lot surrounded by two-story brick buildings. The library, a courtyard, and the main classroom building are on one side. Across the way is Barlowe Hall, a dormitory for single and transient students. A large residence hall with small apartments fills a third area. The architecture has the look and feel of the late 1950s and early 1960s. And, indeed, although the school was founded in the nineteenth century, Mainline Seminary's present campus is a product of the post–World War II period, when the seminary moved to its current site in a metropolitan area in a different region of the nation from that of Evangelical Seminary.

Before we go inside these two schools for a closer look, we must indicate what this book is about and why it is important to understand what happens in schools like these.

Small liberal arts colleges, mega-universities, professional schools, and theological seminaries such as Evangelical and Mainline share certain features in addition to having campuses and physical facilities. We often take these common features for granted: for example, faculty members who (in most cases) must have earned doctorates; a curriculum of studies through which students must pass; and some form of degree to certify satisfactory completion of the requirements. Each also has administrative and governance structures, libraries, and other accoutrements associated with higher education. We recognize them all as schools despite their considerable differences in size and purpose.

At the same time, we surmise that the significant differences among schools are likely to result in variations in educational outcomes for the students. We infer this even about schools that, on the surface, have similar purposes, such as theological seminaries. What makes the difference when purposes are similar? Is it the structure of the curriculum? Is it the quality of the faculty? The quality of the students? The particular pedagogical approach of the faculty? Is it differences in library or other material resources? Just what affects the way students are formed by the educational process?

This book seeks to address these questions, especially the last one, using one type of educational institution, the theological seminary, as the focus of our investigation. Theological seminaries engage in the preparation of men and women for religious leadership, usually as priests, ministers, or rabbis. In exploring the question of formation we have chosen to look not at curricula, faculty quality, governance and administrative structures, student quality, or pedagogy but, instead, at what we believe is a broader but less visible influence on the formation of students: the impact of a school's culture in the educational process. While theological seminaries are only one subset of institutions of higher education, and a relatively small subset at that, we believe that what we can learn about the formative impact of their cultures will prove instructive to educators in other types of institutions and to persons interested in the role of culture in organizational life generally.

What do we mean when we speak of a seminary's culture? We address this question more fully in Chapter 12. There we define a seminary's culture as those shared symbolic forms—worldviews and beliefs, ritual practices, ceremonies, art and architecture, language, and patterns of everyday interaction—that give meaning and direction to the life of the schools and the people who participate in them. Put in dramaturgic terms, a school's culture is a kind of script that guides in powerful ways how the school's various actors—faculty members, administrators, staff, and students—play their roles. Even the school's location and architecture—the "set" that we briefly encountered in earlier paragraphs—contribute to the play. This cultural script, we propose, is a frequently overlooked ingredient in the educational process. It is true that a school's culture is not really a self-contained culture; it is more accurately a subculture of the broader social and, in the case of seminaries, religious world outside the school. Nonetheless, we will use the word "culture" with reference to a seminary's "world" because each of the schools that we examined does in fact seem to have its own unique cultural script that plays an important role in shaping the beliefs and practices of those involved in the life of the school.

Our interest in questions about the formative role of culture grew out of discussions in which we and others have engaged concerning improving or reforming theological education. Many of these discussions have focused on proposals for curriculum revision or pedagogical methods. For example, what should be the content and sequencing of the curriculum? Are experiential or traditional didactic teaching methods more effective? Rarely if at all has the role of culture in the educational process been suggested as a topic for exploration. While involved in many such discussions, two of us (Wheeler and Carroll) were also meeting with a group of colleagues interested in the study of congregations. One of these colleagues, James F. Hopewell, pioneered in the application of cultural analysis to congregations (Hopewell 1987). We were intrigued by Hopewell's work and began to wonder whether understanding the culture of a theological school might provide a new angle of vision on the educational process. In similar fashion, students of organizations generally were also noticing the difference that organizational culture makes in a variety of arenas, especially in the corporate world (e.g., Ouichi and Wilkins 1985). Does Japanese corporate culture, for example, differ from that in the United States? If so, with what results for worker satisfaction and the quality of the products? All of this sparked our interest and led us to speculate about what an analysis of the cultures of theological seminaries might teach us about the role that culture plays in education.

As a start, we began to look afresh at data we were then analyzing for a study of Doctor of Ministry degree programs[1] in American theological schools (Carroll and Wheeler 1987). While we had found considerable similarities in the programs, we had also noted several differences in the educational practices of the degree-granting institutions. To give but one example, schools aligned with evangelical or conservative Protestantism tended to use the lecture method more frequently and have more clearly spelled-out course requirements (such as the number of pages a student was expected to read for a particular course) than did mainline or liberal Protestant schools. The latter were more likely to use experiential pedagogical

methods and to be less exact in specifying course expectations. Are such differences accidental, or do they reflect differences in the cultures of the schools whose
programs we examined?

Full of questions about the role of culture in educational organizations, we decided to test them in a comparative study of theological schools. During the planning phase, we surveyed the literature on organizational culture, consulted with a
variety of theological educators and students of American religion, and designed
the larger project. We also recruited the schools to be studied. In the process, we
enlisted two colleagues (Aleshire and Marler) to join us in planning and carrying
out the research. Since our observations in the Doctor of Ministry study, supported
by extensive survey data, pointed to differences in the educational practices of
evangelical and mainline Protestant schools, we made the two types of schools a
primary basis for our comparative study of seminary cultures, in the belief that
doing so would maximize our comparative interests. If, as we suspected, the two
types of schools would exhibit distinctive cultures, this would facilitate our effort
to understand whether and how culture is an agent of educational change. Also,
the contrasts would methodologically help us to see cultural differences more easily. While comparing evangelical and mainline schools was not the primary purpose of our research, we have learned much from our experiences in the schools
about mainline and evangelical differences, as we note in a subsequent chapter. It
is important to say, however, that in no way do the two schools that we studied
represent the totality of those two broader religious traditions. Such a comparative
study would require a far larger and different research project than the one we
undertook.

Once we decided on a comparative study, we were faced with a decision about
how broadly to cast our net. We believed that the best way to study a school's
culture was through careful ethnographic description. Ethnographic fieldwork
takes time and intensive involvement in a setting. Furthermore, to provide answers
to our questions about the role of culture in the educational process, we needed to
follow a cohort of students through their educational experience—normally a
three-year process in theological education. This further constrained the extent of
what we could attempt. We decided to narrow our focus to two schools, one in
each of the two broad Protestant traditions. For reasons we will discuss later, we
have called them respectively "Evangelical Theological Seminary" and "Mainline
Theological Seminary". We chose the specific seminaries because we considered
each to be a strong, healthy institution. As we emphasized earlier, they are not
representative of all evangelical and mainline schools. They did, however, provide
us with distinct differences in cultural content, as we expected they would. Thus
they allowed us to see how the educational process is affected by differences in
the culture. They also allowed us to see important similarities in the educational
process in spite of differences in cultural content.

Ours is not the first study of a theological school's culture. Sherryl Kleinman
(1984) analyzed the culture of what she called Midwestern Theological Seminary,
a school of a mainline Protestant denomination. Her research, which we consider
in more detail in a subsequent chapter, focused on the way that the school's culture
had the paradoxical effect in certain ways of *deprofessionalizing* its students while

at the same time equipping them for a professional calling. Kleinman's study, however, focuses on only one institution and thus did not take a comparative perspective. Less ambitious in its scope, but also focusing on the culture of a single theological school, is Randall Balmer's (1989) look at Dallas Theological Seminary.[2] Journalistic descriptions of theological seminaries include Paul Hendrickson's (1983) account of his experiences as a Catholic seminarian, Ari Goldman's (1991) chronicle of his year at Harvard Divinity School, and Paul Wilkes's (1991) account in the *Atlantic Monthly* of his visits to a variety of theological schools. Two recent histories of single schools, George Marsden's (1987) history of Fuller Theological Seminary and Robert Handy's (1987) history of Union Theological Seminary in New York, also provide insight into the cultures of the institutions studied.

Methods

A description of how we undertook our study may be helpful. We divided the work among two teams. Aleshire and Marler, whose religious background has been within evangelical Protestantism, took on the task of studying the mainline school. Wheeler and Carroll, whose background is in mainline Protestantism, studied the evangelical school. We made these assignments on the assumption that we would approach our respective institutions as "foreign" territory in which observed differences from our own backgrounds would stand out in greater relief. We lived in student dormitories,[3] attended classes and chapel services, ate with students and faculty members in dining halls, hung out with students in their various leisure spots, attended faculty and occasional trustee meetings, and observed various ceremonial occasions. We also visited churches and other off-campus settings where students, faculty, and their families worshiped and, in some cases, worked. On a number of occasions, we were able to visit churches where graduates were serving as pastors or staff members.

Each researcher spent at least thirty days a year at her or his school for the three years of the study. Most of this was in small two- to three-day units of time, but on several occasions, we spent extended periods at the schools. On several occasions, we were joined by our spouses for the visits. The two researchers on each team tried to schedule most visits at different times so that we could maximize our observation of the school's life. During our final year of fieldwork, we conducted face-to-face focused interviews with students who had enrolled in the year that we began our research. We interviewed most members of the faculty and key administrators and, on several occasions, observed meetings of seminary trustees. Finally, we gathered a substantial file of the material culture of the two schools: student newspapers, faculty publications, memos and other notices that came in the mailboxes which we shared with students, (photocopied) postings from bulletin boards, and the schools' public documents and mailings to constituents. All of this material we recorded in field notes—pages and pages of them stored in computer files[4]—which we shared with each other and discussed at length in person and in memos over the course of our study. We put forth tentative hypotheses about what we were finding and came back to them again and again, discarding some and revising others.

When, in our fieldwork, friendships developed, we permitted this to happen. We tried, however, to follow an iron-clad rule about avoiding engaging in controversies as they arose in the schools. This was not always an easy discipline to follow. For example, students would ask us what we thought about issues of importance to them: theological issues, questions about the ordination of women and homosexuals, abortion, and so forth. Faculty members and administrators also often asked us about what we were finding out in our research and how we were interpreting what we saw. Our guiding principle was to turn the question back to them—ask for their opinions and interpretations. Their patience with our evasiveness was admirable!

The administration, faculty, and students were remarkably open to our study and placed no restrictions on what we could observe or with whom we could speak. They were forthcoming at every request for assistance. Knowing that asking an institution to be open in this way entails a degree of risk on the part of the schools, we promised, when we sought their permission to do the study, anonymity as part of the initial contract. This has meant not only disguising the real names of the schools and their administrators, faculty, and students but also omitting some specific information about the schools and their histories except where such information was absolutely essential to their stories.[5] While such caution would not be typical of many ethnographies, we felt it was necessary to preserve the schools' anonymity. Theological seminaries constitute such a small universe of schools that simply disguising their names while including historical and other similar identifying information would not, we believe, be sufficient.

Two caveats about our focus that had methodological implications should be noted. First, as we have said, the questions that drove our research were centered on the role of culture in the formation process. We were deeply interested in what we could learn that would help us and other educators in understanding these matters. Thus our account is more an applied ethnography than an effort to provide a total account of either school's culture. The latter would have required greater attention to additional aspects of faculty, administrator, and trustee cultures, as well as to governance patterns, fiscal matters, and the relation of the schools to outside constituencies. These are clearly important issues, but to have included them in any detail would have taken us considerably beyond our more specific concern with culture and formation; thus, where we have attended to these broader matters, we have done so with an eye to their contributions to issues of formation. Second, we chose not to use a "before and after" research design in order to measure changes in students from their entry to their graduation. Initially we did consider some form of quantitative survey instrument to provide a "before and after" measurement. We gathered some initial information through the Theological School Inventory and Profiles in Ministry, two standardized instruments designed for use with theological students. Neither proved especially helpful for our purposes. We decided to let the formative process unfold before us and to watch individuals and groups of students as they experienced and negotiated their institution's culture.

Theological Seminaries

For readers unfamiliar with theological education, a word of background may help
to place the two schools in perspective. The name "seminary" (from the Latin
seminarium, meaning "seed plot") was adopted by the Roman Catholic Church at
the Council of Trent (sixteenth century) as the designation for settings where candidates for the priesthood could be nourished and formed in their vocations apart
from distracting "worldly" influences. In the United States, "seminary" (or "theological seminary") is now one of several terms signifying institutions that provide
postbaccalaureate training for men and women for various ministries in churches
and synagogues. Other designations for such schools (hereafter, theological
schools) include "school of theology" and "divinity school," the latter generally
referring to schools that are integrally part of a university. Until the early nineteenth century, most Protestant clergy received a liberal arts education in colleges
such as Harvard, Yale, or Princeton, followed by an apprenticeship of six months
to a year during which one "read divinity" with an ordained clergyman. Concern
for the adequacy of such preparation led Massachusetts Congregationalists to
found Andover Theological Seminary in 1808. Other theological schools were established shortly thereafter, following the Andover example.

In 1993, the Association of Theological Schools (ATS), the accrediting body for
U.S. and Canadian theological education, listed 189 accredited institutions. Another thirty schools were candidates for accreditation or associate members. All
accredited, candidate, and associate schools are either Protestant or Catholic in
religious orientation.[6] Some theological schools are professional schools of a university, participating in the university's governance structures. Others are freestanding institutions with their own governance structures. Some schools, both
university and freestanding, are integrally related to particular denominations and
often receive a part of their financial support from the sponsoring church. Others,
including both university and freestanding schools, have no formal denominational
ties. While the majority of students in denominational schools typically come from
their sponsoring denomination, denominational schools, like non- or interdenominational schools, also draw students from a broad spectrum of religious traditions.

Most theological schools, regardless of denominational or religious affiliation,
are small when compared with other institutions of higher education. Enrollment
in the largest seminary in 1993 was 3,458 students, which translated to a full-time
equivalent enrollment of 2,569 students. The smallest accredited school enrolled
14 students. Overall, 23 schools had a total enrollment of 75 or less, and only 6
had more than 1,000 students. The majority of schools had total enrollments of
between 76 and 300 students.[7]

Women students made up just over 30 percent of the total enrollment in theological schools in 1993, almost triple the percentage in 1973, the first year that
gender statistics were reported and a time when significant numbers of women
began to enroll in theological seminaries. Blacks represented just over 8 percent
of the 1993 total, Hispanics just under 3 percent, and Asians almost 6 percent. Of
particular importance is the age of seminary students. A steady trend of recent

years has been toward older, second-career students. Age data are only recently available. In 1993, almost 30 percent of the men and 43 percent of the women enrolled were over forty years of age. Just over 20 percent of the men and less than 10 percent of the women were under thirty years of age. Many students, therefore, who are entering seminary are preparing for a second or even third career in some form of Christian ministry.

The basic degree offered by most theological schools is the Master of Divinity (M.Div.). Typically requiring three years to complete, the M.Div. is a postbaccalaureate degree designed to prepare a student for ordained ministry, and most denominations require the M.Div. or its equivalent for ordination. While they differ from school to school, requirements typically include study of the Scriptures (often in the original languages of Hebrew and Greek), church history, theology, ethics, and various courses in the ministerial arts—for example, preaching, worship leadership, and pastoral care and counseling. Seminaries also require that students engage in various forms of supervised field education in local congregations, hospital chaplaincy programs, or community social service organizations. Many schools also offer Master of Theological Studies programs for students who want foundational work in theological studies but are not interested in ordination. In addition, many offer a number of specialized Master of Arts programs in such areas as youth ministry, children's ministries, and pastoral counseling. A number of schools also offer the Doctor of Ministry degree, a professional doctorate. University-related schools and a few freestanding schools offer the Ph.D. degree.

We gain additional insight pertinent to our study when we classify theological schools by whether, if Protestant, they are primarily oriented to evangelical Protestantism or mainline Protestantism, or whether they are linked to the Roman Catholic Church.[8] We have summarized some of the differences in Table 1. Evangelical schools are, on average, considerably larger than their mainline and Roman Catholic counterparts. Seventy-two evangelical schools had an average total enrollment of 452 students (314 full-time equivalent), whereas 95 mainline schools averaged a total enrollment of 258 (200 full-time equivalent). The 53 Roman Catholic seminaries, in contrast, are smaller, averaging 142 students (107 full-time equivalent). Another way of considering the relative size of the types is to note that evangelical institutions constitute one-third of the total number of seminaries; they employ 39

Table 1. Selected Characteristics of Theological Seminaries by Primary Religious Orientation

Characteristic	Mainline Protestant	Evangelical Protestant	Roman Catholic
Number of schools	95	72	52
Average total enrollment	258	452	142
Average FTE enrollment	200	314	107
Average full-time faculty	13	15	11
% women faculty	21	8	18
% minority faculty	14	5	4

percent of the full-time faculty; and they enroll 50 percent of the total number of students. The number of full-time faculty members is small in each type of school, ranging from an average of fifteen in evangelical schools to eleven in Catholic. The table also shows the percentages of women and minority faculty members in each type of institution. While none of the three types is especially diverse, mainline Protestant schools have the largest percentage of women and minority faculty members; evangelical Protestant faculties are the least diverse.[9]

This overview, especially the comparisons between evangelical and mainline schools, helps to put in relief the two schools that we have studied. Consider their enrollment characteristics.

Mainline Seminary

The institution that we are calling "Mainline Theological Seminary" is a freestanding school related to a major Protestant denomination. In the year that we began our research, it had a total enrollment of nearly 400 students (350 full-time equivalent). The Master of Divinity program enrolled the largest percentage of students, just under 60 percent in 1989. The remaining students were spread among various other degree programs or were special students. Over 50 percent of Mainline's students were affiliated with its sponsoring denomination. Others were from approximately thirty denominations, mostly mainline Protestant.

In addition to denominational pluralism, Mainline Seminary reflects ethnic and gender diversity. The faculty profile was particularly diverse: Of twenty-four full-time faculty, nearly 30 percent were women, and just over 20 percent were African-American or Hispanic. Compared to the faculty, the student body was more homogeneous. Approximately 15 percent of the students were nonwhite (black, Hispanic, or Asian). Of nonwhite students, blacks were the largest group (13 percent of the total student body). Women students made up just under 50 percent of the total student body. Approximately 45 percent of the M.Div. students were women. The entering class of 1989 that we followed in our research was approximately 80 percent white, 15 percent black, and 3 percent Asian. Their average age (men and women combined) was thirty-eight years.

Evangelical Seminary

Evangelical Seminary, unlike Mainline, is not affiliated with a denomination. Students come from a total of fifty-eight denominations. While members of the Presbyterian Church (U.S.A.) constituted the largest denominational group (13 percent) in 1989, the largest group of students (almost 17 percent) either indicated that they were members of independent churches or did not declare a denominational affiliation. Members of the Assemblies of God and various Baptist denominations were also present in relatively significant numbers.

Like the average evangelical school, Evangelical Seminary has a larger enrollment than Mainline. Evangelical's total enrollment in 1989 was approximately 750 students (full-time equivalent students numbered over 400). Of the approximately thirty full-time faculty members, one was a woman, one was black, and two were

Hispanics. Just over 50 percent of Evangelical's students were enrolled in the Master of Divinity program in 1989. Another 23 percent were in the Master of Arts in Theological Studies, with the remainder spread over several other degree programs. Students were mostly white, and the majority (just over 70 percent) were male. Asians, especially Koreans, constituted a growing ethnic minority. There was a small number of black students. Just over one-third of the women students were enrolled in the M.Div. program, with the large majority in the various master's degree programs. We did not obtain age data for Evangelical students. Our impression, however, is that they are substantially younger than the average age of Mainline students (thirty-eight years old).

The differences and similarities between these two schools that are suggested in statistical profiles will become clearer in the stories and interpretations that we present the following chapters.

Plan of the Book

We have chosen to organize the book much as we carried out the research. That is, we begin by recounting what we observed and experienced during our fieldwork over the three years before we move more explicitly to interpreting and theorizing about what we saw.

Part I contains our ethnographic descriptions of the two schools, first Evangelical (Chapters 1 through 6) and then Mainline (Chapters 7 through 9). We have tried to keep these stories free of explicit interpretation. We intend for the reader to experience as much as possible what we experienced of life in each school and to get a sense of what it is like to engage in theological education at each school. To be sure, what we have chosen to report and the way that we have organized our narratives inevitably involve interpretation on our part, even as what we noticed while at the schools and what we chose to record in our field notes also involved acts of interpretation. Nonetheless, we have tried to be as faithful as possible to what we observed and experienced. Because there were two of us doing the observing in each school, we have been able to check our perceptions with each other.

It will become obvious to the reader that the structure of the two ethnographies differs considerably. We have chosen to report the Evangelical ethnography thematically, while we have told Mainline's story more or less chronologically, year by year. While this may seem odd, we did so because this is the way we experienced the two schools, and to a great extent we believe that it is also the way students experience them. Thus, we did not try to fit them into a common mold. As we note in a subsequent chapter, students at Evangelical are involved in multiple degree programs or different program tracks to a greater extent than is true at Mainline, where the large majority are enrolled in the Master of Divinity program. This means that Evangelical students tend not to experience a common curriculum sequence to the same extent that Mainline students do. Thus, organizing our stories according to key themes seemed more appropriate for Evangelical, while organizing the Mainline story sequentially by years was more faithful to the way that we and the students experienced Mainline's culture. Each school's ethnography was written by the research team for that school, but each was read and discussed at length by the other research team.

In Part II, we give our interpretation of the role of culture in educational formation. In Chapter 10, the first chapter in Part II, we describe the elements of educational culture that we believe are present in each school. This is essentially a look at the common structure of the two educational cultures that we perceive to be present in spite of their differences in cultural content. In Chapter 11 we analyze the process of education and formation that is characteristic of the two schools. Here, too, we believe that there are common processes at work in the ostensibly different cultures. In these two chapters, we draw both on the material presented in the ethnographic chapters (Part I) and on additional material from our field notes. We then attempt in Chapter 12 to situate our research in relation to larger bodies of theory in the social sciences: theories of culture, theories about how culture is produced and the institutions that produce culture, and theories of professional socialization. A final chapter explores some of the practical implications of our research and interpretations for higher education generally and theological education in particular.

The four authors participated variously in the writing. Carroll and Wheeler together wrote the ethnography of Evangelical Seminary; Aleshire and Marler wrote the story of Mainline Seminary. The Introduction and Chapter 12 were authored by Carroll; Wheeler was primary author for Chapters 10 and 11; and Aleshire and Wheeler, with assistance form Carroll, had primary responsibility for Chapter 13. All four of us, however, contributed to and engaged in extensive critiques of the chapters.

PART ONE

Two Theological Schools

EVANGELICAL
THEOLOGICAL
SEMINARY

ONE

The Message

My people are destroyed from a lack of knowledge.
—Hosea 4:6 (posted on a faculty member's bulletin board)

Jerome Allen

All of these guys, you know, they make you work but you're glad for it.
—Ron Biddle

Jerome Allen is working hard. The wide bald spot on his head shines with sweat and his round gold glasses slide down his nose. He paces emphatically across the front of the classroom, gesticulating with both arms in unison at the thirty students who have folded themselves into narrow chairs with writing arms and now sit necessarily still. His accent is heavily southern, but this is no drawl. Allen talks fast. "It's in my heart that you should learn this," he says. "Why? This approach is absolutely central for objective preaching. You have to get the sentence flow. Your grades are great. On the last paper, half of you got a 4 and the other half a 3.5—only one got a 3. I'll encourage you. Think of this as your first day on the job. Limit the time you spend on each assignment to four to five hours. I'll grade you on effort."

"Some of this work is very good. John—may I hand out copies of what you did?" John laughs and says, "I don't know." Allen asks him, "What do I owe you?" and the whole class laughs. "Here," he says, as he hands a student a stack of papers. "It's a beautiful example of the kind of work you can do the first day on the job, complete with blisters."

The students shift awkwardly in their tight chairs to pass the stack of papers to their neighbors. They look uncomfortable in the September heat. Most of them are young men with short hair in T-shirts and jeans or cutoffs. Their expressions are intent, sometimes troubled. They smile briefly when Allen makes side comments:

19

"I don't want to be gross here, but adverbs in Paul are like flies on meat. . . .
Let me illustrate what a proposition is: 'King Edward cigars are smelly and nasty,
but tasty.' "

This is an introductory course on New Testament interpretation. The method
Allen is teaching today, in the second week of the course, is "flow analysis," and
it is—among the several interpretive techniques that the syllabus promises to
cover—the one Allen thinks is most important. He later tells Barbara Wheeler
(BW): "Everything that I do with students is oriented to the same goal, to enable
them to trace the flow of thought in the Scripture, and finally to summarize a text
in one sentence. This does not teach students to become professors but has great
relevance for preaching from the Bible." Once that connection is made, Allen says,
the students share his enthusiasm for the study of the Bible.

This morning Allen's enthusiasm is unmistakable. "Flow analysis" involves dia-
gramming a passage according to a complex set of rules. To illustrate how it is
done, Allen has both distributed John's attempt and written the text on the wall
blackboard behind him. He dances back and forth between the board on which he
scribbles and draws lines and the front row of students at whom he talks with
great energy and earnestness. "Where's the verb in this passage? We don't want
to read it in, as in the NIV [New International Version]. Doing that would be
creative—you can't publish scholarship unless it's creative. But we're looking for
God's meaning." The writing on the board is mostly illegible. (When Allen uses
an overhead projector, he bumps it so often that the image jumps around.) "He is
very intense," a student tells Jackson Carroll (JC) in another class session.

The students' intensity—almost anxiety—is also evident. Their eyes follow Allen to the blackboard, now covered with arrows and phrases to emphasize the
"flow" of the passage; they glance down at their papers, notebooks, and open
Bibles. A few write notes, but none steadily. In their jeans and shorts the students
look very young, and their timid questions sound childlike. Allen, bald and dressed
in a long-sleeved shirt and tie, looks older than he probably is and talks like a
parent: "Whenever you have a problem, call. Because my heart is that you understand. I have empathy. . . . You are my prize possession. It tears me up if you do
not understand it." From all appearances, though, the students do not understand.
Their posture, in sharp contrast to Allen's jittery activity, is frozen.

Allen seems to sense the students' distress. With just a few minutes until the
end of the hour, he abandons the blackboard and puts down John's paper. His tone
becomes even more earnest: "You have to get these divisions so that you can
preach objectively. *God should be blessed by us.* The main point of all of this
passage is blessing, glory." Finally, some of the students seem to respond, to relax—they lean toward Allen. His voice becomes still more intense: "If I were
preaching this passage—and I am—I'd explore the themes of glory, of blessedness. Do you praise God? Why? Does it come from your heart, like cheering a
team, like enjoying a sunset? A-men!"

Jerome Allen is famous among ETS students, who hold a range of opinions about
him and consider him part of the "new crowd" on the faculty. Most view him as
a taskmaster. "He caused marriage breakdowns and marriage breakups," says one

woman student. Brenda Moore, a short pretty woman, very young and very much at the center of campus life, holds him partly responsible for the "near ulcer" she is getting. She quotes one of Allen's famous phrases: He thinks that seminary should be a "spiritual med school—that's tough." Still, she seems to realize that he pushes hard because he cares: "I love Dr. Allen for his zeal, for his love of the Lord."

The stories about Allen's high standards and punishing assignments also stress his kindness. A shy, reserved student tells of an incident that made her "feel very bad" for Allen. He unwittingly rescheduled an exam, at other students' request, that caused her to miss her senior banquet. A speaker at the banquet made jokes about a professor so heartless that one of his students could not attend her own senior banquet. When Allen heard about this, he spent an evening trying to reach the student by phone to apologize, even calling her parents in a distant state in an effort to obtain her phone number.

More common are comments that valorize the hard work that Allen demands. "Some students may complain that the course work is a little demanding at times," says Joe Gardner, who chose ETS over a denominational seminary he could have attended for free. "But I think they're just babies. . . . When I reflect on the times like the class I took with Dr. Allen on New Testament interpretation, boy, I hated it because it was so much work. But, man, it's awesome when you reflect on the things that you learned from that class, how that man just really—it's not like he's trying to brainwash you, but he's really trying to get you to be excited about digging into the Word of God. Because so many people get in there and you think it's dry rhetoric and it isn't. It's very alive and he brings it alive. I mean he makes you see it and it's wonderful. And the same with Dr. Bashford and Oliver. . . . All of these guys, you know, they make you work but you're glad for it."

Another student, David Nelson, who is seriously dyslexic, is "really impressed with Dr. Allen. One [reason] is, rather than getting up and telling you this is what it means, he tells you, these are the tools, and here's how you use them, which I think is far more valuable. And secondly, he is so excited about what he's teaching that it's contagious. So by the time he's through, you're just—you're working your buns off, and loving it, which is, I think, a great quality for a teacher to have."

David feels a special affinity for Allen because, like the teacher, he grew up believing in dispensationalism, a system that divides scripture into periods or "dispensations" and that finds little favor at ETS. The young man was determined to defend his dispensationalist views in Allen's class, but Allen "makes such a good argument for his position [now Allen argues against the dispensational view that the Lord will return before the last age, the millennium, begins] . . . that by the end of the course . . . I really radically changed my whole opinion on end times." Allen does not hide his dispensationalist past. On his bulletin board are cartoons that make insider jokes for those who have mastered the jargon of millenialism: a professor at his desk, with a basket on one side stacked high with papers and one on the other that is empty. The full basket is labeled "Not Yet," the empty one "Already."

Allen has detractors, too. Most of them are women. Allen believes that Scripture does not permit the ordination of women, a position that upsets intense, energetic

Louise Mason, who is planning to be a Presbyterian minister. In a southern accent like Allen's, her voice cracking with emotion, she accuses him and those who agree with him of "doing to us what they accuse [a neighboring liberal seminary] of doing on the other side. They say they bring no prior assumptions to Scripture. But I think they do." Then, she softens: "I do think that if Allen [and other faculty] really thought that Scripture was saying something different about women, they would change."

Janette Cameron, a leader among the first-year students, took action against Allen. While his position on ordination distresses her, her complaint was about the workload in his courses. She says she could handle the demand, learned a lot, and respected him despite his views on women's ordination. But when several students, including some men, broke down and cried, she complained to the dean, who reported the complaint to the teacher. Allen confronted her, asking why she had not spoken to him first. She told him that she found him intimidating. Janette's story, like most about Allen, ends well. When he confronted her, Janette says, he did it "nicely," and he changed the requirements for the course. Even Paula Fleming, perhaps the harshest critic of the school's treatment of women, pays Allen a compliment: "Some professors, like Allen, are clearly opposed to women in ministry, but they don't let it affect the evaluation of your work. I did my exegesis of those key verses in Timothy, and I came out in favor of women's leadership, and he gave me an A."

Paul Bashford

I think they're fountains of knowledge, you know, and they love the Lord so much.
—Mary Lynn

Paul Bashford is also one of the "new crowd" on the faculty. In fact, in both age and length of service, he is one of its most junior members. He may also be the most respected for the combination of intellect and piety. Students mention him more often than any other teacher. Sometimes he is paired with Allen, his colleague in the New Testament department: he is another one of the "guys" who Joe Gardner said make you glad for working so hard, though students more often emphasize the difficulty of the work he assigns—*"very"* hard, says one student, "very challenging," says another—than the amount. "I don't agree with him theologically all the way down the line," says Lloyd Day, an older student who plans to get a doctorate in education, "but as a teacher and communicator, and as someone who really stimulates, scratches your back, digs a prodding stick into your side, gets you to begin research and think and discover for yourself, I think he's an incredible educator."

Bashford is also friendly and accessible. Tim Rothman, who leads the Pentecostal group on campus, says that Bashford "really cares about students . . . he's just . . . , he's very passionate about what he teaches and very intelligent and he's just good at what he does." To Brenda Moore, Bashford and his wife are "like second parents." He was her college teacher and inspired her to go to seminary.

After hearing him preach his candidating sermon at the community church in Whitley, a town about ten miles from campus where he took the job of associate pastor (to Old Testament professor Charles Oliver), Brenda asks plaintively, her eyes wide in her doll-like face, "Where are the men like that who are our age?"

Bashford "is a dynamite preacher," says another student who goes to hear him at Whitley. Perhaps that is why the austere new fan-shaped chapel is uncharacteristically full for the service at 9:40 on a Friday morning. Bashford is slated to give the sermon. A solid block of faculty members and administrators, easily recognizable by their jackets, ties, dresses, and high heels, occupy their usual section, the block of pews farthest from the wide double doors on one side of the fan. Students stream into the other pews, most in jeans or slacks, with books and the winter coats that the cold March weather requires.

An announcement from the dean of the chapel at the end of the previous term made clear what kind of service students can expect on a Friday:

> With the beginning of the spring term, we will have some changes in the Chapel at Evangelical Theological Seminary. Our community Chapels will be held on Tuesday, Wednesday and Friday of each week. The format will center on a worship service with an emphasis on preaching and music. A few special guests, faculty members, and the Dean of the Chapel will conduct the services. This is an attempt to provide consistency and evenness in terms of our meeting together. Monday Open Chapels will continue to offer opportunity for presentation by special groups and concerns, including prayer and praise time.

"Consistency and evenness" seems to mean formality. A musician, dressed in a suit, goes to the pipe organ console. The dean of the chapel, a tall, thin, severe-looking older man with a soft, friendly voice, announces the number of a hymn. Those present take the thick red books from the racks on the back of each row of pews, find the page, stand as the music begins, and sing in slow, square rhythms:

My faith has found a resting place,
Not in device or creed;
I trust the Everliving One,
His wounds for me shall plead.
I need no other argument,
I need no other plea,
It is enough that Jesus died,
And that He died for me.

The dean, Andrew Watson, the recently retired pastor of a large urban evangelical church, gets up from his seat on the dais and goes to the lectern at the front of the platform. He wears a white shirt and a business suit, which set him apart from most of the informally dressed congregation. Bashford and three students, who are also notably dressed up, sit behind him. Watson says words of welcome and then, in the tone of a teacher, "Randy will now lead us in prayer." Randy, a student, goes to the lectern as Watson sits down. He bows his head and recites petitions that begin and sometimes end, "Father I pray." When he is finished, Watson takes his place. As he gets older, the chaplain says, students and faculty members seem to get younger and younger. He tells the story of walking through the halls with several trustees, in the course of which he saw Bashford and said, "Hi, Paul." One of the trustees said, "Andy, it is marvelous that you know the names of all these students." I had to tell him, says Watson, that "Paul" is one of the pillars of the faculty. The audience laughs. Bashford does look very young— he could easily be mistaken for a college student.

Watson resumes his teacher's voice: "Now Ruthie, you come and sing for us, and then Fred will read the Scripture and Dr. Bashford will preach." Ruthie, a heavy woman with carefully curled dark hair, is wearing a black dress with frilly edges. Standing, she picks up a microphone and punches a button on a small tape recorder. Lush orchestral music emerges and Ruthie sings in a low, breathy voice: "I wonder, would I know you now?" The object of the question is Jesus, the mood romantic. The line is repeated over and over.

When Ruthie finishes, Fred reads:

> But if it is preached that Christ has been raised from the dead, how can some of you say that there is no resurrection of the dead? If there is no resurrection of the dead, then not even Christ has been raised. And if Christ has not been raised, our preaching is useless and so is your faith. More than that, we are then found to be false witnesses about God, for we have testified about God that he raised Christ from the dead. But he did not raise him if in fact the dead are not raised. For if the dead are not raised, then Christ has not been raised either. And if Christ has not been raised, your faith is futile; you are still with your sins. Then those also who have fallen asleep in Christ are lost. If only for this life we have hope in Christ, we are to be pitied more than all men.
>
> —1 Corinthians 15:12–19 (NIV)

Fred sits. Bashford stands. He has an animated, nervous manner, holding his hands together but moving them constantly, rubbing one with the other. He blushes as he talks (what follows is a close paraphrase of his sermon):

> I usually don't introduce sermons with personal stories. But my heart beats faster when I talk about the Resurrection, because I am one of those persons who is obsessed with death. I have always been this way; when I was in college, I saw *Harold and Maude* innumerable times. If my wife were here she would tell you that I dream about death all the time, and that I wake up terribly upset. So I like to think that God rose for me. I like to think that so I can sleep at night. But I hope that you can hear the lie in that: The Resurrection was done not for my sake but for God's sake, and my whole happiness is in that. But enough of me.
>
> [He reads from Matthew 28:1–9 (NIV):] "After the Sabbath, at dawn on the first day of the week, Mary Magdalene and the other Mary went to look at the tomb. There was a violent earthquake, for an angel of the Lord came down from heaven and going to the tomb, rolled back the stone and sat on it. His appearance was like lightning, and his clothes were white as snow. The guards were so afraid of him that they shook and became like dead men. The angel said to the women, 'Do not be afraid, for I know that you are looking for Jesus, who was crucified. He is not here; he has risen, just as he said. Come and see the place where he lay. Then go quickly and tell his disciples. He has risen from the dead and is going ahead of you into Galilee. There you will see him. Now I have told you.' So the women hurried away from the tomb, afraid yet filled with joy, and ran to tell his disciples. Suddenly Jesus met them. 'Greetings,' he

said. They came to him, clasped his feet and worshiped him. Then Jesus said to them, 'Do not be afraid. Go and tell my brothers to go to Galilee; there they will see me.' "

Paul heard that story. What difference would it have made to him if there had been no Resurrection? It makes a great difference to those who preach the resurrected Christ. Remember my dream. I awoke in a terrible sweat only last week. I had died again. Now I know you're not supposed to be able to die in your dreams, but I do it all the time. Jesus rose for me; if he didn't, how would I be able to sleep at night? What would I have to say to Woody Allen, who says that the only issues are love and death?

This is what the Corinthians thought. They thought that Jesus may not have physically risen, but that we will go to heaven, or have a super-spiritual life now, or perhaps a thousand years' reign on Earth—that was the Resurrection for them. I can see from your faces that this is not getting to you at all. The light bulbs aren't going on. That's because this gospel way of thinking is so antithetical to the way we think.

The point is this. Denying the possibility of the resurrection would mean something horrendous to God. God would be a liar. If God is a liar, you can't get God's benefits. You can't get the goods of the Christian faith. You can't say that the women got it wrong at the tomb and still offer yourself anything. It robs the gospel of its power.

I could talk about this for forty-five minutes, but I only have time now to make one point: The Corinthians made a mistake about God. They offered people a second-rate gospel about a second-rate God. It's not enough for me when I wake up sweating to know that I have the prospect of a risen soul, a spiritual high, or a thousand years of Christ's reign like the Jehovah's Witnesses. *The issue is the right doctrine about God.* If we preach wrong, your faith is futile, and the end is the grave. You would be one of those deluded sectarians running around the world, believing that Jesus will save them when he can't—a Jesus that has been preached wrong is as dead and as judged as they are. People who believe that are suckers.

I hope that you will take the time to read the best-case scenario in the second half of this text: The women were right. Every misapplication of human possibility has at its root a misapprehension of the character of God. Dear preachers: Please remember that preaching precedes application. The only way is sound biblical preaching."

Bashford bows his head and ends his sermon with a prayer: "Father, thank you for raising Jesus from the dead. Apart from the empty tomb, I would be drowning in success, substances, and self-help. Help us, that we may not misrepresent you or give false hope."

With no further ceremony, the service ends. The people pick up their coats and file out.

Apostles of Criticism: Roy Parks and Reg O'Neil

A dinosaur, a dying breed . . . those of us who define ourselves theologically.

—Roy Parks

Like Bashford and Allen, Roy Parks and Reg O'Neil are spoken of together. Students who admire one usually like the other as well, and the two teachers draw similar kinds of criticism and resistance. The pairing is not surprising: Parks and O'Neil both teach theology and are tall, tweedy, and extremely articulate. They use their command of the language—memorable phrases, elegantly arranged—to say very similar things.

The message from Parks and O'Neil builds on the basic theme that students hear repeatedly from Allen and Bashford. Parks sums up his version of that core message: "I am trying to help [students] to think about themselves and their ministry, whatever it is, and the contemporary world in which we live, from a self-consciously biblical and God-centered position. It's not just a question of laying out doctrines. It's more a question of replicating in themselves the habits of thought that you find in the Scripture."

This kind of theology is endangered, Parks believes. He describes himself and others who "define themselves theologically" as "a dying breed" that makes up no more than 20 percent of evangelicalism. The rest, he tells BW, are gripped by "indeterminacy"; later, talking to JC, he elaborates. Most evangelicals are oriented to the "self movement": "health and wealth" groups and megachurches—extreme forms of "selfism" that cater to the needs of the individual in a kind of cafeteria fashion. He sees much of popular evangelicalism, as represented by many of ETS's own students and some of its faculty, as a milder version. Modernity, he believes, has caused this split between theology and selfism: Evangelicalism is deeply shaped, without realizing it, by the modern world and is in danger of cutting itself off from its roots. Culture is not neutral, as many evangelicals assume; except for a few bits, such as secular humanism, evangelicals uncritically accept culture as an ally and are unwittingly corrupted by it.

The two branches of evangelicalism, Parks thinks, are going to split. He is "pessimistic" about which is going to prevail in most institutions, including ETS. "Modernization," he says in clipped tones, "will do to evangelicalism what modernism couldn't. It will work from within."

At a session of an informal biblical-theological conversation group that Parks has organized (first on an invitational basis for about half the faculty and later, when word leaked out, for all faculty members), he expands on the differences among evangelicals and the origins of those differences. The gathering is held in a colleague's corner office—large but still too small for the fifteen faculty who have jammed in with lunch sacks and soda cans. Parks is delivering a paper titled "Why We Disagree" that represents, he says, a reply to a "rip-snorting attack on moi" in a recent volume on evangelical diversity. Evangelicalism is not unified, he argues: Not all evangelicals belong to NAE (National Association of Evangelicals); not all feel represented every time Carl Henry opens his mouth; not all even subscribe to a "mild generic Calvinism." Parks identifies three expressions, or centers, each with a ground on which to stand. Confessional Calvinism, its ground biblical and theological, was dominant from the end of World War I through the 1970s. Its expression was the "expository voice from the pulpit." From the 1970s to the present, a transconfessional evangelicalism resulted in growing boundaries and a thinning center. The successful evangelical in these terms is the one who has the capacity to embrace diversity. The third center is the charismatic. Here the experience of the Spirit is clearly central, and sometimes the confessional dimensions fall away, as is evident in the widespread acceptance of charismatic Christianity by Roman Catholic and ecumenical groups. The move from confession to transconfession "can be accounted for by the intrusion of modernity into the contemporary world." These categories, Parks continues, are a "taxonomy of our own internal tensions here at ETS. Some—some of us—are confessional, standing on biblical-theological ground and exposition in the pulpit. Then there are those that are transconfessional."

Michael Tucker, who is acting as chair, says, "The floor is now open to behead Roy," but there are no such violent responses. Neil Jertsen, the faculty's most explicitly charismatic member, offers no defense of his "center" but only a refinement of Parks's terms. He urges that "creedalism" and confessionalism be distinguished. Parks replies that there is more diversity—acceptable diversity—in the confessional center, including Baptists whom "we don't mind too much" ("Yes, we do," someone says, and everyone laughs) and, with a nod to Michael Tucker, Presbyterians "such as my friend the chair" who coexist with non-Presbyterians. (One student admirer has identified Parks as "profoundly" Calvinist, as an orthodox Presbyterian would be, but "violently" opposed to the claim that the Presbyterians' highly organized denominational government is a biblical mandate.)

Henry (Hank) Givens, who also teaches theology, signals his general agreement but argues that the history of successive "centers" is more complicated than Parks has made it: "There has always been a tension, built in from the beginning of evangelicalism, between those who emphasize confession and those whose emphasis is on cognitive refinement. . . .Then on top of that there has been the growth of the charismatic movement, which has been taken in." Perhaps, says Parks, but "we evangelicals don't recognize the evils of modern culture. We have posted a fierce guard, inerrancy [a doctrine, widely held at ETS, holding that Scripture in its original autographs contains no mistakes], outside the front door, but modernity has come in the back way."

Parks's dim views of the present state and future course of evangelicalism have attracted a passionately committed following among students of all theological stripes. Adherents take all of his courses, go to hear him speak off-campus, visit him in his office, and broadcast his views to others. These include students who would locate themselves in all three of his theological "centers," and a significant number of women. Parks believes that theologically minded faculty can legitimately differ on the matter of women's ordination; he favors it, but others in the "confessional" camp do not. That range of views is present among Parks's student fans: Mary Chang, a quiet but determined Asian-American who heads the campus advocacy group for women, who has taken all his courses but does not "agree with him about *everything*"; Pamela Willis, who does not have strong views on women's issues, for whom Parks is a mentor and "father figure"; and Sharon Madden, who believes women should play "traditional" roles in home and church.

Despite the general faculty agreement, or a lack of open disagreement, with Parks's opinions and the loyalty of his student followers, Parks is not a popular figure on campus. Many students simply do not know him because they have not studied with him. In recent years, foundation research grants and a special faculty chair have made it possible for him to teach fewer courses than other professors do. Some who know him find him distant ("He seems so shy anyway, interpersonally," says Amy Huchett, whose Pentecostal husband admires Parks). Others find him dour and grim. Fred Constan, an enthusiastic student whom one might expect to be a follower—he wears round glasses and tailored academic clothes like Parks's and loves theology of the Reformed sort—calls Parks "the apostle of criticism," much too "negative" for Constan's tastes. Mary Chang insists that Parks is "not proud and arrogant," apparently defending him against other students who think he is.

Parks's colleagues are generally wary of him. In the spirit of Parks's own mordant humor, they tease him constantly—but respectfully. "Lean, mean Roy Parks," a fellow faculty member says in front of him and a group of students. The group laughs; Parks nods and half smiles his approval. Parksian humor is well established. Notices he prepared for a theology forum say, "Join Drs. Andrew Nagel and Roy Parks. Stimulating intellectual activity will take place, but please come anyway. . . . If it gets really boring, Roy Parks will sing."

Out of his hearing, some comments have more of an edge. One administrator, who knows that he falls into Parks's "indeterminate" category, thinks that Parks has the opposite problem: ideas that are too "definite and non-negotiable." And a young, lonely colleague, who has worked closely with Parks and admires him greatly, nonetheless speaks sadly about him: "I am afraid that nothing warms Roy Parks's heart."

Like Roy Parks, O'Neil has chiseled features, but he is less lean and austere-looking. His face is fuller and his manner more affable. Students know him and generally like him better than Parks, though O'Neil is not a regular faculty member at ETS. He is flying in this semester—the first that BW and JC are on campus—to offer a course, and he is said to be in discussion with the administration about a regular faculty position. O'Neil's reputation from his writing and speaking in other settings seems to have preceded him. About seventy students are registered for his course on theology and culture. Twice that number attend some of the classes.

The course is given in marathon sessions: a three-hour lecture and discussion period one evening, followed by another of the same length the next morning. Because of the size, it is held in an auditorium across the hall from the library entrance, an aggressively plain room with yellow cement block walls and a floor sloping steeply down to a stage at the front. The students, in upholstered seats with paddle-shaped writing arms, sit in clusters of five or six friends together, or in couples that hold hands and talk intensely. Toward the back, more students sit singly, separated by empty seats that fill with latecomers.

O'Neil, looking debonair and sounding cheerful, begins the class with an apology: "It's not an ideal way to do a course. Some of you haven't a clue what I said last time—I hardly have myself." He directs his student assistant, Jeffrey Barber, the head of the student association, to return papers and distribute an article for overnight reading. The article, photocopied from the *New York Review of Books,* is a piece by Garry Wills about the antiabortion movement and Randall Terry, the head of Operation Rescue. Of Wills, O'Neil says, "He's a very perceptive commentator from a left-liberal perspective."

American evangelicalism is dangerously anti-intellectual, announces O'Neil, beginning his eleventh lecture, "Why Evangelicals Don't Think." He illustrates with a story: A southern Californian woman rushes in to ask a question of the members of a panel of which O'Neil was a member. She says, "I have a question so important that all of you must answer it." O'Neil says that he was worried that he was about to be asked about "the five points of something or other." But the woman asks, "How is your body?" O'Neil says that he replied: "In my tradition we don't discuss such things. How's your mind?"

Why don't evangelicals think? O'Neil blames past developments in American evangelicalism—especially revivals such as the Second Great Awakening—that resulted in "the meltdown of truth into feeling, theology into experience, Calvinism into Arminianism." He quotes revivalists: Moody ("My theology? I didn't know I had any"); Billy Sunday ("I know nothing more about theology than a jackrabbit does about Ping-Pong"); Charles Finney, who called theologians "triflers and blasphemers." Toward the back of the auditorium, loud enough for those nearby—but not O'Neil—to hear, a student twice says, "That's a cheap shot."

In addition to those developments, which his outline groups under "piety," O'Neil lists other reasons, including polarization, primitivism, populism, pluralism, pragmatism, and philistinism. Pluralism he finds "on the whole positive, but [it] can lead to nothingarianism, tolerance as the belief of those who don't believe anything, truth viewed as divisive." On pragmatism, the question " 'Will it work?' replaces 'Is it true?'; serving God is replaced with serving the self's spiritual needs." Out of all this a "junkie spirit" emerges, dependent on adspeak and teletruth ("I'm no Luddite—I enjoy television though I rarely watch it"). Evangelicalism "has not been out-thought, but simply was out of it when the thinking was done." Thus, evangelicals are "as moronic as anyone around. We have two-hundred years of history to reverse and plenty to repent of."

O'Neil asks for questions, calling on many students by their first names. As is often the case at ETS, almost all the questioners are men. The only woman who speaks identifies herself as an undergraduate from a nearby college. The questions are deferential and seem designed to show that the asker agrees with the speaker: "Is television unredeemable?" "How can we do evangelism without being anti-intellectual?" Only the student who muttered "cheap shot" challenges O'Neil, asking why a shift from Calvinism to Arminianism is a "meltdown of truth." O'Neil replies, "It's an historical, not a logical link." He declares a recess before the next lecture. As soon as general talking and stretching begins, the challenger fumes to a neighbor, "It *was* a cheap shot. You can't characterize the man [the revivalist Charles Finney] that way. Why doesn't he quote Luther? Luther said some ridiculous things." During the next lecture, the student does not take notes. Finally, as O'Neil continues to talk, the student get up, collects his belongings, and leaves the room.

The next morning the angry student is back, though still he takes no notes. O'Neil asks the students what they thought of the Wills article. There is a long pause. One suspects that students are trying to figure out the "right" answer—what O'Neil thinks. Finally a man speaks up in a tentative tone: "Wills seems unaware that not all evangelicals read the Bible ahistorically."

"But most do," O'Neil replies sharply. "Is the article fair or unfair to Francis

Schaeffer?" Schaeffer, an evangelical writer and head of a religious study center in Europe, was Randall Terry's intellectual mentor, and, as the students learned the night before, was O'Neil's mentor as well. The students clearly do not know what to say. O'Neil has made clear his approval of both Francis Schaeffer and the Wills article that criticizes him. After an even longer pause, a few tentative comments are offered that lean toward judging the article unfair. O'Neil pounces: "It's fairer to Francis Schaeffer than his evangelical critics have been." The students are trying hard to keep up with O'Neil and agree with him, but his techniques of criticizing the ground on which he just stood are making it difficult. "I am in intellectual gridlock," a student says finally. "Every time I try to think my way through these things, every way is wrong. How long did it take you?"

In the next and last class, some of the frustration turns to opposition. O'Neil is denouncing the triumph of emotion in American and evangelical life, as demonstrated into a statement made to him: "Doubtless you are right, but I feel differently." He says that he was "horrified" at the prevalence of "television impressionism, in which Christian discourse is sentimentalized and trivialized chatter," at a major mission conference dominated by "California missiologists." What about communicating with the uneducated, a student asks. He and Roy Parks, says O'Neil, do not believe in the "patronizing" approach of those who "think that the little Third World people need these videos and cannot understand anything else."

The student who asked the question is black, and he is persistent: "But your side, the Reg O'Neils and Roy Parks, seem afraid of media." O'Neil becomes testy. "I have produced documentaries; you can go . . . see them. How many have you produced? But they have limited value. Books change minds."

After the midsession break, O'Neil apologizes for his "grumpiness," but he continues his denouncement of evangelicals who are not "Reformed and Protestant and biblical." The students stand their ground.

> Student: Shouldn't something be done about the fact that words have become so . . . difficult to understand? Outsiders like me who come to seminary have to major in "isms" and "wisms."
>
> O'Neil: You are right about words but wrong about academics, and when you knock them you widen the gap. That will lead to a paraplegic church—all head and twitching limbs.
>
> Student: But academics have to stop making it more complex. It's only their pride and ego that make them do this.
>
> O'Neil: Things are simply going to get more complex. You must realize that. But you can't just plunk ETS orthodoxy on people. There are different versions. The great thing about biblical truth is that a baby can splash in it or an elephant can swim in it. But just because there is pride in the mixture doesn't mean that we haven't been thinking.

As the hour draws to a close, the questions become milder and more deferential. Jim Silver, a bearded student with a "GO NAVY" bumper sticker on his briefcase, thanks O'Neil for his lectures: "Now we can see why America is the way it is."

O'Neil pulls things together with a final prayer: "At the end of the day, our opinions do not matter. All that matters is your truth." The students applaud; the course is over.

TWO

Variations

I notice that most of the faculty is sitting on either side of the room, but only a few of you are in the middle.

—President Vincent at the start of a faculty meeting

The faculty already have well-developed middles.

—Charles Oliver

We also have a developing left.

—Unidentified faculty member

Like a target with concentric circles, three ETS documents move outward from the center to the edge. The "bull's-eye" is the school's Statement of Faith, to which all faculty members, administrators, and students must give assent. Almost as inviolate is the mission statement, six articles that constitute the second circle and define the school's purposes. The third, outside circle is an extended commentary on the mission statement. President Howard Vincent tells JC that the commentary allows people to incorporate different ideas while not violating the basic principles of either of the first two documents. His remark follows a long, often heated discussion at a faculty meeting during which a committee asked for guidance on several proposed revisions to the commentary.

During the meeting Sharp Dunlap, an associate dean who chairs the revision committee, has listed several recommended editorial changes, including one to correct what he assumes is a mistake. The commentary reads, "We shall seek to glorify God and think our thoughts." Perhaps, Dunlap says, the intended wording was "we must think His thoughts." He adds that the error was in original text by the commentary's primary author, theologian Roy Parks. Mark Hornsby, who teaches Christian education, says that this was probably not an error: Parks really meant "my thoughts." Everyone laughs, and Neil Jertsen walks over and whispers to Parks, "There's a lot of 'selfism' in that statement, Roy"—a teasing reference to Parks's criticism of the "self movement" in evangelical theology.

As the joking about Parks's language subsides, Ronald Stoner, a professor of Christian social ethics, asks about the use of masculine pronouns for God and suggests that the document could be revised without using male-dominated language. Dunlap retorts that the document already seeks to avoid gender-exclusive language, but Stoner disagrees, pointing out that it is "loaded with masculine language for God." Many religious communities, he continues, are trying to avoid this.

Margaret Lobel, an adjunct professor, supports Stoner. She cites instances of individuals who have had bad experiences with abusive fathers, individuals for whom the use of "Father" language for God could be offensive. At this, Old Testament professor Charles Oliver objects strongly to any attempt to depersonalize God, even with a good motive. New Testament professor Michael Tucker observes that if bad experiences with fathers constitute a reason for not calling God "Father," then other metaphors for God—such as "King" or "Shepherd"—may also become tainted by sin. To avoid titles for God, including masculine ones, would be to deny the incarnate nature of God, Tucker says.

Robert Harlan, professor of ministry and evangelism, asks Stoner for examples of how he would revise the statement. When Stoner has mentioned some specifics, Harlan speaks in favor of the revisions. Historically, he notes, ETS has drawn students from mainline churches and wants to continue that tradition; since inclusive language is a big issue in the mainline churches, the seminary ought to avoid, wherever possible, giving offense by using male pronouns for God.

Dunlap disagrees. Scripture uses male pronouns for God, he states. Inclusive language is necessary for human beings but not for God: "If the faculty wants to counsel the committee to change the language, the committee would probably reject the counsel."

Stoner then accuses Dunlap of a type of literalism if he means that masculine language is ascribed simply because Scripture uses it: "It is a small but important thing not to deny people an experience of God by using exclusive language." He is frequently out in broader church circles, he says, and when he returns to ETS, "our language seems harsh."

A theologian on the faculty attempts a middle position, noting the metaphorical nature of all theological language about God. Yet, he reminds his colleagues, others in the school's constituency would be offended by a change in the document's language. It is too big an issue to consider in the time available; however, he adds, "we need to reclaim positively various metaphors, including that of God as Father."

The ETS president says that the committee will take the language matter under advisement and, perhaps, the faculty may wish to hold further discussion on the issue, including the language of the mission statement itself. In response, Michael Tucker moves that the faculty determine that there is no need to consider the language of the mission statement about the Godhead. In support, Charles Oliver argues that the documents should not be "time-bound" and declares his opposition to a discussion of the gender of the Godhead: "My mind is made up on this. This issue is one that has been around for a long time. For me to discuss it would be a waste of time."

Although Tucker's motion carries eleven to four, with Paul Bashford abstaining, more than a third of the faculty has left for classes by the time the vote comes. The meeting has run an hour overtime.

As the faculty disperses, one member confesses to JC, "You saw us at our worst." Another says, "I don't know what got into us. This was atypical. Sometimes we just can't do things without conflict."

Robert Harlan

We do a good job of teaching you to exegete Scripture here at ETS, but not so good a job at exegeting culture. As evangelicals . . . we see [culture] as the enemy. But in order to be the salt and light, we have to be in touch with that which needs it.

—Robert Harlan

Graduation exercises have ended, and the crowd is filing out of the hall. Both at the baccalaureate service the previous evening and at commencement today, women have played prominent roles. One gave the student testimony, another preached, and still another delivered the benediction at the baccalaureate. At commencement, a black woman graduate read Scripture. JC greets faculty member Robert Harlan and comments on the high visibility of women in the services. "We're learning!" Harlan replies with a smile.

Harlan is among the faculty members who not only advocate the use of inclusive language but also support the full inclusion of women in seminary life. His wife and daughter received their degrees from ETS the same year.

It is the opening class session of the spring term course on the use of media in Christian evangelism and teaching. Harlan, who is a professor of evangelism and ministry and also director of media education, reviews the course goals. "This is not the course that Jimmy Swaggart took when he was preparing to be a televangelist," he quips. It is not about televangelism at all but about understanding the use of media in evangelism and teaching. Harlan insists that in contemporary, visual society, people can no longer absorb information that is monological, as are traditional preaching and teaching. The course emphasis is both visual and oral. This combination, Harlan says, will be what he attempts to model in his teaching style. As the term proceeds, he explains, the students will produce and present the media projects that constitute the basic requirement of the course. They will also view a variety of media types, learn how media work, and become conversant in the "grammar of media." In addition, they will learn to operate equipment. And there is an affective goal: "I want you to develop excitement about media and their use in ministry. I want you to get the 'media bug.'"

As Harlan speaks, he sits on a stool in front of the class of fifteen students. A music stand is his lectern. The small classroom is designed for viewing media. Harlan, in his late forties, is bespectacled and has a salt-and-pepper beard. His dress, like the students', is casual—no tie, a cardigan, chino pants, and boating shoes.

The three-and-a-half-hour class—7 to 10:30 P.M.—is thirty minutes longer than most evening sessions. The extra time is needed, Harlan tells the students, for the media they will review. His example that night is the film *Parable,* which features a clown riding a donkey. This film, Harlan notes, was highly controversial when it was first shown at the New York World's Fair (in the Protestant pavilion) in the 1960s. "Why do you think it was controversial?" he asks after the screening. "What was your emotional response to the film? Why was it called *'Parable'?"*

Joyce Gremlick, an older woman whose daughter-in-law is also in the class, responds: "It's clear to me that it has liberal theology as part of its background." Other students agree that it points to "Christ the liberator." "Is this bad?" Harlan asks. The students agree that it is not bad, but Lucas Beckley, one of two African-American students in the class, expresses concern that the Resurrection seems to be missing. Others, however, disagree and note that the other main characters—a blue-collar worker, a black, and a woman—"put on Christ" at the film's end. They also note that the protagonists are businessmen who seek to use women and control the others. Harlan remarks that the class assumes that the clown figure is Jesus. "Why this assumption?" he asks. He tells them that it was precisely because fundamentalists made this assumption that they got so angry when the film was first shown.

There is more discussion of the symbolic elements of *Parable.* Then Harlan asks the students to consider the film as a learning experience with two important characteristics: provoking thought rather than supplying full answers, and demonstrating the power of symbols to evoke and support a variety of interpretations.

How might the students use the film? Most say that they would use it with a youth group—one that could deal with the subtleties of the symbols. Harlan suggests that the film would be especially appropriate to show to fundamentalists.

In a later class meeting, Harlan uses more excerpts from secular media—"Far Side" cartoons, Garrison Keillor's story "Gospel Birds," and an Ian Scholes piece from National Public Radio. How, he asks, would the students preach a sermon to a secular radio audience? Students take turns presenting their "translations" of gospel concepts into contemporary forms. Joyce Gremlick tells a parable about a little boy who is adopted into a family "without having to wash his face." His bath, his education, and his grammar came after his acceptance. Students agree that the parable speaks to justification, and Harlan comments, "It sure does illustrate that big fat Calvinist word—sorry about that, Presbyterians." Helen Pericone reads a fairy tale about a prince under a spell who required people to apply for what were supposed to be gifts. Eventually, someone named Grace breaks the spell. "For you Calvinists," Helen adds, "she was irresistible." Others translate concepts about love, conversion, salvation, confession, Satan, and heaven. As the students discuss the assignment, they agree that the academic part of getting their concept straight took time, but the creative part took much more time. The class ends with Harlan noting several books on ways to present theological concepts in different forms.

Harlan was once a missionary in South Africa and is a self-described "liberal evangelical," a description that he is careful to distinguish from "evangelical liberal." One sympathetic faculty colleague calls Harlan a "progressive evangelical." For Harlan, being a liberal evangelical means seeing evangelism and social justice as complements rather than opposites. His liberal evangelicalism is reflected in his membership in the United Church of Christ, a progressive mainline denomination sparsely represented on the ETS faculty. "Students cannot understand how I can be a member of such a liberal denomination," he remarks. He dissociates himself from both liberals and conservatives, defining himself as centrist. Yet Harlan sees his UCC affiliation as quite important, and he is deeply concerned that the school not alienate those from mainstream denominations.

"Ministry should be holistic," he says. This goal influences his view of the "model" ETS graduate. Besides overcoming the division between evangelism and social justice, holistic ministry exhibits the union of the spiritual, the cognitive, and the practical. He worries that the school, with its deep roots in the Reformed tradition, leads students to take a too exclusively cognitive approach to ministry.

In a session of a required M.Div. course on spiritual formation and ministry, Harlan teaches a holistic approach and emphasizes the importance of self-knowledge. "Who we are is how we minister," he says. "We can hide behind a mask of professionalism or behind a clerical collar, or we can gain clarity about who we are: our strengths, our gifts, and our weaknesses. Our gifts define for us our place in the body of Christ." This leads to a lengthy discussion of the results of a questionnaire that students completed at the preceding class meeting. The questionnaire is supposed to help them identify their own spiritual gifts. Citing the highly cognitive approach to ministry typical of the school's emphasis, Harlan remarks that the gift of teaching is the most frequently chosen gift. "This is usually the big winner at ETS," he jokes, adding that if the class were a congregation, recruiting would be necessary, since some gifts would be missing.

Following a spirited conversation, during which various class members discuss their own gifts and those they have seen in others, Harlan asks, "How are some of you Presbyterians, Methodists, and UCCs—like me—dealing with some of the spookier gifts? Gifts like prophesy or tongues?" Students laugh, and one says that he has learned how imbalanced his church background has been in its neglect of many of the gifts for ministry. Harlan tells them that he would like a seminary organized around gifts, helping students to discover theirs and providing resources to develop them.

Asked to name significant persons during their seminary experience, many students mention Bob Harlan. They hold him in high regard as a good and approachable teacher. Lois Boucher, a campus leader who first pursued a career in banking, unabashedly calls Harlan's course on inductive Bible study "the best class I have had at ETS." Julia Best, a soft-spoken Southern Baptist who, with her husband, plans a career in missions, praises Harlan's warmth and caring and regular personal witness to his students. Tony Pierce, whose work schedule and a long commute severely limit his time on campus, especially likes Harlan's use of small groups in teaching. It provides one of Tony's few opportunities for sharing personally with fellow students. Tony calls Harlan "a wise man." Korean student Alice

Kim cites a Harlan course as helping her sort out and integrate what happened to her "in her Christian walk."

Such positive sentiments, however, are not unanimous. The leading campus conservative, Cary Draper, says he would hesitate to take Harlan's courses. Referring to the spiritual formation course, a woman student tells BW that it is "totally lame. There is nothing to it and nothing to say about it."

Harlan chairs an ETS department of church ministry and is credited by a colleague with having strengthened the reputation of that department both within and beyond the school. Harlan himself confirms the low reputation of the department when he took the helm and describes his efforts to raise members' self-esteem. But despite Harlan's contributions, the colleague notes, the department is still neither particularly strong nor well appreciated internally. The theologians and biblical scholars tend to look down on the department's members and to disregard their work. New books by church ministry professors get little attention. In his zeal to protect ETS's Reformed theological heritage, Roy Parks is particularly critical of Harlan, citing him and other supporters of inclusive language as advocates of the dreaded "self movement." Hank Givens contrasts Harlan and others in the ministry division, "who make use of the social sciences," with those on the biblical and theological side, who refer everything to Scripture. This contrast, he tells BW, represents a fairly deep split in the faculty. Not surprisingly, a colleague says, Harlan and several others in his department are much more appreciated outside the seminary than within it.

Michael Tucker

He may be thought narrow by the superficial, for his strict constructionism of the Bible; but only by the superficial. The broadest man is the man who walks in nearest accord with the mind of the Infinite.
—Attributed to Thomas Cary Johnson writing on Thomas E. Peck, 1895, and posted on a bulletin board at the door to Michael Tucker's office

Michael Tucker, who moved against reconsidering the gender-exclusive language of the school's mission statement in the faculty meeting, is a strict constructionist of the Bible. Nowhere is this more evident than in his opposition to the ordination of women, which, in contrast, most of the school's faculty members and administrators support. Tucker is a leader among a small group of faculty members whom one colleague describes as "hyper-Calvinists."

In a short paper prepared for use by both members of the congregation he pastors and his students at ETS, Tucker lays out several arguments for and against the ordination of women to the ministry of the Word. The paper's basis is Timothy 2:12 (RSV): "I permit no woman to teach or to have authority over men; she is to keep silent."

"This clear instruction from a didactic passage must be taken as the testimony of scripture on this topic until and unless it can be proven incompatible with any other didactic passage," he writes.

Tucker will not hear the argument that Paul did not really mean what he said: "Paul does indeed in this passage restrict women in some ways that he does not restrict men," and this restriction applies explicitly to the ministry of the Word. "We do concede," he adds, ". . . that if some allegedly ecclesiastical body exists which has some ordained office which involves neither ruling or teaching, we would have no objection to women filling that office." The New Testament, he also argues, does not teach the equality of all Christians, as supposed by supporters of women's ordination. Rather, it "does clearly teach the *unity* of all Christians," but unity is not the same as equality, and it is not inconsistent with relationships of authority and obedience, which Paul argues for in the text.

In a second paper, Tucker develops yet another biblical argument against women's ordination: Scripture is clear in opposing it. Even in instances where there is no plain directive in Scripture regarding a particular practice—for example, infant baptism or abortion—common sense enables clear inferences to be drawn. The case against abortion, he says, is entirely inferential: "The Bible forbids the taking of innocent human life; the tests in the Bible dealing with the unborn refer to them as people; therefore, abortion is immoral."

Tucker is associate professor of New Testament. He is also the full-time pastor of a conservative Presbyterian congregation in a neighboring state. While this dual responsibility means that his presence on campus is limited, he is greatly admired for putting into practice as a pastor what he talks about in classes. "A hundred years ago," Tucker fan Cary Draper says, "that was the norm." Delores Niblack, who wants to teach, describes Tucker as a brilliant scholar and a great preacher. Although he is so short he can hardly be seen over the pulpit, she tells JC, his sermons are really charismatic.

Tucker is a little more than five feet tall. He himself jokes about his size, posting a photograph of himself in swimming trunks with a reference to Charles Atlas on the bulletin board outside his office. He complements his small build with a trademark bow tie and large glasses. Though his size is not commanding, he attracts attention.

Professor Tucker is a didact, and he advocates an aggressive teaching ministry. He distributes to his students papers he has prepared for use in his congregation. These include such titles as "Some Thoughts on Paedobaptism" (infant baptism), "Why Weekly Communion?," and the one on women's ordination. In a class session on Presbyterian polity, Tucker encourages his students to promote thinking among church members. He tells them about "a little fellow" in his congregation who questioned the observance of Holy Communion two weeks in a row. Tucker says he tries to promote persuasion with his summaries. If Mrs. Smith wants dancing zebras in the worship service, he says, "Let's explore the biblical reasons that we might or might not want to do this." He admonishes careful thought.

Tucker is well-known among students as a master teacher and lecturer. The classes that he limits to a certain size fill up months in advance. In a session of his New Testament course, he lectures for a substantial portion of three hours to the approximately one hundred students who have gathered in the large, tiered lecture hall. Because it is mid-September and still warm, many students dress in shorts and T-shirts. Cole Silas wears a shirt with the printed question "What's so bad about being born again?" The topic of this evening's lecture, Tucker had warned JC earlier in the day, was to be "a boring discussion of the canon."

Like many faculty members at the school, Tucker lectures with the aid of an overhead projector, and he proves to be a master of the technique. His lecture, outlined in detail and replete with diagrams and other illustrations, appears on a screen at the front of the room. He often overlays his outline with blank transparencies on which he writes while lecturing, as if using a chalkboard. The entire presentation is practiced and polished. Students appear to listen intently, despite his characterization of the topic as "boring."

The church has erred, he tells the class, when it thought that it could confer canonical status on books of Scripture; canonicity can only be recognized, not conferred. He illustrates: "When a Ford Escort passes by, you point to it and say, 'Look at that Ford Escort.' You don't make it such but only recognize it to be an Escort. You can't make it a Studebaker." Furthermore, the canon cannot be guaranteed by historical or exegetical investigation. Canon is a gift of Christ, and those who submit to Christ's lordship recognize it. If external criteria for canon could be established, those criteria would be canon, not the books themselves. "When you get down to basic commitments, you simply accept them. You can't argue about them by external criteria. . . . This is a tension inherent in revealed religion." The canon is an authoritative guide for Christian faith and practice.

Later in the lecture, a student asks about the church's teachings on inspiration and inerrancy. When were they formulated? Tucker replies: "From the beginning. If the Bible comes from God's mouth, then God would not have inspired error. This wasn't disputed until much later, so the theology wasn't worked out until the Reformation." One does theology when a challenge arises. "Theology," he says, "is a counterpunch to a punch."

As he describes how the text of the New Testament was transcribed and handed down, often with scribal errors, Tucker calls the scribes "the nerds of the third century." There were also lectors who read while the scribes wrote, and this added to the possibility of errors: "What if the lector was from New Jersey?" he quipped. The King James Version of the Bible reflects many of these errors, though it "is a fine translation of a mediocre manuscript." When a student asks about the reliability of other translations, Tucker indicates preference for the Revised Standard Version (RSV). He says it reflects the highest standards of scholarship and is the most faithful to the original. He finds the New International Version (NIV), a favorite of many evangelicals, "easy to read for people who think *Time* magazine represents a high standard of English."

A 1990 issue of the school's alumni magazine contains Michael Tucker's poignant account of the death of his infant daughter, Elizabeth, from leukemia: He tells how he and his wife were sustained through this crisis by their faith and the ministries of friends and strangers.

Beth's illness was diagnosed at six weeks of age, shortly before her parents were to take her to meet her relatives. For the next eight weeks, the Tuckers lived at the hospital. Having accepted the seriousness of her condition, "each day seemed [to us] a gift," Tucker writes.

During that time, friends from their present church and from previous congregations helped in myriad ways with prayers, visits, and cards. These friends also looked after the Tuckers' house, fed the pets, and did the laundry. Total strangers who had heard of Beth's illness sent cards and told the Tuckers of their prayers for them. "As a result," Tucker writes, "we were able to spend the vast majority of Beth's 14 week life where we wanted to be more than anywhere else—with Beth."

Tucker reflects on what he and his wife learned in the process:

> We learned powerfully that crisis ministry does not begin when the crisis comes. The church's ministry to us in our crisis began many years earlier when faithful ministers, Sunday school teachers, professors, and Christian friends taught us the central truths of the faith.
>
> Had we not already believed deeply in the Resurrection and in God's goodness and sovereignty, our experience would have been almost entirely different, and none of the specific things done for us would have had the effect they did.
>
> No flower arrangement, no card, no casserole, no kind word can comfort the parent of a terminally ill child as can belief in the gospel. The gospel does not remove the pain, but it provides a glorious hope that makes the pain durable.

Reflecting further on the prayers that were offered by friends and strangers during their ordeal, Tucker concludes:

> We can never calculate the exact effect of such prayer, but we were aware throughout Beth's illness that God's grace is real. We were buoyed by a peace that genuinely was beyond our understanding. God was indeed a very present help in trouble. Undoubtedly this was the rich, sustaining power of God in answer to the many prayers of his people.

Some students, especially women, have trouble with Tucker's "hyper-Calvinism." Amanda Sunderbloom, who is transferring from ETS to another evangelical seminary, tells BW what she will and will not miss about ETS at the new school: "I won't find [close friends like] Marge and Juliette, but I won't find Tucker and Allen either." (Jerome Allen, like Tucker, opposes women's ordination.) Tucker's negative views on Pentecostalism trouble other students—for example, Bart Yardley, who is involved in an off-campus Christian fellowship: "Except for Dr. Tucker, I have not found any professors who are strongly anti-gifts [i.e., opposed to the Pentecostals' belief that the Holy Spirit continues to do signs and wonders and give spiritual gifts in the present day]."

Other students, however, are strong in their praise for Michael Tucker. Cary Draper, who would hesitate to take Bob Harlan's courses, has no such qualms about Tucker's. When BW asks who is at the top of his preferred faculty list, he replies, "Michael Tucker, no doubt," adding his comment about Tucker practicing in his pastorate what he teaches in his classes. Following the class on Presbyterian polity that BW attends, senior Kimberly Oliver is ebullient about Tucker's lecture. She declares that no one at Harvard can think like Tucker, and his thinking is wonderful even if one does not agree with him.

Joel Cotton

> His classes give me a warm glow.
>
> —Alice Kim

In a memorandum to the seminary community, President Vincent calls January 15, 1991, "a day of reckoning!" It is the day that the United States forces are to begin bombing Iraqi targets during the Gulf War. Vincent asks the seminary community to meet in the chapel at 8 A.M. for intercessory prayer: "The winds of a great catastrophe are blowing. Come prepared to pray with great intercession for the world's leaders, all military personnel, the community of nations, the community of believers, and for the peace of Jerusalem."

Among those offering prayers at the service is Joel Cotton, professor of mission evangelism and former missionary in Asia. Before he prays, Cotton announces that a recent graduate is in Saudi Arabia as a military chaplain and has baptized thirty-one soldiers since arriving there. Also, he tells the large crowd that has gathered about the medical technician son of a Chinese pastor in Chicago. The son reports that a religious revival is taking place among the troops in the Gulf area. Cotton gives thanks that God is using the horrors of war to spread the gospel. In the prayer that follows, he remembers those two soldiers and then, by name, prays for many ETS graduates in various mission stations in the Gulf and other Middle Eastern settings.

No one epitomizes ETS's commitment to world missions and evangelism more than Joel Cotton. "Whatever subject Cotton begins with, he always gets around to talking about missions," Dean of the Chapel Andrew Watson comments approvingly about his colleague. Another faculty member uses Cotton as the epitome of one way that evangelicals understand what it means to share the gospel: "[T]here are wide varieties of emphases, like Joel Cotton, who will make telephone calls for Billy Graham, hold streetcorner meetings, and pass out tracts and who will force his students into practical, hands-on, cold-turkey evangelism."

Cotton's passion for sharing the gospel has made him the leading advocate in a move to add an evangelism requirement to the school's Master of Divinity curriculum. The proposal is Cotton's idea, the dean tells BW, and there is much opposition to it, some on substantive grounds and, the dean adds, some more procedural. Is it wise to add yet another required course to a curriculum already heavy with requirements?

A hearing on the proposal is taking place before a committee on academic policy. The committee consists of faculty members, administrators, and student representatives and is chaired by Professor Hank Givens. The chairman uses a digital timer that beeps loudly to remind those speaking when their time is up.

The first person to "testify" in favor of the proposal is Cotton. This, he says, is "one of the most important decisions that ETS has before it." While students cannot be completely trained, he continues, there must be a core to their training, and evangelism should be part of that core. "Our Lord said, 'I shall make you fishers of people *[sic].*'" Cotton adds that the school professes to be an evangelical seminary but is one of only two schools in that category that lacks an evangelism requirement. He concludes with a story about a recent graduate who found that he did not know how to lead a person to Christ and called on Cotton for assistance.

Davis Saddler, whose field is New Testament, responds that leading people to Christ—what he would call "personal evangelism"—is only part of the process. Where does a "long process view of evangelism" fit in?

Cotton replies that in his view, evangelism is "95 percent discipleship." In any course on evangelism, personal evangelism, the leading of people to God, should only be the first half; discipleship (teaching the disciplines of the Christian life) should be the second half.

Head librarian Alfonso Bates recalls that Billy Graham, on a visit to the campus, commented that all seminary courses must be oriented to fulfilling the Great Commission—Jesus' command to his disciples to "go . . . and make disciples of all nations." (Matthew 28:19). "Given the diversity of students and their needs and backgrounds," asks Bates, "why should we require instruction in a particular approach?"

Cotton replies that the majority of students these days come from secular backgrounds and that leading persons to Christ is not part of their experience or know-how.

The discussion continues for some time, and eventually Cotton excuses himself to meet a class.

Several students point out that not all courses at the school are oriented toward evangelism. Lois Boucher, who is now working as an admissions representative, says that to prospective students "the missions and evangelism offerings look good; but when they get there, their electives [such as courses in evangelism] often get usurped by other things. Thus you can get out of here, as I did, without any kind of training in evangelism."

Agreeing with Lois, a student comments: "Some . . . object that evangelism is not academic, that we do not learn as much in those courses. They talk as if value is to be equated with academics. But with real people in hurting situations, Bauer and Kittel [two standard reference works on biblical interpretation] may not be what you need."

Bob Harlan speaks in favor of the requirement and suggests that a student be allowed to meet it by taking any one of five courses in evangelism: "Of course one is not sufficient, but I won't push my luck." He adds that in a few years the baby boomers will be entering their midlife crises. He wants to see "our students equipped to make a difference in their lives."

In the discussion that follows, Alfonso Bates worries about "requirement creep" at ETS.

Harlan says that one way to solve this problem would be to require one less course in biblical exegesis—four are currently required. "Of course, my friend Dr. Oliver [of the Department of Biblical Studies] would howl at that."

In a written statement, Roy Parks, who is not at the hearing, objects to the requirement on the grounds that only some are called to evangelism. Davis Saddler, who favors the requirement, disagrees: "We are all called."

Andrew Nagel, who, like Parks, teaches theology, also opposes the requirement and does so as an "Old School Presbyterian." (In earlier divisions within Presbyterianism, the Old School, among other things, opposed the devising of techniques to promote conversions.) Nagel says that as he hears the arguments for the requirements, the concern is that "students leave here without techniques for conversion." Although he hopes for the revival of the church, Nagel states, "I am not sure that I want to have revivalism as part of our curriculum. I am not convinced that I agree with the rationale for this proposal."

Hank Givens adjourns the meeting, saying that there will be a vote by a written ballot of this question at a later meeting. (JC and BW learn later that the faculty voted in favor of the evangelism requirement.)

For many students, Joel Cotton not only encourages involvement in missions but also models an attractive personal piety and warmth. Chuck Hearn says Cotton has "a good heart." Cotton's classes give Korean student Alice Kim "a warm glow" and challenge her in her Christian commitment. Julia Best says that Cotton, her faculty adviser, has taught her that a Christian must be open to God again and again for faith to be real. Her first encounter with Cotton was when she went to his office to have him sign her course cards. "I was only there ten minutes, but we stopped to have prayer eight different times. Every time I would mention the need to choose between this course and that, he would say, 'Well, let's pray about it.' It was weird but nice," she said. "I really appreciated his willingness to open himself to God."

In a talk to prospective students, a recent graduate and now an admissions counselor, Arnold Dillon, describes his first encounter with Cotton. As Arnold drove into the parking lot, Cotton was there with a student. Suddenly both dropped to their knees as if looking for a lost contact lens. Coming closer, Arnold realized they were praying together. ETS, he says, is a community where you can both study and pray together.

Samuel Carlson

> If I could change this place, I would certainly like to see a greater sense that the faculty and administration were on the same team.
>
> —Jeff Gray

The morning orientation session in a lecture hall in Nance Library is called "All You Need to Know." Presiding is Samuel Carlson, known as "Sam"—even to students who never call other administrators or faculty members by their first names. Like other administrators present, he is neatly dressed in a coat and tie—this in marked contrast to the gathered students. Some women are dressed in skirts, and some men in polo or sports shirts and slacks; but many—men and women alike—wear T-shirts and jeans or shorts. One student has on what appears to be bright yellow swim trunks, a T-shirt, and sandals.

Sam Carlson is in charge of enrollment and institutional advancement. It is his office that has been responsible for bringing this entering class to campus, and it is now his responsibility to get the new students oriented and on their way. His manner is humorous and smooth: "Tonight we will end the way things usually do around here: with an ice cream social. We eat more ice cream here per capita than anywhere else in the world. The returning students can tell you all the hot spots—I mean cold spots." He then introduces the dean of the seminary, Morton Diersen, who is also the academic vice president.

The dean produces an umbrella on which is printed the logo "Lausanne II—Manila," a reference to a recent conference on world evangelism held in the Philippines. This umbrella, he says, is a symbol of several things: of rain, of the need for protection that students will experience sometimes at ETS, of the importance of sharing something with others on a walk across the campus, and of ETS's commitment to the world beyond "life on this hill." "You will be tempted, as you spend three to five to eight years here, to forget that world, but you should not. Even here, you have to relate, to let others into your life."

Diersen then reads and comments on the school's policy on harassment, including sexual harassment, and the policy that spells out the school's commitment to the full inclusion of women in all aspects of seminary life. He instructs everyone to practice respect and find joy in both policies.[1] "God," he reminds the entering students, "has created us [all] in God's image." This leads to further comments on the diversity of the school's constituency, the school's commitment to globalization, and the importance of contextualizing theological education: "Seminaries cannot be on a hill anymore."

Following some observations about the curriculum, he changes the subject:

> All your fear of the faculty is justified. They are unpredictable. That is why we make them do syllabuses, which are a kind of contract with you. Some are very entertaining, but watch it, they are making you work while they are entertaining you. With others, it feels heavy. But in either case, you'll work. We are known to be tough. As long as we don't become sadistic, we'll stay tough. You'll get formed, shaped, molded. It hurts. You'll thank God, though—at least three times a year.

The dean finishes, and Sam Carlson asks whether there are questions. There are none. "Good start!" the dean says, and Carlson adds: "It always amazes me that you can tell students how hard it's going to be, and they still salivate to get started. If you made that speech in November, when they are in the middle of it, they would hiss and boo."

Carlson then introduces several other administrators and student leaders who comment on various matters of academic and student life. The final speaker is the head of the campus police force, who warns students about speeding on campus—

a 20 m.p.h. limit is strictly enforced—and other campus traffic violations that result in fines. He concludes: "God bless you. We just know we are going to make money off of you!"

Carlson replies: "They got me. They got Mort [Diersen]. I was a little upset that they didn't get the skateboarder who had passed me. I said [to the officer], 'Let's pray,' but I got a ticket anyway."

Sam Carlson, tall, well-groomed, and in his early forties, is an ordained minister of a mainline Protestant denomination, the United Methodist Church. He is the youngest of the school's senior administrators. (The institutional advancement responsibilities were added to those of recruitment and admissions during this research.) Having graduated first from a nondenominational seminary, he has recently earned the Doctor of Ministry degree from a school of his own denomination. When JC congratulates him on receiving the degree, he jokingly responds: "Well, at least now I have a degree from an official United Methodist seminary." He has previously been kidded about not being a "bonafide Methodist."

Denominational affiliation is an issue at ETS. It is part of the heritage of the founders, who were deeply committed to the mainline churches. Now, however, according to Associate Dean Sharp Dunlap, denominations hold only limited interest for many students, for whom "becoming a Christian" has often taken place in a nondenominational church or parachurch organizations (e.g., Young Life, Navigators, or InterVarsity Christian Fellowship). Dunlap estimates that over 50 percent of current students list themselves as unaffiliated with any denomination, "and we get increasing numbers of charismatics. It is not the tradition of this school to be independent or charismatic. The faculty isn't that way." At an orientation session for students entering midyear, Greg Thomsen, the placement director, tells students that God has not only given them a name (in their baptism) but has also given them a special place where they become what they are supposed to be. Noting the high number of unaffiliated students, he admonishes: "If you are not affiliated, we want you to explore these denominations. This is an interdenominational or multidenominational seminary, not a nondenominational one. Set a course for yourself. Explore the denominations and church life."

Some students believe that the administration's concern for the full inclusion of women is a stratagem to court respect—and students—from mainline Protestant denominations and the larger theological community; others believe the administration is more talk than action when it comes to women. Older student Paula Fleming, who cochairs a group on biblical equality, told BW, "I don't interact with administration row [the hall where most administrative offices are located]. . . . I think we [women students] get lip support from the administration. It is for show. It's not that I think they say one thing and do another. But I don't think they are prepared really to back us up." This, however, is not the view of all women students. Chinese-American student Mary Harris, an Ivy League graduate with one year of law school, views the administration as "100 percent supportive of women's ordination, from the president and dean on down."

Sam Carlson, in particular, seems to be the member of the administration to whom women students are likely to turn when they have institutional concerns. Th.M. student Louise Mason, who is seeking ordination within the Presbyterian Church (U.S.A.), tells BW that she is deeply upset about a particular visiting instructor's attitude toward women. She says she is going to tell Sam that women probably should not be admitted to this program (which involves taking courses with this professor and several others opposed to women's ordination).

Walt Baer, an M.Div. student, is speaking to entering students as a representative of the student association. He tells them that the organization wants to be their advocate as well as an advocate to them on behalf of the administration:

> Often, when we complain—this is true in my own walk in life—we don't have the whole picture. Sometimes I have gotten bent out of shape, but then I talk to President Vincent or Sam Carlson and I've really been disarmed. President Vincent is in his office at seven or eight at night. Dean Diersen comes in on Saturday on his own time. Sam Carlson schedules himself into oblivion.

To this view of the school's administration as hard-working and dedicated can also be added images of rational organization and managerial efficiency. When JC stops by Morton Diersen's office, the dean points to the spreadsheet on his desk as an example of the school's "tight management controls." Administrators are concerned with mission statements; long-range planning; "shared governance" with trustees, administration, and faculty; new markets for students; the school's business plan; new revenue streams; computer models of "what if" financial analyses; and "the bottom line."

Faculty member Henry (Hank) Givens acknowledges the administration's dedication to "the management sciences." Since joining the faculty in the mid-1970s, Givens has watched the school evolve from what he calls a "family model" to a "university model." The founding president and the board of trustees ruled at a great distance. The faculty, he says, was very clearly in control of everything educational. A longtime trustee is more blunt: "Quite frankly, [the founding president] had not been a strong administrator. The faculty had been allowed to run the school as it pleased. The board wanted a president who would give strong leadership from the top."

President Vincent is similarly frank about the administrative conditions at the time of his arrival: "Chaotic." Governance structures and an institutional infrastructure were inadequate or nonexistent. Stacks of donor checks were put in the safe because the small staff had insufficient time to record and deposit them.

The institutional tightening and managerial efficiency now in place have been both appreciated and criticized. Hosea Metsger, who teaches pastoral counseling and psychology, says the administration has made ETS respond to a changing world; however, he wonders whether it will make any difference in the way the school functions, given the strong resistance from many faculty members. Even a harsh faculty critic of the administration acknowledges that the president is a "consummate fund-raiser," but he adds immediately, "The president has no vision: He would not know a vision if it walked into this room." The critics sees Vincent as most at home with master plans and budgets.

Senior student Brenda Moore articulates a similar worry over the administration's vision:

> What worries me most is where the administration is going in the future. I wonder what their vision is. It seems like they are starting so many programs and recruiting so many different kinds of groups. I wonder if they are hurting the core of the school. I wish there were some way that we could all be together on our knees, praying about these questions about the future.

The belief that the administration lacks vision has created a struggle between the administration and the faculty. As one faculty member puts it, "You have one way of thinking about the institution that begins with [the president] and is reflected in the administration, and you get a different way of thinking about it in the faculty. This is what is producing some of the enormous tensions."

From the administration's side, Morton Diersen expresses frustration with faculty resistance to administrative moves: "We have moved into a situation where the board and administration are pushing a faculty that has a built-in inability to respond to changing conditions."

For Sam Carlson, the tension is felt in differences of educational goals. Over lunch with BW, he complains:

> Ministry doesn't get a fair shake in the curriculum. . . . The students are naive—they don't know what they will need for ministry, and thus they don't push the profs for integration. The faculty certainly doesn't see this need. One prayed in faculty meeting that "the students would learn what we teach." They want disciples, and the students want mentors.

BW gives Carlson a summary of a visiting scholar's lecture extolling the intellectual heritage of evangelicalism and calling for renewed dedication to sound scholarship. "The faculty must have loved that—unfortunately!" he responds.

A faculty member with significant administrative experience attempts to put these tensions in perspective, acknowledging fault lines. One is between those faculty members in the classical field and those in the practical; another is between the faculty as a whole and the administration:

> That fault line . . . [is] true in a lot of schools. . . . [I]t is simply in part because faculty [members] have absolutely no idea what it takes to be an administrator. I sort of feel at times like I am an interpreter of the administration to the [faculty]. They'll sit there . . . and come up with schemes of what we could do. And I will say, how do you pay for it? . . . Everything isn't administrative. Put a price tag. Five dollars, two dollars. How do you pay for it?

THREE

Evangelical Culture

My wife and I never were much involved in the American evangelical subculture —
the emphasis on Christian music, Christian books, Christian radio and so forth. Much
of it is okay, but I find that some of it reflects mediocrity.

—Foy Werda

On the table outside the seminary's bookstore, among the various free pamphlets
and brochures, are copies of the *Shepherd's Guide,* a "Christian Business Directory" for the region. Each advertisement in the hundred-plus page book contains a
small symbol—a silhouette of a shepherd and sheep—and this trademark, the
Guide tells the reader, "indicates that the owner of the business [or advertiser] has
signed the statement of faith below." The statement that follows includes confession that "I have received Jesus Christ as my personal Savior, and my desire is to
live my life for His Glory." An acknowledgment that the signer has been born
again is followed by a pledge "to hold the highest Biblical code of ethics in my
business transactions. It is my ambition to treat my clients with the utmost respect
and integrity."

The *Guide*'s advertisements range from abortion alternatives to bridal services,
from architects to veterinarians, from security companies to wallpaperers, from
bookstores to church supplies. Apart from the small shepherd symbol, most of the
ads would be indistinguishable from those found in conventional *Yellow Pages,*
the model for the *Guide.*

Most of the religious symbols at Evangelical Seminary are similarly unobtru-
sive. Such symbols become noticeable only in the spaces that the students deco-
rate. In dorms and residence halls, Christian plaques bearing Bible verses or words
of blessing adorn many doors. Posters, usually vividly colored photographs of
landscapes, flowers, sunsets, or animals with lines of Scripture or religious poetry
in large print, are affixed to the walls of bedrooms and lounges. Religious calen-
dars, picture frames, and other small objects appear on desktops. Sometimes the
religious decorations are homemade: In Covenant House, a women's dorm, where
the most important current notice is taped to the banister at the top of the sweeping

staircase that all students must climb to their rooms, a religious notecard with a hand-lettered exhortation occasionally replaces the official announcement.

Books and Music

> The Evangelical subculture needs to be a bit more particular when it chooses its heroes. The spotlight belongs to those who have spent time studying the Scripture, and not to those who look like, act like and mirror the world in every way except for the extremes.
>
> —Cary Draper (*Didache II*)

One advertisement in the *Guide* is for the ETS bookstore, which occupies a large room on the second floor of Brill Hall. Along with making textbooks and school supplies available to students, the store also offers a broader range of materials to the seminary community and the public. The stock includes theological volumes, Bibles and Bible commentaries, books on pastoral ministry and counseling, Sunday school materials, popular Christian literature, and a large selection of contemporary Christian music.

At the store's entrance, a display of new titles often promotes a "Book of the Month." On the wall behind the display table are posters listing the "Top Ten Christian Books," the "Top Ten Christian Recordings," and a list of the best-selling Bible translations. Shortly before Christmas, a board game, Bibleopoly, is on the table. Patterned after Monopoly, the game "combines the fun of a board game with remarkable cities of the Bible. . . . Once players have earned their 'Cornerstone' by helping a fellow player or doing 'Community Service' they may make offerings to earn the bricks and steeples needed to build a church. . . . The object of the game is to be the first player to build a church in a Bible city."

One shelf inside the store, regularly updated, contains current best-selling Christian books. On one visit, JC learns from Horst Pfister, a staff member, that books on parenting and weight loss currently top the list of the store's best-sellers, closely followed by Frank Peretti's latest mystery novel, *Facing the Darkness*. Peretti is a Christian writer of fiction. "We can't keep enough of his books in stock," Horst comments.

The music section along one side of the store has a large selection of compact disks, LP records, and audiotapes. Classical music is included, but most titles are from popular Christian musicians such as Amy Grant, Michael Smith, and Michael Card. A prominently displayed "Recording of the Month" is played as background music throughout the store. A poster announces an upcoming campus concert by Christian singer Bruce Bennett. The advertisement touts Bennett's lyrics and music as having much more depth and content than "the typical yuppie Christian music."

Don Avery and Dottie Dorset also have a concern about the content of popular Christian music. On the way to a movie, they play a new tape by singer Michael Card. In contrast to their feelings about some Christian music, Don and Dottie tell JC that they like Card's music very much: "It's really scriptural," says Dottie. Don adds that it is much more "God-centered" and presents a sounder theology than a lot of Christian music, which Don characterizes as "man-centered." He wonders whether contemporary Christian music isn't becoming the new hymnody in the church.

The Iron Sharpens Iron board contains a spirited exchange in response to a recent issue of *Didache II,* a student publication. The editor, Cary Draper, has sharply criticized Amy Grant and Michael Smith for inviting questionable (non-Christian) musicians and musical groups on their shows. His criticism followed a *Wall Street Journal* report that Grant and Smith had crossed the boundary into the mainstream. Cary concludes that the singers need to evangelize rather than compromise.

Three articles on the board take issue with Cary's view of the matter: Smith and Grant, the writers contend, are evangelizing "in the world" and are doing what other Christians have to do as they try to live out their Christianity in the secular world.

Lucas Beckley, an African-American student who is very much involved in Christian music both as performer and songwriter, tells JC over dinner that the issue raised by Cary's article is a significant one for Christian musicians: "It's a problem of boundaries," he says—of deciding whether to go mainstream, which may result in compromising one's Christian commitment.

Patterns of Piety

> I really enjoy worship that is freer and . . . music with words that are something you can identify with and truly give God worship.
>
> —Scott King

Appearing in every mailbox, a memorandum from Andrew Watson, dean of the chapel, announces a change in services for the fall semester. Mondays will feature "open chapels" (in contrast to "community chapels," which take place on other days and are typically led by faculty members or administrators). The memo reads in part:

> Many requests have come to me for special emphases in chapel (music, prayer, special worship observances, etc.). Monday chapels will now be available for such activities and will be arranged and presented by various interest groups. Those making such plans must consult with me. . . . I will continue to arrange the community chapel the remaining days of the week. . . . I look forward to a good year of worshiping our Lord together.

Cole Silas tells JC that he, Fred Price, Mickie Long, and several other students have formed a committee to work with Dr. Watson in planning the services— "praise and prayer services," he says. Some students, Cole adds, have not been attending because they believe that "chapel should be just for worship and prayer as opposed to hearing another lecture." The Monday programs will have more contemporary music than the faculty-led community chapels, he continues, and more student involvement, including preaching. Fred Price says that the aim is to get a more charismatic flavor into the services.

In a comment to BW, Sam Carlson gives his interpretation of students' attitudes toward worship:

> I am still surprised to see students in chapel in shorts and even baseball caps that they do not take off. But I remind myself that many of these students are not church people. They come from these parachurch organizations. Chapel isn't church to them—it's like an InterVarsity Fellowship meeting. They like that kind of worship too, songs with the words on overheads and someone playing a guitar, whereas the faculty likes hymns and formal worship.

Chapel today is "open," organized by the spiritual life unit of the student association. Some twenty-five students are present, but other than Andrew Watson, only one faculty member and one administrator attend.

After a long piano prelude, a male student begins with a call to worship: "In times of hunger, you are the bread; in times of confusion, you are the way; in times of death, you are the comfort and the resurrection. Let us celebrate by prayer and singing." As the gathered worshipers sing "Holy, Holy, Holy," several students raise their hands in the air (an act of prayer and praise, especially favored by charismatics, which symbolizes receptivity to the Holy Spirit). Lois Boucher, who is among the students with raised hands, tells JC during an interview that ETS has opened her eyes to different denominations and styles of worship. She is much more comfortable now with raising her hands in worship and would not feel comfortable in a place that would discourage it.

Following the hymn, the student worship leader, a large, tall woman with long red hair, stands for prayer: "I would just like to meditate on God's Word as I read Psalm 100. . . . I would just like to have a time of prayer. I just encourage anybody who is just so led. Think of this as practice for eternity. Then we will have a long time to pray. God really doesn't care if your prayer is silent or out loud."

She falls silent, and other students offer brief prayers: "Father, we just thank you and pray to you . . ." "Holy, holy, thrice holy God . . ." "Father, we give you praise. We invite your Holy Spirit to be here with us now. We thank you, Jesus, that we can give honor and praise in your name." As these prayers are offered—almost all by men—a very tall male student sitting behind BW murmurs, "Yes, yes."

The worship leader introduces a bearded man named Viktor, apparently a student. Viktor is from Latvia. He will "share testimony and tell us how important praise is to him," the woman says.

Viktor begins:

> I come from a country where Marxism is the only religion. I know how great the cost of discipleship is there. I know that people who are disciples lose jobs and possibilities of study, and some have paid with their lives. I became a Christian at fifteen. My parents took me to church. I didn't want to go, to have friends see me, to be known as a crazy believer. I'm so happy to be here. God put me here. Most of you understand it. I want to call you to worship. He gives all. Do not be afraid. Attend chapel tons more and worship. God bless you.[1]

As Viktor sits down, a male student leads in prayer:

Father, with Viktor's words in our ears and hearts, we bring before you gratitude for the freedom of the church in our country. We are ashamed when we think of those who take risks, because we take worship for granted. But it is central to our relationship to you. In exchange for your food and drink, we prefer the sugary sweetness of popular culture. You have forgiven us through the Blood of Jesus. Your Spirit lets us enter the holy of holies. Give us a vision of your majesty like Isaiah's. . . . Bless all of us, all the small groups on campus, all the individuals praying and praising you alone. Conform us to the image of your Son.

The worship leader then asks people to do as the Spirit moves them, standing or not, through a period of singing. Almost all stand, though not Andrew Watson. The administrator in attendance stands, but he does not join in the clapping that accompanies the singing. Some students become quite enthusiastic.

The words to the songs, called "praise choruses," are projected on the wall with the use of an overhead projector. The accompaniment is by drums, a keyboard, and a guitar. Many students raise their hands as they sing. The choruses include:

You are the Lord of creation,
Lord of life.

Blessed be the name of the Lord,
For He is our rock,
He is the Lord.

Jesus reigns on high in all the earth.

The universe is in the hand of the Lord.

The service concludes with a prayer.

Near the end of the fall orientation week, students gather in the chapel for a "Day of Prayer" that includes a time for student testimonies. A male student tells the assembly that his wife took time from her job to take courses during the past summer. To their surprise, her boss paid her anyway. The couple really needed the money, he said, adding that God does unusual things in normal ways.

Another student stands to testify: "I want to praise the Lord for physical deliverance. I worked as a painter this summer and fell from a ladder through a greenhouse roof. I was only slightly hurt. The hand of the Lord protected me."

"I was painting too," a third student reports. "The wind started to blow and I went inside to protect my radio. A huge tree branch knocked down the scaffolding minutes later." Another student, also male: "I spent the summer in Korea and found God at work. I found a real desire of ordinary Christians there to prepare for missions."

A short male student adjusts the microphone lower. It is high to accommodate Jeffrey Barber, the student association president, who is presiding. "What is this," the short student jokes, "harassment?" Then he adds, "I painted this summer too, but I finished the job and nothing happened, so I wasn't delivered." (There is much laughter.) "Two weeks ago, I was headed to another seminary, but things changed. Now that I am here, I am thankful to God and glad that I'll be here for the next three and a half to four years." (Again there is laughter.)

Classes at ETS begin with prayer. Theology professor Henry Givens is lecturing today on the Atonement and prays: "We thank you, O God, for the death of Christ, a powerful and liberating death from the power of sin, and ultimately from the presence of sin. May this once-for-all event become a daily, existential decision for us that we might come to be freed from sin's power and demonstrate in our culture the liberating power of Christ's death."

Professor Jesse Redlin's class on church planting and growth meets for three hours in the evening. Eighteen students are present. Redlin has asked Gayle Penney, a petite second-year M.Div. student, to lead the opening devotional. Gayle begins with a short Bible reading and then asks fellow students for their prayer requests. One student requests a healing prayer for two sick professors. Another asks for prayers of thanksgiving for Cambodian families about whom he has read in a class assignment: They have "confessed Christ" as family units, as contrasted with more traditional "sawdust-trail, individual decisions." There is a request for prayer for a pro-life political candidate who is opposing a senior member of the U.S. Senate. Another student asks for prayers for a new congregation in a town he describes as harboring "the powers of evil." A final petition focuses on a reported Mexican situation in which those who confess Christ become targets of a death squad.

When all prayer requests are gathered, Gayle asks for volunteers to offer a prayer for each. The devotional lasts for approximately fifteen minutes.

A fellowship prayer meeting is set for Covenant House that night, Cole Silas tells JC. Cole cannot go because he has responsibilities with Young Life. The prayer fellowship meets regularly on Fridays under the leadership of Old Testament professor Neil Jertsen. JC learns that tonight's meeting has been shifted to a chapel in Brill Hall and that Jertsen will not be present because of a back problem.

Jonas Keefer, an M.A.T.S. student who is also an accomplished jazz musician, leads the service. Seven persons attend, including JC—four men and two women. Fred Price, Joyce Gremlick, and Alan Posner are among those present.

Worship begins with several praise choruses, with Jonas providing lively piano accompaniment. He belts out the tunes while the words are projected on the wall. Jonas intersperses prayers and choruses. One prayer is for healing for Dr. Jertsen's ailing back. The singing lasts for approximately twenty minutes.

Following the songs, Jonas announces prayer time. He speaks at some length about his belief that the seminary community is still deeply upset over the suicide attempt of a student two weeks earlier. "I had thought for a while that we had been able to come to grips with it," he says, "but I realize that both for myself and many other students, there is still a lot of grieving going on. Also, many of us are still carrying a burden of guilt." Jonas asks those present to pray with him about it. He leads in a long prayer, punctuating almost every phrase with the word "Lord": "Lord, will you lift the burden of guilt from us. . . . Lord, I sat next to Kirt [the suicidal student] for a year and a half in class, and I was not sensitive to his need. Lord, give me greater sensitivity." One of the women joins in and asks for a blessing on Kirt's family.

Following this prayer, Jonas asks for prayer requests from the others present.

Joyce, an older woman whom JC has met earlier in one of Robert Harlan's classes, describes her need for financial assistance to visit her father, who is near death in a Florida nursing home. She wants to see him one more time. The trip is complicated by the fact that her husband is diabetic and blind. Joyce must take him along. "I don't have the six hundred dollars each that it will cost for our airfare," she explains. "I have been praying for someone who will help with the transportation—either offering us a ride to Florida or providing financial assistance."

When Joyce finishes stating her prayer request, Jonas comes over and kneels beside her chair and prays that she may find help. The other woman present also prays, mentioning that the Lord knows that many students have financial needs. She then prays especially for Joyce.

Jonas asks Terry Price if he wants prayer for his work with youth at a nearby church. Terry responds by describing the situation at the church: The minister of Christian education is dumping most of the youth ministry on him; also, the adults who assist with the youth ministry are making noises about resigning. He is beginning to feel overwhelmed.

"But I also have something to praise," Terry continues. "The kids are mostly unchurched. I've been trying to interest them in Christian music without much success. But one night recently, a junior high girl was sleeping over with a friend, and they watched a TV program on Satanism. They were so frightened that they began to write Christian songs to protect them from the Devil. Later they shared the songs with the youth group. And their songs were really beautiful—just right on!"

As Terry finishes speaking, Jonas places a chair in the middle of the circle and asks Terry to sit in it. He complies. Jonas kneels beside Terry, putting his hand on his shoulder. Joyce comes to stand beside Terry. She lays one hand on his shoulder and raises the other hand in the air. Both pray for Terry and his ministry.

Finally, Alan Posner, an M.A.T.S. student and an assistant to Professor Bruce Grantler, moves to the chair in the center. He says his need is not as big as those of the others but he still wants prayers. "On Monday, I have to give a lecture in two of Dr. Grantler's church history classes," Alan explains. "I'm to speak on healing. I've never lectured before, and I've really done little public speaking. I've been working on the lecture for a long time, but I'm really uptight over having to present it. Healing is very important to me, and I see this as a great opportunity to get the issue before the students. It will also help to bring some balance to the topic that I believe is lacking here at the seminary."

Jonas again kneels, and Joyce stands beside the chair. They pray for the Holy Spirit to give Alan guidance. The others also pray. Terry reminds Alan that God chooses that which is weak to shame the wise, and he mentions both Moses and St. Paul as examples. Through his work at a telephone counseling center, Terry says, he has learned that two of the Devil's weapons are fear and feelings of inadequacy. The center provides Bible verses to contend with each of these. Terry says he puts the verses in front of him at the telephone, and they give him courage to respond to the callers. Terry promises Alan that he will give him these verses. The meeting closes with a discussion of when and where the group will next meet.

In response to a question about spiritual support in the school, Timothy Woods says that he and Paula Fleming are "prayer warriors."

> We get together every Thursday and pray. . . . It's a good hour or so that we pray and talk about things. I have prayer warriors both in Maine and elsewhere in the country that contact me from time to time to pray. I have a prayer support group down in my church. So prayer is key with me. I don't think you can do anything without it. . . . [T]here is support on campus to enhance spiritual life.

The large room in Brill Hall is full. Graduating seniors, parents, friends, faculty members, and administrators are here for the annual dinner preceding the baccalaureate service. Don Avery, a graduating senior, invites JC and his wife to join him and Dottie Dorset. Don wants to know if JC has heard their big news: Don and Dottie have just become engaged to be married! Together they recount the details of their decision.

The problem they faced, Don begins, is that Dottie is a charismatic Christian and he is not. They were not sure whether this difference would make for a healthy marriage. It would not be as difficult, Don says, as would be the case if one were not a Christian at all. Still, the differences between charismatics and other Christians are real when it comes to theology and worship styles.

Dottie joins in: "I decided to attend a charismatic retreat held over a long weekend. I tried to get Don to go with me so that he might gain a better understanding of charismatics. I thought this might help us work through some of our differences. Don, however, had just completed work on a difficult term paper and was tired. He decided not to go."

The retreat, Dottie continues, was conducted by a student, an older woman "who is Pentecostal to her roots." The participants were primarily older women.

At the opening prayer session, Dottie decided to lay before the Lord her questions about her relationship with Don. "I prayed," she says, "that the Lord would give me a clear answer. When I spoke my concern aloud, I got an immediate response from a couple of the women who said, 'Drop him. He will be a yoke around your neck.' They asked me nothing about our relationship. I was quite disturbed by their comments. They were so definite."

The next day, an older woman—in her late sixties or early seventies—approached Dottie. Dottie describes her as "a real prayer warrior."

"Do you have a burden that you want to bring to the Lord in prayer?" Dottie recalls the older woman asking her.

Dottie described her relationship with Don and her concern about whether she should continue it. Instead of giving her a quick answer, Dottie said, the older woman began to question her in a loving and compassionate way:

"Is Don opposed to your charismatic faith?"

"No."

"Does he put any hindrance in your way?"

"No."

"Do you want to marry him?"

That was the first time, Dottie says, that she had let herself ask that question, and the answer came back a clear yes. She knew, she says, that this was the Lord's leading. "He had made it possible for me to answer this question with such certainty," she beamed. "I was very excited and could not wait to get back to campus to tell Don."

Don picks up the story: While Dottie was away on the retreat, he had been trying to deal with his feelings about charismatics. "I realized my fear of what might happen at the retreat, but I reminded myself that in the Scripture, God says, 'Have no fear.' It came to me that my real fears about charismatics were not about Dottie but rather about previous experiences during college. Charismatics had put me down because I had not experienced the baptism of the Spirit, nor did I speak in tongues. Dottie is not that way toward me. I realized that I had no reason to fear because she is charismatic."

On the Sunday night after the retreat, as they shared their experiences of the weekend, they agreed that the Lord had been leading them to each other. Definite plans for marriage, however, were not discussed.

Don says he assumed that they would wait until Dottie completed her work—a year hence. He would stay at ETS until she graduated, and then both would go to Indonesia as missionaries. (Dottie shares Don's commitment to missions, and she is open to serving in Indonesia.)

The next morning, the mail brought Don the offer of a full scholarship in a master's program at another school.

When he called Dottie to tell her, Don recalls, she told him that Nina Wahyutomo, her Indonesian roommate, had responded to a report on their Sunday night conversation, "Well, I assume you'll be getting married in August."

"When I heard Don's news of the scholarship," Dottie continues, "all of a sudden, I realized that this was a possibility. The Lord was leading us in this direction."

They will be married in August, just as Nina predicted.

World Missions

> If ETS ever dips its flag on its commitment to missions, if professors no longer teach the necessity to proclaim the Word of God, if students no longer come here with zeal to proclaim the Word, then we will have no right to exist.
>
> —Andrew Watson, chapel sermon

On Saturday evening, students have gathered in Covenant House for the monthly meeting of the World Christian Fellowship. Topics for these meetings vary during the year, such as "The Church in Japan," featuring talks by students, and the film *The Mission,* set in South America. Student reports on Africa have intriguing titles: "Trout Files and Computer Parts: Reflections on Six Years of Making Tents in Kenya" and "An Algerian Adventure."

Tonight Dr. Joel Cotton is speaking on what the meeting announcement calls "the burning question": "Why in the World Is Missions Important to Seminarians on Bell's Ridge?" Approximately forty people, including several children of students, attend.

The program begins with several praise choruses, with the words projected on the wall. One chorus tonight is "Glory, Glory, Glory." The student who presides welcomes the group and jokes about the number of new children swelling the fellowship. He introduces Don Avery, who shows slides of his experiences in Indonesia.

Don is a pillar of the small group of students whose primary focus is world missions. He plans a missionary career as a teacher of theology in Indonesia, where he spent a summer on a mission supported by his home church.

To illustrate that "we're up against it" in Indonesia, Don tells the story of a woman who was cured of cancer by Christian prayers. She then went to a Christian church but did not become a Christian because of pressure from the surrounding Muslim culture. During his stay, he visited the family of fellow student and Indonesian native Nina Wahyutomo, whom Don introduces. Following the slides, when he asks for questions, Don refers those about Indonesian culture to Nina.

Nina, a slight, vivacious young woman, is invited to "share her testimony." She tells how she left Indonesia to attend an American university. When she came to the United States she was Buddhist. Her parents are still Buddhist. With humor, she describes how she became a Christian. During her first spring break, a fellow student invited Nina to come home with her since the dormitory would be closed. When they arrived at the student's home, "her mom opened the door and gave me a big hug, and I was kind of shocked. I have never in my life been hugged and kissed before. And all the time they were talking about Jesus. Jesus will do this and help me in this, and I thought these people must be crazy." One afternoon, following a meeting of a charismatic fellowship downstairs in her friend's home, a woman came to Nina's room "and said Jesus told her to come back and tell me that he loves you. She said she would like to talk, and I said okay." At that time, Nina says, her English was so poor that she did not fully understand what the woman was saying, so she simply nodded—something she did every time anyone asked her anything in English. After that experience, Nina jokes, Christians seemed to be following her everywhere, so much that she got very tired of them. (The audience laughs.)

She did not commit herself to Jesus Christ until later, when, following graduation, she lived with a Baptist family that gave her a Bible. She read from the Psalms: "You knew me before I was born, while I was in my mother's womb." She found herself praying to know Jesus and whether he really was her Savior. Because of her prayers, she felt sure that she did know him. She returned to Indonesia and went through "many experiences, including facing death," and felt that God was with her. (In an interview, Nina tells JC that her brother, angry over her conversion to Christianity and her condemnation of Buddhist symbols as Satan's idols, had tried to kill her with a knife. Their father had intervened. Later, after she returned to the United States, she and her brother were reconciled.)

She concludes her testimony by returning to the verse from Psalm 139. Reading that really shocked her, she says, because her parents had tried to abort her when she was in her mother's womb. They did not want her and "had gone to the hospital to have an abortion, but they did not have enough money, and my father was so humiliated that he would not come back. So, here I am," she says.

Joel Cotton, who is sitting at the side of the room with the other speakers, says, "Praise the Lord!" Others join in. Then there are prayers, including one by Cotton thanking God "for sovereignly preserving Nina's life."

Cotton then speaks. He gives a sermonette on the importance of missions, using the story of Daniel and his companions—Shadrach, Meshach, and Abednego—as his text. They were trained, he said, in seminarylike fashion. While they were in Babylon "the Lord took care of them physically and spiritually." Nebuchadnezzar was like Saddam Hussein, "an autocrat." Cotton laughs often at his own ironic or sarcastic remarks. He says:

> [It is important] to have a heart for the whole world. Someone once said that God had only one son and he became a world missionary. You have a great opportunity to become one too. There is a lot of talk about the globalization of theological education, but it isn't anything new. [He laughs loudly here, apparently at the foolishness of those who think that globalization is something new]. Missionaries have been globalizing theological education for centuries. You are not just preparing for ministry when you're in seminary. This is already a real ministry. Here on campus you are with leaders who will be responsible for thousands of souls. You can have a great impact on them. You can pray for them.

He advises the students to "pray through the campus directory. When you meet people, you will know their names. They will ask how, and you can say, 'Because I prayed for you.' "

Following other stories and a prayer, Cotton introduces a student, Nicholas Betts, who has spent time in Israel and "has come back a changed man." Betts speaks about his experience in Israel, giving an effective "commercial" for becoming involved in a period of missionary service. The meeting concludes with a student-led prayer: "Father, I just thank you for this evening, Lord . . ."

Joel Cotton interrupts the hubbub after the meeting closes to announce that he has just heard from a student who was manning phones at a Billy Graham crusade. He reports that a counselor got a call from a women's prison where nine women accepted Christ through the broadcast of the crusade. A general murmur of approval rises.

Morning worship is moved from the chapel to a large lecture hall in the library so that slides may be shown as part of the service. Students from a summer overseas mission program are in charge. The for-credit, supervised overseas program takes participants into another culture for six weeks of evangelistic ministry and service. As the worshipers gather—about seventy attend—a student struggles to operate the slide projector. He asks loudly, "Someone want to give me a hand here?" Several students applaud in response, and everyone laughs.

The service begins with praise choruses. This morning the worshipers sing "We Exalt Thee" and "Ask of Me and I Will Give the Nations as an Inheritance for You." A well-executed skit on the overseas experience follows the singing. The skit's premise is that all the students happen to arrive at an airport simultaneously as they return from their assignments. They share what they have learned:

- "The power of prayer," says a woman who went to Ecuador. "I was calm and we were safe because people were praying for us."

- A male student tells of his experience of evangelistic preaching in Mexico. "No one was coming to the services. We decided to fast and pray because people weren't coming. We broke the fast when the pastor invited us out to lunch. (The audience laughs.) I preached that night on the Resurrection, and seven people came to Christ." (There is an audible drawing of breath.)
- Harry: "In the Philippines, they have a delicacy. They take duck eggs just before they are going to hatch, and they cook them and then you get to crack open the egg and eat the baby duck—and I don't even like eggs."
- Ben spent his time with a medical team in the Himalayas. He tells how he assisted with eye surgery and how he himself was given a "vision for unreached people."

After several other stories, Jesse Redlin, associate professor of missions and director of the program, appears outlandishly dressed in shorts, headgear, and a collage of costumes. He had intended to go to all the places the students went, he says, but he spent the summer at the airport because he failed to sign up in time. There is much laughter.

The service continues with field slides and closes with a testimony and exhortation from a woman student who has been in Yugoslavia. Near tears, she says:

[The experience] means so much: the change it brings into your heart and life. Everyone needs friends, love, and Jesus Christ. It lets you bring Jesus Christ to the world. Through God we can do things we never imagined. We can witness to people even if we are terrified to do this in the U.S. Even if you do not have a call to missions, you should do this. Even if you never go overseas again.

At the baccalaureate service, graduating senior Judith North has been selected to give the student testimony. A small woman with long brown hair, she is married and the mother of two children. What follows is a close paraphrase of her full testimony:

I apologize for having to speak fast, but I have to pack my whole life story into five minutes. I was baptized and raised in the church, but I was not a Christian: I did not believe in Jesus as Lord. Nevertheless, I was quite religious. I believed especially that the occult world could coexist with Christianity. In my teens, I discovered that I had the powers of precognition. I had out-of-body experiences; I experimented with Ouija boards, Tarot cards, and various occult media. I developed expertise as a hypnotist. I studied apparitions, psychokinesis, and was involved in yoga and ESP experiments.

I sought meaning in all of this, but I found only the "great deceiver, Satan himself." In all of this I thought I was closer to God, but I was deceived. I was hired to teach the occult in a public high school, and I'm shocked that I was never taken to task by another teacher, parent, or student, even when I brought witches to my classes.

During this time, my husband and I went through a separation. I went on a profound search experience: I kept a Bible under my pillow at night; friends prayed for me. Eventually my husband and I reconciled. We went to hear Billy Graham preach, and I felt the Lord moving me to come down the aisle. I remember little that Dr. Graham said, but I know I was called to come forward. Shortly afterward, my husband and later my daughter were also converted. After ten years of marriage, my husband and I renewed our marriage vows.

My experience is a living testimony to the power of God to overcome Satan. I am committed to a ministry to convert New Agers, who are the new occult, to Christ.

I came to this school four years ago. I want to cite Dr. and Mrs. Joel Cotton and Bailey Tyler [a former faculty member] as being especially important in my spiritual walk. Currently, I am pastor of a Baptist church in a nearby state. I have scripted an audiotape on cults to be used by the Billy Graham telephone ministry. In the fall, I plan to enter Stirling University in Scotland to begin a Ph.D. program.

As Judith finishes speaking, there are "Amens" from the audience. Ronald Stoner, who gets up immediately afterward to read the Scripture lesson, says, "Thank you, Judith. Praise the Lord for your testimony."

Right-to-Life Efforts

For evangelicals at large, [opposition to abortion] is the social badge of honor. . . . It identifies you culturally, institutionally as an evangelical.

—Andrew Nagel

The contribution to the Iron Sharpens Iron board is three and one-half typed pages. It is titled, in bold letters, "Racists, Sexists, Anti-gay-*Born again* bigots, go away!" The title is a chant that the author, Lou Shaw, has heard at a protest of an abortion clinic. Lou, a first-year M.Div. student, refers to the clinic as an "abortuary." He is describing his visit to an Operation Rescue protest in which there has been a confrontation with proabortion participants "who were physically and verbally protecting the abortuary." The purpose of Lou's Iron Sharpens Iron piece is "to challenge the media's representation of an Operation Rescue (OR) event by telling a firsthand account of what actually goes on." He continues:

The nation and, I'm afraid, Evangelicalism has a tremendously misinformed opinion of OR based on seeing the organization through the lens of an *edited* 5 o'clock news presentation. Hollywood is 93% pro-abortion (sources available). Is it any wonder that what is seen as the news coverage of Operation Rescue may be biased and not present an objective, truthful account of reality?

Lou's following "Reflections after a Day with Operation Rescue" is detailed and graphic. The report concludes with a call to other students to join him and fellow student Loren Uhler in observing an Operation Rescue event the following Saturday:

We are going *to simply observe* what actually goes on at an OR event, *to pray* that God would bring an end to the killing of 1.6 million babies a year in this country, and *to worship* our God as people helpless against our present Holocaust. . . . *There will be absolutely no obligation or risk of being arrested.* We go to observe and to pray and to worship.

A second article on the board, posted by Loren Uhler, who has been arrested during an Operation Rescue protest, contains a paragraph written by his wife, Tanya:

I had never been to any demonstration of any kind, let alone something having to do with abortion. But when my husband said he was definitely going to participate . . . I just couldn't imagine him there all alone. . . . At the abortuary, I was overwhelmed by the peacefulness of those praying for the mothers and babies. I was also aware of the great spiritual battles going on around us as the "pro-choicers" gathered across the street. I spent nearly six hours at the abortuary and another five hours at the jail where my husband had been taken—mostly in prayer and singing.

She concludes by adding her protest against the biased news coverage that she later witnessed on the television.

Antiabortion protests are regular fare on the Iron Sharpens Iron board. While there are occasional efforts to nuance the reasons for opposition—Sally Trumbell, for example, argues against the tactics of Operation Rescue while taking a pro-life stance—no one openly argues for a pro-choice position. Sidney Bennett, a senior M.Div. student from North Carolina, tells JC that the major argument about abortion among students is not between pro-life and pro-choice but about whether abortion should be allowed for rape and incest victims. Sid, who describes himself as "very conservative," believes that abortion should be allowed only to save the mother's life. "I think," he adds, "that even those who've been raped and incested can find joy and blessing in the baby."

One faculty member tells JC that he wishes that students would be more discriminating in their positions. A supporter of Bill Clinton in the presidential election, he says that he sometimes threatens to put a Clinton sticker on his car. "That would create some stir around here," he laughs, "because when I talk with students about this, they're saying, 'You've got to be kidding! He's for abortion.' I say, 'No, he's not. He's for choice.' "

FOUR

Contests

Students teach each other by friendship and rubbing shoulders with those who are a little different and, you know, those kinds of things.

—Roy Parks

Believers' Baptism

A different step from some of them.

—Student comment about Bashford

One thing that students like best about Paul Bashford is that his views differ just a little from the views of the other most respected professors. His theological pedigree is impeccable. Unlike Jerome Allen, who came from fundamentalism, Bashford was raised in the conservative branch of a mainline denomination, and all the schools he attended are highly approved at ETS. Perhaps this gives him the confidence to take "a different step from some of them," says Tim Rothman about Bashford's gentle approach to Pentecostalism, a branch of evangelicalism that his colleagues often criticize. Tim quickly adds, "He's still pretty Reformed himself"—Reformed being the standard position. A student who finds ETS too conservative and too negative likes Bashford nonetheless because he encourages his students to read works by nonevangelical scholars; yet Cary Draper, famous among his fellow students for theological conservatism, has rearranged his schedule to be able to take as many Bashford courses as possible.

Bashford's popularity is evident at noon one wet March day, as more than fifty students with lunch sacks and cafeteria trays crowd into a classroom too small to offer them all seats. The event is not official, not even sponsored by an organization. Bashford has simply announced that he will explain why, after long study of the Scripture, he has become convinced that baptism should be reserved for those old enough to testify to their faith rather than made available to infants and small children. Students have helped to spread the word by making a poster that sits on an easel outside the cafeteria. Unlike the posters that usually occupy that spot—lettered in a Gothic hand and shaded with pastels—this one has a cartoon of Bashford floating in an inner tube, wearing sunglasses and holding a tall drink. "Come hear Dr. Bashford defend Believers' Baptism!" it says.

Baptism is not an issue on which the school's faith statement takes a position, but infant (rather than "believers' ") baptism is the more common position in the core of the faculty. To justify his stand, Bashford launches into a long analysis of a key passage in Paul's letter to the Romans about "circumcision of the heart." This approach emphasizes "sanctification" ("where there is no fruit there is no spirit"), and it softens a little the severe emphasis, more common in the school, on justification by grace alone: "Justification and sanctification are so closely linked that they ought to be merged into a single word, "justificationsanctification." (Pentecostals like this point. "We are serious about sanctification and the holy life, something that only Bashford talks about here at all," says Trent Lee, a scholarly, intellectual student who is probably the most disgruntled Pentecostal on campus.)

Some students nod vigorously as Bashford makes these points; others raise their hand to argue, most often a very red-headed man, William Emmett, who declares that he is going to defend the Presbyterian and Reformed practice of baptizing infants. At one point Bashford mentions Luther and says to a woman in the front row who seems to respond to that reference, "You must be a Lutheran."

"A Reformed Lutheran," the woman replies.

"She's getting more Reformed as she sits here," Bill Emmett adds.

"She'll be a Baptist by the time I am through," says Bashford, going on to explain that Baptists evaluate the validity of previous baptism. "Baptists are willing to say that your baptism means diddle-squat," he states.

Emmett explodes: "When someone does not show the fruits of faith, you excommunicate. You *don't* ex-baptize!" Bashford replies calmly but urgently. He would baptize the person again.

Bashford—his always ruddy face even redder, his straight hair shaking—winds up the hour with a personal testimony:

> Taking this view has cost me a lot. I gave up my family heritage because I believe this. To this day, my mother says that my pagan brother has had his children baptized but her renegade son, who teaches in a seminary, has not. But I have to tell people that I believe the church is made up of people who have been brought to faith in Christ by the Spirit, and who are willing to testify to the power of the Spirit. We have to preserve the remnant.

Later in the day, BW meets Kate Prater, who is both a student and a staff member. "You should have heard Paul Bashford today," she says. "You would have found that interesting." BW says that she was present, though perhaps not visible, because the room was so crowded. "Well," says Kate, "maybe that topic is not important in the great sweep of things, but in our little world, there is a lot of interest in it."

BW also talks to William Emmett during a class that evening. He seems deeply chagrined. He says that he thinks he may have been rude to Bashford. He searches for a reason that he behaved so aggressively: "For the first time, I felt as if maybe I don't belong, as if my way of doing things may not be the right way."

Modern Theology

You have to watch them.

—Davis Saddler

"People talk about it all week," says Anne Norton of the course called Modern Theology, organized by theology professor Andrew Nagel to bring well-known nonevangelical theologians to campus for biweekly lectures and discussions. In the alternating weeks, ETS professors provide background about the guests' published work and, sometimes, an evaluation of their class lecture.

The course is a major innovation. In the general view, it has been set up to pacify students who are unhappy with Roy Parks's repeated leaves of absence and the resulting lack of variety in the course offerings of the theology department. Only Nagel and Hank Givens regularly teach theology, and Givens's courses are almost all introductory or in his other specialty, the separate field of social ethics. By contrast, students can choose among five New Testament teachers and four in Old Testament. An administrator has a variant theory on how the course came to be given. He thinks that Roy Parks created it because he was tired of teaching the work of "those whose ideas he does not believe"; the course lets such theologians speak for themselves.

Whatever its origins, the course generates discussion, says Anne Norton, who characterizes the major perspectives on it: "There are two camps. One seems to need to define how the guests aren't orthodox and evangelical. The other camp knows that they're not evangelical but is interested in how they've evolved. [The two groups] don't understand each other." The first group makes Anne, who attended an Ivy League university, anxious about how the school will be viewed from the outside. She asks BW, who is attending most sessions of the course, "Did it go all right?" Later she asks again, and when told that the students have been extremely polite to the guests, expresses relief. "Good. Evangelicals can embarrass you sometimes." Rick Harvey, a student with some views considered liberal at ETS, has similar worries. "Well," he mutters to BW after one lecture by an outsider, "people behaved okay."

Louise Mason, who knows from her arguments over the ordination of women how adamant ETS professors can be, is more concerned about what the faculty commentators will say when the outside guests are absent. She tells BW that she does not have a positive impression of the course: "Don't they just invite people in and then tell the students what is wrong with what they've said?"

The Modern Theology course is among the first courses to be held in a newly constructed academic facility. The new building is unpopular with students, though its classrooms are far more attractive and comfortable than those in the old building, with its brown tile walls, harsh lighting, and torturously small seats crowded together. The students complain about the windowless rooms, the noisy ventilation system and, most of all, the amount of money spent on the new center. They think the money should have been raised for scholarships. (Some faculty members, too have taken up this complaint. One, who is held in high esteem by the students, said to BW, an administrator at another seminary, "You've probably found that money for buildings is easier to raise, right? We got a chapel we did not need that way, and now this new academic center. It would be great if we could have that money for student aid.")

The new classrooms, and especially the large central room where Modern Theology is held, do have features that the students seem to enjoy, including the swivel seats arranged in curved rows on an ascending terrace of steps, with continuous desks between the rows. Students swivel to face the platform at the front and lowest level of the room as Andrew Nagel opens the session.

John Cobb, an eminent theologian who advocates a type of theology called "process theology," had lectured the week before. That day Nagel opened the class by asking the students to be "gentle and reverent, but no less bold," in exchanges with the guest. This time he gives no directives. Speaking hesitantly, he says that one reason process theology was chosen as a course topic, and John Cobb invited to speak about it, was "because we have a resident expert here." Professor Davis Saddler was once a process theologian himself, Nagel explains, but he has long since changed his mind.

Saddler, a short, compact man with wavy gray hair, holds his lips pursed in a permanent half smile. He launches his lecture with no informal comments or pleasantries, acknowledging that he has been "to process and back" and will say more about that later. The problem with "worldly philosophies" (process thought is a philosophical and theological system) is that "they have it and they don't," he decrees. They have "general revelation" (the portion of God's truth that Calvinists believe is available to all reasonable people, whether "elect" and saved or not), "but the difficulty for us biblical people is that they give their glory over for creaturely status. First, let's be descriptive. We have to be fair. We were fair last week. We were gentle with Cobb, and he certainly was with us. Some people said to me, 'He's so nice.' I suppose they mean as opposed to lean, mean Roy Parks." The students laugh. Parks is not present, but he was the week before. Almost as many students, however, have come to hear Saddler as came to hear Cobb, though this week a number trickle in after the class has begun. It is possible to slip in unobtrusively because the entrance doors are at the top and back of the room.

Saddler summarizes process theology, drawing on the blackboard curved lines and stick figures meant to show the movement in process thought from the "primordial" past through the "consequent" present to an "emergent" future of "novelty, freedom, and possibility."

"That's what it's about," he says, "the defense of freedom. I do not know where you are in the Calvinism/Arminian scale, but this is hyper-Arminian ["Arminian" is a theological label for systems that give human will a role to play in salvation, a notion that such orthodox Calvinists as Saddler and many of his ETS faculty colleagues reject]. It is really an "anthrodicy" [a term that Saddler has invented to describe what he thinks is the centrality of human effort rather than divine power in process thought]. The point of this system is to guarantee the freedom of the emerging occasion. Thus, there can be no prophecy."

He describes the ideas of various process thinkers, including their unwillingness to limit human freedom and to say that in the future God will be limited to what God has been in the past. "In this view, we are the brains of God's body, the democracy of which God is president." The problem with this is that we have "'no windows sidewise,' as the Scots would say. . . . God does not have a future or a present, but only a perished past. God experiences great loss in this."

A woman student interrupts: "Who can say that God does not have us in the present? In this system, isn't God in every moment?"

"But God leaves you alone in your choice," Saddler replies. "At that moment, God is not there with you. And it does not follow, as the process people think, that a sovereign God leaves you no freedom" (Calvinists teach that God is the Lord over all things).

"What practical difference does it make?" the woman shoots back. "Both ways seem to have freedom. Both seem to have something of God." Another woman asks a question before Saddler can reply further.

A long exchange with the students ensues, much of it about Buddhism, tripped off by John Cobb's description the week before of his dialogue with Buddhists. After responding to a series of questions, Saddler looks out at the class: "How are we doing? This seems simple to me because I have been at it so long. But it must be baffling to many of you."

"Don't worry," says a student. "We are just the perished past."

Saddler resumes his lecture, saying that he wants to give a positive assessment of what "touched me" in process theology, even though later "I left the school." What he liked about process, he says, was its "social" character, the interaction it describes between God and human beings and among the persons of the Trinity. It helped to put aside the "frozen" quality of orthodox theology: "The totally actual God [of orthodox theology] does not know the world but only attracts. How can he care when he's already actualized?"

More than an hour has passed, and Saddler releases students for the customary break. Some leave the room. There is a canteen with vending machines at the new building; however, many will walk the hundred yards across the cold, dark campus to the cafeteria, which stays open in the old building to serve coffee, soda, and its usual wide selection of sweet things for students in evening classes.

When classes were in the old building, instructor and students would often go together for coffee and snacks, talking all the way. Now those who want to talk to the teacher do not leave but descend to the front of the room. They surround Andrew Nagel to ask him technical questions about the "sociality of the Trinity" and listen to his answers about "polytheism" and "modalism." Pamela Willis and her friend Mary Ann Kromer are part of this group. Pamela stands close to Nagel and jumps into the exchange. Mary Ann stands at the edge of the circle. A young man student says to her alone, "I am just realizing that, last week, when John

Cobb talked about resurrection, he didn't mean bodily resurrection. I can't believe that I missed that." Mary Ann says, "You have to watch them."

The break over, the lecture begins again. By 1972, says Saddler, he was "exhausted logically and tired in ministry." At this point, he reconverted to orthodoxy, and now he will give the negative assessment he has formed of process thought. He talks again about its "anthrodicy" and says that he also experimented with the terms "egodicy" and "egadicy" (a joke) to express this human-centeredness. He now believes that process theology involves a "real rebellion against the biblical deity." He gives extensive philosophical reasons for this ("In Whitehead, God is not a legitimate agent; pure potentiality doesn't make choices") and then pronounces: "The God that Cobb has is not the one that I worship. His God is not worthy of worship."

The students' interruptions with questions have an edge of challenge not heard in the first hour, or in the previous week when they questioned Cobb directly. One asks whether the evangelical idea of God also does not involve, as process theology does, "analogical" rather than "univocal" language. Saddler answers shortly and continues his talk, giving more reasons for his doubts about process thought:

> The modern definition of freedom is quite unbiblical. Relational freedom in the Bible comes from being born anew, from seeking to serve, as the persons of the Trinity do. . . . Cobb would do better if he were a biblical theologian. He weights reason and experience. He puts down the Bible and tradition. That is hard to say because he is such a gentle guy, though he can be very tough in professional circles. But I am glad that we don't hear that kind of thing all the time. Frankly, I think it's blasphemous, and then he takes over the name "Christian." Cobb is a great churchman. But without the substitutionary atonement [the doctrine that human beings' salvation was "purchased" by Christ's sacrificial death], he is not a Christian. He is a Unitarian-Universalist. He has no sense of sin. And yet he talks of God as kindness and severity.

In response to a sympathetic question, Saddler repeats his point: "They [process theologians] should all call themselves Unitarians." Angie Harlan, a very young-looking student who asked several of the earlier questions and whose father is Professor Robert Harlan, protests: "Cobb emphasized Christ-centeredness in everything he said."

"But Jennifer," Saddler responds severely, "You have to be tough here. You can't just fuzz out. What did he mean by this? For him Christ is just a good example."

The next questions are from men, and they make clear the questioner's agreement with Saddler:

> Student: What good does this God with no present do for me?
> Saddler: It did me none. It was unsatisfactory. I had to repent, to get down on my knees, to confess my sinful condition. And now I can testify, after thirty-five years of teaching, that if you follow this way, this process way, you will follow impoverishment.
> Student: What does a process theologian preach about?

Saddler: Social issues. Bringing about a social synthesis. A little bit of worship of God. Look what has happened to the mainline [Protestant] denominations.

Angie Harlan is clearly upset at being told that she has "fuzzed out." She is very red in the face. Patrick Clark, a student who looks just as young as Angie and who often asks questions based on his extensive reading in philosophy, looks across the aisle at her and then raises his hand. When recognized, he makes a statement: "Just because a system has antimonies and paradoxes, that doesn't negate it. We have lots of antimonies and paradoxes too." Patrick's challenge seems to make Angie bolder. She joins in.

Angie: I have to redeem myself from the charge of being a fluff ball.
Saddler: I am very sorry I said that, Angie. I should not have said that.
Angie: I am reading from my notes on Cobb: "In Jesus, we have to deal with deity itself."
Saddler: Yes, but Jesus is *not* the Logos [the divine Word made into human flesh] for Cobb.
Angie: But still, the view of Jesus is more complex than being only human.
Saddler: You have to watch them, Angie. It's a legerdemain. It is slightly dishonest. That is a terrible thing to say, but I agree with Machen [a conservative theologian who led a separatist movement out of the Presbyterian Church in the early twentieth century]: What they do is an illegitimate swiping of our terms to hold new ideas. We need to be tough-minded. We need to read widely and see what these persons are saying. . . . Cobb is a sincere person, a wonderful person. He serves the church unstintingly. But his theology is dead wrong. It has biblical overtones, because he uses old terms. He was evangelizing us last week in a wonderful style. But what he says is disastrous for New Testament evangelism. His position is really neo-Zoroastrianism. It is secular, modern evolutionism. . . . I just want to leave you with the joy of exegesis, of biblical theology in the Scriptures. I do not have a great deal of time left, and that is where I want to spend my time. I take my stand on the Word.

Saddler sits, and Nagel stands to draw the class to a close. After thanking the speaker, he addresses the students, making a light joke of Saddler's fervent last point: "Because you're young, you can speculate all you want."

The next day, Patrick Clark makes negative references to Saddler's presentation. Telling BW about a class he visited in a liberal seminary in which "they dismissed the biblical evidence," he says: "It is equally as dangerous as what I hear here— throw things out simply because they are modern, like yesterday with Saddler. . . . [It] surprised me that he was so forward in his condemnation. It is dangerous to condemn. I think that he sincerely does not want people to go the way that he did, but no one in the class seemed willing to take Saddler on." Angie Harlan, however, has gained a reputation as someone who takes people on. Shortly after the Saddler incident, Mary Chang—widely viewed as a progressive campus leader and head of the organization for women's equality this year—identifies Angie as a likely future leader: "Angie Harlan, she makes us all look conservative." Angie's father, however, reports that the confrontation has caused her to question whether she is really an evangelical.

"Meeting God at the Perfect Moment"

As iron sharpens iron, so one man sharpens another.

—Proverbs 27:17 (NIV)

A major change at ETS in recent years has been the increasing diversity of students' backgrounds, says Sharp Dunlap, whose title and formal responsibilities have changed often but who remains the administrator who is most informed about students. Twenty years ago, he says, the majority of students had grown up in churches related to denominations—either conservative ones or the conservative wings of the mainline Protestant denominations—and many had attended conservative Christian colleges as well. Though some students still come to ETS with such roots, many more come from elsewhere: from Roman Catholic backgrounds or homes with little or no religious observance, and from nondenominational campus organizations and congregations where they "met the Lord" for the first time as young adults. An increasing number have experienced the charismatic expressions of evangelicalism toward which ETS has historically been very cool. Many more are familiar with the vaguely charismatic style of evangelical student meetings.

Rick Harvey's background illustrates the extent of this new diversity. He writes about it in the student publication for which he serves as the chief editor, calling his father "an embarrassing hero":

[He was] a country pastor in a small church on the plains of Kansas. He loved to preach. He could have been considered a great preacher. Instead, he was an outcast, made fun of by the local pastors and my classmates. He was a hero and an embarrassment to me.

He cast out demons.

What happened in my house growing up I'll never forget. . . . As I walked into the "counseling room," the woman that my dad was working with began to scream violently. When my dad asked what was wrong, the demon replied through the woman, "Get your boy out of here. He loves your Jesus."

I couldn't bring my friends over after school, even to play basketball in the driveway. The screaming was too loud and I didn't want my friends to ask what it was. I didn't want to lose my friends.

His burden was heavy. Some people were delivered, some were not. He was on the phone sometimes for many hours a day with people from all over the world who were seeking advice. He was the town buffoon. He wanted to be a part of his Baptist peers, but was too charismatic for their theology. He wanted to be a part of his charismatic peers, but was too Calvinistic and critical of much of the charismatic movement for their tastes. Very few people offered to help with the work load, and those who did soon lost interest and he was left alone to fight the powers of darkness.

My dad died over four years ago a broken man. He loved to preach. He had been called to cast out demons in a world that didn't understand. . . .

When my faith gets weak, I remember my dad and all the crazy things that went on in my house growing up. I know what I saw and experienced in my youth. If there is one thing that I know is true, it is this: the name of Jesus Christ and His work on the cross is a violent purge of wicked spirits from the lives of His Saints.

Embarrassment keeps the Church away from deliverance work. My dad needed the help. He wanted to preach. Instead he became a hero and a saint.

With this sort of background and "hero," one might expect that Rick would find himself allied with the few intensely zealous evangelists on campus, students like Len Temple ("our house deviant," one administrator called him). Len covers the Iron Sharpens Iron bulletin board, provided for students to post statements and clippings, with long missives in neat Gothic script denouncing the seminary and most of the churches to which it relates. One such contribution tells of a churchgoing couple influenced by "Pastor Disaster" rather than "Charlie Crossbearer." "Under today's ecclesiastical conditions," Len writes, "the devil could pass as 'Born Again' . . . and become a local church member. I'll wager he already is and has." Len is eventually asked to leave the school for obstreperous behavior in class. After many more articles on the bulletin board ("Woe to him who seeks to please rather than appall," a quotation from the sermon in *Moby Dick*) and some legal wrangling, he complies.

Rick Harvey also protests what he takes to be the dominant orientation of the school, and his work also appears often on Iron Sharpens Iron, but not in the cause of religious rigor or charismatic fervor. Instead, Rick is the most audible voice on the liberal or progressive side of theological, social, and political issues. He takes on a wide range of topics, including what seems to him the low level of controversy among students:

"Iron Sharpens Iron" is a microcosm of ETS: dead politically, dying theologically, and weak spiritually. The fact that no one (including myself) volunteered for Current Affairs chair on the Student Association is unforgivable. The results show on this board. Does no one have opinions on anything but abortion? I'm sure that there is at least one person in this campus that's Pro-Choice. Or is there? I can't believe that everyone here has come to the same conclusion in this issue. Everyone bitches about Len's writing, but no on else in this campus stirs up as much debate as he does. That's part of our education.

Being concerned about God's world is not worldliness. . . . To fight against injustice is to fight for God's justice. For students at ETS not to be concerned about these issues is sin.

Of all the topics that Rick takes on in Iron Sharpens Iron notices and student journal articles, none causes a wider range of reactions than his editorial on "The Perfect Moment," the controversial exhibit of photographs by the late Robert Mapplethorpe. Rick has seen the show and writes about it under the heading "Meeting God at the Perfect Moment."

Throughout the exhibit, I felt a tension within myself that can only be described as meeting God in each and every one of the photographs. My reaction and thoughts about God changed as [my wife and I] moved from photo to photo. . . . [Each flower picture] was filled with a sexual tension, creating in me a wanting to be part of, being in consent with, the flower of God. [The nude studies] spirited questions in my own mind about our taboos about nudity, about our lack of celebrating our bodies as creations of God. . . . [In his self-portraits, Mapplethorpe] made himself transparent for the world and myself to see, a refreshing change from the "Hi, how are you's?" of seminary life. . . . I found myself wishing that I too could be this transparent before my wife, friends, and God.

Finally, the brouhaha. The disturbing pictures. . . . And they were. But, in the midst of it all I felt God all the more. God was my shield, my strength in the time of storm. Sin was staring me straight in the face, distorting sex as God had meant it to be. . . . I had reached the depth of human nature and yet felt God by my side giving me peace in the comfort of the Master. I saw what could very well be myself had God not taken me from the clutches of sin. I saw myself as I really am[:] a sinner like Mapplethorpe, like every other human being on earth.

The Mapplethorpe exhibit is not for everyone. . . . But it can not *[sic]* be swept under the carpet and dismissed as homoerotic pornography. Not only does it capture a time in the late seventies when everything was considered permissible, but it tells us about the world and our God. For me, it truly was "The Perfect Moment."

The editorial is immediately posted on the Iron Sharpens Iron board. The board is large—about four feet high and at least five feet long—and affixed to a wall outside the cafeteria. There are other boards for both student organizational and official announcements, but the material on them changes infrequently. By contrast, when school is in session, something new appears on Iron Sharpens Iron several times a week, and when there is a major controversy, new contributions appear daily. The student association appoints someone to maintain the board and to see that the rules against oversized sheets of paper and unsigned contributions are observed. There is also a limit on the amount of time something can remain posted, so sometimes the board will be covered with replies to an article that has already been removed. To keep up with the exchange, students must consult the board frequently, and they do. On one public occasion, the placement of tables in the lobby makes it impossible to reach the board. An administrator admits that this is intentional, because some of the items currently posted do not, in his view, reflect well on the school.

Responses to Rick's editorial appear quickly. Fred Johns, a frequent poster of comments, generally on the conservative side of issues, writes one line: "Rick, your moment would have been made 'perfect' if Christ returned while you were viewing the exhibit." Cary Draper, an even more prominent student conservative, posts a two-page response, printed in several different typefaces:

That the above article, *Meeting God at the Perfect Moment,* evokes a response of complete disgust for myself is an understatement. In answer I argue that no other source is acceptable, besides the Word of God, as means whereby we may experience God and learn of our own fallen nature; the pornography of Robert Mapplethorpe exhibit offers no redeeming or sanctifying value to the Christian. Rick Harvey has not only discredited himself and his ability to produce responsible Christian commentary, but has also brought shame and disgrace to the entire ETS community. . . .

The ending of Rick's article is perhaps the most disturbing point. He says that the Mapplethorpe exhibit . . . "tells us about the world and God." . . . Do we need the vulgar photography of a homosexual to prove our own depravity to us, or does the word of God not clearly spell it out? The truth about our own falleness *[sic]* is found in the objectivity of the Word of God, not the subjectivity of art. . . .

I offer the question to the student body: are the morals which define us to the world as "Christ's own" to be brought into doubt in such a way as the article by Rich Harvey does? I do not question his liberty to write such an article . . . , but he is also representing the student body of an institution training men and women to take the gospel unto all nations. Twenty years from now, if someone were to read *Meeting God* . . . from the archives of this seminary, what would their impression be of the ETS student body of 1990? . . .

It is . . . interesting how Christ prayed for our sanctification, 'Sanctify them in truth; thy word is truth." . . . It is the word of God *alone* which sanctifies and saves. . . . Perhaps the issue at stake is not the exhibit itself; the real issue might just be whether we hold the Word of God up as the beginning and end of what we know about God and His redeeming and sanctifying plan for our lives.

Helen Pericone's shorter, plainly typed contribution is tacked to the board near Cary's, and it takes the opposite position.

I saw the Mapplethorpe exhibit and I thought it was fantastic—some of the best photography I've ever seen. I thought Rick Harvey's article was excellent and echoed many of the feelings I had. . . .

I decided to see "The Perfect Moment" because I was tired of all the Christian junk mail I'd received asking me for money to help fight the NEA. Rather than judge on hearsay I wanted to make an intelligent decision and exercise my critical brain the way ETS taught me. . . .

I think the basic problem for those who have spoken out so vehemently against Mapplethorpe is the fact that he was a homosexual and died of AIDS. I wonder why evangelicals have such a hierarchy of sins. Why are we more quick to forgive—— [prominent evangelical pastor] of his adultery and not Robert Mapplethorpe of his acting out of homosexuality? As far as I know, our forgiveness should never be conditioned on another's repentance. . . .

I was surprised to see many of Mapplethorpe's works were nude studies of women, especially Lisa Lyon. None of the junk mail had warned me about that. What is it that makes us more accepting of a picture of a naked woman? . . .

There are some Christ-followers who are not afraid to be challenged by those who do not follow Christ and use those experiences for growth. I think Rick Harvey is one. I would like to encourage people at ETS to not be afraid of different people and new experiences.

The controversy in writing stretches over several weeks. Blair Jones writes a letter on the Draper side, though much milder. He thanks rather than castigates Rick, but he raises sharp questions:

Can we, as Christians, afford to simply bask in the radiance of our subtly egocentric beatific visions, "celebrating our bodies as creations of God," emotionally distancing ourselves from the revulsion and horror of the moral destruction of a fellow human being? . . . Rick, I am concerned with what appears to be the erosion of our Christian moral sensitivities. Are we, with ever dulling senses, being inexorably drawn into an adulterous liason *[sic]* with our morally relativistic culture? . . . If we compromise Truth in a misguided effort to gain the right to be heard, what will we have left to say?

One student posts a Bible verse as his negative response to the editorial; another, Brendon Martin, also a frequent writer in student publications, chided him for using Scripture to condemn a fellow Christian. The first student replied:

> Relax! Your point is very much understood, and had my intent in the use of this passage been what was supposed, the point would have been extremely valid. . . . I do not question Rick's integrity as a Christian. . . . I still maintain the relevance of the passage from Romans, applied to . . . the question of legitimacy, *but not applied to Rick himself.* . . .
>
> While all of us get so excited and squabble over Mapplethorpe, scribbling seas of ink all over this board, the misery of the world goes on. I would like to turn my attention to that, and seek the healing power of Christ. As a beginning to this end, if bitter feelings and hurt still linger, I would like to seek reconciliation with my brother, somewhere other than here on the bulletin board. My box number is at the head of the page; I live upstairs in room 64. Rick and Brendon: let's get together.

While these commentaries remain on the Iron Sharpens Iron board, a midwestern jury acquits the director of a museum that hosted the Mapplethorpe show of obscenity charges. BW meets Rich Harvey, who is slight, blond, and boyish-looking and wears the typical neat and casual clothes of a ETS student, and they discuss the verdict. BW says that it may show that people can form their own views, even when they know relatively little about the matter to be decided. "Yes," says Rick, "everywhere but here."

"And Your Daughters"

> Now, this is what was spoken by the prophet Joel:
> In the last days, God says,
> I will pour out my Spirit on all people.
> Your sons and daughters will prophesy,
> your young men will see visions,
> your old men will dream dreams.
> Even on my servants, both men and women,
> I will pour out my Spirit in those days,
> and they will prophesy.
> —Acts 2:16–18

The next year, the student paper has a new name. *Bell's Ridge Times* (whose name came, the masthead said, from the seminary's location on Bell's Ridge) now has the title *Didache II,* and unlike its predecessors (two years ago, the publication was called *The Advance),* this paper contains poetry and boxed quotations. Some of these are key lines from the articles; others are extraneous, such as the following, which appears under the heading "I wish I'd said that . . . " and which is printed without attribution "to protect the guilty": "A lot of folks here talk about being 'Reformed,' but I don't see it happening to any of them." The biggest change is the editor: Now it is Rich Harvey's principal opponent, Cary Draper.

Cary looks the part he plays as leading campus conservative. His fair hair is cut short in military style. He invariably wears the neat, preppy clothes—shirts with button-down collars and leather shoes—that are the uniform of a group of theologically conservative male students sometimes called the "Truly Reformed" by other students. Cary has a solid conservative pedigree. He grew up in several southern cities; his parents attended independent and evangelical churches. He was involved in campus religious activities and decided to let "the Lord . . . be the authority in my life" at the age of fifteen. Originally, Cary wanted to attend law school and then "go into national security," perhaps working for the FBI. Advisers convinced him that he would not like the "red tape." Eventually, he settled on ministry as a profession because he was "good at" his leadership of his Campus Crusade for Christ group. Before seminary he worked briefly for a nuclear weapons plant. He chose ETS, despite its pluralism, which he views as undesirable, because it was outside the South. His study of southern history, he says, had taught him that "one of the reasons for the downfall of the South" was that "plantation owners' sons" spent too much time at home, "hunting, fishing, and horseback riding . . . , and these are all things that I love to do and are . . . really available for me down there." His best friend went to seminary in Mississippi, "and he has proved my theory correct."

Cary is intensely critical of ETS—especially of the students. They do not meet his expectations: "to be well-dressed, or at least neatly dressed; to chew with their mouth shut at the dinner table and be able to carry on a pleasant conversation; and even above and beyond that . . . , to be able to talk about theology and do it in such a way that feelings aren't hurt." He points to handwritten notices on the Iron Sharpens Iron board as examples of his fellow students' slothfulness. "Beyond every other concern here—minority concerns, social concerns, economic concerns—above everything is, are we really learning the Scriptures, are we willing to work hard to do it? And I really don't see that willingness on the part of the students here." He is especially critical of the fact that the school welcomes Pentecostals, who are, in his view, "a different religion" from "historic [*sic*] Protestantism" because they assume that "revelation is not bound between the covers of Scripture." He acknowledges, however, that deciding on whom to exclude from the seminary would be tricky. He cites the case of Joel Cotton, a professor of missions whose personal holiness Cary admires but who does not meet his doctrinal standard.

Cary is a controversial figure among his fellow students. Pamela Willis, who is also from the Deep South, likes and respects him but is critical of his "southern attitudes," and especially of the fact that he and professors he admires still read the work of antebellum southern theologians she thinks are "racist." Paula Fleming describes herself as "charismatic" and "Arminian"—positions Cary opposes—and differs with him deeply on racial matters, but she once had long talks with him. Now, she says, Cary is so busy following "his heroes Barnes[1] and Bashford" around that he does not think for himself. "He ought to follow Jesus instead."

A major student debate centers on whether Cary is a "redneck." "He says he's not a redneck, but he is a redneck," says Pamela. Cary himself keeps the controversy alive. In a public discussion about multiculturalism, Andrew Nagel argues that ETS is in effect three campuses, "one for whites and Asians, one for Haitians, American blacks and others, and one for—" As Professor Henry Givens supplies the word "southerners," Cary Draper calls out "rednecks" from the back of the room.

An issue that arises on Cary's watch as editor of the student paper has to do with the leadership of women in the church. The year before, when the Mapplethorpe controversy was raging, this would have been difficult to predict. The question of whether women should be ordained and permitted to preach is one that almost everyone, including authority figures such as Parks, who favor it, and self-described "traditionalists" like Cary, who do not, seem to agree is an area of permissible disagreement. Cary, in fact, wrote in *Bell's Ridge Times* the year before that the role of women is a "secondary issue," like baptism, on which his "Baptist brothers and sisters" are wrong but, nonetheless, "I shall enjoy [their] company . . . in heaven one day."

What sets off the debate about women in the church is a poster. A woman who teaches regularly at ETS but is not a faculty member places a large poster on the Iron Sharpens Iron board, apparently unaware of the regulations limiting size and forbidding unsigned submissions. Her poster depicts a wall on which had been written a verse from the biblical book of Acts (itself a quotation from the Book of Joel): "Your sons and daughters shall prophesy." In the picture the words "and daughters" have been painted out, and a man dressed in Anglican clerical costume—a round collar, stole, and long surplice—is walking away from the wall with a bucket of paint. Paula Fleming, certain that Cary Draper, who is in charge of the Iron Sharpens Iron board and the student publication, would take the poster down, removes it herself and places it on the board of the women's advocacy organization she chairs. The women's board is newly covered with a locking glass case. It is the only board so protected, probably because of past vandalism attributed to a small group of young, single men who are aggressively opposed to women serving in preaching ministries and make anonymous protests, perhaps fearing the school's antiharassment policies.

The poster set off a storm. "I never thought [it] would cause that kind of reaction," says Paula. "Most students here seem to have had their sense of humor surgically extracted before they came. I missed the line on the application that said you had to do that." Cary Draper and Blair Jones prepare a set of opposing statements, published in *Didache II,* Cary's under the heading "Point" and Blair's under "Counterpoint." The issue between them is not women's ordination as such but the one that Cary had raised before about the use of "images." He writes:

> We who will one day be entrusted with the great questions of Christ's visible church have cause to be concerned over the use of the medium of image. And it would follow that we should have special concern when it is employed by fellow students and a professor to make a point regarding women's role in the church visible (and how men handle certain passage of scripture). . . . Those who support women's ordination are (1) not willing to articulate their position in only that medium which will communicate truth and logical arguments (words) and (2) are willing to employ mediums which, if employed by conservatives/traditionalists[,] would result in possible administrative disciplinary action (per student catalog statement on women . . .).
>
> Will art replace verbal articulation, or dance replace debate? Dumoulin wrote that

"it is easier to look at paintings than to understand doctrine." Our society is character-
ized with intellectual impatience and an inability to think.

Blair Jones, identifying himself as a member of the women's advocacy group,
argues for

> the importance of communicating beyond words, and the cruciality of receiving be-
> yond the printed page. Rather than allowing ourselves to [be] blinded [by] our own
> preconceptions, let us be among the mature, who "because of practice have their senses
> trained to discern good and evil." (Hebrews 5:14). Or will we be like those to whom
> Jesus said "When it is evening, you say, 'it will be fair weather, for the sky is red.'
> And in the morning, 'There will be a storm today, for the sky is red and threatening.'
> Do you know how to discern the appearance of the sky, but cannot discern the signs
> of the times?"

The whole twenty-page issue of *Didache II*—twice the usual length—is similarly
balanced between "traditional" views like those of the editor and "liberal" ones
like those of Blair Jones. Sarah Trumbell points out that Cary is "surrounded by
liberals"—associate editors like her, Blair, and Brendon Martin. But the tradition
of balance is a long one: Rick Harvey gave Cary a prominent column in the
previous year's *Times,* and balance is one of Cary's explicit commitments as well.

The debate continues on the bulletin board. A side issue arises over a short
notice posted by the dean, a rare intrusion by the administration onto Iron Sharpens Iron:

> God's words create pictures that are wonderfully funny, outrageously comical, bitingly
> ironic, festively joyful, if only one's eyes have been opened to see.
>   The author . . . makes the point that only converted people can laugh. There's hope,
> then, for this community which, if we would lighten up a bit in our heavy discussions
> on this board or in *Didache II,* might hear God's laughter. He has seen fit to use humor
> not to make a mere point or two, but a Bible full of them.
>   I think we might want to give it a try and . . . succeed. Converted image-bearers
> really can laugh.

Next to this, a student has placed a handwritten note:

> Mr. van Dierson,
> HA-HA-HA!!!

And Timothy Woods, Paula Fleming's closest friend and fellow "prayer warrior,"
has posted a typed letter to the dean, saying that "whenever I think of this school
I am overcome by laughter and become 'out of control.' Remember[,] Keep the
Faith and Keep Smiling . . . it goes well with your outfit!!!"

Fred Johns has posted a double message. The typed portion reads in part:

> ### Regarding "Point/Counterpoint"
> I am uncertain whether I agree with Blair Jones or Cary Draper on the viability of
> images as a means of conveying the truth. However, I am quite certain that I neither
> agree with nor appreciate what the image in question communicates: a false stereotype,
> and bitterness. What if those of us who are not "partners" were to post an image of a

scowling lesbian in clerical garb painting over 1 Timothy 2:11–12 ["A woman should learn in quietness and true submission . . ."]? This would likewise be reinforcing a false stereotype, and indicative of bitterness.

Handwritten at the bottom of the sheet, and signed with Fred's initials, is a note to the dean: "If I were to post my 'contra' poster, would that tickle your funny-bone, or would it be sexist?"

Sally Trumbell responds to Fred on a small sheet torn from a minister's life insurance company notepad. She is no stranger to these debates. Last year she posted a poem about the pain of being a woman ("Do you have no concept of what it is like / To heed the call and encounter the might of masculine pride?") Cary Draper replied, "Sally, if we are to sharpen each other, we must approach issues scripturally. The world points fingers and casts insults." She countered, "Exegesis is not the only issue. My own views evolved from a traditional mindset." When Sally, who has a tenuous relationship with her supervising United Methodist conference, first came to seminary, she was opposed to anything that she took to be stridency on behalf of women, though she always aimed to be ordained. But since then, she has become strident herself, in the view of many students. Sally and Blair Jones the previous year performed a "turnabout" skit that provoked many objections. They portrayed the seminary as named for a woman and traditionalist men as unhappy with the use of the word "womankind" for all humanity. Blair posted an apology on Iron Sharpens Iron.

Now Sally writes in response to Fred Johns: "Could someone please explain to my poor female intellect what a lesbian looks like just so I'll know when a poster does happen to go up? Thanks." Fred, writing on the same slip of paper, rejoins: "Sally, I know you are aware of the stereotype of which I spoke. . . . P.S. Spare us the sarcasm." But he also replaces his sheet with another entitled "Regarding 'Point/Counterpoint' *Revisited.*" In it, "lesbian" is changed to "woman," and a postscript is typewritten:

> For those of you who have been diverted from the issue, a revision has been marked in bold so that you will not be hindered by the non-issue you were preoccupied with. Please try to understand my intentions: If the tables were turned, you would be hurt. I am hurt by that poster; it is an unloving gesture, one which shows a lack of respect for my position (and very little imagination). I too interpret the whole counsel of God, but reach different conclusions. Please be charitable.

Later in the same week, Andrew Nagel, speaking to theology majors on postmodernism, refers with evident approval to the "culture wars" in *Didache II* among students who hold apparently similar theological views.

FIVE

Students

There is considerable diversity among students. There is a split between those who are academic and those who are practical, though that is kind of a sidelight. There's a split between the Pentecostals and the others, people who don't know what a rapture is. There's a split over the role of women, . . . and there is now a difference over baptism.

—Trent Lee

Ron Biddle

[M]any of the folks in the Presbytery will ask me why am I going to ETS and not one of our accredited schools, and I . . . tell them . . . this school is very Reformed. . . . I'm like a fish *in* water here. I love it, and the stuff that is being taught is solid Reformed doctrine.

—Ron Biddle

The telephone rings in Ron Biddle's apartment. After several rings, an answering machine picks up. The caller hears the opening bars of "Pennsylvania 6-5000" played by the Glenn Miller Orchestra before the taped message announces that the Biddles are not at home. Ron Biddle, a lively, outgoing, articulate young man in his late twenties, is completing his third and final year of the Master of Divinity program at Evangelical Theological Seminary. A member of the Presbyterian Church (U.S.A.), Ron and his wife Charlotte live in married student housing on campus.

The middle child of five, Ron grew up in an affluent suburb of Pittsburgh, where he has spent most of his life except two years in France. When Ron was a seventh grader, his father, a bank executive, went to Paris to open a branch office. Although he grew up attending a Presbyterian church with his family, Ron did not "become a Christian" until the ninth grade. With his mother's prodding, he joined a Bible study led by a new youth minister of his church, Peter Snow. Feeling the Holy Spirit stirring his heart, Ron spoke to Peter as a session was coming to a close:

> And so I went up to him . . . and I say, "Pete, man, we need to pray. How do I accept Jesus?" And he says, "That's great!" "But," I say, "we've got to pray fast because my mom's coming to pick me up." So, we pray this real quick prayer. [At home] I run upstairs and I dig out . . . the Bible I received from . . . the church in the third grade. I dust the thing off and I just start reading like crazy and I pray my real prayer then, . . . and ever since then, I've just been reading and reading . . . and it's been an up and down but mostly up and . . . very much a true manifestation of God's grace in my life, unworthy as I am of it. It's truly humbling and . . . causes my commitment to deepen.

A decision to pursue ordination did not come until Ron's undergraduate years at a small Presbyterian college. Preparing to be an elementary school science teacher, he also helped with the Christian education program. This led him to work toward a double major combining elementary and Christian education. All the while, he recalls:

> My mom would say things like, "Ron's going to be a preacher." I'm saying, "No way.". . . [B]y my junior year, I did an internship at my church . . . with a guy named Duncan Spivy, and I followed him around. That's what I did. I shadowed everything he would do [as pastor]. . . . Well, after that experience, it really hit me. And I was evaluating the skills and talents and how the Lord has worked in my life, and I thought, "How can I best utilize all of the skills and talents the Lord has given me? Could I best use them in the elementary school, or would they be best utilized in pastoring?" . . . I thought about it long and hard, and it came down to the final wire that the pastorate was the important aspect. And so it was at that point that I felt the very kernel of the call, and I started working in that direction.

Ron felt, however, that he was too young and inexperienced to go directly to seminary: "How can twenty-five-year-olds think they are ready to deal with the problems of people that are fifty-five or sixty or deal with divorce and all that stuff? I said, 'No way am I ready!'" So he took the first of two steps to deepen his experience.

First, starting in Seattle the year after he graduated from college, he bicycled across the country alone, speaking and raising funds for Habitat for Humanity and visiting Habitat projects. Second, he spent the next four years working on a commuter college campus for the Coalition for Christian Outreach, a parachurch organization headquartered in Pittsburgh. During that time, he met his wife-to-be, an elementary school teacher. They were married in his second year with the coalition.

Besides deepening his experience, his work with the coalition also gave him advanced credit at ETS. The school sends professors to lead courses at the coalition's spring training program. Advance credit allowed Ron to accelerate his program at ETS.

Why ETS? Ron says that after weighing various options among seminaries, he chose ETS because of graduates he knew and admired: "I was impressed . . . by their level of commitment to God and service to the Lord. I thought, man, you know, that school's got something good." There was also the school's reputation for providing "solid Reformed doctrine." Describing himself as "like a fish *in* water," he tells JC:

> I love it here. . . . When I go into a class and I see a professor standing before me that not only knows his stuff or her stuff, but also has a level of commitment to the Lord God that just emanates from their lives, you sit there and you go, "Gosh, this is really wonderful!" Because I can learn from them academically and also from the whole life aspect.

When reflecting about specific professors, he mentions excitement over a forthcoming course, The Demise of Theology, with Roy Parks. "I think that's going to be an awesome class!" He also praises Scott Hershey, Jerome Allen, Paul Bashford, and Charles Oliver—all professors of biblical studies. "All these guys, you know, they make you work, but you're glad for it." Also singled out is his faculty adviser, Henry (Hank) Givens, who is a member of the nearby Orthodox Presbyterian Church, which Ron and Charlotte attend. Ron helps with the church's boy's group and occasionally reads the Scripture during worship.

Ron appreciates supervised ministry programs, seeing them as important "sifting mechanisms" in identifying students with such "weak emotional structures that they could never minister to anybody."

Community life for married students at the seminary is difficult, he says, especially for spouses such as Charlotte, whose on-campus contacts are limited. Ron says that he makes friends in his classes, "and I . . . bring them down to the place, and she says, 'Ron, I don't understand all of this. You bring all of your friends down and I have nobody to talk to.' " He and Charlotte do play cribbage regularly with another student couple, and they have friends among other couples in their building. Ron also has established strong friendships with fellow workers in the school's print shop, where he holds a part-time job. He and his print shop buddies carry on extended theological discussions as they are "folding stuff." A major topic, for example, is the Arminian versus the Calvinist view of human nature: Methodists and Pentecostals, with their Arminian backgrounds, have a particularly difficult time with the strong Reformed emphasis of the school. "I sympathize with them, but that is where the school is at the present time," he says.

At the upcoming fish fry, a fixture in the school's annual fall orientation program for new students, Ron will be playing trombone in a Dixieland jazz band. "They're . . . folks from [nearby], and I got hooked in with them. We go and play gigs all over the place." He sees people contact as an important part of his education.

> [Y]ou are not only getting your academics and learning to process an exegesis, and how to preach, and all these other little elements that will give you an edge so you can do your ministry effectively, but it's being able to apply that stuff within the community. And I'm very committed to that.
>
> I want to be a part of the PCUSA [Presbyterian Church (U.S.A.)]. I am committed to that. I feel that that's a wonderful denomination, and I think that its heritage is just

something that can't be left to dissolve in the rot of society. I think it needs to be upheld.

Earlier in the interview, Ron has told JC that the solid Reformed theological emphasis of the school "will be helpful . . . especially in the PCUSA." He looks forward to becoming a pastor:

> I would like to be a preacher and use all of my gifts and skills in education and public speaking . . . effectively to spur people on. . . . I would like to see lay leadership really be central within the congregation, that they would have a really solid identity in their Christian faith and be able to do the ministry of the community. And I would just be a facilitator . . . and a teacher, you know, a "doctor of Christian faith," and the whole church would be the family of faith. . . . I think there's something missing in today's twentieth-century Christianity. People don't have confidence in Christianity. They are involved [out of] fear . . . or because they were raised that way, but not by conviction. I would love to have people be convicted by the truth . . . of Christianity.

Zak Korkas

> Life's not fair, but God is good.
>
> —Zak Korkas

Saturday morning breakfast in the ETS dining room is relaxed. No one is rushing off to classes. Zak Korkas is among the students gathered around the table. He and the others joke with JC about his and BW's research on the seminary: They must be guarded in their comments. A more serious worry is about term papers that are due and upcoming exams. The semester ends in two weeks. The major topic, however, is about plans for the weekend and upcoming Christmas parties, including one tonight at Hollis House, a residence for women students. "Lots of food. Come 'pig out,' " the invitation reads. One of the men turns this into a not-too-complimentary joke about the Hollis House residents. Zak and fellow student Elvin Weyl tell about stopping by a nearby karaoke bar—an increasingly popular pastime for students—before going to an evangelical counseling center to serve as telephone counselors. They laugh as they describe some patrons' attempts to sing to the musical accompaniment.

Zachariah Korkas, a short, muscular, dark-haired Californian, is thirty-five years old and a graduating senior. He will complete his Master of Divinity program in three years. Now divorced himself and the son of divorced parents—"the whole dysfunctional family thing," he says—Zak is the father of two children who are in California and whom he sees often. His family was Greek Orthodox, but early in his life, the Korkases joined a Presbyterian Church, not because it was Presbyterian so much as "because it was a Bible-teaching church." Zak has been a Christian since he can remember: "I never doubted who Jesus was in my life. . . . You know, I had my rabbit tracks, where I took off and sinned and did things, but it was [done] . . . knowing the consequences."

After college graduation, Zak ran the family business, a health club, where he was personal trainer and general manager. He continued his involvement in the Presbyterian church, serving as a youth leader. "I've always felt like I was called to the ministry," he says, "and seminary was just a matter of getting here, I guess. I avoided it as long as I could." When did the avoidance stop? "I burned out at work, and then I went through a divorce, and just had to say, you know, what am I going to do? . . . I had a good job offer where I could have made a lot of money doing something else. I just started lining up my priorities, and I said, 'Nah, I've done that thing; it doesn't make you happy.' "

The choice of ETS was influenced by his pastor, a trustee of the school, and the school's reputation as solid, conservative, and interdenominational:

> I . . . came here to basically equip my tool kit for studying the Scriptures . . . I knew that I wanted good exegesis; I wanted good languages; I wanted to be able to go out and teach the Bible for what I believe it is, and in a world that's fallen. . . . I came here for that specific reason, and [the school] had a good reputation for that.
>
> You know . . . maybe being older . . . I didn't come . . . expecting to have some great religious spiritual retreat experience. . . . I mean, people are sinners here too. . . . I knew what I was coming for, and it is an academic structure, so it's not going to be different from any other academic setting, with the competition and things that carry over from how you've gone to school all these years. So I don't think I had any expectations of some great grandeur of a spiritual high.

Biblical studies are Zak's major focus. No one professor has been a decisive influence. He has not dived into anyone's paradigm or become their clone, he says:

> I'm sure I've been influenced by all of them. I enjoy the work ethic, like for Dr. Allen and Dr. Bashford—you know, the teachers that demand the most. . . . I look at this as an investment, so . . . if I'm paying seven hundred and something dollars for a class, I want my money's worth. I just don't want to buy a degree and walk out of here with a piece of paper.

The theology taught at ETS has not surprised him, though coming from California, he had been accustomed to a theology with "a little more dispensational slant to it, not quite so Reformed," he says. "I'm . . . probably not a hyper-Calvinist like some professors may be, but I get along with them. . . . I'm getting stretched. . . . I'm learning. It's painful, but it's good."

He also cites a supervised ministry assignment he created for himself as an important growth experience. Twice a week, he travels to the church where he has developed a men's ministry:

> I really believe that where the church has fallen short is in the area of the men. Because I think if you get a man, you get his whole family. . . . [W]omen have run the church so long. . . . The men aren't doing it, so it creates many problems. . . . I mean, men should be teaching kids in Sunday school, elementary school kids, and they're not. And they should be involved with some type of ministry, and they're not. . . . [If they did], I think it would free women up to seek out what they might be more called to do in ministries.

Describing himself as an evangelist—a "friendship evangelist" rather than a "tract-hander-outer"—he would like to evangelize businessmen, since that is his background. He will probably do so as a Baptist or in an independent church: "I've not been geared to be a denominational person."

As Zak reflects on his experiences at the school, he muses that being here has probably not made him any more committed to evangelism than he was when he arrived; "I've always been evangelistic." But he continues:

> I think I've been refined. . . . You have to be pushed, you know. I mean you have to go through the pain of writing papers and learning languages. . . . So, yeah, . . . I would not want to do what I'm headed to do without being here first. I had to do it, you know. I had to take the hardest classes. You just do or else you're not going to grow. So, yeah, I'm definitely different, wiser, smarter. . . . [Y]ou have to take the time. . . . Jesus went away; Paul spent three years on his own; Moses had a long time away. So . . . I think if you look at this as your time away before you dive in and get your tail kicked in ministry—yeah, you've got to be here.

Amy and Neal Huchett

[I]t was like Pentecostalism was the New Jersey of denominations

—Amy Huchett

It is the Saturday before Thanksgiving. Covenant House is crowded with shoppers taking advantage of a seminary-wide Christmas craft sale. An early snow has added to the holiday feeling. Student wives and staff members have set up tables to display their handmade goods—Christmas tree ornaments, wreaths and decorations, jams and jellies, toys, and other gift items. At one table, Amy Huchett has a large collection of knit goods for sale.

Amy is pretty, with fair skin, wide-set eyes, and long, curly dark hair. Her husband, Neal is slight of build and intense. Both are in their midtwenties and from New Jersey. They are both graduates of Rutgers University and are Pentecostals. They each came to ETS to study, but Amy discontinued work toward the M.A. in counseling after her second year of classes. Neal is a third-year M.Div. student and intends to be a pastor in the Assemblies of God, the Pentecostal denomination to which he and Amy belong.

Being Pentecostal at ETS, with its strongly Reformed theological emphasis, has not been easy for the Huchetts. Amy recalls their first year at the seminary, before they were married: "When we used to eat in the cafeteria, you'd hear comments that people [would make]. I don't think they'd realize that [we] were Pentecostal . . . , and [the comments] were just awful. . . . It just seemed like it was—I mean, we're from New Jersey, so we're used to New Jersey jokes, but it was like Pentecostalism was the New Jersey of denominations."

"Yeah," Neal elaborates, "I think—well, you know, a lot of it is just ignorance." He finds the attitude within the faculty and describes it as "discouraging":

For instance, Dr. Givens did a class on gifts of the Holy Spirit, and the first thing he said when he was talking about it was how [gifts] are misused. But it seems to me he's coming from a Presbyterian background, and maybe the first thing he should have said was how [gifts] are ignored and then gone into how they are misused. So I don't know why he would attack the Pentecostal first before attacking something like that. . . . Sometimes I feel . . . it's like a bunch of people on a sinking ship, throwing stones at . . . the Pentecostal ship that is soaring. . . . [Why not] appreciate what they're doing? They've got more missionaries and more missionary money per person in the denomination than any other denomination. And so to be throwing stones, you know—sometimes I wonder about that.

Amy adds that negativism about Pentecostals even affects some students' choice of whom to date. During her first year in seminary, before they were married, she would hear comments from women friends in Covenant House about various men: "Oh, that guy's really cute! Too bad he's a Pentecostal."

Neal and Amy met in college through Campus Crusade for Christ. Neal, who had recently had a "born again" experience, gave his testimony. "I said to my roommate," Amy smiles, "'That's the one!'"

Born in Virginia while her father was serving in Vietnam, Amy moved with her family to New Jersey and later to Colorado. Raised a Presbyterian, she was active in the church, but "I never really connected with it." Her parents divorced during Amy's high school years, and she returned to New Jersey with her mother, whom she describes as "very, very liberal." Amy's mother is an elder in her Presbyterian church, but the daughter believes that "it's just a cubby-hole-type thing, where . . . she tries to be a good person and all that, but I just don't think that God has made much of a difference in her life." Thus, her mother did not take the news well when Amy "became a Christian" through the influence of Campus Crusade: "She didn't talk to me for a couple of weeks after." Later, after undergoing the baptism of the Holy Spirit, Amy became Pentecostal. Her mother was upset: "She went crazy! 'We don't pray in tongues; we're Presbyterians!'"

Neal, who has lived in New Jersey since he was a small child, grew up as a practicing Roman Catholic. His family took—and still takes—its Catholicism seriously. At the time he went away to college, he was engaged in an intense search for the meaning of life. He had a "born again" experience through the influence of a cousin, a charismatic Catholic, and shortly after that became involved with Campus Crusade. He found the group's emphasis on the authority of the Bible very helpful.

First Neal, then Amy, experienced the baptism of the Holy Spirit during their junior year at Rutgers. For him, it happened on February 28, 1988—"you have to know [the date] when they ask you"—as he read a book, *How to Be Clothed in the Holy Spirit*. "I got down on my knees, and I tried, and I was baptized in the Holy Spirit. . . . [T]he tongues were not really noticeable to me, but I knew that I'd been baptized in the Holy Spirit." When he shared his experience with Amy, he recalls: "She said, 'I've got to have it.' She got on her knees, and was baptized as well. She started speaking in tongues more fluently than I had. She said, 'Just try it, just do it.' We got down on our knees together . . . and it started coming out more for me. So we both, from that point on[,] . . . speak in tongues."

The decision to attend seminary was made while they were on a Campus Crusade mission trip to the Philippines. Both knew, following their conversion, that they wanted to be vocationally involved in religion: Amy leaned toward counseling; Neal toward the pastorate. As Amy describes the decision:

> Not having been raised in an evangelical home . . . I [only] knew of Princeton Seminary, because I was right next to it, and that was about it. We had no background knowing what seminaries were what. So we searched through books, and all kinds of stuff like that, and graduate school guides. And just from what was offered, and the location, and the conservative bent, we . . . [chose] ETS.

The pastor of the church they were attending, who was a graduate of the school, also helped them in their decision.

Did they worry about the Reformed theological emphasis of the school? "Yes," said Neal.

> We wrote a letter to Dr. Parks, because . . . when I applied here, I got five handwritten letters from professors saying, "Do you have any questions?" . . . So I picked . . . Dr. Parks, and one of the questions I asked was about [the baptism of the Spirit]. His answer was that some argue for it and others against it. So it was good enough for me. I'm willing to hear other people—in fact, I want that, to both strengthen me or change me. So I thought that was perfect. What has happened is I've been strengthened in my position here.

Delaying marriage until after their first year in seminary, Amy lived in Covenant House, and Neal lived in a men's dormitory. Both describe the year as an "infatuation period" with the school. "I was just kind of awed by all of it," says Amy. "And I was so excited . . . and learning neat things."

Neal had a similar response: "I think back and, you know, I had never been in an environment where everyone was mostly Christian. . . . And then, here are these guys [the professors], you know they have well-thought-out beliefs. . . . [M]ost of them have some degree of fame for what they believe, at least within the Christian community."

For Amy, the excitement lasted the first year. "Then, I had one more year of classes, and after that, I decided that was enough." Partly it was the pressure of combining academics with a job in a nearby medical center. She also attributes her decision to withdraw to reflection on her spiritual gifts:

> Once I finally started realizing how important it is to be the part of the Body of Christ that you are, and not try to be something that you're not . . . , then I was able to let go of that neurotic obsession with having a masters degree and being a professional and all that kind of stuff. Then I was able to make a . . . more clearheaded decision.

Neil's enthusiasm for the seminary experience remains strong, although after two years, "the infatuation where you're three feet off the ground . . . stops, and that's probably good." He reflects: "Maybe I've gained more confidence in my own theology, so that I don't look at the professors much and say, 'Wow!' as much as I say, 'Well, I think my theology's a little better than yours,' and they say, 'All right.' . . . So you start to lose the Cinderella sort of feel of being in school."

Looking back, he says, "I've worked really hard, and I've found out that my friends also happen to be people who take [studying] probably a little too seriously." Most of those friends he sees at the library. "I don't actually study with them; we just like talking." When asked if he has developed any close relationships with his professors, he responds, "Not at all, no. . . . [I]t's the ideas they give you and . . . you know, just using the books in the library."

He continues to reflect on the school's impact on him: I have had . . . a unique experience. . . . I came here an Arminian, and I am a Calvinist now, and not from the professors so much, but on my own studying, my own research. I've become a Calvinist, meaning that I believe . . . in God's choosing, over and against free will, and God's ordaining all things." Does this mean, he asks, that he has given up on Pentecostalism? Not at all:

> I'm a Calvinist Pentecostal. . . . I mean . . . I agree with the Assemblies of God that if you don't have a vibrant relationship with God that's growing and developing, you have no way of knowing whether you are a saved person. . . . You hear Calvinists say, "Well, now you're saved, so don't worry about anything." I'm so against that. . . . [T]here needs to be a vital, living relationship with Christ.

Neal adds that he should have no problem as an Assemblies of God minister so long as he does not "make a disturbance out of [his Calvinist interpretation]. . . . You can hold [this position]. . . . You might be able to teach it, but if there's a disturbance, they could say . . . 'You'll have to go.' "

His aim is to fulfill his calling "in preaching, and in helping those who are under the preaching to incorporate the Word into their lives and to . . . help them incorporate the change that [this] may bring about."

So, BW asks, has ETS been a good experience? "From one to ten," Neal responds, "I give it about a 9.8!"

Cole Silas

> What's so bad about being born again?
>
> —Inscription on Cole Silas's T-shirt

A first-year student, Cole Silas is attending a New Testament survey class taught by Michael Tucker. The subject for the evening is the formation of the canon and the implications for Scriptural inerrancy. At a break, Cole tells JC that he would like to ask the professor about a matter that has been troubling him in his work with youth: What, he wants to know, should one do when witnessing to someone about the gospel when that person does not accept the Bible as the Word of God? He hopes Dr. Tucker can help him with an answer. When the class resumes, however, he does not ask the question.

Earlier in the same evening, Cole and four other students—Terry Price, Chuck Hearn, Tim Rothman, and Ward Coady—take JC on a tour of Men's Dorm I, where they live. All five are in their first year at ETS. The dormitory, described by a former resident as a "hellhole," houses a gymnasium, where a basketball game is in progress. The tour ends in Cole's room, a spartan space decorated primarily with religious posters. He jokes about how thin the walls are.

Cole and JC talk briefly about an upcoming New Testament class. Then Cole excuses himself to go to a prayer group with the other four students.

The five students were not acquainted before coming to ETS. Assigned to rooms near one another, they took seriously an upperclassman's suggestion that they form a prayer group. Their group is denominationally diverse. Cole is a Conservative Baptist; Terry was raised a Presbyterian but is now involved in an independent Baptist congregation; Chuck is United Methodist; Tim is a third-generation member of the Assemblies of God; and Ward is Episcopalian. They met weekly to pray together throughout their first year and continued to meet less frequently during their second and third years. In the process, they have become very close friends. In an interview near the end of their third year, Terry tells JC that the five still do many things together. Prayer, he says, is the basis of their friendship. Of Cole Silas in particular, Terry says, "[He] is probably my very closest friend. He is an absolute gem of a guy. Nothing pretentious, just a great person and deeply committed to the Lord."

As JC passes the small prayer chapel in Brill Hall following dinner, he hears lively music coming from the room. Looking in, he sees Cole Silas, Terry Price, and three other students—one an African-American, Lucas Beckley—absorbed in a "jam session." Cole is playing drums, Lucas the piano; Terry and the other two are singing and moving with the music. The song in progress is "O for a Thousand Tongues to Sing," rendered in a "gospel rock" setting that JC has not previously heard. They motion for him to come in, and Lucas says, "Let's hit it again for Dr. Jack!" They do so with great verve, following this with another Christian song by the same composer. Lucas and Cole tell JC that they play together frequently for various church groups.

Now in his late twenties, Cole Silas grew up in a Boston suburb and was Roman Catholic until he was eighteen. His parents divorced when he was a fifth grader. His mother has since remarried and is still a practicing Catholic: "My mom and [step]dad have a . . . saving faith. They are still growing."

Cole's natural father, an electrician, traveled a lot in his work and "started getting involved with the wrong type of people. He got involved in drugs and drinking, and [the marriage] just kind of fell apart." He has "been basically unemployed since then." Cole continues:

> [My dad] has been through quite a bit. He has been in prison many times, and he has been near death many times, and God has spared his life. I believe that God is working, is a shepherd over him. It is a prayer of mine . . . that God will watch over him. . . . I have to worry about him. He is in a lot of pain. I know that I can commit this to the Lord.

More than anyone else in his family, Cole has maintained a relationship with his father: "We are pretty close even though we are very different."

When they were teenagers, Cole and his younger brother played basketball at a neighborhood Conservative Baptist church. "My brother and I didn't know it was anything Christian. . . . We just thought it was some guys getting together to play basketball," he says. "Afterward they had a Bible study." Later, on a retreat with the church's youth group, Cole says, "I turned my life over to Christ. . . . The youth pastor really took me under his wing. I was involved in a music program he was doing[,] . . . playing drums and singing." Cole's association in the church grew, and by his senior year in high school, he had joined the church and was part of the youth ministry leadership team.

Attending a nearby college, Cole majored in business but continued his affiliation with the church's youth ministry. He also worked in his stepfather's appliance business, which he did for several years after graduating from college. Although his stepfather offered him a management position in the business, Cole had come to believe that "God wanted me to go into youth ministry."

Because of proximity and having had a cousin and several pastors who are ETS graduates, Cole chose ETS for theological study: "I knew it was one of the strongest seminaries in the country. I didn't apply to any other schools." He is pursuing a Master of Arts in Youth Ministry degree.

Professor Brown Reinhart, who directs the youth ministry program, has been an especially strong influence for Cole, who has served as his student assistant. Cole is also a resident adviser in his dorm and spends fifteen hours a week in a supervised ministry assignment as a team leader for Young Life in a nearby town. "I like to be busy. My call drives me to do a lot of the things I do."

Cole says of his youth ministry program:

[Most classes] have been more practical classes than biblical . . . and that is one reason I am trying to audit at least a class a semester [e.g., Bashford's biblical theology class]. . . . I have a good grasp on a lot of biblical stuff, but I need to be a little bit more grounded in that. I have learned a lot of practical stuff in school. Much of it has been repeat, just because I have been involved in youth ministry all my life. . . . But I have learned a lot from Brown Reinhart, and from classes and from friends.

Cole describes himself as a "charismatic Baptist." "People who meet me think I am Assemblies of God or whatever." He continues:

I am very much involved in music—just music doesn't make you charismatic, but on a scale of Arminian [which would describe many charismatics] to Calvinist, I am probably somewhere in between. I haven't come to . . . know all the differences. I think that God only knows. I know that I am a saved Christian and know that I want to serve the Lord. I don't have to get involved in a lot of different [theological] debates that go on. But I think we can learn from those as well.

As he reflects further on his theological development during seminary, he is especially appreciative of the different theological stances of the professors:

I feel I can learn from any of them and . . . from students who have different perspectives. Almost when you come into ETS, you have to take down a lot of the barriers that you may have had in order to learn from different people. . . . I don't think ETS tries to get over one particular thing, you know, apart from an evangelical stance. Many professors don't agree with each other on some issues.

I think I have definitely grown in my own spiritual walk, in my own theological knowledge, in ministry. I think I have grown in experience even if my theological beliefs have not really changed. I have learned more about what I believe and why I believe it.

Above all, he says:

I have developed a heart for ministry—not just doing ministry for ministry's sake. . . . I want to be there to help kids develop spiritually as much as I can. There is a saying on my door [in the office of the church where he works]: "Reach kids for Christ as fast as you can." If you believe that kids, apart from Christ, are going to hell, then that is the bottom line.

Kate Prater

God made you special.

—Kate Prater's mother

Harvey Cox, a professor at the Harvard Divinity School, has just completed his lecture on Latin American liberation theology in the Modern Theology course. He invites discussion. Kate Prater responds by recounting an experience she had during a study seminar in Brazil as part of an interseminary globalization project. A woman on the trip, a student at a liberal Protestant seminary, insisted that Kate should embrace liberation theology since she had grown up experiencing poverty. Kate told the woman that she saw no need for another theology: "I always thought the gospel was liberating. We have to love and forgive our oppressors. If I took the liberation theology approach, I would be bitter."

Cox replies: "I take you seriously. You don't need [liberation theology's] corrective. . . . Those who do liberation theology in Latin America are concerned about the poor, not about us in North America. They are concerned that the poor should know that God does not intend things to be as they are."

Kate ends the exchange: "I am just trying to understand. I learned the gospel from my parents. I learned from them that God loves me. I do not need liberation theology to tell me that."

A brown-skinned woman with short hair and large glasses, Katerina (Kate) Prater is a native of Texas and the seventh child of migrant farmworkers. She is in her early forties. Her father, a Texan of Aztec descent, and her mother, a Mexican of Spanish descent, had no formal church ties but became Christians through the influence of a farmer for whom the father worked. The employer introduced her parents to the Bible, which her mother read avidly, also telling Bible stories to her children. Her father started Bible study in their house for black and Hispanic workers who were excluded from Anglo churches. Most important, she says, her parents taught their children how to forgive, and they made them believe that education was very important.

The odyssey that brought Kate to ETS included a year in a business school, work as a secretary, and the offer of her "typically macho" brothers—they grew up with the Hispanic understanding that women do not go to college—to help her attend college. Before her senior year at a public university, she married a graduate student, Winston Prater, an Anglo and the son of a Lutheran minister. The two spent time in Germany, where Winston fulfilled an R.O.T.C. commitment. There the Praters involved themselves in a ministry with single soldiers. Military service over, they returned to her university in Texas so that she could complete her education.

Kate, who was a Methodist while growing up, joined the American Lutheran Church with her husband. Later they moved to the Lutheran Church, Missouri Synod. She confesses: I am not deeply attached to Lutheranism. I respect their stand on Scripture, but my husband and I both disagree with the Missouri Synod's stand on women.

The move to ETS was to allow Winston to enroll in the Master of Arts in Theological Studies (M.A.T.S.) program. Kate worked as a faculty secretary and audited courses with her husband. The two planned to become missionaries but, they say, were turned down by their denomination when they told the mission board that they believe in charismatic gifts. Speaking in tongues is not central for her, Kate explains, but is a part of her private prayer language she will not deny.

Unable to secure a missionary assignment, Winston went to work as an engineer for General Electric, and Kate began working for a parachurch youth organization that became part of ETS. The shift made her a member of the seminary's staff, working as youth ministries coordinator in the supervised ministry office. She is enrolled in the M.A.T.S. program, taking one course at a time.

Racism is a central concern for Kate. Recalling an incident when she was called "a dirty Mexican," she remembers her mother's counsel: "God made you special. You cannot hate the people who say this to you." This stays with her, she says, even as she faces "Anglo brothers" at ETS. "I do not hate them in my heart." Those people she feels closest to at the school, she says, are the ones who support the fight against racism. Kate names Jesse Redlin, Brown Reinhart, Robert Harlan, Sheldon Bogard, and Adam Flood, most of whom teach in the Division of the Ministry of the Church. She also adds President Vincent and Dean Diersen to her list.

During Kate's time as a secretary at ETS, President Vincent appointed her to a task force addressing racism at the school. The task force report to the faculty was very painful, she said:

> Some of them, including some very respected people, said racist things, not intentionally, but out of ignorance: things like, "I have nothing against candidates from these groups, but they are just not qualified." I told them how much this hurt me, but I remembered my mother saying not[to] try to win them with hate. . . . I really believe in what the seminary does, but I am not naive enough to think that it is perfect. . . . Even now that I am a student, I still make strong statements. I have told them that they do not know how to do globalization and that there are still racists here. People should not take these racist attitudes overseas. It's like my brothers would say: "Hey, if there's no justice, it's no good."

Kate and Dan have reconciled themselves to not becoming missionaries and have accepted other ways to fulfill their callings:

We had given up everything to go to the missions field. I mean everything. It took a great deal to do that, because at a deep level, having been so poor, I am scared of poverty. Before my husband finished seminary, the Lord said to me, "Kate, you will never do anything because of your need for security." . . . Of course I am paraphrasing what he said. That is when I realized that I really had to give up all material things. Now I know that our greatest joy is to see [that] people know the joy of Christ. We are doing this now.

Winston feels no calling to become a pastor, Kate says, but is content to do his ministry in his quiet way at GE. I do ministry here [at ETS], she adds. She has found that she has always had a special ministry to women:

When I graduate [from ETS], nothing will change. Even before I graduated from college, women would come to me, asking me to be their spiritual director. . . . God has continued to bring women into my life. So I have a pastoral ministry, and my mission is to tell them what my parents told me, that they are all right. . . . I do not think I need ordination for this .

Amos Wayland

First I'm the crazy atheist; now I'm the crazy Christian.

—Amos Wayland

As BW concludes her interview with Amos Wayland, she remarks, "In all my years in theological education, you're the first veterinarian I've ever met in a theological school."

Amos informs her that actually, there is a second veterinarian also enrolled at ETS. Now in his third year as a candidate for the Master of Arts in Theological Studies degree, Amos continues his practice about thirty hours a week while commuting to campus for two courses a semester. Most semesters this means being on campus two days a week; this semester, because he is taking one course as an independent study, he is on campus only one day.

Forty-three years old, Amos is married, with two children. He is a native Pennsylvanian, the middle child in a family of seven. His father, a factory worker, now deceased, was an alcoholic. His mother worked in a department store.

Having first enrolled in a forestry program at a state university, Amos dropped out, then returned to college with "little ambition" and "no interest in doing anything." An encounter with a veterinarian over a sick kitten led him to a career in veterinary medicine: "I really had this affinity with animals." Graduating from the School of Veterinary Medicine at the University of Pennsylvania, he began his practice determined "to be the wealthiest vet. That didn't happen—thankfully," he laughs.

Amos's parents were not involved in church. At one point, however, they insisted that he and his older brother attend a catechism class at a Roman Catholic church. The teacher was a nun whom Amos describes as "tyrannical." That was his first exposure to religion. It led him, during college, to enjoy debating with the "Christian kids in our dorm. . . . I was a professed atheist at the time, and I enjoyed debating them. I delighted in it. I was a very nasty kid."

At age twenty-nine, after several years of "okay" veterinary practice, Amos was depressed. He had no goals:

> I recall . . . coming to work and buying a six-pack of beer . . . and trying to drink it as fast as I could just to get some kind of buzz so I could function at work. [F]inally my wife said to me . . . "That's it. . . . I'm going to drive with the kids in the car, and when I come home, I want you to be gone." . . . And I recall being up in . . . our upstairs room in this little tiny house we had, and sobbing. This atheist, you know, sobbing, desperate, because I had nothing. I had no friends at this point, because I was just nasty and selfish. I remember vaguely calling out something to the effect of "God, help me," and I've never said that word. I had one of those experiences, I guess, like Paul. I didn't go blind, but . . . this just warm feeling came up through me, and I felt hopeful. I felt like all the darkness that was inside was now light, and all the junk was just melted away. At the same time, my wife—something told her to come back— walked into the house. . . . She knew something had happened. And that was it. From twenty-nine to now forty-three, it's just gotten stronger and stronger.

Following this experience, Amos and his wife began to attend a church, although doing so was difficult. First they—by then his wife had also had a Christian experience—tried a Lutheran church, but they left it when Amos and the pastor disagreed theologically. Next came an American Baptist congregation, but again theological differences over the need for a "born again" experience led them to leave. "Now we're about to join . . . an independent Baptist church, I guess, that thinks a little bit more like we do."

Amos's passion for evangelism led him to discuss matters of faith with pastors who brought their pets to his office for treatment. He found that he could use his practice as a ministry: "People seem . . . not very . . . comfortable knocking on a pastor's door, but they feel very comfortable coming in with their animals as an excuse to vent a problem. You can kind of parlay that into a ministry." Over time, the idea of attending seminary began to grow in him:

> I was finding myself unhappy with things in the world. I would be driving to work, and I would find . . . myself preaching in the car. . . . And then I think of . . . the lack of passion in some churches. I'm not big on denominations—I guess I'm a nondenominationalist—but I respect anyone in the pastorate who has a passion for Christ, and I guess . . . I don't show a lot of patience for those who don't. Seeing all that . . . I guess somehow I want to be the antithesis of the pastorate with no passion.

He does not think attending seminary is "an absolutely necessary thing for someone who wants to teach the Bible and declare the gospel as a pastor." However, he believes that the people to whom he wants to witness "really don't take you seriously if they don't see some letters after your name. I guess I came [to seminary] to get letters after my name, so they'll take me seriously about the gospel."

As he considered seminary, he and his wife "took a tour" to ETS. He "wanted something evangelical, yet not fundamentalist. . . . There's quite a distinction between those two lines." The five-hour round trip on his initial visit discouraged him. "I was very depressed. . . . Then I got home and was listening to the radio, and there was this report about . . . something to do with ETS. . . . I said, 'Wow, maybe [God's] saying you better reconsider.' So we did, and it felt very good then. Now I don't think of the ride so much."

The seminary experience has been "very, very good," more than just the letters after his name. "I used to believe you could just read the Bible on your own, . . . but you really can't discipline yourself as well to really learn." He says that for the most part the faculty is "superb." He finds it comforting that students can "sit back, so far anyway, and relax, knowing you're getting, for my way of thinking anyway, orthodox thinking. I enjoy hearing the other schools of thought, but I enjoy them being presented as other schools of thought, not *the* school of thought."

The major negative for Amos is that he has to commute to school: "You plug in for a couple of hours, and you don't feel the seminary experience, whatever that is. I haven't had that benefit. . . . So it's really, each time I come, I feel like, I'm coming from dog and cat diseases, then quickly grabbing my books and I'm here. I forget if I'm a vet or a seminary student at times."

When asked if he has made any friends among the students, he mentions one with whom he "suffered through" Greek: Neal Huchett (whose name at first he has difficulty getting straight). He has also met two others at the church that he and his family attend.

He laments having had few opportunities for conversations with faculty members. Such talks are usually at class breaks or on the telephone: "Like tonight, it will be ten o'clock [when I'm done]. . . . [I]t's like a race to the car, because I know by midnight, I'm going to have the car windows open and the radio on not to fall asleep." He has also missed getting any spiritual nurture from the seminary experience: "There's none of that. The best we do is just grasp onto the prayer before the lecture. That's about it."

What are his plans when he completes his program? He will continue his veterinary practice, using it as a ministry for witnessing to the gospel. At the same, he hopes to start his own congregation, building on a nucleus of friends with whom he and his wife share a monthly time of discussion and prayer in their home. "We kind of felt it wasn't good to get rid of the practice and do ministry full-time, until and unless God makes it definitely sure that's the way."

Ken Schlitz

> There just seems to be no bridge between the resources [that the faculty have to offer] and the students. Maybe there is for those who live on campus, but I have not been able to find it.
>
> —Ken Schlitz

Commenting on a change in class schedules to accommodate working students and commuters, Roy Parks says:

> I think our classrooms are pretty serious business. Now the one thing . . . when a concession has been made in the academic life is that we have moved many of our classes into three-hour blocks. . . . I think it is a concession inasmuch as it doesn't work as well academically. . . . I beat these students to death in one [hour]. I mean my stuff is condensed, carefully phrased. One hour with me is about all students should have.

Although he is only on campus one day a week, Ken Schlitz cheerfully agrees to an interview. Commuting approximately eighty miles each way, Ken is working toward an M.A. degree in youth ministries. It will take him four years to complete it. Meanwhile, he says, he serves part-time as a youth minister in a congregation of the Christian Missionary and Alliance denomination. It is the church in which he grew up.

In his late twenties, Ken has an athlete's build, with short blond hair and freckles. After graduating from a Christian academy, he enrolled in his denomination's college at Nyack, New York, and was married to a fellow student during his senior year.

Ken grew up in the church and a Christian home. His own commitment was a gradual one: "I accepted the Lord [when I was] very young. I was about five years old. Sometime around age thirteen, I was sitting in a church service and felt that God was saying, 'I want you to be in full-time ministry.' I resisted the call because I thought that it was just to pastoral ministry or to missions, and I am not the kind of person to sit behind a desk. Actually, I really wanted to be in forestry." He knew nothing at the time about youth ministry, he continues, but during the last year of college he and his wife had an opportunity to become involved with church young people. "I realized that God gives each of us gifts and things we can use to be in service to him. Now I just can't get enough of ministry to young people."

After graduation, while Ken was still struggling with his call, he and his wife moved to his hometown, where both found jobs—she as a secretary, he in construction. "As we were watching a video about ministry, we saw these kids who had been in college with us and who had gone on to seminary. Now they were in mission. We realized that we could bring people to Christ."

When he and his wife were exploring ministry opportunities within the denomination, an assistant minister position opened in Florida, and things just clicked, he says. He says that he told them, however, that he wanted to get a seminary education and might be there only two years.

When asked in Florida what he hoped to gain from a seminary that he did not already have in his ministry, Ken says he explained that he wanted a practical education. "I felt that I had been overloaded with theology in college, and I wanted to be trained."

He picked ETS because of a friend and the reputation of the school's youth ministry program. Also, enrollment there meant he could move back home and commute to campus. His home church offered him a part-time job—twenty hours a week—and housing. The congregation also pays for his schooling. "You can't get a better deal than that," Ken says.

Ken has a second job at a funeral home—"doing just about everything except embalming, because I am not licensed." He picks up bodies and helps to arrange funerals. The Schlitzes live in an apartment in the funeral home, and he finds it a good work experience.

To date, he does not find his youth ministry program at ETS as practical as he had expected. He calls it "very basic" and hopes that he will find it more rewarding on the advanced level. Ken is also of the opinion that Brown Reinhart, the youth ministries program director, is too busy. "I find it hard to sit and talk with him," he says. "That's true even with other faculty. Everyone is wrapped up in projects and studies. They have a lot to offer, but there just is no bridge between the resources and the students. Maybe there is for those who live on campus, but I have not been able to find it."

Ken concludes that most have been helpful, although he rates an Old Testament course as "absolutely useless." A New Testament course, however, was very well rounded. "I could use it every day," he comments.

He has made "only a handful" of friends through his classes, and those primarily in courses with small groups. Ken does not know the last names of several students he feels close to, and he is acquainted with none of the small number of other Alliance students at ETS.

Faced with a personal or spiritual problem, he would not hesitate to go to Sharp Dunlap or Bruce Grantler: "I have talked with [Grantler] and I feel close with him, and I would feel fine going to the head of counseling, although I cannot remember his name."

Would he commend ETS to others? "I would not have any problem telling the kids in my youth group who go to college to come here," he says. "The professors here do not push their views on you. They talk about dispensationalism, ordination of women, post trib, and all of that. They tell you what the different options are, but they do not press you into a mold."

Ken says that when he completes his program, he plans to be a full-time youth minister: "My major interest is in helping kids who grew up in the church. I grew up in the church, and God was good enough that I didn't reject him. And that's what I want to do. I want to be friends to kids who grew up in the church. I have not ruled out working with a parachurch group, but I have read that it will not be as fruitful in the '90s."

Graduates

> The concern of ETS is for careful, accurate interpretation [of Scripture]. Languages are crucial. Our real goal is to make Scripture applicable in a very proper way, so that it will guide belief and action.
>
> —Charles Oliver

Graduating seniors (125 in number), members of the faculty and administration, and families and friends of the graduates are gathered in a neighboring college gymnasium for commencement. The year is 1990. Jeffrey Barber has been chosen to give the senior address. Jeff, from Fairbanks, Alaska, has been president of the student association. Both he and his wife, Ellen, are among those graduating with high honors.

Jeff begins his address by telling of having also spoken at his high school graduation. He is, he says, much more optimistic about the academic ability of his ETS colleagues than he was of his high school classmates. The purpose of theological education is to produce competent ministers. (What follows is a close paraphrase of Jeff's remarks.)

[While this should] be self-evident, I believe that it is not true of many theological seminaries today. Many schools no longer require biblical languages. Also, many have replaced core curricula with courses that reflect contemporary ideologies. Thank God that this is not true of this school. While ETS takes seriously the contemporary world and global concerns, it does so with a strong commitment to traditional theology and scholarship.

Theological education is important because the gospel is important: Shame on us if the world is more studious and industrious than those committed to the gospel. How can such a precious message be handled with mediocrity? The Christian minister must be a diligent student.

Recalling Paul's admonition to Timothy, he concludes that the minister's calling is to preach and correctly apply the truth of the Scriptures. "We live in a world that believes that what is sinful is normal and what is righteous is strange. But our Lord commands us to proclaim the gospel. Without the gospel promise that God will be with us, this commission would lead to despair. God has called us to a ministry of the Word." There are loud "Amens" from the audience as Jeffrey finishes.

The setting is the same; it is two years later. Albert Ogden gives the student address. President Vincent introduces him as coming "from somewhere between Virginia and Kansas." (A graduate of the University of Virginia, Albert is from Kansas.) He begins with a word to the faculty: "Those who walk with the wise become wise. Thank you for the privilege of walking with you. We will be better because of your deep commitment to Jesus Christ." He continues:

Hidden behind stacks of flash cards, this day has seemed elusive. How naively I approached ETS. I thought that seminary would give me all the answers. I thought that I would be a failure unless I had a whole almanac of answers today: "So, sir seminary graduate," I would be asked, "where did Cain's wife come from?" But I leave with more questions than answers. What has been of value here are the tools and lenses I have gained. I can't think of anything more valuable. With tools we can build well. With lenses we can see well. While I was a student, I worked in campus maintenance. I learned if you want to do the job right, get the right tools. And we need vision for effective ministry. . . . Without tools and lenses, we would spend our strength. With them we can build. . . . We have learned about God, his glory, but also the Bible, church, and world. The faculty [members] have been like so many optometrists. So to those who have stood with us, prayed for us, and encouraged us, thank you. You are our partners. May this school serve Jesus Christ until all nations acknowledge that he is Lord.

The following are excerpts from a letter posted on a dormitory bulletin board:

Dear Filipe and the brothers of the dorm,
Greetings from the far north. Yes, I live 1 mile from the Canadian border now. I miss you big F and the rest of the brothers of the dorm. It seemed really weird to not go to school this Fall. Oh well, life goes on. In case you haven't heard, I was called to be pastor of United Baptist Church in June. It is a very nice church. I couldn't have found a group of more loving, caring, committed Christian people than I have here. They

really love the Lord in this church. The church is pretty good sized for a small town—
150–200 on S. morning, 60–100 on S. night, and 30–50 in prayer meeting. I am very
happy that God called me here. It was quite an adjustment though. . . .

The biggest adjustments have been in the areas of preaching, responsibility and
respect. I now preach no less than 2 sermons a week and have preached 4 in one
week. Initially it was a shock to be expected to preach so much. The responsibility of
providing pastoral care to a good sized congregation is both a challenge and is sober-
ing. I was grateful for my CPE experience at the hospital. The respect I receive is also
hard to take. To go from an obscure, anonymous seminary student to a respected,
looked up to person in the community was a difficult adjustment. . . .

Well brother(s) all is well. The most important news is that I met this wonderful
young lady . . . 2 weeks after I got here. To make a long story short I asked her to
marry me 3 weeks ago, she said "yes," and we plan on getting married either in
December or January. What an answer to prayer she is. . . .

I miss you, brother, and the rest of the gang in the dorm. See you soon.

> Your brother,
> The Reverend James Morgan

SIX

Covenant House

Students are my real support community, and mostly the women from Covenant House. It was so special our year: you could be friendly with everyone.

—Laura Kampen Storey

The Inner Circle

I came here with the idea that everyone would be my age. I found out that that wasn't so. But the women in Covenant House are like me. I have loved them, and it was a treat to be living with them.

—Laura Kampen Storey

The alcove on the second floor of Covenant House has been transformed. The mansion, whose stately ground-level rooms are used for meetings and receptions, is a women's dormitory and guest house on its upper floors. In the alcove, the worn couch, large chairs, and battered television have been neatly arranged. Lois Boucher has donated her coffeepot, which sits on a low table under the window that looks out over Covenant House's circular front drive. Lois, her roommate Laura, and several other women who arrived as new students two months earlier have dubbed the area "the Community-Building Room," a phrase that they all laugh when they use. Within a few weeks, the name has been shortened to "CBR."

The CBR gets heavy use from individual students for television watching and reading. It is also the site for frequent gatherings of the group that created it as a living room: Lois and Laura, whose room is at the head of the grand staircase from the first floor; their next-door neighbor, Anne Norton, who lives by herself in an enormous room furnished for three; and Janette Cameron, her roommate Dot Richards, and Sharon Madden, all of whom live on the third floor. One of the first such events features a demonstration by Anne Norton of her considerable skills as a Highland dancer. Lois and Laura provide music by singing in imitation of bag-

97

pipes. A few weeks later, Laura's birthday is celebrated: The group gives her a sweatshirt with CBR transliterated into Greek (Chi Beta Rho), to recognize both her role in setting up their meeting place and her unfulfilled wish to belong to a sorority in college.

After Christmas, another dorm resident, Marilyn Flexner, contributes a microwave and a popcorn popper. These are used mostly by the women who, like Marilyn, watch television in the evening, singly or in pairs. The founding group has different tastes. They gather in the morning or early evening to make and drink coffee—specialty varieties such as mint-flavored mocha java decaffeinated are preferred—and to talk. Sometimes there is food as well, usually "healthy" muffins. Their meetings (which come to be called "CBR" too, as in "Let's have CBR tomorrow") are not closed, and other first-year students—Marilyn Flexner, Sarah (Sally) Trumbell, Esther Kim—sometimes join in.

But the CBR creators are a distinct group. They are each others' best friends. Lois and Laura, whom Lois describes as alike "as two peas in a pod," have, with Janette, formed a "covenant group" that prays and studies the Bible together. Anne Norton and Sharon Madden are close to all three of them. Others are also knit into this tight fabric: Dot Richards spends a great deal of time with her boyfriend, who is also a student, but still thinks of Covenant House as her social center; and Brenda Moore and Pamela Willis live off-campus but spend a great deal of time with the CBR group. Collectively, they become known as the "Covenant House women," though they are a minority of the thirty or so female students who live there. They are called that even after most of them have moved out of the dorm they dominated during 1989–90, which Laura calls "our year."

The Covenant House women have a great deal in common. They are young—just out of college or, at most, a year or two beyond it. Most are pretty, and all are well-dressed and meticulously groomed: nails polished, hair curled, makeup carefully applied. Those who drive cars have new ones (Anne's is a Grand Am, Pamela's a Taurus), gifts of their parents. Yet they work—in the campus bookstore, at the cafeteria, or on the switchboard, or cleaning house for faculty members. They are "very traditional," says a male student who lives in Leyden Hall, another old building converted into a dorm. They do not stand strongly for women's rights, says an older student's wife, as do the residents of Edwards House, another original estate building used to house women students. Covenant House women, she says, are known for partying, in part because Pamela (the first year) and Brenda Moore (the second) head the campus social committee. And they are marriageable. In the second semester of that first year and the summer after, Dot Richards remembers later, there was a "plague" of engagements and weddings, including her own.

The Covenant House women are both earnest and irreverent. They pray together fervently and argue vigorously about serious issues. Pamela's and Lois's friendship is almost ruptured over the question of what kind of teaching—didactic lectures or experiential methods—can convey theological truth. Pamela says, "You can't just 'share your feelings' about eschatology"; Lois replies, "Yes, but the average Joe congregation member, the average me, for Pete's sake, can't take it straight, just hours and hours of lecture"). But they also build a life-sized, stuffed effigy of one of their most didactic professors, dress him from a used clothing shop in the Covenant House basement, and prop him up for a picture with each of them. At a cafeteria "dorm dinner" where Pamela and Lois sit together, one of them steals food from another's tray while the victim is praying, a move that prompts general hilarity. One evening during a CBR session, a car is heard in the circular drive. Lois and others go to the window. The car bears a bumper sticker: JESUS IS HERE. Who is it? asks another student. It's Jesus, says Lois dryly.

Laura Kampen Storey

Laura Kampen, thin, calm, and usually dressed less girlishly than the others, is the pivot of the group. Her role as everyone's friend and confidante was established early, and it continued through the three years that it took the Covenant House women to complete the "two-year" master's programs in which most of them were enrolled. Laura grew up in the Midwest. Her father was a research scientist, her mother a church musician. The family belonged to a conservative Protestant denomination, and Laura cannot remember ever not being a Christian. As a four-year-old, she says, she prayed for Jesus to come, and she has been making "recommitments" ever since. She attended a state university, where she became involved with a Campus Crusade group. At one of its retreats, a speaker told her that she had leadership gifts and suggested that she consider seminary. She called her mother for advice and discovered that she had been praying that Laura would attend a theological school. She applied to ETS because it was "broad" enough to accommodate her interests in teaching and counseling, because her minister was a graduate, and because she felt it was time to get away from home.

She did *not* come to seminary to meet a man. Since eighth grade "guys [had] been disappointing." And when, early in her first semester, she met Tony Storey, Laura was dubious. He came from a charismatic background, something that her Campus Crusade group had taught her was "from the Devil." But she liked and respected his "spiritual side." So she called her mother again and heard for the first time that the views of the Campus Crusade group were "extreme": My mother told me, says Laura, that speaking in tongues is not a sin. Later, she realized that the group's perspective was dispensationalist, a type of fundamentalism that she did not recognize at the time.

Though Laura and Tony are different in many ways, they went on one date and then more. One day in the library, Tony urged Laura to "trust the Lord to let this relationship go wherever it is leading us," which moved her deeply. She went back to Covenant House and talked to Anne Norton, and increasingly the Covenant House women became involved in the fast-breaking drama. Tony became friendly and popular with all of them. In later years, according to Sharon Madden, serious boyfriends of others in the group were judged by whether they are "like Tony"— that is, willing to be friends with all the Covenant House women and to help keep the group together.

By March, the tension is high. Anne has posted a sign on Laura's door that says, "When will ring day be?" Late one afternoon, BW, staying in one of the Covenant House guest rooms on the second floor, hears shrieks and laughter. She steps into the hall, and Laura shouts at her, "Guess what!" and waves a hand with a new ring. Tony, dressed uncharacteristically in a business suit, and Lois stand by. Everyone but Laura knew that the engagement would happen today. Laura's family helped Tony pick out the ring and mailed it to him, and his and her parents had already met at a "summit conference." Anne even wrote today's date under the question on her sign, but Laura did not notice it. The wedding will be in August, and because Tony is graduating this June, Laura will leave school to go wherever he gets a teaching job. What kind of wedding will it be? BW asks. Laura says to Tony, "What are our watchwords?" Together they chant: "Classy and stately." The ceremony will be held in the evening, and it will be, Laura says, "real worshipful."

Elaborate engagement rituals are nothing new in Covenant House this year. A graduating student was engaged early in the year. Her fiancé took her to the small chapel in Covenant House, lit candles, played a romantic song on the piano, and then asked, "Will you love and serve the Lord your whole life?" When she said yes, he asked, "Will you marry me so that we can love and serve the Lord together?" Another first-year student, Sharon's roommate Marcie, who was engaged before Laura, reported that her husband-to-be first asked her father's permission and then "got down on one knee" to ask her to marry him. But Laura and Tony get special attention. Laura's whole circle plays an active part in arranging this romantic event.

The wedding *was* worshipful, Lois reports later. There was a short speech by Tony, who said that the service was, even more than a celebration of their wedding, "an opportunity to worship God," and when the trumpeter played, Lois thought, "This must be the Rapture."

Covenant House women are both excited and alarmed at the big news the next September: Laura and Tony are on their way back to the school. After the honeymoon, the couple went to Florida, to a private school where Tony had found a job. Within weeks he had resigned: The students had no serious interest in religion; the school would not even permit him to assign homework. The parting was amicable, says Laura, back on campus a few months later and working full-time in the bookstore, but "he's still not over it yet." Tony has been painting houses and contemplating his future. Laura is thinner than ever and looks worried.

Over the next two years, Tony continues to paint houses, tries out a parish ministry internship, and considers other options, such as graduate study or another teaching job. It seems clear that his confidence in his ability to shape his career is shaken. Then he is hired by the seminary as a student recruiter, and he is an instant success in this job.

Through it all, Laura expresses her concern and loyalty (to BW: "This isn't the situation I expected, but I know that I married the right person"). She works in the bookstore and voices her calm moderate views. Speaking to BW about a sister's difficult pregnancy, she says, "It's great to have something to hold onto, besides just the grace of God. Well, I don't mean *just* the grace of God. That's everything. But it's still good to have reassurance." She and Tony join an Orthodox Presbyterian church, more because it is a "very warm church" whose people "just love us to death" than for its conservative Calvinist theology, though she "sees the logic" of that too. She does wish it had a more moderate position on women: "I can see why they have problems with women's ordination, but I wonder if they would let me do the kind of things I can do." Paula Fleming and other leaders of the campus women's group would not consider Laura much of a feminist, but she is a moderate in the Covenant House group. Perhaps her moderation, along with her warm interest in others, is the reason she plays such a central role in the group. Laura's place at the center of the network becomes most evident after Anne Norton announces her engagement.

Anne Norton

Like Laura, Anne had come to ETS because her ministers were graduates, but she did not grow up as Laura did in a nest of evangelical churches and schools. Her father, a developer, had once attended a liberal seminary, but he fell into a "skeptical circle" and lost his faith altogether. After one of their frequent family moves, Anne and her mother and brother attended a conservative Presbyterian church; Anne liked it, joined, and was shaped in a "scriptural view of Christianity" by a Sunday school teacher. In undergraduate days at a "seven sisters" women's school, she joined InterVarsity, a struggling religious organization on that campus, and soon became a leader. Life as a Christian at college was "culture shock," but Anne dealt with it, eventually becoming best friends with her roommate, who was an atheist—and a Democrat.

Anne—dark-haired like Lois and Laura, less conventionally pretty, but animated and interesting-looking—is both the most cosmopolitan member of the Covenant House circle and the most conservative. In Covenant House and on campus she is widely known for "class": She has a cappuccino maker in her room and uses it often; her clothes are made for her; and she and her mother, to whom she is very close, have registered as interior decorators so that they can shop in design centers.

Anne, says Laura, has "seen a lot," and Anne gives plenty of evidence of urbanity. At her college, she reports, "we have bulimia, anorexia, homophobia—you name it . . . [and] co-ed dorms . . . men living there but not paying." She describes these features without adding any judgments; in the same even tone, she recounts the arguments that were given for the college's annual Christmas service by her side (InterVarsity) and those opposing it, noting that, as her opponents argued, the college was indeed a "diverse campus." She regularly takes courses at nearby, more liberal seminaries, where she says she learned that "syncretism" (a process that evangelicals criticize in liberal and new religions) affects evangelicals too: "Even the cognitive Reformed way assimilates the Renaissance." She also has a keen interest in world events and heads the current affairs committee of the ETS student association, which at her instigation provides the *New York Times* for cafeteria reading.

Anne takes a dim, often humorous view of some of her fellow students' evangelical tastes and ideas. Looking at snapshots in which all the people have red eyes from over-strong flashbulbs, she laughs, "They're demon-possessed!" She says that she "hates" popular Christian music: "It's so sloppy and fluffy." On a more serious level, when a fellow student attempts suicide by setting himself on fire in a field near the school (he is saved by a farmer), her concern focuses on subsequent medical care. She says she has heard that he was being treated for schizophrenia rather than manic depression—his real problem, she maintains—and shows impatience with theological explanations for his action. Sally Trumbell, who lives in Covenant House but is far from the center of its social circle, says that she has "heard that some people say that Kirt's problem was that he did not have enough faith," that he would never have attempted suicide if his faith had been strong. "Who says that?" Anne snaps. "Who would say something as stupid as that?"

Although urbane and quick-witted, Anne has a deep piety, and her views are by no means liberal. Her reason for keeping up on world affairs, she writes in the *Bell's Ridge Times* in the fall of her second year, is "to affect our world through prayer. . . . Our God is powerful, mighty and sovereign in this world . . . . I am not helpless in the face of an international crisis. I have the most powerful tool to effect change, prayer to a personal God." She asks how BW's pacifist son views the Persian Gulf War. BW says that he feels that his antiwar organizing efforts have failed. "I feel a lot like him," says Anne. "I am very convicted about the power of prayer, and I have been praying for peace as hard as he has been organizing."

Anne's views about women's roles are very conservative. She opposes not only ordination but also women teaching men. Scripture, she believes, counsels women to be submissive:

> Submission of women in the church to men may be difficult when equality is supposed in the world. Even so, I have found that accepting a supportive role in the church is corrective of my desire for public applause. . . . Every day of my life has been an observation of the implication of 1 Peter 3:1–2. My parents were married while both of them were Christians. Then after their marriage my father renounced the faith. My mother struggles in trying to submit her life to God in a marriage that is unequally yoked, and she lives with the strong conviction that God has called her to stay with my father and to live a life in which she does not try to win him over by talk but by the behavior of her life so that he may see her reverence for God.

At the end of her second year, her degree not quite complete, she applies for a job as a nonordained minister to women in a large southern Presbyterian church. She is interviewed but not, she thinks, taken seriously, chiefly because of her youth. The committee raises scriptural objections: Titus 2 (a passage Anne often cites on women's roles) suggests that older women should teach younger women. Anne counters with Paul's advice to Timothy on teaching his elders. She says that only grace enables anyone to minister, and she would pray for grace. When she returns to campus and learns that she did not get the job, she is furious at the unfair treatment and says that she now knows what racism might feel like.

Anne decides to stay at school for at least another semester to finish her degree. And then, as the school year opens, she makes a stunning announcement: She is engaged to marry Albert Carr, a quiet, red-headed transfer student who has been on campus for only a semester and is not known to the other Covenant House women. She tells her roommate, Brenda Moore, that she is immediately moving out of the large third-floor room they shared during their second year; she has rented an apartment in married student housing in anticipation of her winter wedding. Several departures from Covenant House at the end of the first year—Laura and Dot Richards were married, Janette transferred to another seminary, and Sharon took an internship leave—had broken up the second-floor CBR center, and Anne and Brenda's amply furnished room, with its couch, fireplace, laser printer, coffeepot and cappuccino maker, had become the second-year substitute. The room was more exclusive than the alcove (the invitations to BW to come for coffee were just as frequent), but other inner-circle members such as Lois, who had become the resident assistant in charge of Covenant House, were welcome to drop in.

Brenda is stunned and, says Sharon, takes Anne's "defection" very hard. Lois, relaying the news to BW, is solemn. This engagement is not accompanied by the enthusiastic laughter that accompanied Laura's "ring day." The reservations are of several kinds. First, the speed of the decision worries Anne's friends and her mother, who is openly opposed to the match. Second, Albert's personality seems to them an unlikely match for Anne's: He is quiet, apparently shy, and "gets all stressed," according to Lois. Third, Lois worries that Anne's strong theological views about women's roles may be too large a part of the decision: Anne, she says, is trying to live out her own idea of submission—and she is torn between her mom and Laura on one side and him on the other.

Anne is clearly troubled by the lack of enthusiasm for her choice. She earnestly says to BW: "All these things couldn't have happened like that if it weren't the Lord's leading, could they?" She cuts almost all ties to her friends. She simply "dropped off the face of the earth," says Sharon, reporting the somewhat wounded feelings that she, Brenda, and Lois share.

Only Laura is not cut off. Her position is not exactly on "one side," as Lois reports. By Anne's own account, Laura is helpful and supportive, an alternate authority to her disapproving mother and others: "Laura tells me that Albert provides the guardrails on my highway. Isn't that a nice metaphor?" Lois and Sharon are hurt, even angered, by Anne's abrupt departure, but they express great admiration for Laura's ability to stay friends with both them and Anne.

Even Laura is shocked by the next development. At a party for Anne at the bookstore, where Laura works full-time and Anne is a part-time clerk, Anne blurts out that she and Albert will not return after the wedding but will move to the seminary from which he transferred. Laura, who is slated to be Anne's matron of honor, knew nothing of this plan, which Albert insisted be kept secret. She is deeply distressed that she is not permitted to tell their other friends. Her anxiety abates as Anne changes her mind and begins to tell others.

Despite the widespread reservations, Anne holds firm. She believes that her relationship with Albert is God's plan. Albert has similar views. Shortly after he met Anne, he asked God for a sign of her interest and told himself that if she appeared at the library on a certain evening, that would be the sign. She did appear.

Laura gives a shower, inviting the Covenant House crowd, which is "very awkward," by Sharon's account, because Anne's unhappy mother is present. The wedding takes place. Only Laura and Deborah Rickles, a new student known to none of the inner circle, attend. Anne and Albert move to his former seminary, where Anne takes a job in the admissions office. They return in June for her graduation but do not attend the party that the Covenant House women throw for themselves and their families and friends in the basement of a church close to campus.

Sharon Madden

The three other long-term Covenant House women, Sharon, Lois, and Brenda, do not marry during seminary, though Sharon comes close. Sharon—gentle, thoughtful, well-spoken, and an excellent student—was raised by evangelical parents and attended a Christian college. As a teenager she aspired to become the first woman pastor in her conservative denomination. By the end of college, however, Bible studies had convinced her that women should not be senior ministers, and she had given up the idea of ordination for herself, though not the goal of ministry. Her college friends and advisers "forced" her to apply to ETS. She has loved seminary, both her classes and her friends.

Her views of the church and the ministry are clouded, however, by a searing experience during her second year. She left campus to serve as an intern in a midwestern church, conservative but allied with mainline Presbyterianism. Soon she discovered that her supervising pastor was having a string of affairs with women in the congregation; before she could confront him, he began pursuing her as well. She became frightened and asked her father, a civilian employee of a law enforcement agency, to come take her home. She told no one of her plan to leave and departed at night, leaving a letter giving her reasons with a trusted church member. Once back at school, she joined with other women in the congregation to bring charges against the minister in church courts.

Reentry was difficult. Most people were extremely sympathetic, including the dean of students, whom she had called for advice when the situation in the Midwest became difficult, but Sharon was still badly shaken. The responses of some of the male students to Anita Hill's testimony (about Clarence Thomas) infuriated her, and during the hearings she would not eat in the cafeteria because of their comments. While still not a strong advocate of women's ordination, the thought of the minister who harassed her makes Sharon realize, "I would rather have Mary Chang in the pulpit, never mind what her gender is." (Mary is the quiet but extremely articulate leader of the campus women's organization.) She will not seek ordination herself partly because she agrees with Roy Parks, whose ideas she greatly admires, that the professionalization of clergy leadership has been a bad thing.

One result of her bad experience is the way it clouded her subsequent relationships with men. Her popularity resumed as soon as she returned. One suitor presented her with a ring after a short string of dates, but she thought that he and others thought less of her for having been involved in the harassment case. (One administrator told BW that some of the less mature and more rigid single men view even young widows as "used goods" and would hesitate to date them.) She was so troubled that she considered not returning in September for her third year.

But Lois, Brenda, and Laura have prevailed on her to stay, and things smoothed out. She is resident assistant for Covenant House (Lois's job the second year). Her sense of humor reasserts itself. When Sam Carlson, the enrollment manager, complains that the cafeteria is selling stale, day-old doughnuts at full price, she tells him that she feels the same way about the two-year-old course-on-tape that she is taking at full tuition. Faculty member Roy Parks, whose course it is and who happens to be at the same table, though he is on leave, quips that the course was stale already when he gave it.

Sharon becomes increasingly serious about her new boyfriend, Graham, although she finds "it's hard to date in a fishbowl." The pressure is so great, she reports, that she and Graham start saying they will just "live together" rather than get married. They say it's fun to watch reactions. "Of course, when Dr. Cotton [the saintly and much-admired professor of missions] asked us, we did not say that to him." By year's end Sharon and Graham have announced their engagement. They will be married after her graduation and return to campus in the fall for Graham to finish his degree.

Lois Boucher

As it turns out, none of the Covenant House women have actually lived in Covenant House for the whole three years between entering and graduation. Laura and Anne left to marry; Sharon left on an internship. Lois Boucher, who was resident assistant for Covenant House her second year, moved out midway through the third year into an apartment in the neighborhood. She became deeply enmeshed in campus life and was part of a tight-knit group of students employed in the cafeteria. After finishing her academic work, Lois accepted a job in the seminary's admissions office. Energetic and enthusiastic, she is more practically oriented than her close women friends, taking many courses in education and children's ministry and raising sharp questions about the propositional kinds of theology and teaching that Anne, Sharon, and others consider the only correct ones. She had come to seminary to prepare for children's ministry, and while there she developed an interest in missions, traveling to Israel and working in Mexico and inner-city Washington. She sees her work for the seminary as temporary and still hopes for work in another country or a city church.

Brenda Moore

Of all the Covenant House circle, only Brenda Moore actually has a ministry job for the year after graduation. Brenda was raised in a conservative denomination and attended a Christian college where she met Paul Bashford, then in his first teaching job. When she came to ETS at his urging, she lived in his house while he and his family were on sabbatical. Though she became part of the Covenant House inner group right away (she gave the party where Laura met Tony), she did not actually move into the dorm until her second year.

Brenda is blond, curly-haired, blue-eyed, freckled, and extremely pretty, almost doll-like. She is a magnet for men, some of whom want feminine sympathy. (During Brenda's first semester, BW observes two men approach her: "I'm sick," says one, "and we both need a mother. Will you be our mother?"). Many others want to date her (some of these are "absolutely vetoed" by Sharon and Lois). None finally meets her standard, though each time a relationship collapses, other suitors immediately make their interests known. Women also find her admirable and engaging. Sharon says that she envies the intensity of Brenda's prayer life and that after praying with her she understands why Brenda relates so well to so many people: Brenda really cares for the "whole person," says Sharon, not just the part that affects her own life.

Along with (on occasion) Anne Norton, Pamela Willis, and Sharon Madden, Brenda goes to Whitley Church, where Charles Oliver is pastor and where her mentor, Paul Bashford, has been installed as associate pastor. Like most of her friends, she thinks that Scripture bars the ordination of women: "It's not that I would not speak to someone who believes in the ordination of women, but those of us who are more conservative and traditional are more comfortable together. I am very grateful for Anne. The fact that we agree on this allows us to share a great deal." At the same time, when leaders of the campus women's group invite her to a lecture by a Christian feminist on justice in family life, she goes, and she is impressed. She says that it makes her think that "maybe our biblical idea of the family isn't so biblical after all." Later that semester, Brenda questions BW about feminism, patriarchy, and a book by Susan Faludi on the backlash against the women's movement. Someone gave her the book, and she is reading it.

Despite these explorations, she seeks and gets the kind of job that the "traditional" women say they want: an internship in women's ministry in a very large evangelical church. (It is important to Brenda that she work in a church. She and Anne, she says, will not work for parachurch organizations.) At graduation Brenda's future direction is better set than any of the others': Laura is still working at the bookstore, her degree incomplete; Anne may move back to campus with Albert next year or may not; Lois's commitment to her job is tentative; Sharon will work to support Graham.

Brenda has attained her professional goal, but she cries many times as her years at ETS draw to a close. Tears fall during the graduation ceremony, at the church basement party, and while cleaning up later. She is very sad to leave her much-loved Covenant House friends.

The Outer Ring

I'm a square peg in a round hole here.

—Janette Cameron

Community. There's no community. And that, I think, would be difficult—I certainly don't have any answers . . . different people living off-campus and working.

—Marilyn Flexner

I no longer feel connected to ETS.

—Pamela Willis

I am the odd person out, no matter how you look at it.

—Paula Fleming

Jannette Cameron

Janette Cameron looks and acts like an inner-circle member and is generally accounted one. She is beautiful—tall, with wide-set eyes and long straight blond hair that gives her the look of Alice in Wonderland. She wears the printed cotton dresses that the Covenant House women favor. She is the third member of Lois's and Laura's covenant group, and her upbringing, in an upper-middle-class suburb of New York City, has many features in common with Anne's and Laura's. At home she attended a mainline church, and she credits a "real radical" woman minister, "who I might not agree with about a lot," with "recogniz[ing] me and my call." In college she became part of the Fellowship of Christian Athletes because she admired many of its members. She was, she tells BW, "swept up by the joy" of the proceedings and liked how demonstrative the Christians athletes were.

When she arrived at ETS, she became an instant leader. Janette has a gift for giving smooth, cogent meditations and was frequently asked to do so in student prayer and praise services. In one, she talked about freedom:

> We are free. My ministry has been feeling like a burden, and I prayed hoping that God might tell me to forget it. But when I prayed, I saw that God loves me so much that He would be willing to let me go; only divine love gives us that kind of freedom. That brought me back to God, realizing that He loves me enough to let me go.

Even more popular is her singing. The whole CBR group gathers to hear her practice, accompanied by Laura on piano, the heartfelt "contemporary" religious songs she will perform in chapel.

Janette stands out. She confronts Jerome Allen—successfully—about what seem to her to be oppressive teaching methods. She views with alarm the keen desire of so many students to marry quickly: "You have to be absolutely clear here. Everywhere else I have been, men are afraid of the big *c*-word. But here it is more like, 'You seem nice. Will you marry me?' Each fall they look over the new crop and try to snap them up." She plans to be ordained in the Presbyterian Church, a fact that causes conflict with her roommate, Sharon Madden. "I'm always the liberal," she says, defending a class presentation by a guest that some students thought had New Age overtones.

Still, when she makes it known that she is transferring to a Presbyterian seminary at the end of her first year, there is general distress. Janette seems so much at the center of things that it is hard to imagine the group without her. The ETS president's wife, for whom she has been cleaning house, is as upset as Janette's friends. The general view is that the move is necessary because antievangelical members of Janette's presbytery might block her ordination if she completes her degree at ETS.

Janette gives BW other reasons for leaving. She is transferring because she does not like ETS: "I am a square peg in a round hole here. I did not even know what the word 'evangelical' meant before I came here, and I am not sure that I am one." She is bothered that some professors "summarize doctrines in one sentence." Her views diverge on issues other than women's ordination. While Janette herself is "no radical" on abortion, she found that she could "support a friend [from elsewhere] who decided to terminate a pregnancy this year. She asked me what I thought, and I told her that I might have made a different decision. But there was no problem in being her friend after that." Janette knows that she is much more conservative than most mainline Presbyterians, and except for the radical woman minister, she has received little encouragement from her denomination. She asks BW, a Presbyterian, how to respond to certain tricky questions that her supervising committee might ask.

(Janette's experience at the Presbyterian seminary was rocky. She was uncomfortable with the evangelical students she met there. Their views she found "fundamentalist," yet she was much more conservative than her other classmates. She considered leaving. Then things began to fall into place. She developed an interest in ethics and decided to organize campus events at which liberals and evangelicals could discuss issues. She got more involved in the denomination and took an internship in a Presbyterian church. Janette reported to BW by phone that she was settled and happy. Shortly thereafter, Lois heard that she was dating a man from a conservative Presbyterian denomination that does not ordain women. By graduation, the consensus was that she would soon become engaged. Even the Covenant House women who oppose the ordination of women were taken aback by the irony of this development.)

Pamela Willis

Pamela Willis, who had enrolled a year before the CBR group formed, never lived in Covenant House, but she quickly became part of its life. During the first year, when Anne Norton occupied her enormous triple room alone, Pamela, who lived off-campus in a house where she helped with the cleaning, sometimes stayed after late evening classes. She became a frequent guest at CBR and an almost integral part of the group. She is like its core members in significant ways: She greatly admires Roy Parks, for instance, and thinks of herself as theologically orthodox. She shares their good manners and taste for nice things. She and Laura prayed together during Laura's first year.

Pamela is also different. She looks distinctly different. The Covenant House women almost always look collegiate or very feminine—jumpers and turtlenecks, or dresses with floral prints and white collars. Other women students dress with greater variety. Jeans or slacks are common in the classroom, often paired with sweaters in pale pastel colors and designs, with lace or ruffle decorations and—most common of all—a small bright gold cross held by a short, thin chain. Many wear their hair shoulder-length or longer and carefully curled. Thus the standard look, especially among the younger women, is a sort of casual delicacy. In such surroundings, Pamela stands out. To one Modern Theology class session, Pamela wears a bright yellow bomber jacket; her blond hair is precisely and modishly cut, shorter on one side than the other. In the period before class, she engages in an intense conversation with Mary Ann Kromer, another student.

The conversation focuses on Pamela's decision to take a job at the United Parcel Service, where several ETS students (none of the others women) work because of the high pay and tuition assistance the company offers. She will go directly from this evening class to her night shift, which begins at 11 P.M. "It's skilled labor," she has told BW earlier. "There are a few other women on the line. Most of them aren't too butch. Mary Ann very much disapproves. Her husband died, you know, and, I think, when he was dying, she very much gave in to his whims; now she thinks women should be like that."

Mary Ann is making her disapproval clear in this conversation. She admonishes Pamela: "You consistently do things that do not safeguard your femininity." Pamela considers this criticism without bristling. She tells Mary Ann that she may have a point. She says that when she first came to ETS, she met a male student who later told her that "he never asked me out [because] . . . I do not always wear skirts." Actually, Pamela is wearing a skirt on this occasion, a black-and-white one, but it is very, very short. The skirt, big bright jacket, and hair cut shorter on one side than the other make her by far the most dramatic-looking woman in the room. Her good looks and avant-garde style often get noticed. At the opening picnic one year, a new student points Pamela out to a friend and says, "I would really like to meet that woman. She dresses so stylish and funky. Isn't it odd how you are sometimes attracted to people by how they look?" When this conversation is reported to Pamela, she laughs and says, "Too bad it wasn't a man."

Pamela is also known on campus for her outspokenness. Most students seem to try to play down BW's and JC's presence, but Pamela regularly points it out and teases them about what she suspects is their different view of things. "We had hot-and-sour soup in the cafeteria the other day," she tells BW. "It had tofu in it—very progressive. You must be having some influence around here." As an M.Div. student, she is one of the few women in many of her classes. (Pamela has no interest in being ordained but no objection to other women seeking ordination, and she thinks that the school should support both those who approve of women's ordination and those who do not.) In class discussion, she frequently asks questions and makes comments. This contrasts sharply with other women students, who are mostly quiet in class. When she feels that she has an important point to make, Pamela pursues it rigorously.

In a Modern Theology course, she engages guest speaker James Cone, author of well-known books on black theology:

Pamela: You state that "God loves us because we are black." Doesn't God love us because of Jesus' death?

Cone: Who taught you to ask that? [He laughs and points to Roy Parks, who is sitting in the middle of the classroom and looks enormously pleased.] I recognize that point. I had dinner with that brother. . . .

You know, you can know too much theology. Your question comes from a struggle. Mine does too. Those who use that language of yours oppressed my

people. I have got to ask if you've come to terms with that. You have to stay
with that a long time. You can't talk about Jesus' death on the cross unless you
talk about real death, about those who are dying. Jesus died for those who are
dying now.

Pamela: Didn't Jesus die for all of us?

Cone: Now there you go again.

Pamela: Jesus died for the poor only?

Cone: Since I am leaving you and you'll have plenty to reinforce you, I have to tell
        you that the problem with your universalism is what it covers up. You try start-
        ing with a particular. If you start with the universal, you'll never get back to
        the particular.

After this exchange, Pamela tells BW that "[Cone] really hacked me off. He
said he was reacting to anti-intellectualism, but then he used it when he was questioned. He tells us to use common sense and the Good Book. What would his
colleagues say to that?" A student approaches her to say that he has enjoyed her
participation in the course. She responds that she liked a question of his about the
problem with premodern views. Such views, he says, are a problem only if they
spill over into fundamentalism. Pamela replies lightly: "Any view is fine with me
as long as I can go out and drink beer and talk about it."

Notes frequently appear in BW's mailbox, suggesting that she and Pamela go
out for a "brewsky." Often the invitation includes a movie. Pamela is intensely
interested in cinema, especially art films, and literature, in which she majored in
college, where her favorite teachers were radical deconstructionists. Along with
Mary Chang and Susie Jacobs, she has organized Inklings, a literary group that
reads and discusses the work of C. S. Lewis and Dorothy Sayers and their circle.
She would like to be a religious journalist after she graduates. Despite her aggressive style of class participation, she is terrified of addressing groups of people, so
she does not want to teach, much less preach.

Pamela grew up in a fundamentalist family. Her father, a stockbroker, was also
a lay preacher in a dispensationalist sect. When guests in their home questioned
the literalism of their church's doctrines, her mother became convinced that some
elements of their orthodoxy were wrong. This caused much religious strife at
home, which dampened Pamela's interest in religion for a long time. She came to
ETS "on a whim." Her father was opposed because the school is not dispensationalist, though he helps to support her; her mother is pleased. Her father does
not want her to become a pastor, though he told her that he would attend her
church at least once if she did.

Pamela now goes to the Whitley Church, along with many other ETS students,
several of the Covenant House women and, recently, Roy Parks. This group likes
what pastor/professor Charles Oliver calls Whitley's "faithful ministry of the
Word." The "mild generic Calvinism" that Parks says characterizes the seminary
is much in evidence at the church, not only in the preaching but also in the prayers. On the Sunday that Paul Bashford gives his inaugural sermon, Oliver gathers
concerns from the congregation and shapes them into prayer. For relatives of congregants who were close to, but not affected by, recent tornadoes, he gives thanks
that "in this case, God has seen fit to spare them"; he also gives thanks for the

improved health of several relatives, noting that healing has taken a long time and that it occurs "in God's time, not ours." For a woman in the acute stages of leukemia, he asks that she be given "a sample of the healing that awaits us all." About the accidental death of a high school student the night before, he says "such things seem almost necessary" to bring young people to an awareness of how they are leading their lives; he asks that teenagers in the church be enabled to use the opportunity for witness.

Pamela and some others do not like the sentimental Victorian hymns Oliver favors or, sometimes, his highly expository preaching style ("The man does not even know what application is," says Pamela).

Pamela is a mixture of typically evangelical and unusual traits. She is theologically and politically conservative (Dick Cheney, the then U.S. secretary of defense, is one of her heroes) and ardently pro-life. She goes regularly to a clinic nearby "to engage in dialogue with pro-choice women demonstrators." Yet she avoids the girlish styles of dress and behavior that make ETS women popular. She has sharp views about what she considers the racial insensitivity of her fellow students. She likes to participate in the structured "ecumenical" dialogues with liberals, Catholics, and Jews that the National Conference of Christians and Jews sponsors for seminary students. Some very orthodox students at ETS are not comfortable with her forthright manner. One, an Orthodox Presbyterian who also works at UPS, says that he has avoided forming a friendship with her because "she seems too bright-eyed and bushy-tailed."

Gradually, Pamela drifts away from the Covenant House crowd. She maintains a close friendship with the Stanfields, a student couple also living off-campus. She often cares for their young son. The Stanfields are charismatic Episcopalians. Jim is tall, calm, good-humored, and planning to become an Episcopal priest. Miriam Stanfield, almost as tall, is famous as Jerome Allen's best student ever—she graduated with a nearly perfect record. The Stanfields share Pamela's commitment to pro-life activism in a civil style and to interfaith dialogue, as well as her sense of humor, love of stylish things, and relaxed attitude to drinking off-campus.

By the time of graduation, as Pamela leaves to work as assistant to an evangelical writer and speaker (Roy Parks helped her to get the job), she "no longer feels connected to ETS." Her life has become only classes; otherwise, it is "pretty well lived between the dogs I take care of [at the house she lives in off-campus], UPS, and Whitley." She and her parents, who come to her graduation from their home in South Carolina, are not included in the Covenant House party in the church basement.

Marilyn Flexner

Marilyn Flexner was one of the original Covenant House occupants during "our year." She contributed a microwave oven to the Community-Building Room in the alcove, and she spent a good deal of time there watching television, but she never did feel connected to the inner circle or to anyone else at ETS. Her background is very different from those of the other Covenant House women. She was raised a Roman Catholic, the third of four children. When she was a child, her parents joined an enthusiastic Catholic renewal movement, the Cursillo; early in her teen-age years, they divorced. Marilyn describes her childhood as "troubled . . . pretty wild . . . unhappy . . . a lot of anger."

While in college, Marilyn lived at home and worked her way up in a law firm from secretary to paralegal and office manager. She was involved in the youth group of a Congregational church, but she did not "make a commitment to Christ" until much later, in her midtwenties. Her mother had joined a Christian weight loss program that "centered around Scripture and seeking God's kingdom," and that led them both to a charismatic Episcopal church, where, after a few months' participation, Marilyn made her commitment. Her leadership ability in the church's youth group prompted a young priest to urge her to consider seminary. ETS was his only suggestion—it was the school he would have attended had his bishop not vetoed it. Marilyn did not want to be ordained, however; she wanted to work with youth, and ETS had a program with that specific focus. Her interest in kids, especially troubled kids, grew out of her own early unhappiness. "I've experienced a lot of things that they are experiencing—abandonment . . . and anger, certainly."

When she arrived at ETS, she seemed lonely and unhappy. Her looks contrasted sharply with those of the other women in her dorm. She dressed like a college student in jeans and shirts, wore little makeup, and did not curl her hair. Within a few months, her looks substantially changed—she lost weight, acquired a new haircut, and grew considerably more cheerful. BW asks her why. "I am blessed to be able to go home every weekend," she says. The youth ministry program has a lighter workload than some others, and that gives her time to stay "in control," to go home to her family, and to attend her home church. During her whole time at seminary, she never "connects" with any other church.

At the end of the first year, Marilyn accepts an internship in a distant city on the staff of a group home for abused teenagers who are now preparing for inde-pendent living. The experience is the high point of her seminary training—in fact, in her interview with BW about her seminary years she wants only to describe the internship:

> It was tough. . . . It's a model home—we all ate dinner together . . . . We were teaching them life skills. . . . Some of [the kids] had [criminal] records . . . , but their major problem was probably abuse. . . . The purpose of the program is to minis-ter to their spiritual needs, but I think that in order to do that, you need to provide for their physical needs, and that providing for their physical needs will open them up for their spiritual growth. . . . I think it's a subversive ministry. It's not—there's not a lot of conversions or that type of thing. But there were a few kids that I can think of that had real healing take place, that I attribute to the will of Christ, because we are there as a staff because of Christ, ministering because of him, and the kids know that.
>
> It was a very intense community living experience out there. I ate with at least twenty people every night for dinner, and was very close. I made some really good friendships. And, knowing that I was only going to be here another year, I haven't really reached out, or tried to get involved in anything here. I didn't want to live on campus.

Back at school after the internship, Marilyn becomes even more detached than she was during her first year. She finds a house to share with other young Christian adults in the area—none of the others seminary students. "We lead four separate lives. We live in the same house together, but it's not what I had experienced [at the group home]." She does have campus involvements. She works in the cafeteria and travels with other ETS students—including Lois Boucher and Brenda Moore from Covenant House—to Israel, and serves as student and teaching assistant in the youth ministry program. But she continues to go home every weekend, and she has no seminary student friends. Her advisee group rarely meets, and she was the only student to show up at two meetings of the Episcopal students that is supposed to exist. Asked by BW how ETS should change, she says, "Community. There's no community." At the same time, she cannot imagine how, with frantically busy schedules like hers, students could build or be organized into a closer community.

Marilyn does not blame the school for what she has not found. She says that it has been "a good experience" and that she has "grown a lot in my relationship with God and with others and myself." She thinks the seminary has given her "a well-rounded, good, balanced education," and she is glad that she has had to take theology and Bible as well as youth ministry courses. Her whole focus, however, is on what she will do after seminary. She plans to live at home and to explore whether she can set up a group house for troubled teenagers like the one she worked in. If that does not work, she will do what she planned when she came to seminary: look for a youth ministry job in an evangelical church. For the time being, she will work as a volunteer with the youth group of her home church. "It's something I am committed to," she says.

Paula Fleming

Paula Fleming, says Patrick Clark, a young, talkative student with vigorous intellectual interests, is something like the opposite of the Covenant House women. On the question of women in ministry, Patrick "goes back and forth" between Paula and Brenda Moore to test his developing ideas (he has interviewed both of them for his paper on the subject). Paula herself likes to emphasize how different she is:

> I am the odd person out, no matter how you look at it. I am a woman. I am older. I am Arminian [the theological position that emphasizes the role of human will in accepting the gift of salvation and thus runs counter to Calvinism's insistence on "irresistible" grace alone]. I am not Pentecostal, but I am definitely more charismatic, in that I take more heed of the Spirit all the time.

Paula is thirty-seven, a large, handsome woman who is married and has a nine-year-old son. She talks fast and has an emphatic manner. She was born into a midwestern family, the daughter of a welder who was involved in labor unions and state politics. He was an "embittered agnostic": His first wife had died after "some stupid Lutheran minister" had suggested that she wouldn't die because he

needed her so much. The rest of her father's second family, including Paula, belonged to a very conservative denomination, from whose perspective "this school
[ETS] is on its way to liberality and hell," especially because it admits Pentecostals, though ETS's inerrantist views of the Bible are respected. Paula went to Bible
college, preparing to teach Hebrew and steering deliberately clear of Christian
education courses. From the start, she wanted to be a church leader in some nontraditional way. A professor in college suggested ordination, but Paula dismissed
the idea as impossible in her denomination.

After college, she went to work to earn money for further study, met her husband (a printer), and convinced him to join a Baptist church with her. They moved
to the ETS vicinity when he got a job here. Paula had always thought that she
would do something of a professional nature for God, she says. She attended a
prayer service where a Methodist friend gave a testimonial. During the talk, she
says, she heard a voice inside, not her own ("I know the sound of my own voice").
It said, "I want you to do that, Paula. Go back to school."

So she did, to ETS because it was nearby and she did not want to uproot her
family for something she was unsure about. She is very critical of the school's
treatment of women like her who plan to be ordained and are advocates for
women in ministry (Paula succeeded Mary Chang and Susie Jacobs as chair of the
women's equality organization). Though she was the only woman in many of her
Bible college classes, she says that she gets more grief here than there: "The
[ETS] professors are essentially supportive of your efforts . . . , whether or not
they think you should be doing this." Yet, she continues, they convey their feelings
about women in ministry by failing to call on women or make eye contact. She
adds that some are very supportive, and a few, like Jerome Allen, are very fair
even though they make their opposition known. The students are another matter,
she reports.

Paula commutes to the campus from a distance and has only a few close student
friends. One is the iconoclastic Timothy Woods. Tim reports that he and Paula are
"prayer warriors"; for an hour or so every week "we pray and talk about things."
Of Tim, Paula says, "[He] thinks that no woman should be ordained, and no man
either, unless they have the gifts for it." But most of her views of her fellow
students are intensely critical: The students are the worst. And they get worse in
each crop of incoming students. They are tolerant of women only if they are
invisible and silent. They think of themselves as guardians of the only truth." She
says that she wants "to say to those guys [the ultra-Calvinist students and faculty],
'You search the Scriptures, when the author of Scripture is standing right in front
of you.' I know the jots and tittles in Scripture well enough to know that there is
usually a lot of leeway." These guys want to drag all of Scripture through a few
difficult verses. I want to fit a few verses into the pattern of the whole Bible."

Paula is even more critical of the women students:

> The women students are the worst. I keep asking, What they are selling out for? I hate
> to say it, but I think that they think that the prospective husbands will like them better
> if they are opposed to women. But you know, it is not going to help them. They are
> going to have to stand before the judgment alone, not with a man. And they are going
> to be asked, You, with all of your gifts and abilities, why didn't you fill a pulpit?

When the Covenant House women graduate, Paula still faces two years of work toward her Master of Divinity degree. She has completed her supervised ministry assignment in a congregation. An odd thing, she says, is that some of the fundamentalists who joined that church have become her supporters. She thinks that she will become a pastor, though she has not yet taken the steps to begin that process in her newly chosen American Baptist denomination.

MAINLINE
THEOLOGICAL
SEMINARY

SEVEN

Year One: Encounters

This is not the first "call" you have received, and it most assuredly will not be your last—but for this time in your life's journey, there is a special work for you here.
—Academic Dean Harriet Hercon, fall orientation address

Moving In

The second floor of Barlowe Hall, Mainline Theological Seminary's dormitory for single and transient students, begins to show signs of life two days before fall orientation. Two large standing metal fans bring sound and motion to a long, dimly lit hallway. An Asian woman emerges from her room in bathrobe and slippers, a towel over her arm, and heads for the bathroom. This dorm originally housed men only, as is clearly evident from the four urinals in the "ladies'" room.

Several other rooms on the hall are obviously already occupied: The name "Alice West" is printed on a piece of white paper on one door, along with a laminated message board with a floral design. Across and down the hall, a door is partly ajar. A woman lies on a narrow bed reading; over her head is a large, glossy poster of a muscular man. The name on the door is "Lucille." She has a message board like Alice's, but it is not decorated.

Two male students carry boxes of computer equipment into a room about four doors down from Alice West. They huff and puff. Nearby, a faculty member who heads up the deaf ministry program at MTS stands in a doorway talking to a new student, her mother, and her fiancé. They are hot and sweaty from unloading and unpacking in the non-air-conditioned dorm.

The student, Tess Lytle, has long, blond hair, dark brown eyes, and a refreshing frankness about her. She wears bi-aural hearing aids, signs some, and reads lips very well. Tess is twenty-four, a recent college graduate from a small midwestern town. "I am preparing for the diaconate with a special emphasis in deaf ministry," she says proudly when introduced to Penny Marler (PM).

119

The next day Tess and Judy Ponder, who "just moved [in] down the hall," stand talking in the passageway. Judy is short, with brown hair, lively eyes, and a pleasant smile. She is dressed in cutoff blue jeans and a T-shirt. As they chat, a girl with long, curly blond hair walks up. She is Alice, a third-year student who lives on the second floor; she's Alice West, of the floral door design. She says hello, signing it at the same time, and explains that she is also in the deaf ministry program. Judy states that she is "just an M.Div. student."

Later that afternoon, Tess, Judy, another new student named Sam, and PM go downtown. Sam, is twenty-six, tall, and plump, with blond, thinning hair and a spotty complexion. He wears wire-rimmed glasses, and his speech is slightly slurred. He smiles a lot and talks a lot. From time to time he exclaims, "I can't believe I'm really here in the city!" Sam graduated from college last spring and is interested in youth ministry.

On the way, Judy talks about herself. She lives in eastern Pennsylvania, and she came to seminary to become a pastor. Her inspiration is a woman who was pastor of her home church several years ago. Judy worked a few years after college as an activities director at a nursing home. She is twenty-eight years old. Judy, Sam, and Tess are all at MTS with some financial assistance through the school or their local church. They worry about expenses. Judy is not sure how she will pay her tuition next semester. Each of them is looking for a job. Tess, through the help of the associate dean of students, thinks she will have a twenty-hour-a-week job in the bookstore. Judy is investigating an after-school program for young people at a nearby church. Sam has made a connection about a youth ministry job.

The students talk about how they will afford to eat weeknight suppers and weekend meals. Breakfast and lunch are served Tuesday through Friday in MTS's refectory; on Monday, only lunch is offered. In the middle of the conversation, Tess says, "I've never heard of a 'reflectory' before." Judy replies, "It's a refectory." Tess asks what that means. Sam adds, "Something like reflection?" "Yeah, at night and on weekends all we can do is 'reflect' on our food," Judy laughingly says.

On the busy downtown streets, vendors tempt late summer tourists. Tess stops at a booth where war veterans are urging passersby to sign a petition against the "desecration" of the American flag. She signs it; the rest of the group walks on. Later, on the way back, Tess asks, "Is there something wrong with me signing that petition about the flag?" "No," Sam and Judy say together. "Well, nobody else signed it," Tess observes. "Well, I feel differently about it," Sam offers, "but there's nothing wrong with you signing it if you want to."

"I just think that we ought not to burn the flag that so many people died for," Tess says. "Well," Sam replies, "it's just that I think as Americans—believing in freedom and all—that we ought to be able to burn the flag." "Oh," Tess responds. Judy says not a word.

Tess talks about missing her fiancé and how she cried when he drove away. She says they have set a time to intentionally "think about each other" every day because they can't afford frequent telephone calls. Tess goes on to say that she is not sure she will stay at MTS more than a year.

"Sometimes I think that I should just go home; I left a good job for this," Judy offers. "[But] it's worth it," she continues. "If it wasn't a struggle, it wouldn't be worth it." That leads her to more talk about the female pastor she so admires, and how sometimes churches do "horrible things" to people. Her pastor was forced to leave the congregation, she says, because the rural people were so unaccepting of a woman pastor. "But she had integrity," Judy remarks, and she comments that she has encountered some seminary students who had none.

Orientation

"The mission of the Seminary is to educate persons for the various forms of ministry and to provide theological leadership on issues facing the church and the world," students read in the catalog. MTS is related to a major Protestant denomination and "is committed to a form of theological education both loyal to its denominational heritage and supportive of the ecumenical movement toward a united church."

The principal task of ministry is "to proclaim by word and deed the reconciling and liberating gospel of Jesus Christ to a broken world." This ministry has its foundation in "God's saving action" and in "Jesus Christ's life of service." Jesus, the mission statement continues, "brought salvation to sinners, preached good news to the poor, release to the captives, recovery of sight to the blind and liberation to the oppressed."

As a "laboratory of learning," the seminary "attempts to demonstrate how rigorous intellectual pursuit can be centered in a worship of God that leads to caring relationships within the community and informed concern for the world without." To this end, "administrative and educational policies"

> affirm the dignity and worth of every human being. Mainline Theological Seminary is committed to inclusiveness of race, sex, nationality, economic status, and age; it is committed to working toward the goal of a barrier free environment with adequate facilities and assistance for persons with handicapping conditions.

This conviction is visually highlighted by the choice and arrangement of pictures in the catalog.

MTS's public relations material since the mid-1960s has included a recurring graphic design—a rectangular grid composed of irregular boxes, all bounded by a stark, white border. The pictures in the grid change as the constituency of the student body changes. In the 1989–91 catalogue, the grid appears opposite the school's "Mission and Ministry" statement. In the upper left box (the largest square), a white male student leans forward over a book. In the upper right, a white female stares ahead intently with her arm resting on an open notebook. In the middle left box, a baby-faced white male puts finishing touches on a clay figurine. In the middle right, an African man in native headdress stands in front of a library stack. In the lower left box, a smiling Korean student is dwarfed by a large seal bearing the word *oikoumene*. In the lower right, a middle-aged white female takes notes in a large classroom.

On the sidewalk at the corner of the parking lot, a male student with blond hair braided in the back holds a big poster-board sign that reads "Orientation," with an arrow pointing toward the administration building's main entrance. He's quite a center of attention because he is wearing a cap with an animal face—fuzzy hair, nose, and whiskers—forming the front brim.

New students are lined up in the hall outside the registrar's office to get their photo IDs made. They vary in age. Some are just-out-of-college types wearing neat shorts or jeans and T-shirts. Others are middle-aged and wear dark suits and carry briefcases. Still others are preppy types with sports coats and open collars. All the women over thirty-five or so wear contemporary summer "Sunday dresses"—plain, straight shifts or neat skirts and blouses—and hose. Most of the students are white.

Judy and Sam approach Tess accompanied by a tall, slender woman with short brown hair. They introduce her as Arlene. She is wearing a white T-shirt with a half watermelon painted around the front collar. Arlene is single, thirty-three years old, and claims Texas as her home. For the past several years she has been deeply involved in a church—in a nearby city—that she describes as "real active in peace and justice." It has a "sister church" in Nicaragua and is a "sanctuary" congregation for Third World social and political refugees. Arlene says that her participation in this church—along with "this idea of being a missionary/martyr all the way back to grade school"—led her to MTS to specialize in urban ministries through the Master of Divinity program.

Everybody picks up registration packets and helps themselves to juice, coffee, or tea from two long tables set up in the narthex of the chapel. A couple of faculty members mill around; also, a fully outfitted clown tries to strike up conversations. No one pays much attention to the clown.

Following a service of worship, Harriet Hercon, the academic dean, welcomes new students to MTS. She wears a plain shirtwaist dress and is deeply tanned. Her dark brown hair frames her chin and bounces noticeably as she speaks. Hercon has two agenda at this initial "dean's meeting": one, to let these new students know that this will be her last year at MTS; and two, to talk about MTS's inclusive language policy.

Dean Hercon begins:

> Why would an academic dean who is perfectly happy with her work, is convinced she is at the best seminary in the [denominational] system, and prefers living in [this city] to practically anywhere, accept a position as faculty in another [denominational] seminary? . . . One would assume that academic deans must by definition be rational creatures, so insanity must presumably be ruled out.

She says that her work as an administrator has been "varied and intensely interesting" but that "it easily expands to take all the hours I can give it." Harriet explains that she is also a "teacher and a scholar," and that work, "just as easily as administrative work, expands to take all the hours I can give." "Deans are Janus-faced creatures," she observes.

A decision had been forced upon her, the dean continues. Last spring her teacher and mentor announced his retirement from a prestigious chair at another school, and "I have been honored with the invitation to be his successor." She smiles and adds that the decision has not been an easy one. "I love this school and have been grateful to have been 'called to this place' these past seven years. I feel deeply interwoven with the work here, and I have much affection and esteem for my colleagues. Struggling with the call was enormously difficult," she concludes.

These personal words over, the dean moves to the second issue: "generous language" at MTS. She refers to the student manual section stating that "linguistic sexism—the assumption that the male is normative, the dominance of masculine imagery and grammatical forms, or any other usage that diminishes the equal dignity of women and men—is to be avoided in the writing of senior papers and other papers as well."

"Generous language," Harriet Hercon says, "is language that includes everyone—excludes no one." Why is inclusive language important? Precisely because, she argues, the way we talk to one another makes a difference. Language, after all, "reflects, reinforces, and creates reality." Her hand and arm movements complement her message: When she talks about inclusion and generosity she opens her arms, as if welcoming, and then pulls them slowly toward her, as if embracing.

The president's home is on the seminary campus in a thicket of trees. Older students joke to new ones about "seeing President Jack [Stewart]" in his bedroom reading the paper. They have a fairly clear view into the upper story from the back of Barlowe Hall. And dorm life in warm weather, when windows are open, includes cries of "Archie-e-e" as the presidential cat is called in for the night.

President Jackson Stewart hosts a reception for new students at his home the first night of fall orientation. The back patio is crowded with students debriefing their first day at MTS.

One group of students is particularly animated. The members obviously know one another, but they welcome a stranger who joins and asks about their backgrounds. A tall, lanky man with thinning brown hair introduces himself as Tommy Reiss, a sports editor. He is thirty-one, grew up in a middle Atlantic state, and has lived in Florida and Virginia. His religious background is mainline Protestant, although, he remarks, his wife is "one of them there Baptist dippers." Tommy decided to leave the newspaper business for the ministry as the result of an intense spiritual experience in a charismatic prayer group.

Standing next to Tommy is a forty-year-old man with curly brown and gray hair and a mustache. Patrick has pale, clear eyes that almost twinkle when he smiles or laughs. He describes his Protestant background as "very conservative." His call to ministry was successfully evaded, he says, until he had an industrial accident and was disabled for three months. That's when "I started a very inward journey that ended up with me following the call."

Evan Shanks is "the old man of the group." He's very short and looks to be in his late forties. An M.B.A. who spent "twenty-six years in the finance world," Evan worked for several companies and ended up as chief financial officer of the real estate division of a major regional corporation. "During all that financial success," he states, "I was married and divorced twice." In the end, financial success was just "not satisfying." His current wife encouraged him to follow up on his interest in ministry. He did—and after a couple of years of night courses at a

Baptist seminary, he decided to quit his job and pursue a Master of Divinity full-time.

The only woman in the group is Susan Arch, thirty-two, red-haired, married, and the mother of an elementary-aged son. Her background is in nursing. She explains that she's "seen a lot of child abuse and spouse abuse" and thinks women and children need an advocate and role model in the ministry. In fact, she sees herself as a nurturer and defender of these "special minorities."

James Englehardt completes the circle. In his midthirties, he is from the upper Midwest and is dressed in pressed khakis and a button-down plaid shirt. He wears his ash-blond hair short and combed back. Jim grew up in church, and his "turning point" came during a men's retreat at a small college in the East. During midnight communion, he says, "something was calling me." He explains that his "marriage was in the toilet," and he just "felt so empty." So he walked out to the school's football field. "I just went to my knees and started crying," Jim recalls. "I said, 'Jesus, take my life.' " And immediately afterward, "I felt the physical presence of Jesus Christ standing over me, and it changed my life." But a new course was not instantly clear. After a rough year and a divorce, Jim moved back home, got a good job as a computer programmer, and remarried. He attended a local seminary part-time for about a year before deciding to pursue his call wholeheartedly.

Patrick and Evan explain that the members of the group already know one another well because they were together in the summer, preparing for a special program combining M.Div. and pastoral work. This program was developed "as a method to integrate better student pastorates into the educational design of the regular curriculum." Each student pastor enrolled serves as the "sole pastor to one or more congregations." The program begins with a seminar offered during the summer prior to the first year.

Students in this program attend classes at MTS for three consecutive days each week for four academic years. Housing is available on campus for two nights a week. Participants are encouraged to adapt class assignments to the parish setting. The student pastors meet as a group with a faculty person for two years and field supervisors for two more years to discuss concerns about their congregations and classroom-congregation "integration."

After Tommy complains that the English test taken earlier was "too picky," Patrick takes up the issue of Dean Hercon's "inclusive language" talk. "I think that 'generous language' sounds paternalistic," he says with mock seriousness, then he laughs along with Evan, Tommy, and Jim. Susan glares and simply says, "That's not what she meant!"

Harriet Hercon listens to a small group of new students tackle questions about culture and Christianity after viewing the film *The Mission* as part of orientation. The movie focuses on the evangelization and treatment of South American indigenous peoples by European missionaries and governmental emissaries. Questions have been passed out before the film: "What is the integrity of the Indian culture from the European perspective? From the Indian perspective?" "What were the issues involved in the European/Indian relations (racial, cultural, economic, and religious hegemony, land, resources)?" "What do we mean by Christianity? How is it related to transformation?"

Peter Tomas, a twenty-three-year-old M.Div. student and son of a minister from the West Coast, speaks up first. "I didn't like the film," he states decisively. "It was insensitive to indigenous people." Peter further observes that *The Mission* brings up the tension between particularism and universalism. Somehow, he concludes, an emphasis on the universal tends to cancel out the particular. Looking away from Dean Hercon, he says, "I don't really like 'inclusive and generous'— sounds paternalistic. I live in my culture [and the best I can do] is engage yours in dialogue."

A middle-aged woman enjoins, "You shouldn't just withdraw from foreign missions, though. I'll not apologize for my culture and tradition. It's important to know the boundaries."

An M.Div. student from Virginia in his midthirties says he found the European missionaries very "rigid."

A forty-two-year-old Unitarian recalls a phrase from the opening segments of the film. "Before God came to the Indians . . . ," the narrator began. This student talks about the arrogance of that position and says colonizing people ought to ask for "forgiveness" for such an assumption.

A middle-aged widow listens intently. She has dark, expressive eyes, a soft, almost musical speaking voice, and shiny, jet-black hair cut in a short bob with bangs. She says that she cannot forget the Indian women and children in the film: the innocent, the victims. And when she thinks of the priests, all she sees are "agents of a European government," not priests of God at all.

A new doctoral student from Liberia sums up a lot of the conversation with a sigh: "Ministry is tough!"

Hercon, who has been quiet to this point, asks: "What is Christianity? . . . Maybe a first thought is: It's the institutional church. Instead, the film seems to say that it's more forgiveness, love, acceptance across cultures. It's [how] an image of God takes root in other cultures, and the way it expresses itself."

"Like through the flute or pipe," the Liberian student comments. Hercon smiles. Another student concludes that the message of the film is that we both "suffer for one another [and] need one another."

Classes Begin

The purpose of seminary is not an educated clergy but an educated congregation. . . .
The practice of learning is so you can give something away.

—Harriet Hercon

Several students gather for breakfast on the first day of classes. The refectory at MTS is located below the classroom wing. It is a large, rectangular room; like other rooms in the building, it is painted a mixture of off-white and green. Toward the back are two glassed-in auxiliary dining rooms, a partitioned cafeteria line, space for carts holding trays and flatware, and a half-dozen long rows of tables. This area is sheltered by a lowered acoustical tile ceiling, so it tends toward dimness. The front part of the room is filled with scattered round tables, a portable podium and, sometimes, an upright piano on rollers. This half is brighter, with an "airy" feel due to the windows and a higher ceiling.

A big, genial, red-haired M.Div. student, who was a lay minister and a farmer before "I got the calling to the full-time ministry," comments on the seating patterns: "All the whites except for a very few sit toward the windows, and the blacks sit back in the other end." He adds, "Now at breakfast it doesn't matter, but at lunch it does."

A new student lifts his breakfast tray from the chrome tracks and moves toward the cash register. As he offers a picture ID that indicates his meal-plan status, the plump black woman checking cards says, "No, that's six; you'll have to put one back." The student flushes red around the ears and nervously returns a piece of fruit.

"Five Things Mildred," the watchdog for meal-plan violations, is a legend among students at MTS. All resident and commuter students at MTS who stay in Barlowe Hall for one night a week or more are required to purchase a meal plan. They may select "five things" from the cafeteria line at mealtime.

At the breakfast table the first day of classes, Robert Keithley, a second-year student who lives in Barlowe and hails from Mississippi, tells this story to first-year students Terrence Nunnally and Boyd Arthur: "One time I got the wrong bowl [on the salad bar]. Mildred's even got rules about the right bowls for the right [number] of things. She came out of the kitchen right to my table and told me I had the wrong bowl," Robert recalls. A small bowl counts as "one thing," and a larger bowl is "two." Clever students tend to select the smaller bowl and really load on the ingredients.

PM notes that she took only four things. Take five, advises Alice West. "I always get my five things. Even if I don't eat them all. You can always get an apple or a carton of milk to take back to your room [for] later. Or I give one of [the] five things to someone else."

The lower level of Dunavant Hall, the classroom building, contains the campus bookstore, a post office, a lounge for commuting students, two classrooms, and an art studio, which is a laboratory for religion and art classes and also the base for artists-in-residence. There, too, is the entrance to "the tunnel," an underground corridor leading to the chapel and administrative offices. Dunavant's basement is easily the most-traveled space on MTS's campus. Two prominent bulletin boards, one by the bookstore and the other by the art studio, regularly display a variety of announcements.

As the fall 1989 semester begins, Dunavant has been newly renovated. Much of the building had been closed during the previous academic year for asbestos removal and redecoration. By fall, the work is nearly completed. Classrooms are freshly painted and ready for use. Room 107 can hold about eighty students at new desks neatly arranged in rows. The furniture, the paint, and the carpet are taupe and muted grays. This is the largest classroom at the seminary and is used for Introduction to the Old Testament; Mission and Ministry; and Church History.

These three courses are taken by virtually all first-year students, and enrollment in them this year includes only a few students that are not part of the entering class.

The main door to Room 107 is in the middle of the side wall, and to enter one must go around the rows of desks facing toward the front, on the left. The other side wall, opposite the door, has windows onto the sloping front lawn. Room 107 is a traditional seminary classroom: plain furniture, muted colors, artless walls. The teacher's desk at the front holds a portable lectern. Attached to a chalkboard spanning the width of the room is an old map rack. The room is neither an ugly nor a memorable space for learning. Although new, the student desks are not a universal hit. Large individuals have trouble sitting in them. To alleviate the problems, three oblong tables with straight chairs are set up at the back of the room.

Since this room is used for most core courses of the first-year students, a fairly regular seating pattern prevails in all the classes. Most of the African-American students cluster on the front left, not far from the door; the student pastor group sits toward the right front, along the windows. Many of the commuter students, who often come to class in suits or business attire, sit along the wall on the side by the door to accommodate their sometimes late arrivals or early departures from class. The students who live in Barlowe Hall tend to sit near each other toward the center or center-right, toward the windows and away from the doors. On a typical class day, students dress in many ways: suits, shorts, sweats, and jeans. Attire frequently conveys more about what students do apart from class than expectations about what should be worn to class.

Mission and Ministry, September

MTS has a series of courses called Mission and Ministry that deal with different aspects of church, ministry, world, and theology. Three of these courses are required during a three-year M.Div. program. The classes are team-taught, and this fall Harriet Hercon and David Parsons are in charge. Occasionally both professors are present in the classroom, but frequently one takes over in the absence of the other.

Harriet Hercon turns to the blackboard and writes: "What does theology have to do with the mission and ministry of the church?" She then instructs the more than fifty first-year students to form small groups of three or four and come up with an answer to the question.

One spontaneous group consists of a male M.R.E. candidate, about thirty, wearing dark eyeglasses; a middle-aged African-American M.Div. student; and PM. The younger man recently received a master's degree in "Instructional Technology"; the older is a full-time civil service worker and is one of a few in the class who arrives in jacket and tie.

"What does she want us to do this for?" the M.R.E. student asks. "Isn't this what the whole class is about?"

"I think that she wants us to think about it first—to see what we know," the other student responds.

"I don't like this," the younger student says, pausing, then continuing: "What does theology have to do with the mission and ministry of the church? What is theology? . . . Well, I think theology is what you think about God and how God works in the world. You really can't do 'ministry' unless it has something to do with God—otherwise, it's just helping people."

The M.Div. student agrees and adds that theology is the whole reason for being a church. Without a theology, he says, there really is no church. The pertinent question to him is that of the kind of theology dictating the "kind of mission or ministry you do."

The M.R.E. student brightens: "Yeah, that wasn't so hard. I think that's the right answer. Don't you?"

Hercon calls the class back together and immediately draws two stick figures on the board. One she labels "Bob," and the other, with a skirt, she labels "Jane."

Bob never once asked the question "What is theology?" Hercon says, explaining that he is not a very happy man. She draws a frown on the stick figure's face. Bob thinks "life is sometimes hard" and also believes that "to be human is to be hurt." Bob knows that "life is crowded over with problems," she concludes.

Hercon tells the class that Bob is an alcoholic. One day, a friend invites him to Alcoholics Anonymous. Through AA, Bob gets the feeling that "things might be better after all." The teacher says Bob's friend is not responsible for this feeling because he never tells Bob about God. Bob just has an experience of a new power and calls that power "God".

Harriet Hercon starts to draw Bob's encounter with the power called God. She stops and says, "How do you draw God? I never know. I just draw circles." And she puts a spiral of circles over his head. "Bob can get through one day at a time because he has encountered this power," she says.

"Bob goes to a church," Hercon says, drawing a stick church, a square with a triangular top and a cross. "He begins to learn the tradition, [and] he talks about what happens. The minute Bob starts to ask questions about faith, he becomes a theologian. [Because] witness is always first; theology is second order. [Theology is] critical reflection on witness."

Now Hercon moves to Jane, who as a black woman feels like a second-class citizen. She feels like there is always a "crazy obstacle in her way," says Harriet, drawing a wall next to the female figure. Jane worked for a company that treated her badly and made her feel worthless.

In the unwinding story, Jane goes to church where she encounters a power that helps her. Jane reads Psalm 18 about God helping people "jump over a wall" and thinks, "Maybe by God's help I can leap over my walls."

"Did Jane's encounter with the power change the people in the company?" Hercon asks. No, she says, they were just the same; they did not see the wall or the power that Jane knew would help her leap over it. Hercon tells how Jane learned about the NAACP and about empowerment. Jane started going regularly to a black church and eventually changed jobs.

Hercon says that Jane found out what happens in a community of people through the power of God. Jane hears people at her church talk about God being on the side of the oppressed, and, Hercon notes, Jane begins to talk about her own faith. Jane will not use male language for God, but Bob will, a reflection of what Jane learns in her church that is different from what Bob learns.

Drawing some quick "connecting lines" between Bob and Jane, Hercon says, "Bob and Jane meet. Both are so enamored with the power of God in their lives; each finds an opportunity to witness to the power of God." Then Hercon faces the class and asks, "Whose theology will be right?" She concludes that personal contexts both shape and reflect a person's theology. "There's always room for one more theologian," she observes. It's like making a cake, she continues. You need a lot of different ingredients—flour, salt, shortening, eggs, sugar—and so it is with theologies and theologians; they are made up of a lot of different elements of experience.

"Theology," Hercon tells the class, "is mixed up with one's own personal experience, culture, and society. You will understand things through who you are." "My hope," she says, "is that everything you learn here, you will share with people in the church. If Jane wants to understand Bob, she must understand his experience of tradition, Scripture, and reason. If Bob wants to understand Jane, he must understand her experience of church, language, and word." The task of students, Hercon concludes, is to understand all the elements and "put it together theologically."

Old Testament

Marvin Miles teaches Introduction to Old Testament each Monday afternoon. The pace is quick and the volume of material heavy in this one-semester overview. About sixty people are enrolled; many of them are also taking Mission and Ministry. Attendance is consistently high. On this September afternoon, Miles is teaching without coat and tie and lectures with limited reference to notes. The students have come from lunch; many of them bring soft drinks and snacks to class. Even though this is only the second or third session, students have adjusted to Miles's quick-witted asides. Miles, who is not ordained, has become "Marvin" to many of them.

The first half of the class introduces students to the technical considerations involved in studying the development of Old Testament literature. Students busily take notes, and questions are primarily for clarification.

At the start of the second half, Miles writes the word "firstories" on the board. He tells the students that it is important to understand that first stories are not written as history—rather, they are stories about a world "before the world came to be known as it is." As such, they have a certain fantastic character to them and describe events and activities that do not readily fit into the world as it is now known. For example, in the Noah "firstory," every kind of animal on Earth can fit into one boat. He further notes, however, that this ancient world of first stories is not a discreet world completely different from the present world. The "firstory" world overlaps with present reality. Miles distributes sheets that provide a structural outline for the "firstories." As he begins to talk about Genesis, chapter 1, he tells students that the story is "not meant to be a bag of information." It is meant to provide a coherent understanding of the world.

Miles says that the six days of creation and the eight separate acts of creation comprise a story that develops like an architect's rendering. The story teaches that creation is an ordered place where chaos does not reign. The creation story is written in terms of days to help establish rhythms as life has come to be known. Miles interprets the text with considerable reverence, commenting on possible ancient as well as modern meanings.

The teacher explores the understanding the ancient Hebrews might have had of the "great" and "lesser" lights (Genesis 1:15–16) in a world in which some of their neighbors worshiped the sun or the moon. In this story, the God of the Hebrews makes light itself before dividing it into lesser and greater lights; thus, the text is in large part a polemic against treating the sun and moon as divinities. He continues with commentary for modern readers on the creation of man and woman. "Adam is a generic noun, and thus best translated 'humanity,' " Miles says. God speaks on the sixth day because—with the creation of the man and the woman—there is now someone with whom to talk. Miles says that the central meaning of humanity's creation in "the image of God" points to the capacity of people to share communion with God and also signifies that people have the right and responsibility to represent God in the world.

Four weeks later, on an October Monday afternoon, Introduction to Old Testament is dealing with the legal literature of Exodus, Leviticus, and Deuteronomy and the movement of the Israelites into the land of Canaan. Miles describes some of the issues related to Pentateuchal law, then students discuss an article assigned for today's class. The author is James Cone, an African-American theologian who has said of Exodus in *A Black Theology of Liberation,* a book MTS students read for another course: "The entire history of Israel is a history of what God has done, is doing, and will do in moments of oppression. Though God acts in history, only the community of faith is able to perceive God's revelation." The assigned article deals with faith, liberation, and the willingness to risk everything for human freedom.

In the discussion, an African-American student says that he thinks that the article is dated—that Cone omits a large part of black culture and writes as though blacks can be "put in one box." Later, a white student wonders whether Cone's article does not focus on blacks' liberation to the exclusion of other groups' liberation. In response, another African-American argues that liberation emerged from reflection on a specific situation—from speaking to a particular need. Since liberation theology speaks to a particular situation, Cone does not mean to exclude other particular situations.

After this exchange, Miles lectures about the history of the ancient Israelite movement into the land of Canaan. The material he is dealing with begins with the exodus from Egypt under Moses, continues with the years of wandering, and concludes with the conquest of the Promised Land. Battles abound in the biblical accounts; the most famous is Joshua's capture of Jericho, where the city walls fall down before an outnumbered Hebrew army.

He begins by drawing a distinction between "documentary history" and "symbolic history" and suggests that earlier biblical scholars were perhaps naive in not taking account of the difference and in applying the same interpretative principles to both. The conquests of Joshua, including the battle of Jericho, are, according to Miles, symbolic history and not to be dealt with as though they were actual history.

Miles elucidates his argument by leading students through an analysis of the Israelite ascendancy in Canaan. He relies almost exclusively on the archeological evidence—an evidence that to him indicates no radical cultural discontinuity during the time period in question; apparently, then, no outside cultural group, such as the Israelites, gained control through the battles described in the Bible. What he describes is a shift in settlement patterns from 1300 to 1100 B.C.E. (Before the Common Era). In this shift, fortified city-states diminished as a rural culture dominated by villages emerged. Miles speculates that the Israelites were already living in the surrounding area and across two centuries gradually gave up nomadic existence in favor of a more settled, socially consolidated agrarian life.

"If this hypothesis is true, then why is there (a story of) Joshua at all?" Miles answers his question by referring to an article by his faculty colleague Roland Pritchard, who argues that the Joshua story emerged as an attempt of the monarchy of Israel (hundreds of years later) to establish nationalistic policies. After analyzing the theories and staking out his own position, Miles looks intently at students and says, "I wish it weren't so complex, but I am personally happy with the conquest not occurring as depicted. I would rather deal with Joshua as literature than to have to deal with 'the God of Joshua.' "

Students begin asking questions, exploring one possibility after another that would retain as actual history the story of Jericho and its walls. "I'm not going to preach that," a student sitting next to Daniel Aleshire (DA) says at the end of the class with regard to Miles's conclusion that Joshua fought no battle in which Jericho's walls fell.

Mission and Ministry, November

The semester is closer to its end than its beginning. Outside, the fall foliage has grayed, and the last leaves blow across the grounds. In Room 107, Mission and Ministry is completing a long look at the theological formulations of the early church fathers. Today, after opening by reading a psalm, Harriet Hercon surveys her students: "We worked through dry old Kelly [a text on early Christian doctrine] for seven weeks, and many of you must have said, 'How long, O Lord, how long?' " The class laughs.

Dean Hercon "flows" through her class. Her hair is manicured. Her dress is tailored. Her demeanor is professional, warm, and embracing, her speech articulate. She moves freely, avoiding stationary locations as she teaches. She seldom misses a student's raised hand or fails to acknowledge a questioning expression. Hercon has a way of teaching as if she were a tour guide showing visitors the secret delights of places she dearly loves.

"This is a course on Christian identity," she says. "We've been exploring it in the context of the early church fathers, and with this unit, we turn to explore it in the context of James Cone [see earlier in this chapter]. The primary issue in Christian identity is salvation. The issue of salvation is as strong in Kelly as it is in Cone." Hercon says that the concept of Christian identity is both diverse and unified. The single theme is: God has saved us in Jesus Christ. But interpretations of the Trinity, sin, and Christology influence how the idea of salvation is dealt with by various theologians, resulting in diversity around the idea of salvation. "Listen to the diversity, argue as you will, but listen to the rich diversity around this common theme," Hercon implores the students.

Turning to face the chalkboard, Hercon writes "Early Church" on one side and "Cone" on the other and proceeds to use the two to show diversity on key theological and interpretative categories. First, philosophical background: For early church theologians this was Greek Platonism; for James Cone it was existentialism and Marxism. She writes these terms on the board under the proper heading. A second category is Scripture. Early Christian theologians interpreted Scripture with Platonic assumptions and used them to buttress their arguments; Cone uses Scripture interpreted by a hermeneutic of liberation. The early Fathers focused on Adam as a Platonic type; Cone focuses on the Exodus and God's identification with the poor. Another category is tradition. Early theologians appealed to the arguments of even earlier Fathers. Cone, by contrast, uses a wider tradition because he does not want the twentieth-century church to trace its tradition through "a thin white line." His tradition includes black experience, culture, and history because, he argues, the Spirit is at work in oppression and liberation.

Hercon continues this comparison in terms of other key theological categories. Of sin, she says that the patristic writers treated it as a willful turning away from God that results in lust, ignorance, and death. Original sin is a condition infecting people from birth, and all are guilty because of Adam; the church fathers viewed sin as "original and individual—but not so much communal." Cone, on the other hand, views sin more as a communal matter, as oppression that estranges people from the community as a whole. Some people "are treated as having done something wrong when you haven't. You are just black, and original sin is the action of a racist society against your blackness." In his scheme, to be white is to suffer original sin.

It is almost time for the break, and Hercon shifts from her comparison of patristic theology and liberation theology to a description of the required paper that is due soon. The seven-page composition will identify, describe, and react to one of several doctrines. A final section will discuss how one could use or share this understanding of the doctrine with a congregation. She lingers on this last point, speaking with more passion: "Everything you learn here is for someone else. The purpose of seminary is not an educated clergy but an educated congregation. . . . The practice of learning is so you can give something away."

After a break, Hercon continues the comparison between patristic theologians and James Cone with reference to Christology—the nature of Jesus Christ. For the patristic scholars, Christology dealt with how the humanity and divinity of Jesus are understood. Cone's focus is different. For him, "the christological importance of Jesus must be found in his blackness. . . . The definition of Jesus as black is crucial for Christology."

This comparison sets off an intense, racially tempered, but not antagonistic conversation. "Wasn't Jesus born to a middle-class family?" one student asks. When others respond negatively, a white woman remarks, "I feel like I can't say anything right anymore." An African-American who had defended Cone's idea of Christ replies, "I can't be the person to cure white guilt."

In concluding the class session, Hercon talks about how theologians invariably understand religious truth in the context of their own time. That, she says, "is what all theology should do."

Graduate Days

Each fall, MTS hosts its graduates for a week of worship, workshops, an awards banquet, and a number of smaller "reunion" groups such as African-Americans, women, and retired professors. This year, the featured speaker is United Methodist Bishop Murial Adams. The promotional brochure says that she has been a pastor, is "very active" at the regional and national levels of her denomination and, most recently, has focused her ministry "on AIDS-related issues."

Bishop Adams is short and plump, with clear, mahogany-colored skin and closely cut salt-and-pepper hair. She rises to preach and announces her sermon title, which is also printed in the bulletin: "We've Said It Often Enough: Can't God Hear?"

"God does hear," she declares. "It is what God hears that is disturbing." Bishop Adams leans against the pulpit: "The deeper question is that of theodicy. The word of God comes to us and implores, 'Don't you hear?' The onus is on us and not on God." Then she tells stories about visiting a poor district in India, about the movement of the Spirit in Nigeria, and about a friend of hers, a bishop in Bolivia, who "risks his life" daily in ministry. God hears those people, she concludes. "God speaks in all languages." God is speaking, but "are we listening?"

"We are so comfortable; we have no business being this comfortable," she continues. Real charity means giving, but it also means confronting "justice and sacrifice." Only "through suffering by the power of the Spirit are we enabled to participate in the vision of a just society. We serve such a bold God to be so timid. Are we listening?" she asks again.

Bishop Adams takes off her glasses and begins to move from the pulpit to the floor of the chapel. She talks about a children's choir she recently heard. It was a large choir, she recalls, over one hundred voices. Black children and white children were singing, "I am a promise; I am a possibility; I am a promise with a capital *P*—I am a great, big bundle of potentiality." She repeats the refrain slowly as she walks down the final flight of stairs.

She stands before the congregation, "I am a promise. Isn't that marvelous? Are we listening? Can we be bold enough to speak out? I am a promise, I am a possibility." Then, echoing the rhetorical style of other powerful African-American preachers, she builds a litany of facts about people in poverty and suffering children around the repeated lines, "I am a promise. I am a possibility." As she concludes, the congregation breaks into applause and everyone stands. PM glances to the end of the pew, where Terrence Nunnally stands clapping; a single tear rolls down his cheek.

The congregation sings, "How firm a foundation, ye saints of the Lord, / Is laid for your faith in his excellent Word! / What more can he say than to you he hath said, / To you who for refuge to Jesus have fled?" Joe Pepper, president of the alumni association, asks the preacher to dismiss worship with prayer. He puts his arm around her shoulders and squeezes as she comments that the hymn "didn't use inclusive language [for God]." When Joe doesn't respond, Bishop Adams laughs and asks, "Will these women ever be satisfied?" Then everybody laughs.

After the prayer, a graduate of MTS, now a pastor, plays the piano and sings "His Eye Is on the Sparrow." The tall, lean, dark-suited man performs with passion and freedom. The black members of the congregation—and a few, more tentative, white congregants—respond with shouts of "Amen," "Come on!" and "Well!" Marian Findley, a first-year M.Div. student focusing on urban ministry, raises her hands, closes her eyes, and sways back and forth to the closing chords.

The MTS Association of Black Seminarians hosts the African-American graduates' luncheon in Drayford Hall. The room was redecorated during the recent renovation that was part of "the largest fund-raising effort in the history of the school." It is rectangular, carpeted, and bordered with rich, dark moulding. Next door is the paneled Board of Directors room, with dark, lacquered seminar tables. Adjoining is the new glass, chrome, and marble art gallery. A creeping brown stain discolors the ceiling tiles outside Drayford Hall. Commenting to a crowd of donors at the dedication several days later, Jack Stewart quips, "God is telling us to build arks, not buildings."

As the crowd trickles in after worship, PM sits down by a first-year student pastor, the son of a preacher, originally from Florida. In conversation, Charles recalls that his bishop urged him to go on to seminary and get the "wilderness experience" over with so he could return and "move right into a larger church situation." So he and his family packed up and "made the journey . . . to get the full wilderness experience."

Charles also follows up on an earlier conversation that took place in a reflection group following the Mission and Ministry class. He says he is having all kinds of trouble with his pastoral assignment: "It is hell." He pastors four churches, and the largest is jealous of the time he spends with the smallest churches. The larger congregation, he continues, insists that since the smaller ones cannot contribute much to his salary, he should spend less time with them. Charles is angry; his eyes widen and he shakes his head as he says, "They're trying to hold my salary back. . . . I just want to tell them that they are heretics." Of the demand to cut down on the time the smaller churches get, he declares, "I'm not going to do that."

Marian Findley joins the table. She is wearing jeans, a pink oxford button-down shirt, and the heavy canvas backpack that marks her as a commuter student. Marian, twenty-nine years old, is one of the few Roman Catholics at MTS and has arresting smoky-hazel eyes. She is a first-year student and one of the three elected on the second day of orientation to the seminary's Community Committee, a faculty, staff, and student group concerned about the racial/ethnic and commuter/noncommuter mix.

Marian leans toward PM: "You really missed an interesting Community Committee meeting." The minorities on the council, she explains, got really mad because "the administration" had already picked Asian-American relations as the topic for an annual, all-campus retreat, without input from Asian-Americans at the seminary. A "bunch of whites," she says, had planned the retreat and intended to "carry it out" by involving the Asian-Americans at the later stages. "There was a big stink," Marian notes and presses on: "They claim to be so inclusive around here but they are really not." In her view, MTS is under "white dominance." Whites "let" the minorities have some power, but on their own terms, she concludes. PM asks what happened. Marian says that the committee voted to refuse to ratify the plans that were being handed down to "rubber-stamp." She reports that it voted to give the Asian-Americans more control over the process and recommended that the planning group be made up of Asian-Americans. Marian adds that people are still mad about the process.

Lu's Suicide

> Incline your ear to my cry, for my soul is full of trouble, and my life draws near to Sheol.
>
> —Psalm 88 (NRSV)

It is the Monday following the Thanksgiving holiday. As DA approaches the quad on this spectacular morning, Professor Glen Fisher sees him, approaches, and says, "I have just heard some tragic news. We lost a student this weekend." Lucille Dudley had committed suicide. Had DA known "Lu"? DA says yes and asks Professor Fisher if he remembers any other MTS student who had committed suicide. This white-haired teacher of long tenure at the MTS looks to the ground, thinks a moment, shakes his head, and says he cannot remember another suicide during the past twenty years.

Lu is a fourth-year student and, as the semester begins, has a room on the second floor of Barlowe Hall. She appears to take delight in showing the ropes to new people. During orientation week, Lu accompanies PM and a group of first-year students to a local restaurant for dinner. When they are seated, Lu says, "Can we have real drinks?" None of the first-year students say anything, apparently because alcohol use is a sensitive issue to them. Some do not think seminary students should drink. Others, who normally would have a drink, do not know whether or not it is appropriate for them as new seminary students. When the server comes to the table to take orders, Lu asks, "What kind of beer do you have?" As the selections are described, Lu seems to be as interested in the responses of others around the table as she is in the available selections. She laughs a little and says, "Oh, well, I'll just get a glass of wine." No one else orders an alcoholic beverage;

the issue is not discussed except that later, Tess comments, "I can't believe that she did that."

As the students sit around the table waiting for their food, Lu begins giving advice, much of which seems harsh, even frightening. "MTS is really hard," she says. "They make you work. They say you have to do two hours of homework for every hour in class. When they say that, it's no exaggeration." Lu also talks about different teachers, and when the first-year students mention the names of two faculty members, Lu rolls her eyes, describing one of them as a "tough broad and a strong lady." She continues by sharing her opinions about faculty, courses, and seminary life. Referring to one administrator, Lu says: "They ought to get rid of her. She's two-faced. We have had our run-ins." She warns these—by this time—rather amazed first-year students: "You've got to watch out who you fraternize with around here."

Once when PM asked Lu where she was from, she replied, "From all over. I was a ward of the state and I grew up in foster homes everywhere." Another time she said, "You just don't know what kind of stuff I've been through in my life."

Lu seems to value tough people and exudes a certain toughness herself. She speaks in a low-pitched voice, which she says has caused her problems because people mistake her for a man on the phone or incorrectly assume that she is lesbian. She told PM, "I'm not really as tough as I sound; I've just been through a lot of stuff."

Lu is more than an opinionated, gruff person. When the food finally arrives at the restaurant, Lu holds out her arms to Judy and Tess, who are sitting on either side of her, and says, "Shall we pray?" She then gives thanks for the food and the fellowship and God's provision. Students do not know Lu so much by her appearance or voice as by her contradictions. Gruff, bossy, given to rough speech and strong opinions on the one hand, she is, on the other, a person of noticeable religious affection and concern about other students.

Lu has a history of struggle with psychological problems and had admitted herself to the hospital in mid-November. She signed herself out of the hospital to go to her foster parents' home during Thanksgiving break. On Friday, she dressed in a snowmobile suit, put some food in the car, drove off to a deserted country road, and killed herself by carbon monoxide poisoning.

On Monday, the first class day after Thanksgiving break, Marvin Miles begins Old Testament class in a somber tone: "I am the bearer of bad news. Lu Dudley, a fourth-year student, went home on Friday and killed herself." He continues, "She was not what I would call fragile but has lived a life of torment. She was manic-depressive." Finally, Miles tells the class that he wants "to take some time to work with this, because I need to." He reads from Psalm 88 (NRSV):

> God of my salvation, when at night I cry out in your presence, let my prayer come before you. Incline your ear to my cry, for my soul is full of troubles, and my life draws near to Sheol. I am counted among those who go down to the pit. I am like those who have no help, like those forsaken among the dead. Like the slain that lie in the grave, like those whom you remember no more, for they are cut off from your hand.

After the psalm, he reads a passage from Romans 14 and prays, "Oh Lord our God, Jesus our Savior, we pray for your servant Lu, who took her life." After other petitions and a long pause, he closes the prayer with one final phrase: "We feel so damn helpless." When Miles finishes his prayer, he dismisses the class for a break and leaves the room; when class resumes ten minutes later, he begins the task of lecturing on the assigned text. Several years later, a student, reflecting on most memorable seminary events, recalled the time Marvin Miles "came into class and told us about [Lu's] suicide, and he broke down in front of us, reading from the Bible with such passion and hurt, you felt he was one with what he was saying. And he was. We felt one with him in the whole thing. That, I will always remember."

On Monday evening a group of students attend a "gathering" in Barlowe Hall lounge scheduled by the two seminary deans. Most of the thirty people are dorm residents or others close to Lu. Dean Anderson describes this meeting as an occasion—similar to those in African-American tradition—when people gather at the home of the deceased's family. Since the dormitory was Lu's home, the dean of students says that the lounge would be the proper place to gather. She invites students to share various stories about their experiences with Lu, to suggest hymns to sing, and to read passages of Scripture. The meeting lasts about forty-five minutes. A number of students talk about feelings of grief and pain surrounding Lu's death. There are also stories of encounters with Lu: Some recall her brashness and abruptness and her capacity to intimidate others; some recall fun times and Lu's desire to be a source of enjoyment to others. Daniella Byrd reads a Bible passage and comments that Lu had a spirit that yearned to be free but was somehow trapped. She concludes, "Now that spirit is free." Several students' comments reflect a sense of guilt. They seem to think that if they truly cared for one another, and if the seminary community really were a "community," something like Lu's suicide would not have happened. Some students pick up on Daniella's imagery of freedom—of liberation and an end to the oppression that Lu had felt.

The comments over, Dean Thomas asks the group to stand, form a circle, and sing "Kum By Yah." This is an emotional time. Every time the song is about to end, someone starts another verse. When no one can think of more words, the group hums the tune several times. Finally, as if he were the pastor in charge, Mitch Tabor leads in prayer. Then Alice West tearfully suggests that students bring flowers to Lu's door, or put notes on it, or find other expressions to celebrate her presence within the seminary community. "I think we should try to give her a party," she said. The people leave the lounge slowly.

By midnight several notes are taped on Lu's door. More have appeared by morning, and a variety of items are left in front of the door, including a flower in a bud vase, a stuffed animal, a box of felt-tip marking pens, and a cross formed from two wide-leaved pieces of straw. One note says, "May God's presence surround you." Another one reads, "I hope your shoulders are always loose and comfortable, and you have a personal masseuse in Heaven. Thank you for the advice about the room." Still another says, "I don't know, Lu, I just don't know. I hope you know now."

During the regular chapel worship on Tuesday, a special prayer is said for the friends and family of Lucille Dudley, and a memorial service is announced for later in the semester. Tuesday afternoon, Harriet Hercon is in the midst of summarizing the work of Leonardo Boff, the second liberation theologian discussed in the Mission and Ministry course. She explains a technical concept Boff uses, *perichoresis,* to describe a sense of love and mutuality, of interpenetration and self giving. To illustrate the term, Hercon says, "In Lu's suffering we suffer; in her death we feel pain. When things go badly with someone you love, they do not go well with you." Hercon makes frequent references throughout the class to Lu's suicide, to the hurt that Lu had felt, to Lu's experience with foster parents who did not care for her properly, to others who abused her, and to the seminary's loss as a result of Lu's death.

The memorial takes place in the chapel on Wednesday of the following week. Extra chairs have been set up in a large aisle on the right side of the nave, and by the time the service begins, the space is full. The worship follows the "service of death and resurrection" in the hymnal used at MTS.

President Stewart's greeting includes special words for Lu's foster father, who will speak later. The congregation sings, "The strife is o'er, the battle done." After the hymn, Bailey Douglas and Alice West approach the chancel. Bailey, wearing a white robe with blue stole, sits on a stool, accompanying himself on the guitar as he sings "Fire and Rain." Alice, dressed in long, loose pants and a sweater, signs the lyrics, written by James Taylor. Prior to the singing, Alice explains, her voice at the edge of tears, that Taylor wrote "Fire and Rain" after a friend of his committed suicide. She quotes part of the lyric, "I've seen fire and I've seen rain, but I always thought that I'd see you again." The congregation is moved. Some students have tears in their eyes, and a few are openly weeping. After the song, Professor Mary Miles reads from the book of Job and talks briefly about Lu, describing her as a struggler who experienced much pain: "Lu is not in pain any longer."

Gilbert Dabney, professor of preaching and a distinguished African-American preacher, delivers the homily. He recalls Lu as a person with a deep hunger, and he shares personal experiences with her as his student. Lu, he says, was "not the easiest person to get along with." He then takes off his glasses, looks over the congregation, and says, "And you know that, too, if you ever encountered Lu. That's what you did, *encountered* Lu." Laughter moves through the congregation. He talks about Lu's hunger for learning, her hard work, her academic success, and her deep troubles. He notes later in the sermon that her suicide called for understanding and "mercy more than judgment."

The sermon concluded, Jack Stewart introduces three other speakers. One is from Lu's home congregation, another is a denominational official, and the third is her current foster father. Lu's foster father explains that he and his wife had been foster parents to Lu for about four years and that the relationship had been a roller coaster. He cautiously says that in situations like this one, people always think about the "what ifs" and the "if onlys." He expresses his desire that the students know several things about Lu. The first is about her background. She had grown up as a ward of the state. Through her life, she was in and out of seventeen different foster homes. She had been sexually abused, beaten, nearly starved, and forced to do hard manual labor in some of those situations. He describes her as a moody, angry, suspicious person who could also be sensitive, open, and honest. Second, he talks about her illness, a manic-depressive syndrome with which Lu had struggled for many years. She had seen a number of therapists and had taken medication on and off, but it remained a psychological condition from which she was never free. Finally, after recounting some of the events and the obvious planning that led to her suicide, he looks out at the congregation and says: "Now I want you to hear me. I am going to tell you something that I think will be important for you to hear. . . . I want you to know, and hear me now, that you are not responsible." He pauses, looks around, and says, "Who knows why, now? Lu was doing well this semester. Typically she was a procrastinator and always had unfinished work. But when she died she was totally caught up." He concludes by saying, "In reaching for God, Lu was crucified by her own past."

During Holy Communion, worshipers sing "On Eagles' Wings," "Here I Am, Lord," and "When We All Get to Heaven." The whole service lasts almost two hours. While some slip out, most people stay.

In mid-February of the next semester, the dean of students decides that something should be done about Lu's dormitory room, which has been vacant since her death in late November. The door, previously decorated with gifts and messages, is now bare. Dean Anderson asks students from the dorm to join her in planning a service that would signal a release of Lu's dorm room for future use. The dean distributes and describes a ceremony "of release" that she has found. Susan Arch has brought material as well. The discussion weighs a number of options, and the group finally agrees on a plan including candles, incense, music, memories, and refreshments.

Later that month, around eight o'clock on a Wednesday morning, a table with fruit and several large votive candles is placed outside Lu's former room. Susan Arch brings a green plastic bowl filled with water. About ten people gather outside the room. Dean Anderson wears an alb and a multicolored stole. The printed order of service is titled, "Ritual of Release for Room 216." Candles are lit in the hall, and individuals are asked to follow Anderson into the room and place the candles wherever they choose. Once inside, the people hear a passage from Ecclesiastes. A prayer is said. Anderson invited persons to share experiences they had in this room. Four people talk; one mentions that he set his candle where Lu always kept a bottle of wine, and he describes her alcohol problem. Another talks about Lu's gruffness but recalls that she always got a hug from Lu before leaving the room. The group members join in a unison prayer that was used at Lu's memorial service and has been printed in the "Ritual of Release." Anderson then declares the room reopened for use as a place of rest and study for seminary students. She takes an evergreen branch, dips it into the green bowl, and sprinkles water around the room. The students sing "There's a Sweet, Sweet Spirit in this Place." In conclusion, Anderson says that the door to the room will remain open for the rest of the week and asks people to pick up the candles and put them back on the table.

The unlit candles and fruit remain on the table throughout the day. People eat from the table, often standing in front of the door, looking into the empty room.

Spring Semester

In the spring semester, virtually the same group of students who had been in Old Testament and Mission and Ministry gather in the same classroom for Church History. The professor is Cliff Mims, who is in his first academic year of teaching. He is finishing his Ph.D. dissertation and with this class takes on his first core requirement course: Church History from the Reformation to the Twentieth Century.

Mims, wearing a tie and looking at the class through brown-rimmed glasses, is noticeably young—much younger than many of the students. Today's class is about Luther, Calvin, and the theology and history of the Protestant movement. Mims begins by asking: "If you would go to a middle-class church and ask them about Calvin, what would you hear?" Students respond in random order: "Predestination." "Restrictive." "Elitist." "Sovereignty of God." Mims comments, "Not very good things." He tells the students that "predestination" does not occur until Book 3 of Calvin's *Institutes of the Christian Religion* and that the term "sovereignty of God" never occurs in the *Institutes* at all. He notes that John Wesley, who is often cited as non-Calvinistic, once said that his theology was only a hair's breadth from Calvin's.

With these disclaimers, Mims invites the class to "look for the true Calvin" and launches into a detailed lecture on the differences between Luther and Calvin. Luther came first, while Calvin was a second-generation reformer. Luther was from German peasant stock, Calvin from the rising middle class and educated in aristocratic ways. Luther was earthy—a people's man; Calvin was ascetic—never really popular with people. Luther was no humanist; Calvin was trained in classics and, by the sixteenth-century definition, a humanist. Luther married a former nun and addressed the medieval Roman Catholic Church; Calvin married the widow of an Anabaptist and wanted to order Protestantism.

As the lecture proceeds, Mims comes to Calvin's doctrine of predestination. He explains that we "need to understand predestination as reflecting Calvin's perspective that all have sinned and deserve spiritual death, and by sheer grace, God's benevolence, God elects to save some." Several students groan audibly as Mims follows this comment by reading a text from Book 3 of the *Institutes*. Many of these students seem offended by this doctrine and spend the final twenty minutes of the class arguing against perceptions of predestination.

By late spring, the semester that started with the theology of Martin Luther and John Calvin ends with an overview of twentieth-century American Christianity. The MTS campus blooms in spring. Dogwood, azaleas, and flowers are abundant. The view outside Room 107 is green and bright by late April. Mims is behind in the material he wants to cover. Earlier, he had discussed twentieth-century developments in American religious life, including the fundamentalist/modernist controversy.

Today, Mims reviews the development of twentieth-century "evangelical Protestantism," noting that from the 1960s through the 1980s, evangelicalism grew while mainline Protestantism declined. "Why?" he asks, and then partially answers the question as he continues. Perhaps, Mims suggests, in "issues of authority, race relations, class distinction . . . evangelicals have offered alternatives to the prevailing culture." They offer authority as opposed to a lack of it; identity, fellowship, and community as opposed to anonymity. Mims says that while evangelicals offered alternatives to culture, they also embraced part of it.

At this point, students interrupt with questions seeking to distinguish fundamentalists from evangelicals and to draw distinctions among evangelical groups. As students use words loosely, Mims interjects, somewhat emphatically, an admonition to refer to religious groups as they choose to be identified. "We may think Wesleyan Methodists are fundamentalists, but they do not. We have to understand how labels in the classroom can become labels in the parish."

Mims moves on to the emergence of Pentecostalism. He traces the roots of the twentieth-century charismatic/Pentecostal movement to the mid-nineteenth century, specifically to Phoebe Palmer's "Tuesday Meeting for Promotion of Holiness" and to the idea of "entire sanctification," which led to a popular understanding of "second blessing." Ultimately, division arose over the role of "second blessing" in Christian experience. The "entire sanctification" group, known as Holiness people, were marginalized within Protestant denominations and subsequently left to form their own Holiness churches. In the twentieth century, Pentecostals split from the Holiness churches because the Holiness groups did not accept the Pentecostal insistence on a second baptism—usually associated with speaking in tongues.

Students engage in a discussion of their own understandings of twentieth-century evangelical and Pentecostal styles of religion. Several describe Pentecostal worship as more informal, spontaneous, and interactive. In the midst of the conversation, one African-American student comments that verbal responses to the sermon—talking back—and the emotionality of worship services in black worship should not be interpreted as Pentecostalism.

Mims resumes his lecture, following a clear outline and occasionally writing words or phrases on the chalkboard. He communicates information in an orderly manner and invites questions, and one has the sense that he is constantly negotiating the tension between covering a body of material and allowing time for student discussion. With limited minutes left in this session, and only a few more classes before final exams, he turns attention to his summary analysis of what he calls "the crisis in the mainline."

Students are invited to assess why mainline Protestant denominations are experiencing problems in the latter half of the twentieth century. Various respondents offer their own analysis or what they have heard or read. They attribute the "crisis" to the charismatic movement; the loss of religious zeal; stands on justice issues that alienate constituents; operating practices of congregations that underprogram and shut down in the summer; cultural influences, particularly pluralism; enculturation that fails to reflect any difference between church and society; the emergence of new social organizations that meet needs once met by churches; a shift away from traditional values along the mainline; and the lack of mainline religious demands on church members.

Mims nods and encourages these responses, then forwards his own three-point assessment. First, the mainline denominations have so identified with the culture that on many important religious issues they do not want to take stands that may offend. The result is that the churches become increasingly neutral and people lose their sense of religious identity. Second, as the crisis has become more severe in the last half of the century, denominations have circled their wagons, become less ecumenical, and not addressed the kinds of issues that contribute to the growth of conservative churches. Finally, mainline denominations have difficulty calling their members to "anything that is really compelling."

"Goodbye, Harriet"

The refectory is filled with students at various stages of their lunches. Barlowe Hall students laugh and talk over trays filled with the inevitable "five things"; commuter students with sack lunches and moderate helpings of MTS fare engage in what one student calls "table theology"—serious debriefings of classes; and student pastors—commonly known as the "SPT blob"—drink coffee, discuss church problems, and share the latest jokes. Shortly after noon, Harriet Hercon is coaxed to a table near the center of the room, where an impromptu "stage" has been set up: lectern, floor mikes, and upright piano. There is a brief chaos. Chatter increases, then slowly subsides; chairs are shifted for a better view, and lunch debris is gathered and put away.

Glen Fisher begins the festivities in his usual wry manner. He pulls the microphone toward him slightly, puts his hand in his pocket, and looks right at Harriet Hercon, his pale blue eyes twinkling and crinkling slightly at the corners as he smiles: "I'm here as testimony to the fact that there is life after deanship," referring to his stint in that role. "You miss meetings, chauffeur-driven limousines, and Jodi [the inveterate secretary of MTS deans]." Pausing for laughter, and hearing it rippling in the back of the room, Glen nods his head and says, "And oh, Harriet, you have also left a secret society at MTS—the Sisters." At that moment four women faculty members—Betty Trotter, Susan Johnson, Lucy Knight, and Trudi Darsa—strut to the front wearing flamboyant hats ("girl gangster" styles—black, ivory, feathered, and trimmed in gold braid), strings of faux pearls, and even a red feather boa. Harriet nearly doubles over with laughter.

Betty Trotter, who teaches pastoral care, leans into the microphone to read a short ditty that includes a litany of "bye-byes" that are obviously inside jokes because hardly anybody but Hercon laughs. Among others, there are "bye-bye clothes" and "bye-bye St. Scholastica." Trudi Darsa presents the departing dean with "a small token to wear when you do liturgies with a Native American flavor." She pauses and adds, "Of course, there are no Native Americans at MTS." Harriet just shakes her head.

Lucy Knight, lecturer on religion and arts, wears an ivory hat, cocked coquettishly, with a red feather boa dramatically slung over her left shoulder. She tells a story about the dean and a dinner dance. Hercon blushes appropriately; the "sisters" preen.

Susan Johnson tells a slightly more serious story about how she was introduced to Hercon after a lecture. Johnson acts it out a bit: "Dr. Hercon, meet Susan

Johnson, who is applying for the position in pastoral care and counseling at MTS." Johnson recalls saying that she was not finished with her dissertation yet, and Harriet responded, "Oh, my dear, we're looking for someone much farther along." As things turned out, the search was extended, and Susan reconnected with MTS and Hercon through another faculty member. "Harriet, you've been a healer to me," Johnson concludes, "and I will allow no other dean to call me 'my dear,' and you're the only person who will ever, ever call me 'sweetie.' "

As the "Sisters" leave the stage, Betty Trotter says loudly, "Sure, our new dean is qualified, but does he shop at Talbot's?"

Fisher takes the floor again and quips, "Harriet is a dean who's about to lose her faculties." A few people groan audibly. He continues, "So Ben Somers has been chosen to represent the faculty in tribute." Professor Somers, in his usual dark suit, crisp oxford-cloth shirt, and perky bow tie, prepares to speak. Glancing at Hercon and pulling a pretty straight face, he makes jokes about the Sisters and the precedents set for the next dean.

After the laughter dies down, Somers says he has a short speech with three points, "a beginning, a middle, and an end." His first point is "novelty": "Harriet doesn't just bring novelty, she is novelty. In church history novelty is heresy. She is the first deaness—we have to use it quickly before we can't anymore—and she is Reformed and always to be Reformed." Among other "novel" accomplishments, he notes, "She overcame the inertia of academic ways of doing business by computerizing this faculty, and she always singled people out for encouragement." The second point is "memory." Hercon was always good at reminding professors to remember where they came from, he says. Despite Talbot's and dinner dances, she "wasn't flamboyant." She had her feet on the ground. The third point is "loyalty." Somers finishes by talking about "Harriet's remarkable loyalty to Christ and Christ's church and this institution. Loyalty to building a kingdom in a world in need of hope." He smiles warmly at her; she smiles back.

Fisher takes the stage again and makes comments, some of which are hard to hear. Then he introduces a representative of the Community Committee who presents Hercon with a piece of stained glass commissioned from the artist-in-residence. The dean walks up to receive it wearing Knight's red feather boa, which she dramatically tosses over her shoulder as she approaches. She accepts the glass graciously and holds it up for all to see.

Bing Harrod, an assistant administrator, is introduced as "Aaron to her Moses." He holds up a framed, poster-sized, black-and-white picture of Hercon. The photo is from January 28, 1985, the date she was arrested for demonstrating against South African apartheid. In the picture, her hands are behind her back and she appears to be talking with the officer on her way into a paddywagon. Harrod quips that Hercon was saying, "But I just want to discuss theology."

Next, Hercon's secretary, Jodi, presents her with a handmade box that her husband tooled. Inside are a number of items: tape; fingernail polish (for runs in hosiery); different colored Magic Markers (for scuffs on different colored shoes), and a memo to remove her furniture from the office.

Finally, President Stewart takes the floor. He begins by talking about how creative and energetic Dean Hercon is: "She had at least ninety-eight new ideas a week, and in the time she's been here, that's 35,872 new ideas, three of which were good, one every six months that we could get the faculty to adopt, and one that would actually work." The faculty laughs and she does too. "Working with Harriet is interesting," Stewart continues. "I made commitments before I knew what I was doing. Would this feminist use feminine, wily ways?" He laughs and nods his head vigorously yes, while Hercon is wagging hers no.

"I've saved the worst 'til last, however, and I've hesitated to finally tell," Stewart says ominously. He continues,

> There is a bit of thievery going on. A wonderful woman died and left her apartment to MTS. When they began to look over the cache, I was informed there were some Victorian pieces that might go well in the dean's office. There was a certain clock that Harriet spied, and she said, "That is a presidential clock." I agreed. So Harriet said, "I will tend it for you until you move [your office]." Well, I kept waiting for that clock to be delivered, and she came to think of it as her very own. Sometimes justice must be done. This week I retrieved the presidential clock in fear it would go [with her]. And as compensation, I'd like to present you, Harriet, with a small gift.

Of course, it is the very same clock. Hercon takes the timepiece, smiles sweetly, and says, when asked if there is anything she'd like to say, "Alma [Stewart, the president's wife] is the epitome of what we hope for in community at MTS." President Stewart laughs loudly. Harriet Hercon looks around the audience slowly and adds, "I love you all and will carry you in my heart." She sits down with her clock to thunderous applause.

David Parsons gives a short, and fittingly warm, benediction: "Sister Harriet, may nothing separate us from your love and each other. Amen." Everyone is asked to join in a song composed for the occasion by the president of the Community Committee. The words are printed on pink paper; the tune is "Darlin' Clementine," and it seems a fitting end for a memorable tenure.

EIGHT

Year Two: Working Things Out

Miles's Installation

Classes are just beginning, but on this September Tuesday the major activity at Mainline Theological Seminary is the installation of Marvin and Mary Miles as tenured professors.

The ceremony in the chapel, filled to capacity, begins with an organ fanfare—"Trumpet Tune in D," by David Johnson—and a full-regalia academic procession. Marshal Tory Campbell holds the mace before him as he somberly leads the faculty down the center aisle. He wears a cassock under his black academic gown; two white collar tabs peek out at his neck. Reaching the front, Campbell turns to direct his colleagues into the pews— senior, tenured professors to one side, and all junior people to the other. The faculty in place, the assembly stands to declare:

> From the ends of the earth we have gathered together
> The poor and the rich, the joyful and the sorrowful,
> The honored and the despised.
> All are gathered in one community, reflecting the love and life of God.
> We have come from many worlds. Let us worship God as one!

"In Christ there is no East or West . . . ," the congregation affirms in rousing song. Then Gerald Adcock, the new academic dean, moves to the chancel and invites Marvin and Mary Miles to join him. MTS's "Rite for the Induction of Senior Professors" is a solemn occasion. Adcock, a tall, middle-aged man peers over his half-frame glasses as he reads from the orange-colored order of service:

> Mary and Marvin, the mission of Mainline Theological Seminary is to educate persons for various forms of Christian ministry and to provide theological leadership on issues facing the church and the world. Do you affirm our primary commitment . . . to prepare persons for ministry, both ordained and lay; and do you understand preparation for ministry to involve the full development of the intellectual, spiritual, and behavioral dimensions of each individual?

"I do," respond the Professors Miles. They give the same answer, or "I will," to a series of similar questions.

Dean Adcock declares: "On behalf of your colleagues and of this entire community, I welcome you as senior professors of Mainline Theological Seminary." Tory Campbell rises and directs the other senior professors to the chancel, where both Professors Miles stand. The worship bulletin explains that the senior faculty will "move forward to shake hands with the newly inducted professors." Handshakes, however, quickly give way to embraces and softly spoken congratulatory words. Marvin and Mary Miles are deeply moved. In a response, Marvin says, "I did not realize the personal effect of this installation. . . . It is as close to ordination as I will likely come . . . , God willing." The remark evokes laughter. Neither Marvin nor Mary Miles is ordained.

The Mileses' tenure has come five years after the couple began teaching at Mainline Seminary. Each has an earned doctorate, and together they share one faculty position. Their initial appointment was the first such arrangement at MTS, and the issues surrounding their induction as two individuals with one professorship claimed the careful attention of the administration and faculty.

The service continues with readings from Luke 10 and Genesis 11. The Genesis passage is the Tower of Babel account, in which God confuses "their language, that they may not understand one another's speech. So the Lord scattered them abroad from there over the face of all the earth and they left off building the city" (Genesis 11:7–8, RSV). In the text from Luke, Jesus commissions seventy followers and sends them "ahead of him, two by two, into every town and place where he himself was about to come" (Luke 10:1–2, RSV).

Marvin Miles moves to the pulpit to preach. Babel, he says, is the story of the human family's attempt to make itself invulnerable by securing its own existence. God takes away human "sameness" so that people will understand that human unity is not in sameness but in relationship—relationship with God and community with one other. He notes that language shapes reality, saying, "We struggle with language more than anything else in this place."

He turns to the Lucan text: "Babel's ending is our beginning. The God who scatters calls us away from exclusion to engagement, from refuge to vulnerability. God does not will a community of sameness but a community of covenant. The God who sent apart in Babel is also the God in Luke who says that community among people can be established." He ends his sermon, "Thanks be to the God who scatters."

Daniella Byrd, an African-American student, sings the gospel hymn "Beams of Heaven as I Go."

The congregation prays responsively, "O God, we thank you for the human family; for people of other faiths and races; for the variety of human experience and the gifts we bring to one another."

Rick Santos, wearing an alb and stole and the only faculty member not in academic regalia, presides at a service of Holy Communion. As the congregation recites the Lord's Prayer, Santos, who is Hispanic, prays in Spanish.

A unison prayer concludes the ritual: "God of our fathers and mothers, we give you thanks for this feast of reconciliation. Now we join our voices in gratitude for our life together, for the world which we share, and for the experience of Christ's presence among us. Amen."

The service lasts significantly longer than the scheduled hour, and most of the people go directly to a community lunch in the refectory. They are reminded as they leave the chapel that Mary Miles will deliver her inaugural lecture there at one o'clock.

Shortly after one, the chapel is nearly full again. Mary Miles is in academic gown, her short blond hair contrasting sharply with her black robe. She moves to the lectern on the right of the chancel. Miles explains that she is taking the occasion to present rationales for her two primary scholarly interests: Second Temple Judaism and biblical anthropology. Her address is a metered, deliberate academic discourse; she argues points, raises critical issues, and provides correctives.

After addressing some issues concerning Second Temple Judaism, Miles shifts focus to criticize what she considers an implicit "white male" perspective in the discipline of biblical anthropology, a perspective she finds inadequate for understanding several issues. As she draws to a close, her pattern of discourse changes. She says:

> Marvin and I have been trying to embody the things I have been talking about—mutuality, interdependence, etc.—in the ways we have worked these past eleven years. We have shared one position, and our nine-year-old and seven-year-old have a different experience of growing up because of it. There has been a less clean separation between family life and professional life, and both children have benefited from that.

She looks at her husband, sitting in the front left section of pews, then turns to the rest of the congregation: "I want to thank Marvin personally. In this patriarchal world, he had everything to lose and I had everything to gain by the arrangement of our shared position." With this expression of gratitude, she walks down from the chancel into the congregation where Marvin is sitting, then reaches out and kisses him. They embrace. By the time she reaches Marvin, the entire congregation is standing, clapping, and many people throughout the chapel have tears in their eyes.

The Art Controversy

> I live among my subjects. I walk a lot, take buses. I look at people. I have good visual memory, and I do not need sketches to remind me what people look like. . . . I am white, but many of my subjects are not. I have lived most of my life in fully integrated neighborhoods. . . . I often paint human figures; many of my figures are nude, mostly female, some erotic. As a swimmer, I spent my childhood around naked bodies. Nakedness is natural for me.
>
> —Artist's comments

> [Y]ou don't have to be a Rembrandt to notice that a large percentage [of the artist's paintings] have more of a pornographic slant than anything else. . . . [M]asturbating virgins and revealed breasts are not my vision of Black women of integrity. Concerning the male models in the painting, the closest facsimile I've seen to these brave souls

can be found in most anthropology books illustrating Neanderthal and other prehistoric specimens.

—Student editorial about the art exhibit in the *MTS Journal*

MTS is one of several North American theological schools that takes art seriously. Exhibitions are frequent, as are opportunities for students to participate in creating art. Worship in the chapel routinely uses visual arts—especially pieces made by students. Lucy Knight has been at MTS for more than ten years and has given art a voice in the school's theological reflection. At the dedication of the seminary's Munger Gallery, she said, "We now have a public space to help us focus on the issues we face as a community . . . through the ability of art to transcend the material from which it was made."

A brochure says that MTS's Arts and Religion Center is dedicated "to demonstrating the inter-relationship between the aesthetic and spiritual aspects of human existence." An exhibit earlier in the fall depicted the struggle, trauma, and pain of urban life, particularly of the urban poor. Knight shares some positive newspaper reviews of that exhibit with DA and shows a videotape of a critique aired on a local public television station. The critic noted that the exhibit was both good art and good political commentary and rhetorically asked why large, well-funded galleries in that metropolitan area had not paid more attention to such works. During the conversation about these positive reviews, Knight talks about the next exhibit, featuring two artists. Both artists, one a painter and the other a sculptor, are independent thinkers who, in Knight's mind, have gone their own way without significant support from the arts establishment. She thinks the two have something in common with ministers, who at times must go their individual ways in pursuit of truth—notably when the community cannot provide support or affirmation. The new exhibit is mounted by late October.

The paintings of one of these independent-thinking artists are all of African-Americans, both men and women. Many contain nudity and postures or activities that are clearly erotic. The artist has written that for her, nudity is a normal human occurrence; for many MTS students, particularly the African-American students, the nudity and eroticism are viewed differently.

Mitch Tabor writes in a guest editorial in the student newspaper that the art raises two questions for him: First, "if . . . an accomplished artist in the 1990s has this distorted perception of Black people, then what of the white seminarian who has no extensive contact with Black people? . . . The other question in my mind was, what was the position of MTS concerning pornography? Would it be okay for a Black artist to portray pictures of naked white women and men?" Mitch is not against art. He talked once, while eating at a local hamburger joint, about a trip to Mexico, where he observed the faith of poor people and the beauty of Mexican basilicas. "[It] . . . was phenomenal," he said. "Beautiful. Beautiful works of art. Their faith was so deep. It was so inspiring." Art touched Mitch, but these paintings offend him. Doreen Clark, another African-American student, says these pictures show "black people in a very depraved state." Other African-American students seem generally united in their judgment that the erotic images in these paintings are inappropriate, if not pornographic, and that similar pictures of white men and women would likely never be exhibited. This perception leaves black students with suspicions about latent racism at the seminary. White students have little to say about the paintings, other than to sympathize with the African-Americans distressed by them.

Broad comment greets the works of the sculptor. These works, all similar in appearance, are placed in the quadrangle between the main buildings on campus. They consist of discarded objects—typewriters, broken TVs, bicycle tires—welded or fastened together and coated in a resin that gives the appearance of hardened slime. Some sculptures have legs; others incorporate discarded lawn or office chairs. The artist wrote in the exhibit brochure that he had "an empathy/excitement/disgust/reverence for these elements that have been produced by humankind. The daily process of making art is how I get in touch with my humanity. The identification with the refuse of man's throwaways provides an arena for all of this."

One evening during this exhibit, apartment-mates Jenny Sherrod and Judy Ponder throw a party in their Grant Hall quarters for three other students who have birthdays within a few days of each other. The seminary's apartments, while much roomier than the dorm rooms, are small, with a living/cooking/eating room and a separate bedroom. This is a typical seminary-issue apartment: nondescript institutional paint, a vinyl-covered couch and chair, and a formica-covered dinette table and desk. Jenny and Judy have personalized the space very little.

By 11 P.M., when the party is going well, some thirty people are present. Not everyone can fit in the living room. Conversation spills out into the hall and down the steps. People are animated, laughing and joking with each other. Several prospective students visiting campus have come. Soft drinks, chips, dip, some beer, and a jug of wine are on the table. Frequent jokes are made about alcohol at MTS—mostly for the benefit of the prospective students. Drinkers lifting plastic cups of wine or cans of beer look at DA or the prospective students, and one says, "Be sure to tell them there is no alcohol at MTS." People laugh, and a few raise their glasses to toast the remark. Several people drink a little wine or beer; no one drinks very much.

A birthday cake is presented, and after the mandatory singing of "Happy Birthday," the honorees cut and distribute it. In the middle of more jokes, conversation, and eating, Alice West steps onto the couch and asks for everyone's attention. The next night, she says, a group of students will meet at 11 P.M. to create "art" for the campus. She invites everyone interested to come and to bring along old type-writers and pieces of junk. And, she concludes, "If anybody knows how to make slime, bring some." People laugh loudly.

The students have already had some fun with the sculptures in the quadrangle. One night earlier that week, they put the names of faculty members beside several sculptures—as though these unusual forms represent their teachers. The next morning, the faculty generally enjoyed the humor, and some professors had their pictures taken next to the assemblages of junk named for them. Thursday night the students who respond to Alice's invitation gather to make their own "sculptures." They use an abandoned TV from the Barlowe Hall student lounge, a broken toaster, and other discards found around campus, along with cardboard, cans, and balloons. The products of their work are irreverent imitations of the sculptures in the formal exhibit, and the students intersperse their creations among the "real" sculptures on the quadrangle.

The next morning, word comes—presumably from a middle-level administrator—that the student work must be removed. The students are complying around 9 A.M. Friday when President Jack Stewart walks by. He pauses, then invites the students to leave their art in the quadrangle. At his office, Stewart enlists three other seminary administrators as "art critics" to judge the students' works. During lunchtime in the refectory, the "critics" present their award for the best student sculpture. The "award" is an old teapot with a softball shoved into its mouth. It honors "the artist in resonance"—an allusion to a statement describing the current exhibit as allowing people to "resonate with the enigma represented by postmodern life."

A panel discussion with the sculptor that had already been scheduled takes place the next day. Clint Emery Jr., a student who sat on the panel, later reports that the artist looked at the student work after the discussion, seemed to enjoy what he saw, and asked if he could take some "student junk" back to his studio.

The Language Controversy

> O help us all to know you, Lord,
> and hear the message of your word
> in peals of thunder, cries of pain,
> our time, O Lord, in sonic boom and beating rain,
> through every sound your voice is heard,
> and we are called to serve you, Lord.
>
> Our Father, who has made us all
> your children, hear us when we call.
> Save us from self-destruction here,
> from selfish hatred, inner fear,
> from famine, pestilence and sword.
> Send peace within.
> —Order of Service

William Abraham Newman, a professor at MTS for decades, wrote these words in an earlier era, to be sung to the tune "Melita"—most familiar from "The Navy Hymn." During a time of national unrest, Newman had used a melody associated with the military as the music of a prayer for peace and racial justice. Newman is retiring from the MTS faculty at the end of the fall semester and is preaching in chapel one last time in November. He has requested that the choir sing his hymn text, and his request unleashes a battle on campus—one engaging students, faculty, and administrators.

The struggle started during choir practice the week before the service. The MTS choir consists of students who earn one hour of credit for a semester's participation. Requirements include weekly practice sessions and performance at chapel services. The choir customarily changes all masculine terms for God to gender-inclusive references in the choral texts it sings. Newman's hymn text has no pronouns, but its use of "Almighty God," "Lord," and "Father" is to the choir—and the larger MTS community—an exclusive, masculine form of address for God.

Choir members engaged in an intense debate during the practice. Jenny, a sociable, thoughtful, attractive West Coast woman, later summarizes the opposing arguments: Some students objected to singing the hymn because they believe that the seminary chapel should model only inclusive references to the deity; others thought the choir should sing the hymn as written because, in Jenny's characterization, "everybody knows he [Newman] is a little different, so sing the song and let the man retire, and we'll get on with our work." The disagreement in choir practice grew so intense that several people walked out. Jenny did not leave the practice, but she chose not to attend the chapel service. Some students and one seminary administrator who did attend walked out during the sermon.

The order of worship for the Newman retirement service includes the unpublished hymn text on the back and an explanation by the author under the heading "Language":

> This hymn is addressed to a masculine deity; therefore all terms of address are coherently masculine—God, Lord, Father. To have changed only one of these, "Father", to another masculine title, such as "Almighty God", would have changed nothing. In worship, we should address one deity, if we are monotheists. As monotheists, we would worship either a god or a goddess. . . . [P]oems, like this one, are addressed to a personal deity, one who has children. Since this parent deity is also called Lord and God, the corresponding parent is Father. Others are free to compose hymns addressed to a goddess, but to be good hymns, they should be unified.

Students who are upset over the singing of the hymn organize a kind of protest. They tie small ribbons on safety pins attached to cards that read:

> Please wear this ribbon to affirm the value of diverse God-images, the legitimacy of diverse theological traditions, and the inclusion of diverse peoples within the community of God. Our understanding of God is enhanced by feminine imagery; feminist/womanist theology challenges us to a fuller understanding of our faith, we benefit from full participation of women in church.

The card looks like a bookmark, with the text covering its length in columnar fashion. Jenny is wearing a ribbon and, the week following the chapel service, gives one attached to the explanatory card to DA. Several students are still wearing the ribbons days after the service.

Newman decides to underscore his case by circulating through campus mailboxes a five-page paper entitled "Tradition and Change." He argues the point about coherent language made briefly on the back of the service bulletin, and he continues by asserting that the Christian community has had difficulty distinguishing between fact and fiction.

> Cultural pressures and ethical considerations have forced upon the church a change in posture in its attitude toward women. This is being done as carefully as possible so that no one will think any ancient doctrines have been abandoned. Scripture is twisted

in all sorts of ways to prove that monks like Jesus and Paul were ancient advocates of equal rights for women. In *fiction,* we are devoted traditionalists while in *fact,* ignoring Paul's admonition that women should keep still in the church and all the other implications.

Newman's paper moves to a more personal and perhaps accusatory section:

> When I preached in chapel recently, I broke none of the rules given in "Guidelines for Inclusive Language." The bombshell was not in the "guidelines." I used my own hymn which was composed against Kipling's segregationist hymn—such "rantings as the Gentiles use and lesser breeds without the law." I also used Whittier's famous hymn because I thought the church was in need of forgiveness, and I know of no better way of expressing this need than that composed by Whittier. . . . I knew there was a parade in the Seminary. I knew that there were some major trigger words that fit into the parade and others that did not. A good word was the masculine term, "God." A bad word was the masculine word "Father." It was considered chauvinistic to use one masculine word, but not the other. I also knew that people seldom think when they are on parade, and they are not able to discuss things with passersby. They have just learned a way to move but I want people to stop parading long enough to think about the way they are going when they march.

The paper concludes with a final word to this community in which Newman has labored for decades: "This is not the first time I have stood in front of a parade. . . . I have no interest in determining the way the parade should move from here. I trust people whenever they begin thinking. I worry about militant parades that are formed too quickly."

The inclusive language policy Newman mentions was adopted by the faculty in the mid-1980s. Former academic dean Harriet Hercon underscored its importance with her orientation homily on "generous language." Given recent events, Dean Adcock has sent a memorandum to all MTS students citing the formal text, a part of which reads:

> [L]anguage reflects, reinforces, and creates reality. Because all [seminary degree program] papers are intended to be expressions of the faith, life, and ministries of the church to which God calls women and men, it is important that the language of these papers represents as full an understanding as possible of human reality. For this reason, linguistic sexism—the assumption that the male is normative, the dominance of masculine imagery and grammatical forms, or any other usage that diminishes the equal dignity of men and women—is to be avoided.

All examples in the formal policy refer to written statements about people. The policy contains no statement about masculine references to God. Last year, in her last orientation presentation, Hercon did talk about references to God even though these are not cited in the policy document. She said that students may "slip" from time to time in speech but should adhere to the inclusive standard in written papers. Inclusive language is a major aspect of Mainline Seminary life. Patrick Landes, a student pastor of a small parish, says, "The lack of inclusive language . . . is really taboo. I mean, I can get away with it at church, but not here . . . because someone is going to call you to task on it."

Trudi Darsa, the faculty member who has overseen chapel services for three semesters, responds to Newman's long memo with one of her own the next week. Her paper, addressed to "The Worshiping Community," comes with a cover letter from Dean Gerald Adcock commending it "as a contribution to an ongoing discussion." The dean also notes that the faculty has voted to discuss the question of God-language at a special December meeting. In her reflection, Darsa reviews Newman's position, then argues that Newman

> confused linguistic analysis with metaphysical propositions. The three letters G-O-D in English, when placed together in the sequence, "God" become only one thing, an English word in the English language. . . . The English word "God" is not the same as the ontological reality of Divine essence. Newman understands the word "God" to be a male noun. Even so, the use of a male noun in worship does not mean that the ultimate reality it expresses contains substantial maleness.

Darsa asserts that the argument from coherence in language can be misleading—that the personal nature of God (which Newman called the God who had children) does not require a single gender. She refers to German theologian Jurgen Moltmann's concept that the God who "both begets and bears his son is not merely a father in the male sense. He is a motherly father too." Darsa writes: "But some of us have a radical vision. . . . [T]he day may be at hand when the living God will surprise the church with a new content for the ancient name of 'Trinity.' "

In a more pastoral note to the seminary community, Darsa observes, "The real issue for an inclusive community is how to include those who differ with inclusivity. Inclusiveness also means a constant search for liturgical material from all the riches of the tradition." She is relinquishing responsibility for the chapel services at the semester's end, and she concludes by thanking those who have helped her and attended worship during her oversight. "Finally," she writes, "my special gratitude to all faculty colleagues for your participation and words of grace during this time. God/ess Bless!"

The *MTS Journal* Debates

MTS's annual community consciousness-raising event—an on-campus winter retreat—focuses this year on abuse within society and the seminary community itself. The agenda includes a plenary address on domestic violence, a series of workshops, and roundtable discussions. Workshops deal with incest, female and male survivors of abuse, forgiveness, sexual aggression, and ethics both sexual and legal. Discussions cover adult abuse and both women and men as abused children. Unlike last year's emphasis on Asian issues, selected by the administration, the abuse theme was chosen well in advance by a faculty/student committee. Participation and interest are high.

Sarah Kent, who represents a women's group concerned with theology, ritual, and ethics, leads a workshop and delivers the concluding plenary address. She argues that since Jesus' death on the cross was not necessary for salvation, God is a "divine child abuser." This brings most students and faculty members to their feet: Some stand and applaud; others walk out. The strong, polarized response to Kent resumes a couple of weeks later in the *MTS Journal*. This debate, in turn, sparks others—so many debates that a new section, "Voices," is added to handle the correspondence.

The *MTS Journal* is a thirty-seven-year-old weekly campus newspaper funded by the Community Committee, its editor selected, paid, and supervised by the committee's executive body. Or that is the historical arrangement. A change takes place during the fall semester. Months of poor attendance at Community Committee meetings and grumbling among student members about the inordinate power of faculty and staff representatives produce a change. An ad hoc group drafts a new constitution. Encountering little opposition from faculty or staff, the committee reorganizes as the Mainline Theological Seminary Student Council. After that, the *MTS Journal* is accountable to a communications committee of the new council. The newspaper becomes—as its mission statement says—entirely student-run.

Orthodoxy and Feminism

The *Journal* debate over Sarah Kent's address opens the third week of January. An eight-page, stapled, powder-blue edition containing "News and Opinion from the MTS Community" appears as usual in mailboxes, on a display rack outside the business office, and in the glass-walled commuter room. Thomas Melvin, the president of an evangelical students' group at MTS and author of a weekly column in the *Journal,* launches the opening salvo. Thomas writes:

> She [Sarah Kent] considers the cross as the ultimate symbol that promotes Christianity as a religion of hate and violence. . . . And she portrayed Jesus' death on the cross and resurrection as being unnecessary to our salvation. . . . I don't disagree with Sarah's call for justice, for freedom from oppression, for equality of all persons, male and female of every race. I do disagree with any call to rush to some new and glorified future that depends on human initiative and not God's initiative. Such a call is contrary to Scripture, to human reason, to human experience, and makes a mockery of the faith of millions of people. . . . When people get "right" with God; when people abide by God's law; and when people begin living in the "power of the cross," then the human race will live as brothers and sisters in the peace, love, joy and harmony that God has intended from the very beginning of creation.

Holly Sturdevant, a fourth-year student, responds. Holly was on the organizing committee for the retreat. She is an avowed feminist and serves as the straight gatekeeper for a student organization for gays, lesbians, and bisexuals (announcements of meetings instruct interested individuals to call Holly for information about times and places). She is physically striking: of medium height, and trim, with dark almond-shaped eyes and dark auburn hair. Out of concern for thrift or hip-chic, Holly usually wears outdated, secondhand clothing. She needs little prodding to take Thomas on:

> Sarah Kent takes a critical and scholarly look at the doctrine of atonement, and suggests that such beliefs are related to abusive human actions. For this, Thomas Melvin accuses her of seeing "no love in the Christian church today, only hate and violence."

. . . If Thomas takes God-talk seriously, as he claims to, then perhaps "God"—as understood by people; "God" as a particular patriarchal ideological construction—just might be part of "the problem." A God who demanded the excruciating death of his *only* child might not be the means of salvation for an abused person. Such a "God" most decidedly is not salvific for us. For the church to perpetrate a traditional doctrine of atonement, all the while mostly being silent on matters of abuse, is to participate in the ongoing victimization of millions. If abuse is not the church's problem, what is?

A couple of weeks later, Thomas replies:

If we view God only as "particular patriarchal ideological construction" . . . then we do not know God. Perhaps this limited view of God is why God is not understood by a great many people, including those persons who see only an abusive God in the atonement. . . . Do we get rid of God because of our imperfections? I would hope not for it is only through God/Christ that we have a chance to achieve perfection. People who abuse people will reach out for anything to justify their actions, and this includes religion.

Clint Emery Jr., Holly's boyfriend, who is reading Christopher Lasch on the decline of public discourse in America and trying to do his part to improve intellectual debate at MTS, makes a solo response to Thomas in the next issue. And as with many articles this semester, friction of one kind leads to others. What started as a debate about the nature of the Atonement moves to more typical MTS concerns about feminism, justice, liberation, and praxis.

Thomas writes that as we "view God only as a 'particular patriarchal ideological construction' . . . then we do not know God." I couldn't agree more. Patriarchy distorts reality; it is sinful. Much of Christian theology is imbued with this sinful ideology. It is traditional Christian theology—and not dreaded feminist iconoclasts—who distort our understanding of Ultimate Reality and in the process participate in creating an unjust social order. Feminists respond to patriarchy, they don't create it. . . . Thomas notes that "humans are less than perfect." . . . Of course, we will never liberate ourselves fully (and in this sense liberation is spoken of as a gift from God). But this knowledge does not preclude commitment to liberative praxis. The question is, will the church—including persons at MTS—oppose or support the process of liberation? What will we say and do on behalf of abused persons?

Racism

Ironically, another letter in the same *Journal* issue mutes the clamor over Kent's lecture. An anonymous member of the "community of the African diaspora" uses this theological debate as an opportunity to remind white community members, especially liberal ones, of their silence about the exhibition of African-American figures:

This "inclusive," "Christian" community was not disturbed by the exhibit and made no protest against it. Where were the White "liberal" seminarians who raise their hands in class to proclaim their sorrow and remorse for not having been born to an oppressed people? Where were all the feminists who say that they are in solidarity with their Black sisters? One must conclude that the seminary community condones and supports this image of the African diaspora. . . . Not only are the Black seminarians in great anguish, but so are the human beings that clean and maintain your buildings, the people that prepare your food, the persons that maintain your book accounts, the individuals that handle your mail, the instructors that teach some of your most challenging classes. When have they ever betrayed you?

The anonymous writer closes with a challenge: "PROTEST AND REMOVE [THE] DEROGATORY DEPICTIONS OF AFRICAN LIFE FROM THE SEMINARY WALLS . . . NOW!"

The next week, the *Journal* includes a letter signed, "Agitate, Agitate, Agitate, A Spiritual Walker Concerned about Racial Justice." The letter begins with a quotation from C. Eric Lincoln: "The power of racism is the power conceded by those respectable citizens who by their action or inaction communicate the consensus which directs and empowers the overt bigot to act on their behalf." The writer tells about an MTS student who "called me a TOKEN" and another who "asked me if EGYPT was in Africa." This "Spiritual Walker" says that the seminary is not about the business of spreading the gospel to "all people regardless of race." The writer adds, "We spend so much time at this seminary discussing inclusive language only to exclude a vital part of everyone's culture, the African-American." Quoting John 10:10, "I come to give you life that you may have it more abundantly," the writer concludes, "Where is that abundant life that was mentioned? I don't see it. Maybe I'm blind; even if I am, my glasses come from the oppressor. . . . WAKE UP!"

Disable-ism and Ageism

The "Spiritual Walker's" letter prompts a response, although probably not the kind the author had in mind. Alice West expresses distress about the use of words such as "deaf," "dumb," and "blind." Using these words as adjectives to define an intellectual capability instead of a physical capability, she argues, only shows the writer's ignorance and insensitivity. Like most contributors, Alice argues from experience: She knows persons who are deaf, blind, and mute, and they are "at least as insightful as the population at large." She finds it "a sad irony that persons wishing to call our attention to perceived injustices would choose to use stereotyping language in an effort to make their points." After all, "how much integrity is in a call to make just that which is unjust, when the call itself is an injustice?"

While controversies continue around insensitivity to women, blacks, and disabled persons, a second-year student vents frustration in the *Journal* over a decline in "academic integrity" at MTS. Peter Tomas questions the grading practices, teaching techniques, and evaluation procedures and concludes: "It is my feeling that an uncritical commitment on the part of this seminary to the 'education' of second-career students has undermined the commitment to high standards of scholarship."

Now "ageism" enters the debate. Age is a particularly sensitive issue at MTS, where the average student age is closer to fifty than twenty. A half-dozen letters from second-career students appear in "Voices" over the next several weeks. One student lists his preseminary credentials, which include enrollment and/or teaching in "at least 14 college and university programs"; another maintains that "we are self-motivated, know why we are here, and have a strong commitment to our seminary studies." A student who successfully pursued a Masters in Theological Studies while working full-time in a high-profile management job, and is now in the M.Div. program, accuses Peter of "an elitist, uncritical bias toward part-time, second-career students."

Passions run high. "I have witnessed some vicious and quite personal attacks against Peter. . . . I don't wish to become the next target of such abuse," says the writer of an unsigned letter supporting Peter. Still, there are lighter moments. A contributor who signs himself "An Arizona Cowboy" pleads: "Join me in repenting, my dearest brother Peter, for the hour is short. . . . Will you put on your sack cloth and ashes and join me in prayer by the gate of our temple, at 10:55 A M., on April 17?"

While most students emphatically stake out their particular social and ideological space in these debates, at least one wonders where she fits. This student describes herself as "a low-income, single parent" struggling like "many of my abused and marginalized sisters." In recent issues, she observes, "I have been told not to address issues concerning the Black community because I am not Black." She wonders where this leads. Should people ask others to verify their racial and ethnic heritage before joining them? Or, in matters of class, should people ask to see income tax returns before forming relationships? And now, she concludes, "I am told that I must be a certain age [to] have any intelligence."

"Ducking and Covering"

> I think that survival in a place as diverse as this involves a certain amount of ducking and covering.
>
> —Second year, white male student

Public controversies rage in the *MTS Journal* during the spring of 1991, and at the same time, a quieter form of protest becomes evident in individual interviews with six white male student pastors. Most of these men admit that they knew MTS was "probably more liberal" than they are when they entered. In the interviews, they describe what it is like for them in a seminary where being "politically correct" requires "being open to radical feminism," "confessing the sin of racism," "rejecting the [denominational] stand on homosexuality," and "worship[ing] as dogma, God's preferential option for the poor."

Tommy Reiss is married, has two boys, and is currently the pastor of several small rural churches two hours from Mainline Seminary. Tommy talks about his seminary experience as a struggle to "see God from the perspective of other people." On issues of race and feminism, he says, this has been hard. For example, he struggles with his response as a white member of the community: "Is it my responsibility to penetrate the black community and interact with my black brothers and sisters, or is it my responsibility to withdraw and let them work out their anger, or should I make myself available to be a scapegoat for their anger?"

On women, Tommy says, "I thought, well, I can deal with women. I found out these are not women. These are WOMEN. What's going on here? I thought I could speak this language." Mentioning a class on feminist theology, Tommy laughs a little and repeats a joke about how "they open their prayer by speaking in tongues and barking at the moon." Still, Tommy admits that he is becoming more sensitive to issues of gender. "So I'm learning," he says. "I mean my [bishop] is a white woman. My [area supervisor] is a black woman. The times are changing. That's not bad but I need to understand how to deal with that. . . . The bottom line is [that] it has been good, [but] to get to the bottom line has been painful and frustrating."

The lack of humor in dialogue is a familiar theme. Boyd Arthur, who is married and commutes from "on the field," says, "I just feel like everyone has an agenda. And I feel like a lot of people bring their agendas to seminary" and take everything "extremely personally." This is especially true, he says, of women students. Then he tells a story:

> I was sitting in the M&M class last spring and Susan Johnson was doing her thing, supposedly on pastoral care. She was quoting pastors of churches in the 1800s, and she got to one who happened to be a woman. That woman said something to the effect that we shouldn't be so preoccupied with trying to change the church and trying to change . . . the family. It was a woman's place to please the man, and we need to get our priorities in order. And, you know, I just thought that it was extremely hilarious. It was like so much doom and gloom . . . before [patriarchal or sexist statements] and then she comes up with this woman who was saying the same things. And when she finished, there was a silence, and I just said, "Amen."
>
> I was sitting in the back and off to the right of the large classroom in Dunavant, and it was like everybody up and turned and looked. I felt daggers were just coming into me like flying nails. After it was over a couple of people came in and they were kind of laughing and saying, "If we didn't know who you were, and what you were doing, we would have thought you were crazy."

Women can make jokes, this student observes, and black students can too: "But me, I can't do that," he said, concluding that at MTS, being white male and middle-class is taboo.

A younger, newly married suburban pastor agrees. Lester Spotsworth sees a "lack of patience, and a real anger" at MTS that comes from "not being heard." When PM presses him about the identity of those who are unheard, he says, "there are lots of people who feel that way," but "I would think that the majority would be white males." Asked why this is so, he replies, "Well, I guess historically and experientially, white men have been the oppressors in our culture. [And so] white men are probably the ones who need the most radical conversions, [yet] I have had difficulty identifying myself with typical white male oppression."

At MTS, some white males admit that they feel more like the "oppressed" than the "oppressor." Tommy Reiss says, "You cannot marginalize anyone [more]. . . . We white males feel absolutely marginalized. Stomped on, spit on, emasculated." Still, all these students feel that their seminary experience has stretched them in some important ways. As Tommy sees it, "I learned through it to recognize the

'hot buttons,' which is vitally important if you are going to function in a parish."
Tommy continues:

> It has been a good learning experience, a valuable learning experience, but I can't say
> that I will cherish being kicked in the stomach emotionally. It bothers me that they're
> hurting. It bothers me that I am a part of their pain, but it bothers me personally that
> they blame me. And, you know, maybe they have a point and I am not sure that I
> would be forced to examine myself on these issues so intently without the motivation
> or prodding of their anger.

Jim McClaren, a shy, bearded rural pastor, is more cautious: "You have to be so,
so careful sometimes."

All of the students who talked to PM in the spring of 1991 about their own
struggle with "white maleness" describe themselves as "more conservative," or
"more orthodox," than most students at MTS. These students agree that their experience at MTS has made them more—not less—sure of their theologically conservative positions. The shy rural pastor puts it this way: "My foundations are still
my foundations, but I have added a couple of new rooms onto the buildings."

Working It Out

> The educational philosophy of MTS is one that integrates all learning around scripture
> and the traditions that provide the church's identity in the gospel of Jesus Christ.
> . . . Furthermore, the educational process is designed to bring into complementary
> relationship classroom and field learning experiences.
>
> —MTS catalog, 1991–92

Arlene Jervis

Arlene is dressed very conservatively this morning. Her beige blouse fastened at
the neck with a small brooch, rust-colored sweater, and dark wool A-line skirt are
a far cry from the bright watermelon T-shirt and denim skirt on the first day of
orientation. She and PM walk to the bus station about a mile away for the twenty-
minute ride to Evans Street Church. Arlene is an intern at this inner-city congregation as a part of her urban ministry program. She says she is supposed to be just
"observing" this semester, but that is hard: "I couldn't just sit by and do nothing."

A homeless, middle-aged black man is cooking bacon in a frying pan on a
small, very worn camp stove inside the bus shelter. He has a round face with very
shiny cheeks and a toothless grin. A portable radio propped up on the shelter's
bench belts out a rousing black sermon. On-campus students are familiar with the
man: He cooks, sleeps, and plays solitaire in a number of alcoves on the main
road leading away from the school. Arlene comments on the radio preacher's sermon and receives a smile and a pleasant, garbled response. She says she has
brought him food on some Sunday mornings, but he always refuses it politely.

Arlene came to MTS from an activist, downtown "peace and justice" church in a large East Coast city. The emphases on liberation theology and Third World issues at MTS are in line with her own goals. Early in her life she dreamed about "being in Central America leading or facilitating a base community" or "being in a church that's real involved in social issues." On the ride to church, Arlene talks about some of her concerns regarding this urban ministry placement.

Arlene is excited about the possibilities at Evans Street. She explains that it is "like a lot of inner-city churches." In the late 1960s, it merged with two other congregations to survive a loss of members and the decay of the urban neighborhood. The current pastor is new, and Arlene is very enthusiastic about him— particularly because he attended a conference on healing that she helped to plan and he sat with her. (Arlene smiles at PM from her place in the choir when the pastor brings up the conference in his sermon.) She is impressed that the pastor was willing to come here with his wife and children from a larger, suburban congregation. "Turning this church around," Arlene remarks, "is a very tough job."

The young woman says that Evans Street has not really been very involved in "radical" social activism, primarily because the church is filled with "government-type" people. She worries that members concerned about the status quo will resist the kinds of issues important to her. Will she "offend" them with her more radical ideas? Arlene confesses that she is not sure how one motivates lay people to be socially active, although she's interested in trying.

Evans Street Church is about a mile northeast of the central business district at the edge of a now-deteriorating neighborhood commercial zone. There are some signs of new life. A few apartment buildings have been spruced up and have "gone condo." The strip of once-abandoned commercial buildings is being renovated for an assortment of antique stores, art galleries, and "yuppie-style" restaurants with striped awnings and brass trimmings.

The church building is of the same 1960's style as the seminary. The exterior, all vertical lines, is dominated by a tall rectangular tower with exposed chrome and cream-colored moulding inlaid with colored glass in bright reds and blues with a bit of gold. Inside, the sanctuary looks a lot like MTS's chapel except that it is about twice as large. There is a large cross on the back wall toward which the choir turns to face during the singing of the Doxology.

Arlene introduces PM to several church members whom she has gotten to know well. These include a trial attorney, a couple of investment brokers, some university students, and a few activist types employed by local social agencies. A glance through program listings in the church newsletter confirms the decidedly professional tenor of the church. Educational opportunities include sessions on "Looking Back through the Decades" (on the evolution of medicine); "Children: Their Needs, Our Responsibility"; "Petra: The Host City" (slide show about archaeological discoveries); and "Looking Ahead to the Future" (on the environment). The sole change of pace is "Singing the Gospel and 'Old' Hymns of the Church."

The service of worship is typical of mainline, heavily professional congregations: litanies, announcements, a choir anthem, the offering and Doxology, and a sermon (on the role of faith in healing and overcoming pain and suffering). When worship is over, Arlene and PM eat a quick lunch and return to MTS. On the way, Arlene talks enthusiastically about the Maundy Thursday service she is planning for the church. She is using a "feminist litany" from her large collection of liturgical materials. Along with her zeal for social justice issues, Arlene has a passionate interest in corporate worship. She attempted to organize a "feminist liturgy" group during her first semester, but nothing ever got off the ground. After that, Arlene put her energy into a women's Bible study, the seminary's spiritual life committee, and a women's covenant group.

Arlene admits that she had high expectations for "community" when she came to MTS. "The forming of community has been disappointing," she says. "I haven't connected quite as well as I wanted to." She mentions Lu's suicide the year before as "totally draining"—a stark reminder of the failure of community. She recalls that her first-year classes helped to compensate for a lack of community. One high point was the research for a paper on "tongue-speaking," a phenomenon that attracted her because of the intensity of the experience. "I thought, God, I want something like that, an event that can take you and shake you," Arlene says.

Chapel services also provided some spiritual fuel during the first year. She was moved by the "spontaneity and creative liturgies" of Trudi Darsa, the chapel elder at the time. And when it came to community, she says she concluded that "what you need you can just go out and create. I'm better at just going out and getting what I need—making myself do that. I feel better. If I focus on somebody else, those feelings [about lack of community] would go away."

In her second year, Arlene combines her spiritual and community-seeking activities with her continuing social action interests. She cochairs the MTS social action committee and notes that people have "a lot of energy for that." What she recalls most vividly are the controversies:

> I got real involved in being with people because of shared interests. I could list all of the PC [politically correct] people. Toward the end of the year, I remember having conversations with people and realizing that I was real tired of all of the divisions and all of the camps. You know, if you can't agree with somebody politically, you don't like them as a person; I mean that whole idea. . . . So [I] became more and more involved in my church, getting more of my fulfillment there.

Evans Street Church, at first a target for Arlene's reforming zeal, becomes a place of succor. She is involved with the children's music, a shut-in ministry, a growing singles group, and "just fellowship." Over a casual meal with PM in a local Persian restaurant in late 1991, Arlene says that her church is "doing mostly inward, nurturing things" because "that's where they are right now and that's what I've needed to do. It builds trust, and now I feel like I can say things I haven't said."

Arlene admits that now she looks "more realistically" at issues, asking, "How do they apply to lay people in my church?" But in case it sounds as if she is no longer concerned about social justice, she is quick to add, "The issues are still real when you see men washing red paint off the statue of Columbus." Native American issues are currently on the front burner for the social action committee at MTS in anticipation of Columbus Day. So, Arlene muses, "I haven't changed much; I was already left of center. If anything, I've moved more toward the center because that's where most lay people are."

Janet Cable

A woman with lovely silver and ash-brown hair stands in the pulpit of Oak Grove
Church near the center of a village famous for its historic stand on abolition. Her
hands are planted firmly on either side of the broad, wooden pulpit, the sleeves of
her eggshell-colored robe draping over the corners as she leans forward slightly.
A large wooden cross hangs around her neck on a rough, dark cord. Her face is
pale, and her rose-colored lipstick calls attention to her mouth—and so do her soft
but steady words. She begins:

> I think my daughter, Amy, kind of wrapped it all up with a question to me late one
> night. She said this, "Mom, I know you have a strong faith, but something that always
> bothers me is this: If Jesus came to give us new life, to save us from our sins, and if
> he is really alive today and in the world, why is there so much misery and unhappiness
> still?" That's quite a question to have posed to you, isn't it? And I wish I had a
> profound, wonderful, all-encompassing answer to that question. I am going to tell you
> a story this morning that I think sheds some light on a possible answer.
>
> This is a story that goes back to the days of World War II. There was a group of
> Laplanders that hadn't heard about the armistice. Now, at that time of the year
> in Lapland, there was darkness just about twenty-four hours a day. And the people of
> Lapland continued to live their daily lives as if the war was in full swing. That meant
> that the people huddled together and lived in fear daily. The war was over, but there
> was no celebration for these Laplanders until months later. Now you notice, while it
> was still dark in their lives, the Allied victory had already been accomplished.
>
> You know, I thought about that, and I thought about Mary Magdalene and the other
> women coming to the tomb of Jesus in the darkness of early morn. The resurrection
> victory had already been accomplished, but the reality of what happened had not sunk
> in yet. And you know, I think that today, in the midst of our fast-paced, busy world,
> with all of the pain and the separation and despair, we have to wonder if the reality of
> the resurrection experience has sunk in with us yet.

Janet Cable is a third-year student on a pastoral track. She is fifty-four years
old, and this is her second try for a divinity degree at MTS. Her journey to ministry has taken several detours.

Janet was baptized into the Lutheran Church, and her grandfather officiated at
her confirmation: "We wore white robes and we knelt at the altar, and I can just
remember feeling so close to God and thinking this is what I want to do. I want
to do something so I will feel this close to God for the rest of my life." She did
not know what to do until much later. The summer between her junior and senior
years in college, Janet read a book about a woman minister in upper New England.
She comments wryly, "If you made it into ministry in those days, you were sent
to the far reaches of the earth. You know, never heard from again. So I knew
it was possible, but I didn't know anybody, any women who were going into
ministry."

When Janet was twenty-two, she enrolled in the Christian education program at
MTS because somebody told her "a lot of women go into religious education."
She did not enjoy it, so she petitioned the faculty to switch to the divinity pro-

gram, and she was admitted. She recalls loving the classes, particularly systematic theology and existentialism. "But anyway," Janet says, "to make a long story short, while I was at MTS, I met this handsome young man who just stole my heart away." She married him and, with thirty-five credit hours toward her degree, dropped out of school.

In the years that followed, Janet had three "great children," but her relationship with her husband became harder. She says he was intensely jealous, but "I had been raised that when you make your bed, you lie in it. So I tried for years to hang in there. And it just didn't work out." She and her husband separated in 1977 and later divorced. For a time, Janet worked at a nursing home at night and at a local school during the day. Finally, she got a full-time job at a long-term care facility; she started out in personnel and was soon promoted to director of admissions.

"I never, never got rid of the feeling that I was called to ministry," Janet explains, and she was always involved in church. She taught an adult Bible class for seventeen years, and she took classes in "lay speaking." Then, in the late 1980s, the long-term care facility came under new management. Janet said that the emphasis shifted to marketing, to dollars instead of people. About the same time, her pastor approached her about a year-long project: taking a small church nearby that "needs a lot of nurturing." The time felt right, so she agreed.

Janet reenrolled at MTS in 1989 and has not looked back. She is presently the pastor of two churches about 150 miles east of the seminary. The Archway Church meets in a small sanctuary dominated by warm, dark mahogany furnishings. A large poster on the back wall says a lot about this "family" church. It is covered with pictures of adults of all ages and children eating together, playing games, and working together to build the new cinder-block fellowship hall that sits on a small rise next to the church.

Janet says that the people of Archway were at first very resistant to her, a woman minister. Another woman had served as pastor several years earlier, and reportedly, that was not a positive experience. The first woman was followed by a male pastor who "bonded well with some of the people." When Janet arrived, the Archway members were not very happy. Strangely enough, she says, during her first year, all of the primary antagonists were ill for one reason or another. This situation gave Janet a natural opportunity to visit them in the hospital and in their homes. Her nurture and love at the personal level are what won them over, she concludes.

At the same time, Janet struggles with issues of feminism and servanthood in her seminary classes. She explains:

> I am not a liberation theologian because they start with identification with the poor and the needy and then build their faith. I still start with Jesus Christ, but I think, like Bonhoeffer said, "He was a man for others." And therefore, the church must also really exist for others. So, I can see the idea of servant ministry. You know, that's an excellent model for ministry, and yet the feminists say, "Don't talk to us about servant ministry. It's servitude and submission, and that's where we've been, under somebody's thumb all of our lives." And I know that's true in my own life. I know that's true. So I think

you have to be very careful about what you mean when you talk about the servant role. I believe that we're called to be servants, but I don't believe we're called to be doormats.

Janet is not comfortable with inclusive language for God, and she is not convinced that abusive relationships are good reasons for eliminating the male pronoun for God. "I mean, I lived in a really bad marriage for a long time, but I didn't transfer that to God," she argues. "I have to admit that I am not a feminist."

Oak Grove Church is an attractive, Federal-style, redbrick building located in a historical district. This congregation is the product of the merger of a black and a white congregation in the mid-1970s. The sanctuary is very beautiful, with grand, carved wooden staircases that cradle the balcony in the back and open onto the main floor on both sides. There are seats for about 250 people, but on Easter Sunday Janet counts fifty people a good crowd. Presently, the congregation is about 50 percent black and 50 percent white, and "they are the most open, loving, nurturing people."

Janet smiles and says, "Here I am in an atmosphere like that, and then I go into MTS, and there is just a lot of hostility in some of our classes. . . . Open anger." On the anger of African-Americans at MTS, she continues:

And I had trouble understanding that anger at first. And I think now, even though I don't like it, you can't blame them for having it. It's so easy for the white people to say, "It's all changed." It hasn't, you know. And in a sense, it is the same thing that I guess the women feel. That we still don't have the opportunities to the point that we should. . . . One thing that I did learn through my divorce, I think anger is a very destructive thing for you more than anybody else. It may hurt a lot of other people, but you're the one that it really destroys.

Janet talks about her own trouble with David Parsons in a course on global mission and ministry. She says that his anger in class is palpable. When it looked like she was going to have Parsons as her systematics professor, she tried to get out of it. The registrar, whom she respects, told her that she ought to rethink the decision. That surprised her, and Janet said she felt ashamed. She stayed in Parsons's class, and "Something happened to both of us. . . . He must have such a love for theology that it just kind of poured out of him. And, you know, he kind of like dances with it when he really gets caught up in it, so that you feel him as well as hear him. . . . He made light bulbs go on in my head."

Some "light bulbs" have also gone on for Janet in her ministry. She and the members of Oak Grove want to turn their church into a training center. Their dream is that church groups—particularly youth groups—might tour the old town, visit its Civil War museums, explore the surrounding area, and then come together for periods of reflection on ecological responsibility and racial justice.

Jenny Sherrod

Jenny Sherrod has shoulder-length chestnut hair, hazel eyes, and a nearly classic Roman profile. She is a California woman with a free-and-easy way about her.

Her first sermon as a student pastor at Caulfield Church—a congregation in a prestigious older suburb—reveals her whimsy and her passion and empathy for others. She asks whether people on trips to the West might have seen clumps of brushes blowing around and thought: "Wouldn't it be easy to be a tumbleweed?" She follows up, "Sometimes we want to just go wherever the wind blows, be happy and carefree, but life just isn't like that. It seems no matter what we do, somehow we can't help but get a little bruised and battered."

Jenny touches on the lectionary reading about Thomas, the doubting disciple. "Sometimes," she says, "we have good reason to doubt the presence of God," especially in an age where everything can be reduced to scientific explanations. Then Jenny shifts to the movie *Flatliners*. Several medical school students, she explains, "decided to explore what it is like to die and come back." They discovered a "power [they] could not explain," and their experience with death taught them the importance of life and relationship.

Jesus commissioned disciples to continue his journey after his death, she reminds the worshipers. For Jenny, "carrying the example of Christ" is done in community by "sharing our stories and supporting one another." Most important, "we share the sins and we share the forgiveness."

Jenny tells about reading Toni Morrison's *Bluest Eye* for a class: "The book is about a poor, young black girl who wishes she could have blue eyes. If she had blue eyes, then everything would be different. She would be pretty; her parents would stop fighting, her father would stop drinking, her brother would stop running away. The book ends with very little hope for this young girl." This story about racism and hopelessness, however, leads Jenny to another story about racism and hope.

Maya Angelou is a kind of heroine to Jenny Sherrod. Jenny has read Angelou's autobiography and her poetry and has heard her lecture twice. Maya Angelou had a "tragic childhood full of abuse and abandonment," yet she still "believes in people." Angelou is convinced that she is "a child of God," Jenny says, and what makes her so special is "her love for all people, as children and creatures of God." What is the lesson? Jenny sums it up: "As we share our lives and our love with one another, we are sharing the Body of Christ."

Jenny Sherrod grew up in a congregation in California. From her early teens through college, she served first as a "youth representative" and later as a "young adult representative" on several councils and committees in her church and on her denomination's regional level. Jenny's home church is, in her description, "liberal," and not surprisingly, she was encouraged through the years to consider the ministry as a career. She laughs and tells PM in an interview in early September 1990, "My pastor would always say, 'Whenever you want to talk about it . . .' and I said, 'No, no.' "

For several years after college, Jenny drifted—much like the tumbleweed she describes in her sermon—from job to job, potential vocation to potential vocation. Her college degree was in elementary education, but after student teaching, she says, "I knew I didn't want to do this." Jenny considered counseling, resort management, and park management. She had no models for counseling, and management was not appealing because of the hours involved and the lack of "spiritual enrichment."

She settled temporarily on a day-care job and moved in with her sister. "The day after I moved," Jenny remembers, "I went to church." At the church she became friends with a retired high school teacher. Jenny laughs and says, "Her mission was to find Jenny meaning in life." Her new mentor was very involved in local and regional church activities, a "lay minister" of sorts. This woman finally convinced Jenny to try seminary and the ministry.

Jenny got a slow start at MTS. She was also accepted at another school and did not make her final decision (which was based on financial aid) until the last minute. She missed orientation completely, and when she finally got to campus, Jenny says, her welcome was less than enthusiastic. She went to the admissions office because she had been impressed with the friendliness of the director in telephone conversations, and was greeted, "Oh, you're here." Then she found her adviser, who said, "Oh, you showed up."

"I cried after every required reflection group following the Mission and Ministry course that first semester," she recalls. That class, with Harriet Hercon and David Parsons, was, by most student's reckoning, very tough. For Jenny, the small group debriefings were excruciating. "They would talk about things and I didn't know what they were talking about," she said. "I started really feeling bad about myself. . . . Sometimes I wonder if I am intelligent enough to be here."

Several things did help that semester. Jenny became good friends with Judy Ponder and Terrence Nunnally, and she started dating a second-year student. Still, in an interview with PM, she recalls, "I expected more community than there was here. I really didn't feel like people cared until the last two weeks in the first semester after the suicide." She sits back a minute and thinks about what she is saying. "Well, it was partially because of Lu's suicide and partially because I got warmed up to everybody and everything."

Jenny became engaged at the beginning of the spring semester, and defining and redefining that relationship occupied much of her time. The next fall, Jenny moved into an apartment with Judy Ponder in Grant Hall and learned a great deal from the other woman, she recalls. By this time, Judy had become an indispensable part of campus life. She was given responsibility in working with the maintenance crew and also managed a light meal program at night in the refectory. Judy's industry and organizational skills became a model for Jenny.

By the fall of 1990, Jenny is very involved on campus. She is active in the Social Action Committee, a feminist reading group, a women's covenant group, and the chapel choir, and she is secretary/treasurer of the Community Committee (later renamed the Student Council). And true to her background, she is also increasingly involved in a local church. This semester she works in the youth program at Caulfield Church. At the same time, she and her fiancé begin to rethink their relationship, and during that semester, they decide to break their engagement.

When PM asked Jenny about significant events or experiences at MTS, she first said, "Working at Caulfield," then said, "Living with Judy." While for other students the second year was a time of conflict and testing, for Jenny it was a rebuilding year. Her student pastor position at Caulfield had a lot to do with this.

According to Jenny, the church that she grew up in is "liberal, a lot like Caulfield, but her home congregation has not dealt with homosexuality, as Caulfield is attempting to do. Caulfield takes part in the sanctuary movement, supporting Central American refugees fleeing oppression; sponsors the Caulfield Peace Ministry, an independently funded peace network supporting neighborhood-based services in Puerto Rico and Zaire; and shares its facility with community education and social service groups. And the church is linked to a nationwide "ministry with lesbian and gay persons and their families." A special committee lobbies denominational agencies and officials on gay and lesbian rights issues, raises money for a fund "which helps an HIV-infected [member] pay for his AZT treatments," and works with other community programs that support gay and lesbian persons.

Involvement at Caulfield puts Jenny in touch with the struggle of the gay and lesbian community. Because it is one of the few congregations in the area with this emphasis, Caulfield attracts many gays and lesbians, both couples and singles. Jenny has increasing opportunities for dialogue about this ministry; her easygoing way and empathy for others builds natural bridges, and she has a mentor, too, in Nan Webster, the activist pastor of Caulfield Church, which operates out of a two-hundred-year-old Gothic-style building.

By the third year, Jenny follows Holly Sturdevant as the straight gatekeeper of a reorganized MTS student group for gays, lesbians, and bisexuals. Besides her duties at Caulfield, she also volunteers in a food program, a kind of Meals on Wheels for people with AIDS, many of whom are very ill and very much alone. She gets support in these involvements from her closest friends. Judy Ponder also volunteers for the AIDS food program, and Terrence Nunnally is doing his field placement with that organization.

In a sermon on peace and justice one Sunday in late 1991, Nan Webster provides an image that captures the spirit of Caulfield Church and of Jenny Sherrod: "We are listening for that vision of the reign of God, and, for a moment, we glimpse it and there is awe. As we glimpse it, we see that we are the secret—a whole bunch of angels with muddy feet."

Mitch and James: Interracial Witness

A large, silver bus lumbers down a narrow, country lane past white tract houses. Ahead on the left is a neat frame church building with a long, rectangular attached fellowship hall. The driver maneuvers the bus—oh, so carefully—onto the shallow, soft shoulder of the road and stops.

Mitch Tabor is standing with PM on the front walk of the Wileyville Church. This jovial, ebony-dark man with laughing eyes and broad, beefy shoulders straining his "preacher suit" laughs and motions to the driver. "Go ahead and pull it up in the yard!" he yells. We watch as the bus eases back a bit and then bounds quickly forward across a slight depression and up onto the greenish brown grass. Rows of pale faces bob in the windows as the bus shifts awkwardly.

James Englehardt, his wife Marie, and twenty-eight members of the Exeter Church make their way off the bus. PM glances at the order of worship that will be used later. Mitch points to the middle of the inside page: JESUS COMMANDS . . . 'That you love one another; as I have loved you, that you also love one another.' " He says that what they are doing today is "historic." He has called the local newspaper to invite coverage. The papers, he reasons, cover the bad things that happen in the black community, so why not the good things? Mitch asks the question, yet shakes his head and shrugs as if he is not so sure it possible.

Mitch was called into the ministry when he was fourteen years old, but he didn't "surrender" until he was thirty-one. He was at a Baptist church in Pittsburgh, Pennsylvania, and he recalls, the pastor started "prophesying and speaking in tongues and pointing at me. And when she started speaking in English, she started saying that I was going to be a minister. A man of God." Mitch adds with a laugh, "I decided to spend the rest of my life proving that I wasn't going to be." He tried many jobs, including counseling and teaching, without achieving satisfaction. It took a personal crisis and a visit from a pastor to bring him to a decision.

The pastor who visited Mitch's home, prayed with him, and heard his public testimony about God's call was white. And the church the minister led, which Mitch joined, was also white. "So I became the only black member of that church. . . . It was wild. These people were so loving and warm and caring and it helped me with an area that I had problems with—in believing that white people could really be Christians, really love Jesus." Eventually, he says, "they voted me in as a candidate for the ministry." That pastor, Mitch explains, "taught me everything there was about how to be a pastor—a loving, caring pastor."

Mitch had to face some painful choices. "It had to come down to whether I was going to serve God or serve my wife who went into the Jehovah's Witness movement," he recalls. "So I had to make some personal choices there." Mitch and his wife divorced. Following the urging of his pastor, Mitch visited MTS. He liked it and enrolled in the basic pastoral program.

How has seminary changed Mitch? When he came, he says, "the whole idea of theology was not even in my vocabulary." What's more:

> I was so glad that I had no theological background per se until I got to MTS. Because it enabled me to embrace liberation and theology to the point [that] I have embraced it. It became so apparent to me in the beginning of my relationship with theology that this could be the only way that all people, despite sex, race, and gender discrimination, could be freed through Christ. It fit with my worldview. . . . [I]t was like something that you knew in your heart all along.

Writers like James Cone and Dietrich Bonhoeffer have been particularly meaningful. "It was like drinking water, . . . like drinking clear water," Mitch declares.

Mitch says that he has become more open, ready to hear different points of view, even more liberal. By "liberal," he means "more apt to listen to others," which is something he has learned in his parish: "I think more than anything, I have learned that what other people were saying [is] important. . . . I have learned that in the parish, and I have used it. I have applied it to MTS."

Then there was the trip to Mexico. MTS has involved faculty, staff, and a few students in intensive educational experiences in several Third World countries. In the fall of 1990, many more students wanted to go than MTS could send. So a group of students successfully lobbied the administration—and a few faculty members—for an immersion experience in Mexico, with class credit, during the January term. Mitch went, and he says, "It changed my life."

> Because I saw people who had nothing. [Yet] their faith was so deep, so inspiring. It is one thing to read about something, but when you see it in action—and you see Christ working in a people—then you realize you have a mission. . . . [Now] I don't want to be a part of anything that doesn't work for the people of God. When I went down there in Mexico and saw the base communities, it became more than just a political struggle . . . I realized that it was more than just some academic idea.

Mitch says he got in touch with "the potential of what you can actually do." And at MTS, in his role as president of a black seminarians association, he began to make some changes.

The only way change is possible, Mitch argues, is by starting from a "spiritual point of view." "There's no black and there's no white," he states. "If we're going to be clergy, Christian educators, we need to begin with a spiritual point of view despite our differences and diversities." He says he took some ideas about cooperation between whites and blacks at MTS to the black seminarians group and "got opposition." Some members said, he reports, "Well, we can't let white folks in our meetings." Yet some changes took place anyway. The black association and the "mostly white" social action committee planned several well-received joint activities. In the spring of 1991, the ABS sent invitations for their annual banquet to the entire campus, faculty, and students. One graduating senior told PM that this was a "real first" at MTS.

While Mitch was building bridges between blacks and whites at MTS, James Englehardt was struggling with ways to promote interracial dialogue and justice. He is another student pastor, tall, thin, and blond, a very clean-cut midwesterner. Although he and Mitch were born and reared in different places and very different social and religious cultures, their paths to ministry are remarkably similar. James's call—after midnight communion at a men's retreat—was unexpected and, like Mitch's, included an audible summons from God. Both James and Mitch were pursuing other vocations without much sense of satisfaction, and neither of them responded to their call immediately. Both of their calls led to painful decisions about first marriages. James, like Mitch, is divorced and remarried.

Also like Mitch, James was encouraged to consider MTS by a pastor-mentor, and James has been "changed" by experience with base communities in a Third World context. He participated in a denomination-sponsored program in Nicaragua the summer between his first and second seminary years. Exposure to liberation theology influenced James in what he calls a "leftward" direction. He recalls a lecture by Rick Santos during a seminar for students in the student pastor program:

> It was in the summer of 1989 when the group of us first came together. . . . [Rick] was talking about Nazareth, how it was no accident that Jesus came from Nazareth because Nazareth was just a little backwater town, had a bad reputation, and that Jesus

the Savior, the Son of God, came out of this little marginal town. [Rick] used that to go on [and argue] that Jesus is the liberator of the oppressed. Because Jesus came out of a people who were oppressed and abused. I will always remember that. . . . I guess this theology of liberation was the first time that theology really made sense to me [at] a really practical level. And I told Rick, after the lecture that he gave us, that I wanted to learn more about that . . . theology that is just really down and dirty with the people.

"The people" whom James works with most closely are the members of the Exeter Church. Exeter is nestled in rich farmland a tortuous three-hour drive north-west of Wileyville. The congregation there traces its roots to 1788; overall, there is a feeling of stability upheld by prosperous country tradition. The church building is dark red brick trimmed in crisp white. A large, modern education building with classrooms, a well-equipped kitchen, and a roomy fellowship hall have been attractively added on. The interior of the sanctuary is all dark, carved mahogany, and the ceilings are stenciled in fading pastel designs edged with gilt.

James has accomplished quite a lot since becoming the pastor of this three-hundred-member congregation. Currently, he is promoting an $80,000 project to replace a rotting (and dangerous) porch and to make the education building handicapped-accessible. James believes the church "has potential," but he is frustrated by its lack of interest and involvement in outreach and ministry. "You know, I have come to the conclusion," he says, "that these people don't have the foggiest idea what it means to be a church. To them it's basically a social club, and it's an institution that their families have been associated with for generations, and they want to keep it going because it's always been there." What, James wonders, might motivate them to look outside themselves?

The racial and social justice debates raging in the *MTS Journal* spark much discussion among the student pastors. The way Mitch tells it, James looked at him one day and asked simply, "Mitch, what do we do? . . . Really, tell me the truth. What can I do?"

James and members of the Exeter Church have traveled to Wileyville for joint worship with Mitch and the Wileyville congregation. The Exeter people get off the bus and make their way into the white frame building. People are literally crammed into the Wileyville sanctuary. Blond wooden pews that ordinarily seat about eighty persons are completely filled. Church members spill over into the aisles, against the walls. Choir members in pressed white shirts and black skirts sway to the "jazzy" sounds of the piano. Behind the choir, in a centered recess, are two pictures, one a traditional portrait of Jesus and the other of Jesus and the twelve disciples at the Last Supper. Two brass vases with red and pink artificial flowers are arranged attractively on the ledge below.

After an hour of testifying, singing, and reading Scripture, and the baptism of two babies, James speaks. He begins: "This gathering is a sign that injustice, hatred, racism, violence, and death do not have the final say. . . . This gathering is a sign of hope in a nation that says with its lips that all people are created equal, which says with its actions that some are more equal than others."

"All right!" Mitch responds loudly, and James pauses a bit awkwardly.

James says that all people are created in the image of God and that "the color of our skin is the sign that God's image is expressed in diversity and variety." He talks about Jesus' relationship to his disciples, how they ate together, argued with each other, and loved each other. Jesus gave his disciples a new commandment "to insure unity within the family after his death," he explains. It's about loving God and loving your neighbor as yourself.

James continues by recounting how the denomination originally took a strong stand against slavery and how, after awhile, the church began to "soften." "Whites," James says, "began to feel uncomfortable worshiping with blacks."

"My Lord!" Mitch shouts.

"Blacks were forced to the back pews or to the balconies," James says. "The sin of racism has split our great church. . . . I don't think that is what Jesus intended when he commanded us to love one another. . . . We have let Jesus down." He asserts that the true test of faith is not following a doctrine, creed, or idea but living a certain kind of life. "Remember, love is not a feeling," James says, "it's a way of acting." He concludes, "And as long as there are churches like Wileyville and Exeter that are willing to overcome the racism that divides us, there is hope."

The communion table is painted white, and the words "In Remembrance of Me" are carved into the front panel. On top of the table are a brass cross, two unlit brass candlesticks, a large stoneware cup with a white cloth folded neatly across it, and a plate with a loaf of bread. Preparing for communion, Mitch says:

> What you have when you come here today is from prayer, it's from having two men from different parts of the United States and believing in one Jesus Christ. Believing that the blood of Jesus Christ which flows in each one of our veins is the love that conquers all. That conquers racism. That conquers prejudice. That conquers hate.

After the communion prayers are said, Mitch Tabor and James Englehardt stand side by side. The members of this congregation, black and white, rich and poor, old and young, rise from their seats, coaxed row by row by women in dark skirts, white shirts, and white gloves. Each person receives the bread, then the cup.

"The Body of Christ," Mitch whispers.

"The Blood of Christ," James intones.

NINE

Year Three: Resolutions

Faculty Retreat

> Ineluctably, the new term is approaching. Conversations with several of you recently
> revealed new energy and high expectations for the new academic year.
> —Academic Dean Gerald Adcock at Fall Retreat

Gerald Adcock, the academic dean, expects the new energy and high expectations
he detects to enliven the annual fall faculty retreat that precedes the orientation of
new students. For the third consecutive year, the retreat is being held at a Roman
Catholic facility about two hours from campus.

In late August, the days are still hot, the trees fully green. The meeting room at
the retreat center is on the lower level. An outer wall is glass, with doors opening
to an open area under a wooden deck extending from the floor above. In the room,
the tables are arranged in a rectangle, with a large space in the middle. President
Jack Stewart and Dean Adcock sit at one end of the rectangle; Oliver Wilfred,
assistant dean and registrar, sits to the left of the dean, and Clifford Mims, who is
to make a major report, is on Stewart's right. The rest of the faculty fills all
available spaces on the other three sides of the tables. The attire is informal: open
collars, shorts or skirts, athletic shoes or sandals. Variations in dress reflect individual perceptions of "casual."

Ben Somers, who teaches church history, begins the afternoon with a review of
ideas developed in faculty papers during the previous academic year. Somers is
young, at least by some faculty standards, and has a trim moustache. He distributes
a one-page summary of his observations. First, he says, "our faculty has wide
divergences as to the character and logic of the theological task—and, I suspect,
the character and logic of the church. Before we get to talking about globalization,
we have enormous 'local' divergences that make genuine conversation difficult,
since we do not share the same starting points." Second, his written summary
contends, the MTS faculty has "an unsettled sense of mission: Our attempts to
write a mission statement last year suggest that we do best at identifying the

functional character of our common work, and less well when we try to articulate *substantive* theological principles or impulses." Finally, he notes, the faculty members have a "tendency to talk through our differences. . . . We do not live together, most of us do not worship together, and we only occasionally work as a team . . . since our pedagogical models—and the specializations within which we have been trained—still are largely and perhaps unavoidably individualized."

The faculty is invited to react to Somers's observations, but the conversation is not lengthy. The group is more anxious to share feelings about an "immersion" event scheduled for the end of the academic year. Cliff Mims reports on plans for the event that have developed during the summer. Every Mainline faculty member will live part of one week with a family in a depressed rural area and part of another week with a family in a depressed urban area. The professors will attend community churches and meet with community organizers and local residents in an attempt to sharpen their understanding of conditions that few of them know firsthand.

Several faculty members admit to fears about going into cultures of poverty. Rick Santos says that as a Latino and a "street kid," he fears white middle-class culture more than that of poor people. David Parsons, an African-American professor of theology, says that "the fear that black people have is different from the fear white people have, so there cannot be one general conversation about fear! . . . Fear is always race- and class-specific."

One person, reporting on an earlier such immersion experience, observes that people in Third World cultures seem not to think about doctrine so much as to struggle with the tasks of survival. Cynthia Binder, who is new to the faculty, replies that she finds it inappropriate to speak of Third World peoples as "not thinking." They think, she says, but not in European, white, Western, male terms. The give-and-take continues until Dean Adcock stops the discussion to announce the schedule for the evening.

During the evening session, considerable time is spent on the death of a seminary administrator early last summer. Hollis Dirks died, apparently of complications of AIDS, although that term is never mentioned. Betty Trotter, a middle-aged woman professor of pastoral counseling, recounts an excursion with Dirks to an art gallery because he wanted to see "some beauty." Alvin Mitchell, a retired professor who is teaching this academic year, tells about taking communion to the very ill Dirks, then spending the evening talking with him. Mitchell comments that he never knew about Dirks's sexual orientation during all the years they worked together. Others share other reflections about Dirks: He had an alcoholic father, an abusive family, and became involved in church as a young man. One faculty member, familiar with the background, says that had Dirks's home congregation known of his sexual orientation, the man would have been charged with homosexuality and denied a ministry. Several people note Dirks's temper and his effort to control it. They recall his acts of kindness toward students and also the high level of student frustration he could cause.

Students generally think highly of the MTS faculty. James Englehardt has the impression that most of the faculty members are "open and tolerant." Tommy

Reiss, the student pastor of a small church, says that "somebody observed to me when I got here that . . . the faculty is much more middle-of-the-road than the student body. The students are, on one extreme, much more conservative than the faculty, and on the other extreme, much more liberal." He wondered whether the faculty sets out "to mainstream" students.

A cohesive picture of the faculty's view of itself as a unit is hard to frame. Living arrangements, office locations, and other institutional factors mitigate against social or religious interaction apart from formal work and committee meetings. There is no faculty lounge, and most MTS faculty members live in different, some quite distant, communities. Their offices are in four different campus locations. (Those in the Gregg administration building and the Dunavant academic building are of moderate size, and most have windows. Another group is along the tunnel linking Gregg and Dunavant. These are small, and several are windowless. A fourth set of offices are converted dormitory rooms on the same floor with students in Barlowe Hall. The beds are gone, but the built-in dressers and closets are still there, along with new bookshelves. These are the most spacious faculty offices at MTS.) While they do not complain about offices or lack of gathering space, some faculty voices speak of a "lack of community."

The faculty lacks a unified view of itself, of the interrelation of members, and of faculty influence on students. Marvin Miles thinks that by acting out their "commitments . . . in the classroom and in worship and in community life," long-term MTS people (professors and administrators) validate "the deeply held conviction" of less permanent residents. Ben Somers worries that students are "often caught between the conflicting . . . voices of authority they hear." Students, he says, "come [here] much more open than they leave. . . . [F]or whatever reasons, this is not a place that broadens people."

Mary Miles observes that MTS has multiple visions and voices. The school, she states, has a "feminist vision of mutuality, proximity. . . . We've got a South American liberation voice . . . about changing structures. . . . We've got a black liberation voice. . . . We've got a very conservative strain in the faculty that adheres to tradition and says that salvation comes through the traditional means of the church." For the conservative group, in her perspective, sin is understood as failure to submit one's whole heart to Jesus, whereas liberationists and feminists understand sin as being too submissive, too passive, and not trying to change the structure.

Matthew Lincoln, a longtime professor well-known throughout the denomination, perceives that a homogeneous faculty "is a thing of the past, and quite frankly, I don't think we will ever recover it in the form we had it in [the mid-1960s]."

The "effect of the faculty's pluralism" on students worries another professor, who reports that he loses sleep over the issue. He says: "I would say [that] the negative side of pluralism . . . is a kind of confusion. . . . [S]tudents will have experienced different conceptions of salvation, of the gospel, and [of] the character of the church and its place in the world." Tory Campbell, a senior professor, resonates to his colleague's concern. "I hope the faculty can remain diverse but not destroy itself in terms of polarities," he says. "[We] have some heavy-duty work to do on this."

The Mail and the Classes

Living the questions of faith requires our head. But it also requires our heart and our hands.

—Clint Emery Sr.

Students quickly catch up on campus activities as they empty their mailboxes during the first week of the fall semester. They learn that the main catalog and the CD-ROM containing religion indexes have been relocated in the library reading room. Another library notice invites everyone to an open house marking the retirement, and the birthday, of Florence Lawler, an MTS student in the 1970s who later became a full-time librarian.

A pale gray-and-black flyer from the MTS evangelical association announces a "revised schedule of speakers," including faculty member Cliff Mims on the topic "What Does It Mean to Be an Evangelical?"; noted evangelical author Carl F. H. Henry on "Where Evangelical Theology Has Been and Where It Is Going This Century"; Matthew Lincoln on "The Authority of Scripture"; and other lectures on personal evangelism and spirituality.

A news bulletin from MTS's Arts and Religion Center previews an upcoming exhibition on angels and the urban imagination. The exhibition features "seven artists whose response to contemporary urban living has resulted in works of mythical power and spiritual conscience." The opening includes a slide lecture by a guest artist on conscience and angels. A pale yellow flyer announces a tandem library exhibition entitled "Angels Lesser Known": "illustrations of unusual angels, artistic depictions of angels by ethnic and racial minority artists, angels in Islamic and Armenian art."

Next in the pile is a flyer proclaiming, "Good News!! The Gospel Choir Is Back!" Students can participate in this choir and get credit by enrolling in the MTS chapel choir. The flyer says the gospel choir will rehearse and sing with the chapel choir on occasion, but at other times it will practice and perform on its own. The invitation states: "If you have questions as to exactly how this will work out . . . so do we! But Dean Adcock is willing for us to give this a try. . . . BRING YOUR BEST VOICE AND YOUR LOVE FOR GOD."

"The Healing Ministry of the Church" is handwritten in heavy black letters across the top of a shocking orange sheet from a lay resource center at MTS. Below the headline is a copy of the front cover of the book *The Journey toward Wholeness: A Christ-Centered Approach to Health and Healing*. Kathleen H. Hofeller, M.A., Ph.D., will offer a course covering such topics as "The Mind/Body Connection"; "Prayer and Healing: Historical Perspectives"; "Forgiveness and Healing"; and "The Role of Guided Meditation." A note penciled in at the bottom says, "MTS students and staff receive a 50% DISCOUNT!"

A lavender flyer titled "An Urgent Call for Peace in El Salvador" announces a "National Call for Prayer, Fasting and Action to Christians in the United States in the month of September" by the Committee for National Debate for Peace. Rick Santos is organizing a group from MTS to "participate in a vigil" on September 19. The notice encourages students to urge "church members to write to their congressional representative . . . to co-sponsor HR 1346, 'Peace, Democracy and

Development in El Salvador Act.' " It concludes, "Pray for the church to hear the cry of the crucified people of El Salvador. With Jesus, let the church oppose the social structures that cause and sustain the affliction from which the cry of the people of El Salvador arises."

The first fall semester edition of the *MTS Journal* has two lead stories. One is about the new dean of community life, and the second is on an urban symposium. The Reverend Heisik Park, the new community life dean and faculty member, is the first Korean woman graduate from another denominational seminary to be ordained to the ministry. The article says that although "she had a number of options when choosing to work on a Ph.D., she chose to study at MTS because her first priority in ministry is working with people."

MTS is teaming up with a denominational agency to sponsor a symposium on drugs, violence, and community organizing through the church. Besides guest lecturers and group discussions, the article says, "field trips will be arranged to visit models of community empowerment—housing groups, drug rehabilitation groups, labor organizations, political lobbying groups, community organizing groups, refugee rights groups, and local churches with solid social witness ministries." An additional mailbox notice in pumpkin orange advises students that they should "disregard the student registration fee" for the symposium. Students with class schedule conflicts are advised to "discuss [it] with the course professor(s)."

A final flyer announces an upcoming meeting of a support group for "gays, lesbians and bisexuals." A rectangular, rainbow-colored sticker is affixed in the upper right-hand corner. Interested persons are asked to call Jenny Sherrod.

Religion and the Arts Class

On a Monday evening, forty students gather around a display of black-and-white angular drawings taped to a blackboard spanning a large, rectangular classroom. This course deals with contemplative drawing and selfhood and is one of the few course offerings that meet the religion and arts requirement for all graduating Master of Divinity students.

Lucy Knight, stylish in a tailored white shirt and belted, dark-colored straight skirt, reviews student attempts to draw a chair with the aid of a viewfinder. She says, "What's important here? There are relationships to the bounding edges of the format. There is the concept of shared edges, and there is the relative relationship of the parts." One student describes the difficulty of holding a viewfinder and drawing at the same time, then dealing "with the layers of negative space." The technique, Knight explains sympathetically, pushes one to engage the "whole brain."

After a fifteen-minute break, class discussion turns to the creativity and pain of art as "birthing." Leaning forward on the lectern, Knight asserts, "The patriarchal church denies birthing images; creativity requires birthing." A woman sitting close to the front raises her hand and speaks authoritatively: "People resisting the arts are patriarchal and patronizing."

Referring to a reading by Matthew Fox, Knight draws parallels between an organic and cosmological way of viewing the world and the artistic act. A black woman responds, "I feel good about the expression of a holistic worldview, especially the creation piece; you know, you are the creation and the creator. There's no need for a hierarchy to tell you what to do."

Knight moves to application: "Okay, so you recognize this creative ability in yourself and yet you know the world is full of problems. What do you do as leaders of churches?" Another African-American woman responds, "You bring people in to be cocreators; that way, they're included." With sudden animation, Knight responds: "That's an approach! I've always thought you could open up fellowship halls in churches and have opportunities for poor, indigent street people to come in and make something with their hands. That's what I call 'power with.' " A young white male adds, "That reminds me of an empowerment model of counseling; I'm learning that here, too."

The Global Church

After a midmorning break, David Parsons's Global Church class straggles back into the room. Several students arrange chairs and papers at the front table that ordinarily serves as a base for the portable lectern. Peter Tomas leans forward and whispers a warning to a few Barlowe Hall friends within earshot: "These panel discussions are not very creative."

A middle-aged student pastor distributes copies of a handout containing three items: a poem, "originally written in Xhosa," entitled "You Tell Me to Sit Quiet"; a news article from a December 1986 issue of the South African *Weekly Mail* about "illegal statements" that cannot be made "at the dinner table, in casual conversations, or even in private notebooks" without the prior permission of a "cabinet minister"; and an etching of a black township. The four-by-five inch picture is striking. A large, white, open hand—palm up—is in the foreground against the figure of a black man wearing a too-small hat and a large dark coat. The man slumps forward. The background is filled with rows of tiny shanties, topped by smoking chimneys and bounded by a very tall wire fence. A bold STOP sign appears in the upper right corner. The handout is not discussed or referred to again.

Another student, a commuter and a pastor, informs the class that the panel will address themes from Albert Nolan's book *God in South Africa*. He admits that his first thought after reading about the situation in South Africa was, "What can I do? I can do nothing. I'm powerless against the apartheid in South Africa because [according to the reading] the oppressed are called on to take up their own voice." He continues by saying that it is necessary to examine our "personal and communal motivations for [joining] the struggle" because "guilt and anger [are] not faithful responses. The problem is mistaking my voice for God's voice."

The middle-aged student pastor to his immediate left stands and says, "I sat in my nice, rural setting, in my two white churches, and thought, 'What can I do?'" He admits that he "sat by and [just] watched time go by." He smiles. Now, "I have realized [that] in my life there must be some change. What can we do?" First, "we must look at what's already in place." He says that most mainline denominations agree that "apartheid is not biblical" and, along with the World Council of Churches, encourage their congregations to "divest with corporations doing business with South Africa." But, he concludes, "what we're saying is not what we're doing." He sits.

The next student tells the class about an "aggressive preacher program" that his regional judicatory instituted on the issue of racism. He talks about a 1990 meeting with a white South African clergyman, "who let [us] know what was really going on." This clergyman, he recalls, described a communion service in a South African prison. "[He told us] that traditionally the person [who was] least important drank from the cup first. So, he gave the cup to a black and then to a white man. . . . After communion, [the white man was] holding hands with the minister and a black person—the oppressor standing with the oppressed. During the prayer, things changed."

Roger, the next student on the panel, talks about racism in his denomination. "We say we don't exclude, but we do. [There is] racism in our church structure." For example, he says, a cluster program teams white and black churches, but "90 percent of the conveners and chairs are white pastors." The white pastors "sound patronizing," making comments such as "They [the black churches] could benefit from our resources." Even when the black and white churches have the same number of members, he adds, the black churches are treated as "smaller or poor." And while many black churches have had a white pastor, "[we] don't give a white church a black pastor." He continues:

> In 1967, a black minister was appointed to a white congregation [where] my own family [attended], and I wasn't baptized in that church because my family wouldn't let me be baptized by that black minister. . . . One Sunday, two Klansmen came to the church in full regalia, and no one in the congregation said a blessed thing. They just whispered and looked [around] anxiously. The black pastor walked back to the KKK and said that it was all right to be here [as long as they] took off their hoods [because it was] improper for men to wear head covering in church.

There is laughter around the classroom. "He [the pastor] said if you challenge institutional evil—the system—you are cast out," Roger says, looking around the class. "How [do you] respond?" he asks. Without waiting for a response, he concludes, "[You] talk about it or take a stand."

The last presenter, a younger student with long, curly black hair and a reputation as a social activist, states: "There's so much to know, it's confusing. . . . I've sought out organizations in the city that have information about South Africa. Reagan and Bush [are] not in favor of sanctions [against South Africa]. Bush is trying to lift sanctions now. We need to speak up and let people know that [sanctions ought to continue] until a one-vote-per-person system is implemented in South Africa."

This student proposes a campus committee to protest the lifting of sanctions. He indicates a small stack of papers: "I have fact sheets and information that you can sign up and send in for." He says there are "three different denominational committees that oppose lifting sanctions." He has a directory with names and addresses. Peter Tomas leans forward and whispers, "How 'denominational' of us." Terrence Nunnally laughs and rolls his eyes. The speaker invites everyone to come up after class and sign up. Several students sitting near the front hang around and look through the material; most gather their things and head for the door.

Old Testament and the Arts

Thirty desks are pushed back against the walls of a large classroom to make a space for twenty others arranged in a semicircle around two tables. One table bears equipment (VCR and monitor, overhead projector, and microphone). The other is low, four by five feet, and set with pottery plates, a large mug, four wine cups, and a serving bowl. Unleavened bread and some vegetables and herbs are on the plates and in bowls. The food is later identified, discussed, and tasted as elements of a Passover meal; and of the dark, reddish purple liquid in the single mug, Professor Roland Pritchard says, "Dry household here: grape juice!"

Four students sit or kneel around the table. They are all in Hebrew dress: solid, neutral-colored robes, some with bits of color in sashes or stoles. Their head coverings are shoulder-length, and they wear sandals or are barefoot. Most of the students sitting in the larger circle are also in costume. A few are dressed in the Hebrew style. One white male comes as a soldier, with a breastplate and gold-colored helmet held by a prominent gray chin strap (more Roman than the intended Egyptian style). Several women come as cattle, wearing white tunics covered with black or brown spots, caps with cardboard horns and oblong ears, and blackened noses. A few students have on dull brown tunics with signs identifying them as locusts; one student dressed in blues and greens has poster-board wings and "dilly-boppers" (glittered balls on long springs) attached to a headband. She says she is a gnat. A couple in green outfits with yellowish spots look something like frogs (and later they hop a bit), and one student in gray wears an androgynous poster-board mask with hollow cheeks, a long hooked nose, straggly black hair, and red (blood) on the forehead. The professor and a couple of older students are not in costume.

The class is Old Testament and the Arts, and the session topic for October 31 is Moses and the Exodus. Instructions for this class session were distributed the previous week. Students were directed to "dress as your favorite Egyptian, Hebrew, or plague," to read certain sections of the text (*The Bible and Its Painters*), and to review the handouts provided. Class handouts were many: photocopies of paintings, including *An Israelite Marks the Doorway with the Blood of the Lamb,* by James Tissot; *Miriam's Song,* by Sir Edward John Poynter; *The Plague of Frogs,* by Gerard De Jode, and *Moses Smites Water from the Rock,* by Luke Yuan Tu Chen; the text of G. F. Handel's *Israel in Egypt*; a reading from Exodus 12; the text and tune to "Go Down, Moses," illustrated by a picture of two male Africans in manacles and chains; copies of the "Passover Haggadah," compiled by a Presbyterian church in Pennsylvania; the text and score of "Lift Every Voice and Sing," by James Weldon and Rosamond Johnson; a passage from the "Exagoge" in both Hebrew and English; and a copy of the poem "Moses" from *The Weather of the Heart,* by Madeline L'Engle.

Class is led by the four students in Hebrew garb at the table set for the Passover meal. A "Haggadah picture" from fourteenth-century England (a miniature on parchment) is projected on the overhead screen. One student explains, "Seder is made up of a lot of symbolic actions and foods." She and her colleagues around the table touch or pick up each foods on the table and talk to each other about its significance: "Unleavened bread. We remember we left so quickly; there was no time to watch the bread rise. As the Angel of Death passes by, we have the roasted egg, symbolic of the temple offering—the spring offering. . . . It worked. We're saved. . . . Four wine cups: the fourfold promise." The class is invited to follow along as the group moves into the recitation portion of the Seder. The "youngest child" (another group member) asks "the four questions," which begin, "Why is this night different from all other nights?" And to further answer questions about the context of that day, a Hanna Barbera cartoon video called "Moses" is shown.

As the class goes through each section of the Seder, paintings are shown, poems read, and recorded songs played. Each is discussed. Commenting on *The Submersion of Pharaoh's Army* by Lucas Cranach the Elder, the student in Roman soldier garb observes: "Looks like a medieval war [scene] with masses of people struggling in the mud." Of a clip on the Red Sea crossing from C. B. DeMille's *The Ten Commandments,* he says, "Here the cinema version is like the Keystone Cops." Everybody laughs.

The next piece is a woodcut from the Gutenberg Bible entitled *Moses Raises His Staff.* Janice says, "Dr. Pritchard, water that high is not possible." He responds, "The accounts in Exodus are mixed—from wagon wheels being bogged down to poetic versions like God's nostril's blowing a breath and the water standing in walls. According to the Talmud, water stood up to three hundred miles and could be seen all over the earth; all other water parted in sympathy. [The point of the] Jewish tradition of the crossing is to celebrate the character and wonder of the event. Artists capture this better than historians, [which is] the important point of this whole course. In texts on how to explain how this happened, commentators are caught up in rational details. Artists have naturally and intuitively seen that [celebrating the wonder] is the important part of the story. They have their own ways of making the mysterious familiar."

The class closes with a recording of "Wayfaring Stranger" by Emmylou Harris and a prayer read in unison: "May the One who broke Pharaoh's yoke forever shatter all fetters of oppression, and hasten the day when war will be no more. May God soon bring redemption to all humanity, and may we be freed from violence and from wrong, and be united in an eternal covenant of peace with all people everywhere. Next year in Jerusalem! Amen!!" A "Frank and Ernest" cartoon appears on the handout below the prayer: A Moses character stands on a low mountain ridge in sandals and robe with shaggy hair and beard. He holds two tablets with Roman numerals, one through ten. Below is an apparently endless crowd, and three characters stand out in front. The speaker wears a large, turbanlike headdress—perhaps priestly—and says to Moses, "WE FEEL WE'RE BEING OVER-REGULATED."

Preparing for Ordination Candidacy

It is early Saturday afternoon, and Arlene Jervis's apartment is unusually cluttered with papers, opened bags of potato chips, dirty plates, empty glasses, and a couple of pizza delivery boxes. Three women besides Arlene sit on the floor or lean against the sofa. They arc Carol, Felice, and Lisa, who is part Filipino. Everybody but Lisa lives in MTS's Grant Hall, the dorm with small apartments typically reserved for married students and their families. This year, nearly half the occupants are singles—most of them third-year students.

The women are reviewing material for an approaching candidacy retreat required by the ordination process in their denomination.

"I heard the most wonderful sermon one time on the idea of living on the cutting edge of time," Arlene says. "And this minister was able to kind of create this image of us just constantly being right on the edge of time. [It's] like the kingdom is right here."

Carol: "That's one way of looking at it."

Arlene: "It's, like, right before us. It's right with us. But we're still caught in this stuff behind us. We're not really able to get free and break loose from it."

Carol: "Yeah. Right."

Arlene: "It's right here. And that's how he talks about that 'already but not yet' kind of thing, where you're always moving along that edge."

Lisa: "Did any of y'all ever have Hercon for any[thing]?"

All nod assent.

Lisa: "One of the stories that she [told] that always, well, which I always remember was about the already and the not yet. She was saying that she went on this trip and was in the desert driving with her sister, and it was dawn and the light was starting to come up, and it was pink all around her. And she said she thinks of that as her analogy for the 'here and not yet' because she knew the sun was going to come up, but you were in the midst of this other—you know, on the brink. And that's how she described it. I always thought of it like that—that it was a goal, and the glimpses were rays, some little rays coming in every once in a while."

Felice: "But some people argue that Jesus ushered in the Kingdom of God and those of us who choose to believe in Jesus, as Christians, are already a part of that kingdom here on earth, and that we are to manifest the kingdom mentality in our lives."

Arlene (interrupting): "I guess I am talking [about] the real, eternal kingdom [that] we're never quite getting to, though. I think you are right. It's also here in our midst."

Felice: "So you don't think the Kingdom of God is something that is going to, you know, like Revelation . . . suddenly the clouds are going to open up and this huge giant Jesus is going to—"

Arlene: "No, but I think that the world really is going to be renewed."

Felice: "That's interesting, talk some more about that."

Arlene: "Well, I think that the understanding of Revelation is that it was meant for a community [that] was struggling. A struggling community that was being persecuted, and this was the language that was being used. It was a language to give them hope."

Felice: "What is the Second Coming, then? I mean, you are bringing up some issues that I never really thought of as far as the Kingdom of God so, . . . I mean, some churches that I have been to teach that the Kingdom of God is the Second Coming. And just those people who are perfect will be able to enter this wonderful kingdom."

Carol:"To me it's just when life is going to—when the brokenness is going to be healed."

Arlene: "Reconciliation. And we'll really see God in each other. I think that's where we will really see God. Not that there's going to be this thing, and we'll say, 'Oh look, there's God over there.' I really think that God has a purpose for the world, and that is what we're kind of struggling toward."

After a couple of hours of theological talk, the women discuss shared rides to the retreat site and "what to bring." "Well," Carol says, "there's a list that we're supposed to have." "Yeah," Arlene, "we're supposed to have a hymnal." Someone adds, "Anybody who wants to bring stuff for helping with this research, you should bring it. I will bring the commentary. And don't forget your Tampax. We're all going to have our period. We've already discussed this. Everybody is going to be menstrual." There is lots of laughter; Arlene shakes her head.

The Issues Retreat on Racism

> The realm of God is and always will be a pretty mixed neighborhood.
>
> —Arlene Jervis

It is late January 1992, and the parking lot is filling again. Students and faculty make their way to the campus refectory to register for the 1992 all-campus issues retreat—this year, on racism. The theme is "Image of God—One in Many/Many in One." There are no plenary addresses on the agenda and no outside "experts" on the subject. The program is evenly divided between worship, small group reflection, and "creation sessions."

Students are offered a dizzying array of creative opportunities for expressing their feelings and exploring their thoughts about racism. Three drama sessions focus on three different biblical stories or themes: Creation, Babel, and Pentecost. Other choices include interpretive dance, poetry writing, storytelling, collage making, and creative meditation with clay. Other sessions are titled "Music: Brokenness and Healing through God's Word," "Journaling for Insight, Self-Care, and Change," and "Music in the African-American Tradition." Those interested in liturgical statements can explore "anti-bigotry prayer." "Extroverts" who are not comfortable with traditional forms of prayer can meditate through multimedia. Students or faculty members lead most groups.

Opening Worship

Sunlight plays across the seminary refectory floor. In a large center area—a twenty-foot circle formed by a pressing, mostly white, crowd—diverse actors jump and twirl to a cacophony of sounds. David Parsons is dressed in bright African robes. As he careens around the perimeter, he exposes a well-muscled calf in energetic kicks. Two African students in tribal dress punctuate the dance with drumbeats and responsive chants. Simultaneously, several Korean women in intricately embroidered silks sway to the strains of harp and ching.

This dramatic invocation, entitled "Primeval Chaos," concludes with a responsive reading: "And God saw everything that God made, and behold, it was very good." Then there is silence. Slowly, the chords of an African-American spiritual are heard, and an a capella tribute to God as Mighty Spirit fills the room. This is the "Good Creation," according to the printed order of worship.

Suddenly, the scene shifts. The Good Creation is disrupted. The drum, harp, and ching make discordant sounds as an account of Babel is read: The people of the earth set out to build a tower to the heavens to "make a name for ourselves," and the Lord acts to "confuse their language, that they may not understand one another's speech." The liturgist, Dean Park, instructs the congregation to shout at one another, in their native languages—spoken or signed—"Babel! Babel! Babel! Babel! A name for ourselves! A name for ourselves! A name for ourselves!"

A black woman walks to the center of the circle and begins to sing, "Sometimes I feel like a motherless child." The congregation grows quiet. Then a black-haired woman in pale pink moves slowly in a Korean Han dance, guided by taped oriental music. The woman's face is impassive; her flowing arms and hands are expressive. The worship order says that *han* means sorrow and pain.

The final scene is Pentecost, and the liturgy states that this event restores the Good Creation. The account from Acts is read aloud: "And there appeared to them tongues as of fire, distributed and resting on each one of them . . . and [they] began to speak in other tongues." Everyone is urged to call out "Christ is Lord"— first in English, then in different languages, and finally all together. One voice, many voices: African dialects, Korean, Spanish, throbbing drums, clanging cymbals, and the fluid motions of American Sign Language. As the English-speaking majority joins in, the room vibrates with sound, energy, and motion. No voice dominates now.

In the last days it shall be, God declares, that I will pour out my Spirit upon all flesh, and your sons and your daughters shall prophesy, and your young men shall see visions, and your old men shall dream dreams . . . ," the people proclaim. After reciting the Lord's Prayer in many voices, worship ends in affirming song:

We are one in the Spirit; we are one in the Lord . . .
And we pray that our unity may one day be restored.
And they'll know we are Christians by our love, by our love.

As the final note fades, people—standing or sitting—hold the hands of their nearest neighbors.

People leave the worship circle slowly. Later, in a reflection group, an older woman remarks on the power of the service. She says she was particularly moved when "Christ the Lord" was shouted in many languages. Her comment leads to a discussion about the value of distinctive cultures and languages. Doreen Clark, a third-year student, who organized a successful black student campaign to remove a pale-skinned Nefertiti doll from a donor display her first semester, asks why it is necessary to give up other languages to be American. As a black woman, she is saddened by the loss of African languages. The student facilitator of the group, an ash-blond, thirty-something man in jeans and a sweater, says, "We ought to be a melting pot." Doreen looks askance and says, "Well, most of the time it's more like a salad bowl: Toss on top twelve black people for our benefit."

Reflecting on Racism

Reflection groups meet twice during the retreat, once on Friday morning after the opening worship and again on Saturday morning before the closing worship. At the first, PM sits with a group of thirteen students, mostly in their second and third years, and Tory Campbell, professor of preaching and worship. After introductions, handouts are passed around. One includes several lengthy definitions of racism as discussion starters; the other is a flyer for a Martin Luther King holiday service sponsored by area churches.

Students look over the definitions, some of which characterize racism as:

- "the use of power to isolate, separate, and/or exploit others."
- "pervasive, insidious, affects entire societies."
- "having the power to carry out systematic discriminatory practices through the major institutions of our society."

Group members informally share their responses to or experiences with racism. A second-career student engaged in an inner-city ministry to children and senior adults tells about facing racial discrimination in the United States civil service system. He says, "You don't realize what's going on around you." An older student, a candidate for a second master's degree at MTS, talks about his experience with Native Americans: "It was sick; the way they were treated was less than human. . . . Power is really the issue; being born into the power class, white and male." Another student speaks up: "[When] I worked with the state employment service . . . I noticed that they would call a white man 'sir,' and a white woman 'Mrs.' or 'Ms.,' but a black man or woman, they would call by their first name."

A first-year student in a pastel sweater and gray pants says his father's church hired the "first black minister to pastor a predominantly white church in [the state]." This means some things are changing, he states. A third-year student working in a rural parish shakes his head and tells this story:

> I moved to [his area] from [a large city]. The racism is almost worse, but you don't see it. [Blacks and whites] mix in the schools, but they all live in separate neighborhoods. There are two churches in the area, one black and one white, and they do things together like hymn sings and dinner on the ground. I was eating with three sweet little old ladies and one asked another, "Whose idea was it to invite the dark people?" The other lady shushed her. And it kind of scared me. Of course they're not the kind to burn a cross or do anything overt. But it was so pervasive in them, though with a veneer of sweetness and respectability. It's a cancer.

Doreen thinks a minute and responds, "Well, it's a valid question. I wouldn't consider it racist." Another group member interrupts, "Except this tone . . ."

Then Doreen tells the group that she had asked a similar question when her maternal grandmother died. Among the mourners were some white people. She asked her mother, "Who are they? Why are they walking around this house?" Her mother replied, "They're your kinfolk." Well, Doreen says, "that ended that." Her grandmother's father was white, and her great-grandmother was Native American. Doreen says that was a real revelation for her: "I have to deal with that myself. I have to free myself up from prejudice. I still have problems with white people. [But] we're all kin when you look at it."

The conversation turns to relationships at MTS. The older woman says she had reservations about this retreat because she remembers another, known as the "racist" racism retreat, four years earlier. "I sat down at lunch, and I was the only white woman at a table of black seminarians," she says, "and I knew that I was not wanted." Doreen looks at her and nods her head slowly: "Uh-huh. I've come to the point that it's all right for me to be black and you to be white. But you have to remember what that means." After a few minutes of uncomfortable silence, Campbell dismisses the group.

The reflection group reconvenes on Saturday morning. Much of the debriefing focuses on the Friday "creation sessions." The new editor of the evangelical column in the *MTS Journal* alludes to the Sarah Kent lecture last year and comments that the retreat was "more unifying this time." He likes the emphasis on the "affective domain, the heart." This single, middle-aged man went to a drawing session and said it was a powerful experience. He drew a "risen Christ weeping over a fence standing between a black and a white person." The fence in his picture represents the church. He concludes, "That symbol of racism will stick with me for the rest of my life."

A young black student says it wasn't so easy for him to draw because he is "not artistic" and was ashamed even when told to just "let it flow." But another student, a woman, "helped me out," and "I put mine [his art] with the others and somehow it blended. It wasn't as bad as it looked." Separated, it looked ugly; in the group, it seemed to fit. Several people commented on the power of seeing the beauty of diversity in unity.

Near the end of the conversation, the older student pursuing a second MTS degree comments on a session titled "Telling Our Stories." He says it was powerful, and he's "ashamed we don't do more [of it]." Another student, also in that session, agrees. He wants to "suggest it [doing more personal storytelling] to the administration." A tall, thin, bearded third-year student responds with some passion: "I don't mean to contradict you, but it's an issue of power. We don't need to 'ask permission' of the administration. We need to unify our own thoughts and efforts and then take it to the administration. We take the power." The older student responds, "It's not us over against the administration. . . . The group interested in storytelling ought to just get together and do it."

This discussion about organizing at MTS is followed by a brief closing prayer. Group members form a circle and hold hands. The facilitator asks if someone will lead. The person who volunteers prays for courage.

The Aftermath

The first issue of the *MTS Journal* after the retreat features a large, boldfaced announcement of "an ongoing dialogue on racism at MTS." "Look for signs around campus regarding our discussions as we attempt to address our concerns and plan action on this issue that is vital to our community," the notice says. Later that semester, a third-year student who is concentrating in urban ministry and was a regular at these dialogue sessions, tells PM that "it's mostly white students."

A reflection group involving Professor Betty Trotter has continued to meet. The next week that group publishes a list of "individual resolutions" in the *Journal* "in order both to make our commitment public and to encourage others in the community to keep the graces of the retreat going." Resolutions cited include: "to have at least one thoughtful conversation a week with a person of another culture"; "to get to know more about the many backgrounds of at least one person"; "to continue journaling about racism"; and "to be a part of the voice of passion against racism from the majority side."

In the February 3, 1992, issue of the *Journal,* the seminary's Council on Racism "invites all in the MTS community who have experienced racism to share the nature of their experiences in an *MTS Journal* format." The group seeks "stories of hurt and healing; of being held back and moving ahead; of despair and hope." The only qualification, they say, is "that you are honest with yourself and wrestle in the article with issues of racism."

The invitation is accompanied by articles from two members of the council. One begins, "What do I do, as a person traditionally associated with power? I'm white, male, middle-class, Western, and Eurocentric. . . . I agonize over considerations such as when to speak and act, and when to be silent and listen." The author concludes, "I must risk receiving the anger of the very people I am trying to hear and change for and with. I know also that I must risk the anger and rebuke of the systems of power into which I fit."

The other article, "Reflections on our Judeo-Christian Heritage," starts with a story. The author explains that she was in chapel last fall when Ben Somers was officiating. In his communion prayer, she writes, Somers said, "We, who are the children of Abraham and Sarah . . ." The student says that she could not hear any more and that within a few moments, "I began to weep." What was so upsetting? The primary feeling, she recalls, was that "he's not talking about me." She felt "excluded from the community." Although she knew, she continues, that the statement referred to "our Judeo-Christian heritage," that did not help "because I couldn't get beyond the matter of race and class in the biblical story. . . . I could not dismiss the thought that persons of African ancestry had, to a great extent, been 'shafted' in the Eurocentric biblical interpretation, and to some extent here at MTS. This was yet another moment of cognitive dissonance."

Mitch Tabor is the only person who takes up the challenge to address racism. The next week, his article "People of Color" is front-page copy:

> When I first heard this new title [people of color], I sort of took it in stride. This was another label that the Euro-American power structure used to keep its supremacist ideology intact. Besides, "People of Color" is not so abrasive. It doesn't have the negative overtones such as "nigger," "spic," or "chink." And it is also very inclusive; you don't need to say Latino, Asian or Black—just lump them all together as "People of Color"; they will get the message. The one thing that really perplexes me is that with Euro-American hunger for power and control of human destiny, how could they

afford to be left out? Isn't white a color? Are white people truly colorless? If so, then we the "people of color" are really in a fix. Because if we as Christians (of color) abide by the Golden Rule, then it's our bounden duty to somehow, someway, get these poor souls some color.

Then Mitch goes on to write about marketing "skin melanin" and legislation to make "out-of-season 'sun tanning' a secured benefit in each health plan." In closing, Mitch says, "WE AFFIRM THAT ALL PEOPLES ARE PRECIOUS IN THE SIGHT OF GOD AND SHOULD NOT BE DEPRIVED OF CERTAIN INALIENABLE RIGHTS, THOSE BEING LIFE, LIBERTY AND PURSUIT OF COLOR." And as a kind of postscript, he adds, "Don't delay!!! Don't be excluded in this new age of inclusiveness!!!!" After the serious, confessional tone of the retreat and the pronouncements that followed, the campus had a big laugh. James Englehardt says later, "Only Mitch could get away with this." No other articles on racism appear during the semester.

The MTS Pattern

[I]t's been exciting to watch my passions grow and change.

—Sharon Paige

Sharon Paige is a wife, a mother, a full-time seminary student, and an artist. At age sixteen, Sharon recounts, she attended a service of ordination, and at the close the minister asked "young men" to come forward to dedicate themselves to Christian ministry. She sat still, of course. The preacher then asked for "young men and women to come and dedicate themselves to church-related careers." And Sharon remembers that "for some reason, I found myself walking up. I mean I just had to do that." She was brought up in the church, baptized as an infant, and later confirmed like most of her friends. So this act, Sharon concludes, "is my version of the altar call."

Sharon majored in religion at a small liberal arts college, but when it came to church-related careers for women, "all that was available was being a director of Christian education." She says she lacked the gifts (or interest) for that role. She married and moved to Hawaii, where her Navy husband was stationed. After military service, her husband, Robert, "wanted to come to seminary to sort things out." The Paiges moved to MTS so he could enter the Master of Arts in Theological Studies program. Robert finished in a couple of years, and they moved again when he took a government job.

During this time, when she was raising two young sons, church and another interest—quilting—occupied her "free" time and provided considerable meaning. Church involvement was always a part of Sharon's identity, but the quilting tapped an affective, feminine, and spiritual part of her. She was chair of the worship committee of her congregation and a lay representative at her denomination's judicatory level. Eventually, she combined her passion for quilt making with a love of liturgy, theology, and Scripture and became a freelance liturgical artist.

Sharon talks about the way quilting has educated her and how it prepared her for the ministry. In an interview at her home, she shows PM a series of quilts and talks about the process of creation. About one, she says: "What I was trying to do here was struggling with light and dark. Trying to talk about darkness, and also doing some meditating work [around] seeing God as much in the darkness as [in] the light. [Thinking about] darkness as night where you see things as opposed to the blinding light of the sun." Her work on the quilt is really a way to "deal with racism," an effort she started before arriving at MTS. "Instead of talking about light as your ultimate good," Sharon continues, "[I was] trying to find beauty in the darkness . . . trying to find people in darkness."

Art and life frequently merge for Sharon. She was finishing a quilt filled with Marian images, which she describes as "about newness," when she ran into an old friend, one with whom she had answered the altar call to Christian service at age sixteen. This male friend had gone into the ministry, and he encouraged her to follow her early dream. Sharon explored the idea with her husband, who was supportive. The family moved so that she could attend MTS.

PM asks Sharon, "If you were going to image your movement through MTS, what images come to mind? How would you quilt something like that?" Without hesitation, she says, "It would have to be growing and coming alive kinds of images." Sharon cuts a long horizontal piece of paper, gathers her colored pencils, and sketches a quilt pattern of her journey through seminary. She talks as she draws the first-year segment:

> [It's] like a timeline . . . contained and together with some little sparks at the beginning before I start. . . . Okay, now we're going to be getting into seminary here. . . . Then there's going to be some kind of murky stuff as I got started and wasn't sure and as I was frustrated with these huge classes. And the fact that I felt I wasn't being heard. . . . That's it. I'm boxed in. That's me. But I was being excited by what I was learning, so it wasn't total. . . . I would put some little bright lame stuff in there and a few odd lines because it's not all negatives by any stretch. Mostly first semester. My second, we get to my Psalms class, and I start to wake up.

The first panel is all regular geometrical figures: rectangles, squares, triangles that fit together just so. The initial colors are dull browns and dark greens, and Sharon colors "herself," a little square box in the middle of it all, purple and brown with a bit of bronze. Toward the end of the panel, an irregular rectangular box bisects the panel at a dramatic angle. Here she writes some Hebrew letters representing a Psalms class with Mary Miles. Sharon's quilt design seems also to fit the experience of other students.

Remembering the First Year

A group of five graduating seniors, including Sharon, meet with PM and DA to talk about their experiences at MTS. Memories of orientation vary. Linda Lewis is not sure how important orientation was. "I didn't really feel that it formed community, and I think that was part of the intention," she says. Another student only recalls being "packed in" the large classroom in Dunavant "to watch television sets," and he remembers the film *Places in the Heart*. Terrence Nunnally follows that up: "I remember that some guy in my small group said after we watched *Places in the Heart* that he couldn't relate to any of the people in the movie because nobody was a functional white male."

They also remember settling in and going to classes. Among the initial concerns from on-campus students were dorm conditions and a lack of refectory service at night. Social life, on the other hand, is remembered positively. Jenny Sherrod mentions the women's Bible study group. For four of these students, Mission and Ministry was the most important experience of the first year, although the course was not easy for them. At first, Jenny Sherrod remarks, "I hated it. Felt like an idiot every time I left, but to look back on it—it was formative."

Tommy Reiss talks about the Mission and Ministry class with PM and DA in another small group meeting: "I remember the first Mission and Ministry class; we went through seven weeks of disconcerting hell." And it was David Parsons who made the most impact on him: "He offered prayer for the midterm, and I don't remember what he said but I just remember the gentleness of it, and I was really touched." Tommy mentions a quality of Parsons that many other MTS students emphasize: "When he would stand there and tell the class the problems he had with white people, and all the pain that he had suffered in racism, I came to realize how much I had played an unwitting part in that. I came to understand things that I had always rejected before, and that was very opening to me."

The "disconcerting hell" of Mission and Ministry is discussed at length by a group of black students with PM over dinner. Doreen Clark says, "Well, I thought Mission and Ministry, that first session of M&M, was the most ridiculous course I have ever had. There were all of these foreign terms that I had never heard of in my life. I mean, talk about God and economy and all of this. . . . I felt lost. I felt stupid." An older, male student pastor recalls, "There was some racist tension because some students complained to the dean about Parsons. They were saying his teaching was so above their head but, you know, Harriet Hercon was teaching the same class."

A second career commuter student—who admits to never really finding his "place" at MTS—recalls that issues of race "undermined" the class his first year:

Harriet read a poem one day, evidently by a black female student, and the poem praised black and condemned white. The black came first, and black is beautiful, and black is rich. White is cold; white is ice; white is hard. And when she finished reading that poem, there was just stone cold silence. I think a lot of the white students were blown away by the antagonism reflected in the poem, and I thought, oh my God.

Leticia Payne, the woman who wrote the poem, was so frustrated with the racism at MTS that she left after the first semester. The curious thing, this student observes, is the absence of such tension in a course on racism he is now taking, and "there are a lot of black students" in it.

Betsy Spring, another third-year student, an artist and currently the pastor of a rural congregation, gives her interpretation of the tensions in Mission and Ministry the first year:

I saw the anger. It was very painful, and I thought, why are they doing this at the seminary? Here we had the model. We were working together, and they are destroying it. . . . And then suddenly, I realized that this was the safe place to let all of that out

. . . that we could be trusted to absorb that pain and help them to work it through. And then, in a sense, grow also. . . . So I came full circle with that. But it was a very painful road for me.

The first year was full of "murky stuff"—things got stirred up, and there was a certain lack of clarity. The settling period came more quickly for some, such as white on-campus students and student pastors.

Like Sharon, many students say they felt "boxed in" because of a lockstep curriculum, the demands of their families and jobs and, in the experience of some black students, the need to adjust to a white majority religious culture. Second-career students, especially, did not like the "huge classes. I felt really alienated by the structures in which you sat in large classes and had stuff handed to [you]," says Sharon. "I was used to being in control of my life. I wasn't in control of anything." Married students struggled to "help the family settle into the new." Sharon remembers:

My favorite story about that is I am studying for an Old Testament exam and one of the little terms that we had to learn was "murmuring motif"—like the murmuring in Egypt . . . when they murmured in the wilderness. And the night before the exam, I sit down at my dinner table and my son says, "Why can't we move back to Seattle where people are kind? [where] I don't have to deal with these horrible [local] people?" I said, "Murmuring motif."

Commuter students talked about the same tensions. A third-year M.Div. candidate, a full-time youth minister, recalls: "I had to resign myself to the fact that I was going to do my full-time job, and I [had] to be a father and a husband. . . . [M]y life was compartmentalized so that I did only seminary here [on the campus]."

Commuter students also had trouble fitting MTS worship experiences into their schedules. But for on-campus students and those in the student pastor track, chapel services were important. They liked the style of Trudi Darsa, who was the elder of the chapel at the time. Arlene Jervis says, "I mean, chapel was like a lab, really. You always learned something." She saved all her worship bulletins. Students borrow ideas from the chapel services. When PM attended Easter services at the parishes of students that year, two student pastors used versions of a "Remembering Our Baptisms" ritual from the first chapel service of the fall semester.

Daniella Byrd, a soft-spoken black woman with large, expressive eyes, also comments that chapel felt like a class, but this is not a positive thing for her. Limiting worship to an hour was problematic: "I don't feel that you can box the Holy Spirit up and do a good worship in an hour." Doreen Clark adds, "I always feel kind of apologetic when I walk into chapel." Four other students nod their heads. Doreen says that she has never felt included in worship services, and part of the reason is an attitude that if you don't do it their way, you're not doing it right. So she seldom went to chapel after the first semester, she says.

The end of the first year, a graduating student told PM a story about a conflict between Trudi Darsa, in her role as chapel elder, and certain black students. An African-American worship service had been slated for the spring semester. Darsa involved some black students in planning that special event. As the story goes, the students wanted an all-black gospel choir to sing for the service, and Darsa insisted on the chapel choir (which is mostly white). Her grounds were "inclusiveness."

For other students, the inclusiveness of chapel was significant. A female student pastor and active choir member remembers "a real diversity reflected in the services" the first year. She recalls a point in a particular worship service when "the sopranos were singing their part and the tenors and basses singing their part and the deaf ministry people were signing. . . . I just looked around and watched all of these people doing their own thing, and it all came together so beautifully." That is "one little vignette," she concludes, "that will stay with me forever about the strength of diversity and the beauty of diversity."

Remembering the Second Year

In the interview at her home, Sharon continues to sketch her MTS quilt into the second year. She talks as she draws: "Now that we're over here, [I'll] try to get some stuff going . . . a few more angles. These are a little less predictable, a little more exciting, a little zippier."

Other conversations with students reflect similar patterns. Doreen Clark says, "I think the second year for me was getting more into the groove of things. Getting more into the routine of things; more into what I needed to do to hang in." She was named to a committee to shape an inclusive language policy and found her voice as a part of that group. She argued that the black community at MTS could not afford to let the issue of inclusive language for God divide black women and black men.[1]

Doreen says that "the blacks at MTS really have been on the cutting edge, pushing the institution to be what it is supposed to be—and what it thinks it is in terms of pluralism, diversity, inclusiveness, and so forth." But being on the cutting edge, Doreen adds, means that "sometimes you bleed and you don't realize it." The debate over race at MTS helped Doreen "in recognizing my own blackness because I looked for what was missing." Other black students conclude that the talk about diversity and inclusiveness built black solidarity and highlighted the fact that the institution is still predominantly white. "Regardless of what happens, we need to stick together, period," says a black student pastor.

White students, especially student pastors, struggle with other issues although some dynamics are similar to that experienced by black students. Boyd Arthur says he really struggled with negative attitudes about white males at MTS. "What really hit me was the Mission and Ministry class. . . . Because for the first time in my life I really felt people were pointing fingers at me [for] being white and male." He had a family and a full-time job as a youth minister in a suburban church, so it was easy for him to "duck and cover." In the spring of the second year, however, everything changed. Boyd reports that the third year of Mission and Ministry, called "The Global Church" and led by David Parsons, "caused me to look at my motivations in ministry."

He started teaching his church youth about justice issues. Now, he says, "We've got a totally different youth group." The young people do not want parties for themselves anymore, and he is concentrating on more than numbers. He tells about how his young people gave a party for residents at a local convalescent home and "adopted" an elderly black man, an amputee. They even raised money on their own and bought him a television set. Arthur's eyes shine: "They turned me completely around."

"The core of where I really am is stronger," says Jim McClaren. He sees his MTS experience "as a challenge of faith, in one sense, without a loss of faith." Much of what he got came "from late-night sessions." Asked by PM about the content of those conversations, he replies, "Well, we have done women's issues, and we've done sexuality issues in the middle of the night. We would come out of a class and somebody would say, 'I felt abused,' and we'd talk about that." There were conversations about the Atonement, the Bible, and child abuse, and always freedom to agree or disagree, without pressure to "accept each other's perspective."

Tommy Reiss nods his head in agreement. "That speaks to a truth . . . that it has been more liberating to be heard than to hear." He is convinced that at times he—as a white male—has not been heard. Sometimes, he says, people seem to assume that "I want them to believe like I believe, and I don't [want that]. I just need to be heard."

Finding a group or place where one can be heard is a common theme in the second year, according to the students' reflections. Arlene Jervis and Jenny Sherrod find that place in their congregations. Others, such as Sharon Paige, find it through Third World immersion experiences and, increasingly, in classes. And a few students, including Mitch Tabor and James Englehardt, find that experience through a combination of church, fieldwork, and classroom.

Sharon continues to sketch the quilt pattern. The middle section of the timeline is taking shape. The angles are sharper, more defined, almost jarring. "Mexico comes in," she says, "and then Israel takes off from there because it was very much some of the same things." Sharon shades in a brilliant elongated triangle of red, orange, blue, gold, and green that bisects the paper dramatically. This represents the student-organized immersion trip to Mexico. Connecting spring 1991 with fall 1991 is another triangle representing her summer trip to Israel, with dark green for the Palestinian flag, black and red for Palestinian women's dresses, and gold for the desert.

She talks about several vital connections she made during the second year. Although Sharon found her "voice" in the Psalms class, that voice took on richer meaning through a Hebrew course the following summer. "I would be so excited I couldn't study the last thing before I went to bed or I couldn't sleep at night." In January she went to Mexico and saw liberation theology in action in base communities. Inspired by that experience, she designed special paraments for MTS's chapel. The next summer she toured Israel with an MTS program. Sharon says that both trips stressed social justice concerns that she had always passionately held. However, connecting those concerns with artistic and biblical issues was new for her.

Tommy Reiss says that his "overriding sensation" in the second year was "that the magic was gone. . . . What's happening is a new vision. It's a vision of the end of the tunnel, but it's also a vision of the ministry. . . . [T]he tools that have been in the box for the first four semesters [are] starting to come together."

One third-year student connects a "loss of vibrancy" to the departure of Harriet Hercon. After the former dean left, what helped this student, she says, was Susan Johnson's course in feminist theology. "There was just lots of celebration of who we were as women," she recalls. Susan Arch had originally been in the student pastor program but dropped out because of conflict with lay leadership in her rural church. "I just felt beaten down," she says. Experimentation with women's ritual and frank discussion of women's issues provided the healing she needed.

The Third Year: The Gospel According to MTS

Sharon talks as she draws a chaos of fine, dark lines, many intersections, and then colors them in quickly with a rainbow of colors. She explains:

> And the image that gets started on this last paper that I am dealing with is the image of the spiderweb. I like spiders because they're spinners and weavers. . . . I'm trying to do something that would express some of the interconnectedness of the experiences that I am now having. That should happen at the end of an education—the way that my concern for social justice intersects with the longing for working with biblical images . . . [making] connections between the biblical story and our story today.

Sharon is graduating from MTS this spring, and she has been accepted into a doctoral program in Old Testament. She sees her time at MTS as a "growing and expanding" period. She says, "I am doing things that I didn't think I could do, [but] the kernel was [always] there."

Reflecting on their MTS years, several student groups toy with a question put to them by DA: "What is the gospel according to MTS?"

"The good news is justice for all," Arlene Jervis says.

"Diversity," another student states.

"Appreciation," Arlene adds. "Whether we actually see that and live it or not, that's still the message."

A graduating student who has lived and worked on campus for most of the three years offers: "Why don't we just have an eleventh commandment, 'Thou shalt not offend'? Because [not] offending people, [not] wounding people's sensibilities regardless of whether they're black or white or conservative in theology, here, seems to be the only thing that really matters." Terrence Nunnally, another campus resident, calls this MTS trait "peace-agree." Many things never get dealt with here, he explains, because people are concerned about harmony, unity, and a kind of inclusiveness that really excludes people.

Peter Tomas, who dropped out of the M.Div. program and switched to the Master of Arts in Theological Studies program, says he does not like "inclusiveness." When PM presses him on what he means, Peter says, "Inclusiveness implies, somehow, that there's room for everybody, but there's not room for everybody in that tent because some people have more power than other people have." He compares it to a "Republican big tent" and continues: "The tent has a name on it, and you have to go into it and kind of surrender all of these things at the door. And to me, that's 'inclusive.' It tends to mute diversity; it is tolerance without justice."

These students contend that diversity entails honest dialogue, something, they say, that is not always practiced at MTS. Peter illustrates: "For example, I know students who are gay, who will never talk about being gay. We are then not a diverse group by virtue of sexuality because there is a large body of people who have no sense that [such] diversity exists within our community." Peter says that he watches people's faces and "sometimes they disagree but they don't say anything. . . . Nobody wants to be called a heretic. Nobody wants to be called a racist."

Sharon Paige listens to Peter talk about his frustration with the notion of inclusiveness at MTS. PM asks, "What about you, Sharon?" She responds carefully, "I was wondering, are we simply dealing with a vision of the kingdom as the perfectly inclusive, perfectly diverse unity? And the fact that [in] every earthly kingdom our human structures always fail?" In that sense, she notes, there is an ongoing struggle over how people are left out or included. In the end, Sharon says, it is the struggle at MTS that students talk about as valuable, and it is the lack of honest, open dialogue—struggle—that they complain about as harmful.

In a group interview with four student pastors, Tommy Reiss talks about the relationship between diversity and inclusiveness at MTS: "We've got a racial rainbow here on campus; we have a rainbow of gifts, graces. . . . But I don't think that all the people on [each] end of the rainbow appreciate and are comfortable with the people at the other end." PM asks why. Tommy laughs. "Other than original sin?" he asks. Pressed, he continues:

> I think that part of it . . . I will speak for myself. I am more comfortable with folks who are different from me now because I have been exposed, I have dealt with some of their issues. I have heard some of their issues. I have felt some of their pain. I am in no way black. I am in no way female. I am in no way physically challenged. But I have been with people who are, and I am challenged by the reality of their experience to include [them] in my theology and in my ecclesiology and in my existential being.

Tommy says that he is thankful for the diversity at MTS; however, he adds, "I stop short of saying that I am inclusive because I am still not fully comfortable with the people who are wildly different."

DA asks why race, age, and gender seem to be the real points of contention at MTS. Tommy says he thinks it is a matter of awareness. Something becomes an issue at MTS because it is "made an issue," he observes. For example, he says that "denominationalism has not been an issue up to now." However, an ad hoc student group recently formed to protest a working paper on new concepts of fieldwork structure and supervision written by a new professor of practical theology. Many students are not of MTS's parent denomination and object to what they view as a strictly denominational approach to church-based student work. Will they continue to be "included" at MTS?

On the issue of homosexuality, Tommy adds, MTS is not truly inclusive "because denominationally, we are not ready to take a stand." So the issue is spoken around, with a pretense that gays and lesbians are not a part of this community.

What, in Tommy's view, is the gospel according to MTS? "I feel strongly that

MTS has given me the tools to work with, and to work on my own faith. . . . I think the seminary has given me a fuller understanding of, and an appreciation for, the gospel of Jesus Christ." He laughs a little bit and adds, "Now to me, the gospel of Jesus Christ is one thing; to other heretics, it may be another thing."

Another student pastor says that the "gospel according to MTS" is fairly simple: "There are two things. God does have a sense of humor, and it is possible to be good and dear friends with people who you disagree with theologically." He looks at the redheaded woman next to him and smiles warmly. "Carol," he says, "is one of the best friends that I have ever had, and we see eye-to-eye theologically on very little except that God does exist." She smiles at him and adds, "And God died on the cross." "Yes."

This admittedly conservative student pastor says, "My heart was set on going to [another seminary], and I was accepted, and I wanted to go there. I was all ready to go." But, he says, a problem came up about student employment, and further, "something just stopped me from doing it." He believes now that if he had gone, "I would [have been] with a whole lot of other people who thought like I thought" and "my views [would] have calcified." MTS, he concludes, "has been an exciting experience for me, and I am glad I came. I hope this is a kinder and gentler me than I would have been if I had gone to [the other school]."

Final Faculty Meeting of the Year

The last faculty meeting of the year takes place in early May in the board room, a recently renovated space that is both comfortable and attractive. The whole faculty can easily sit around tables arranged as a hollow rectangle. A side table holds refreshments. Some faculty members bring baked goods, and they are on the table as well. This Monday is a beautiful spring day, and flowering shrubs are visible through the large windows that span the entire wall opposite the door.

The academic dean and president typically sit at the end of the table closest to the only door into the room. Behind them, a combination bulletin board and white writing surface hangs on the wall. A few professors sit in the same place at every meeting; others take chairs next to persons with whom they entered or beside colleagues who greet them.

A full agenda awaits. The faculty must vote on recipients of student awards, approve the nominations for next year's committees, review plans for summer school, and adjust the class schedule for the next academic year. Action is also required on position announcements for two faculty vacancies and on a recommendation from the academic personnel committee regarding tenure for theology professor David Parsons.

The meeting begins with recognitions of faculty achievements, an opening feature at almost every faculty meeting: Mary Miles has a grant for archaeological study in Israel; Cynthia Binder and David Parsons have recent publications—one a contribution to a Bible commentary series from a feminist perspective, and the other a book on aspects of African theology. After congratulatory gestures and words, the meeting moves to consideration of draft position descriptions for two faculty vacancies. The vacancies were created when Ben Somers accepted a professorship at another theological school and Glen Fisher resigned to become the pastor of a prestigious congregation.

Attention turns first to a position description in Christian ethics. The draft is from the faculty personnel committee, working in consultation with the academic dean, and focuses the position on social ethics. Cynthia Binder begins the discussion by stating that one of the two positions must be filled by a "woman of color," and these position announcements should not be worded in such a manner that they discourage these women from applying. Oliver Wilfred and Matthew Lincoln respond that they think the drafts contain phrases intentionally worded so that women of color would not be discouraged.

Ralph Hermann, a black professor, interrupts to ask Binder whether by "woman of color" she means "black woman." Binder nods affirmatively. The draft description has been written with specific references to competencies that would complement those already present within the faculty. Roland Pritchard suggests that the ethics draft be revised using more general language so the description itself would not discourage potential candidates. The draft also includes a requirement for a Ph.D. degree, and someone asked whether this might deter minority candidates who might otherwise be qualified. Gerald Adcock speaks in defense of the Ph.D. stipulation in the document "because it reflected language of earlier position descriptions." David Parsons says, "If we want black women, why not state in the description particular areas they would address, such as womanist ethics."

This comment prompts Adcock to write notes while verbally agreeing to add "womanist ethics." He also suggests adding the statement "Ethnic/minority women are especially encouraged to apply." Pritchard again recommends that the specialization area be made more general, not more specific. Howard Street, who is also in ethics, says that he is uncomfortable with some language in the description because it suggests too much overlap with his own area. The academic dean ends the discussion by saying that the comments will be considered by the personnel committee in revising the position description.

The second faculty position is in church history. After comments about whether designation of a "research area" should remain, Mary Miles says, "My concern is that both position announcements say 'business as usual.' The descriptions feed Eurocentrism." In the midst of subsequent comments about the Eurocentrism of the second position description, Ralph Hermann says, "I want to ask a question." Then he makes a statement: "We need to make sure that this person is not brazenly, openly racist and sexist." Hermann makes it clear that he is talking about the faculty member now vacating the church history position, and he refers to comments made when that professor was interviewed for the job. Hermann says that Ben Somers, when interviewed several years earlier, expressed anger over the advantage recent women and black Ph.D. graduates had over recent white male graduates. Hermann takes this and other comments as indications that Somers is racist, and he expresses frustration that the seminary hired him anyway. Beth Dickerson looks straight at Hermann and says, "I find what you say libelous." Hermann responds, "I'm telling you, it happened."

The exchange is tense. "We need to move on," says Gerald Adcock, but Oliver Wilfred resists this procedural ploy. "One of our colleagues has had his character questioned," he says. Beth Dickerson asks Ralph Hermann for corroborating evidence concerning his accusation against Somers.

"There may or may not be corroborating information about what [Somers] had said," Hermann answers. "Others may not corroborate because people do not tell what they see." Again the dean calls the group to the next item on the agenda, and this time, conversation ceases. Cliff Mims, a departmental colleague of Ben Somers, leaves the room briskly at this point; he returns to the meeting room about ten minutes later.

The mood shifts as the faculty considers committee and program reports; a more subdued tone settles in. At this point, various faculty members make announcements or issue invitations to summer events.

Mary Miles asks whether the faculty wants to make a statement about the jury acquittal of the police officers accused of beating Rodney King and about the ensuing riots in Los Angeles. The members decide to send a common letter to the President of the United States and to denominational officials and theological schools in southern California. Howard Street suggests that the letter be circulated to students and graduates of the seminary. Gerald Adcock then asks for three volunteers to draft the text of the letter. Matthew Lincoln volunteers, but no one else does. Adcock asks Mary Miles and David Parsons if they, along with Lincoln, will draft the letter for the faculty. Dean of Students Park says that the letter should be translated into Korean, and Cynthia Binder suggests that Rick Santos translate it into Spanish as well.

The last item requires the deliberation of only tenured professors. Junior faculty members and administrators who attend faculty meetings leave at this time. A motion is formally placed before the senior professors that David Parsons be recommended to the MTS governing board for tenure and promotion. Roland Pritchard makes the motion on behalf of the faculty personnel committee. He reviews the materials Parsons prepared as part of the application for tenure and comments that he thinks Parsons has matured both as a teacher and as a scholar. Edgar Lampston, an African-American professor with many years of service at MTS, says that Parsons represents an "important bridge between Western theology and African heritage." Matthew Lincoln and Beth Dickerson both add positive words of support.

The faculty votes by secret ballot; the dean receives the ballots and asks two faculty members to help count them. The vote is unanimously in favor of tenure. Parsons, who had been excused from the room earlier, is summoned. Adcock announces the unanimous vote of the faculty, and the faculty applauds as Parsons returns to his seat in front of the windows. He smiles, and he nods to individual colleagues as they make eye contact with him. Several people sitting near Parsons stand to congratulate him. Three or four colleagues embrace him, then a kind of receiving line forms around Parsons. People shake his hand, offer congratulatory words, or hug him. The faculty then trickles out of the room.

Graduation

O God, you are like a weaver in our lives. Out of the expanding energy of creation
you have spun each of us into a unique, colorful strand with our own special hue and
texture; you have woven us together into a single family that blankets the globe.
—Call to Confession, Service of Word and Table, Commencement Day, 1992

May 11, 1992, is commencement day at Mainline Theological Seminary. PM
rushes to the 10:00 A.M. service of Holy Communion that is traditionally led by
graduating students. This year, the service takes on special meaning because many
students are unhappy with the selection of the graduation speaker, who is a member of the MTS board and a government official. A protest was raised earlier.
Holly Sturdevant wrote an article in the *MTS Journal* about the choice, calling it
predictably "male, pale, and stale." Jenny Sherrod and another female M.Div. student organized a petition drive to change the speaker. No change was made, although administration officials offered assurance that they would take the suggestions seriously in picking future speakers. For some, one student comments, the
student-led worship is "the real graduation service."

A third-year MTS student, soon to be a graduate, makes room on a back pew
for PM. He leans over and whispers, "Campbell said they only ran off seventy-
five," as he pushes his order of service into PM's hand. The chapel is full. There
are students, a few faculty members, and family members—children, husbands,
wives, mothers, fathers, and even grandparents.

The chapel is colorful, too. What must be Sharon Paige's paraments, the over-
flow of her Mexico immersion trip, adorn the pulpit, the lectern, and the table.
They feature stylized animals in primary colors on a white background. And there
are shiny kites suspended all around: stars, sunbursts, moons in whimsical geomet-
ric shapes.

The service bulletin is five pages long and was designed by Holly Sturdevant.
It has bold graphics: a stylized Aztec-like sunburst; a trio of ravens pecking at a
pile of bones; a descending dove with an olive branch; a group of men and
women, some working and others sleeping, in front of a communion table; the
figure of a woman standing with her arms reaching up toward the sky; and a
woman working at a table with paper and glue.

The Scripture reading is 1 Samuel 3:1–18, the call of Samuel. In a pantomime
of the text, an older woman student reclining on a makeshift cot at the front of
the chapel is disturbed three times by the call "Samuel, Samuel, Samuel." At first
she believes someone else is calling her—a fellow student, a friend—but she dis-
covers that she is wrong. Finally, this pink-robed Samuel realizes that the Lord is
calling her.

The story of Samuel and Eli, begun with the reading, becomes an ongoing part
of the service. Without warning, a voice calls over the public address system,
"Arlene, Arlene," or "Robert, Robert," or "Alice, Alice," and every time, the student stands and asks another, "Did you call my name?" And always, the student
replies, "No, I didn't call."

After a brief call to worship and a hymn, "This Is a Day of New Beginnings," the liturgist, a female M.Div. student, leads a call to confession: "When we are honest with ourselves, we must admit that there are times when 'our bones are dry, our thread of life is snapped, and our web is severed from the loom.' Let us confess together our separation from our truest selves, from our sisters and brothers, and from the Source of Life." The congregational response images God as a "weaver in our lives." Each person is unique, though woven together into a "single family that blankets the whole globe." Nevertheless, the reading continues, "we admit that we have rent the fabric of your design. We have allowed ourselves to be bound by the narrow contexts of race, age, sex, and ideology. Open our hearts." Then comes assurance: The liturgist continues, "God forgives us, encourages us, and frees us to love others. Thanks be to God."

The "sermon" for the morning takes the form of three meditations. The first, given by a second-career student, is entitled "Jesus Wept for Jerusalem." A tall African-American man with salt-and-pepper hair and wearing a dark suit begins by "praising God" for the opportunity to "pursue this field at this point in my life." He paints a vivid picture of "pain and suffering" in the cities and says that "Jesus looked at the city and he wept." But "Christ was in urban ministries," this minister continues. "He talked. He loved. He had compassion. He gave hope to those in the cities. . . . Let us be peacemakers. With God in my heart, I plan to be that urban minister that cares. May God bless us all in the Resurrection. Amen."

Alice West Chompa (recently married) smiles broadly at Terrence Nunnally. Terrence has a beautiful, mellow voice but is a bit shy about singing solo. For this special service, Jenny Sherrod and others have coaxed him into singing "On Eagles' Wings." Tall and almost elegant this morning in a white starched shirt, a multicolored tie, and slacks, the light catches his small, gold earring as he tilts his head and sings. The chapel is very, very quiet as he finishes, pauses, and sits.

Alice, wearing a white robe, preaches the second short sermon, "Valley of the Dry Bones," based on the biblical text of Ezekiel 37:1–14. She reads the text and tells a story from her first year at MTS:

> I remember my first year here, the last day of finals, I was sitting in the library working at my desk and a woman came in to take a test for Hebrew. She had just picked up her robe and her cap, and she came into the library with her cap on her head. She picked up her blue book and marched into the reading room, where she sat and took her test. [When she was finished] she put the blue book under her desk and burst into a joyful rendition of the Hallelujah chorus and marched out the door. And many of us here today have that feeling.

"We come to celebrate the amazing grace of God that has pulled us through when we didn't know if we could make it," she continues. "But we're just beginning our journeys." Referring to Ezekiel's vision, she says, "Everywhere you look, you will find people who feel like 'dry bones,' who don't know if they could make it another day." Such people, she says, "are all among us"—parishioners, people in the streets, children, and the poor. "We are called to prophesy because we have experienced the Spirit of God," Alice asserts, and "don't just stop with the bones." She ends with a call to put flesh on the bones—to change the system, to "prophesy to the institution" and cause social change.

The final meditation, "The Call of Isaiah," is given by a fiery African-American student pastor. He reads from Isaiah 6: "Then I heard the voice of the Lord saying, 'Whom shall I send and who will go for us?' And I said, 'Here I am, send me.' "

"Something happened to us when we came to MTS," he says in a booming voice:

> We came wanting a vision of God. And from my experience, I came with one idea of God but now God has opened my eyes and I see God for myself. . . . The Lord stayed the same, but everything looks different to me now.
>
> When Isaiah was called, he [said] that he was no different from the people whom he was called to prophesy to. He said, "Woe is me. . . . Lord, I am a racist. Lord, I am a bigot. Lord, I am a man. Lord, woe is me!"

But the Lord today, the preacher contends, "is shocking our perceptions so that we might get a hold of the beauty of God." This tall black man says he does not know who it was—it might have been Trotter or Hermann or Mims—but "they came and they touched our mouths," and "we are free now." Now, he says, "I can proclaim a word of God, to tell her people that there is good news. After all of this studying and all of this reading and all of these testimonies and all of this arguing and getting upset with one another, we say it's all over now. Have mercy. . . . I feel like the saints when they say something got a hold of me." He leans close to the microphone and says, "I hear voices saying, 'Here I am, Lord, send me.' But you know, once we get out there, we're the people of God. Yes, we are. Struggling to bring about God's kingdom." He reminds his listeners that even when "our dreams get crushed" the vision is there to cling to. "In the year that George Bush ran for reelection, I also saw the Lord. Amen!"

A song is sung in preparation for the prayers of the community. Then, spontaneously, people pray for the "gifts of our artists," for those "who taught us on the two immersion trips to Mexico," and for those in the student community as well as those in the church's ministry.

Heisik Park, dean of community life, is the celebrant for communion. A responsive prayer is read.

Dean Park begins: "We dream, O God, of community. But in waking hours we forget such hopes. Our dreams we call 'alien'; our sister and brother we call 'stranger.'

The people: "You call us by name. With arms outstretched as on a cross, you call us to yourself, and you name us your own people."

"Arlene, Arlene, Robert, Robert, Alice, Alice . . . ,' a voice booms. Soon-to-be graduates stand all over the chapel.

"Is that you, Lord?"

"Here we are, Lord, send us."

PART TWO

Culture and Educational Formation

TEN

Elements of Educational Culture

The two seminaries we have described and discussed differ along many dimensions used to analyze theological and religious institutions. Mainline Seminary's home is a tight ring of buildings in an affluent residential section of a large city; Evangelical Seminary is spread over a tract of more than one hundred landscaped acres in affluent exurbia. Mainline is affiliated with a single religious denomination, though it welcomes students and employees of all faith traditions as well as those with no formal religious ties; Evangelical has no links to a particular religious body but requires its faculty and staff to sign a specific statement of religious beliefs. The pattern of faculty training is different. All but one of Mainline's faculty members earned their doctorates in one of the two dozen historically Protestant private universities that offer advanced academic training in theological subjects.[1] More than half of Evangelical's faculty hold degrees from other kinds of institutions: European universities, public universities, and conservative Protestant seminaries. Although both schools attract students across a wide span of age, the student bodies differ too. Mainline's is dominated by students coming to seminary from other careers; Evangelical attracts many students within a year or two of their college graduation. And the experience of students in the two schools is different. Many students at Mainline move through their degree programs in the cohorts in which they entered, taking courses together in sequence and completing the program in a specified number of years. At Evangelical, where virtually everyone takes less than a full-time course load, students plot individual paths through the curriculum, with the result that those who enter together follow different sequences and finish at different times.

Even more prominent than these formal differences is the contrast between the religious views and values that characterize the two schools. On the bipolar, liberal-to-conservative scale that is frequently used these days to analyze American religion, the seminaries we studied are far apart. In choosing our research sites we were careful to select institutions that are *not* viewed as extreme examples of their theological position. A number of seminaries are widely judged to be more conservative than Evangelical and more liberal than Mainline. Nevertheless, on theological questions, such as whether biblical authority can ever be challenged or whether the salvation that Christianity promises is available through other religious traditions as well, the division is equally deep and neat: Most of those associated with Evangelical come down on one side, most of the denizens of Mainline on the other.

The theological and ideological differences between the two schools also show in many details of their educational programs and common lives. There is very little overlap between the sets of authors, primary and secondary texts, and journals and reference works that are standard for each institution. Each relies on a different group of publishing and religious goods companies for books, music, and other supplies. With a few exceptions (Billy Graham and Pat Robertson, Bishop Desmond Tutu and William Sloane Coffin), the names of the religious leaders whose activities are followed in each institution would not be recognized in the other. It is highly unlikely that any donor to one of the schools could be persuaded to make a contribution to the other, or that a local Protestant congregation that has hired a graduate of one would even consider an application from a graduate of the other. In most respects, these two Protestant seminaries operate in separate intellectual, religious, and social worlds.[2]

Yet despite the salient differences, the structures of the educational cultures of the two schools and the processes by which they accomplish their purposes are remarkably similar. *Structurally and functionally,* the two institutional cultures are very much alike. Even though they are knit into very different larger cultural fabrics, both schools do their work of forming the views, capacities and values of their students in the same ways.

In this chapter we describe the elements of the dominant and alternative cultures we found in the two schools. In the next we outline the process of formation that we think is common to the two cases.

A Central Message

Both institutions we studied have a normative goal, the stated aim of shaping students' capacities to accomplish certain ends and of forming their views and opinions in favor of some objectives and against others. As we have already indicated, the goals of the two seminaries are greatly different in substance and content. But they are structurally similar. Both rest on bedrock convictions about what a world conformed to God's wishes would look like and on critical judgments about how the world (and the church as part of the world) fails to live up to that ideal. Both are also enmeshed in patterns of behavior that are assumed to be consonant with the ultimate goal.

The goal of Evangelical Seminary is to bring a missing religious discipline to Christian and social life and institutions. God's plan for the world and the redemption of human life is an orderly and reasonable one that is inscribed in the Bible. The obligation of human beings, in return for the inestimable gift of salvation, is to learn that orderly plan and accept the grace that enables them to live by it.

Secular society and liberal Christians who have ignored the biblical plan for life must be shown its superiority to the human-centered principles they have endorsed. Even more pressing, evangelical persons, agencies, and churches must be re-called to observe God's covenantal plan; they have too often permitted the corrosion of modern technology and sentimental, self-indulgent piety to undermine the necessary discipline and order of truly biblical Christian faith.

Thus, students at Evangelical Seminary are taught the methods of rigorous study of the Scriptures ("tools" for the Christian life, in the words of the student graduation speaker), and they are shown and urged to adopt careful habits of life that are consonant with the noble plan that Scripture instructs them to observe. They are warned away from persons, ideas, and institutions that seem to have given in to humanism and the emotional excesses of revivalistic religion. They are urged instead to associate with colleagues and organizations that are disciplined in their manner of life and faithful to the tenets of a "reformed" faith that emphasizes God's supreme power, humanity's low and sinful state, and the authority of the Bible and its message of saving grace.

The goal at Mainline is also the reform of Christian and social life, but along other lines. In the regnant view at Mainline, the world and the church are missing not order and discipline but inclusiveness and justice. God's intention for the world is that all should have access to its resources—not only material resources but also intangible goods, such as freedom and equal regard. Structures and attitudes that deprive some groups of the goods to which they have a right are deeply sinful. Redeeming grace becomes available as prejudices are changed and unjust structures are replaced with others that require the inclusion and equal treatment of all. American society and the mostly white, middle-class mainline Protestant congregations that Mainline graduates will lead exclude and oppress many because of group characteristics such as race, gender, class, and sexual orientation. They require profound restructuring and reorientation, a "shatter[ing]" of "all fetters of oppression . . . [that we may] be freed from violence and from wrong, and be united in an eternal covenant of peace with all people everywhere. Next year in Jerusalem!" To a lesser extent, the denomination that sponsors Mainline Seminary is guilty of these same sins and thus requires restructuring.

To this end, students at Mainline are exposed to pluralism and challenged to confront their own deep prejudices and intolerance. Changed themselves by these proleptic experiences of diverse and just community, they will, it is hoped, lead their congregations, denomination, and other social organizations toward the peace, inclusiveness, and justice that God intends for all.

The cultural goal and the assumptions, fundamental convictions and patterns of behavior it entails form the *message* of each institution, a set of normative judgments and intents that play a central, organizing role in the school's common life and educational program. This message is not, of course, the only set of goals and associated values and ideas that gets aired in the school community, but it has a unique status: It functions as the pivot of the institution's culture, anchoring the culture and orienting the educational agenda.

The pivotal message was not hard to identify in either institution we studied. In both institutions it is widely acknowledged that there is a dominant cluster of views and values. The power of the dominant perspective is evident in the amount of everyday discourse about it and the tone of that discourse, in special attempts at humor, in official characterizations of the school. Its consequences for everyday life are repeatedly demonstrated in certain patterns of action, and it is negatively acknowledged in each school's taboos—the list of topics that are not mentioned, claims and ideas from which there is no open dissent, and forms of behavior that are not permitted.

At Evangelical Seminary the dominant view is named repeatedly. The label most frequently used to sum it up is "Reformed." Many informants—students and faculty members—volunteered the judgment (without our even asking whether there is a dominant view or approach) that the school is "overwhelmingly Reformed in orientation" or "very Reformed," that it has a "strong Reformed focus," and that the "faculty is fairly heavily Reformed." With some regularity, students and faculty also identify the seminary's emphasis on "cognitive" approaches.[3] Not everyone who describes these dominant motifs embraces them personally. Most speak of them with admiration and approval, but some feel constrained or even suffocated by the central emphasis on Reformed and "cognitive" ideas and values. Almost no one, however, belittles them; even the opposition is respectful. Perhaps the sole exception was the student named Len Temple, the "house deviant" who posted diatribes on the Iron Sharpens Iron bulletin board about the hypocrisy of the school and its academic norm, browbeat professors, and was asked to leave. And no one at all seems to question that Reformed motifs and "cognitive" methods and values are central in the school.

These two features of the pivotal message at Evangelical—the Reformed theological focus and the scholastic emphasis caught up in the term "cognitive"—are the target of a certain amount of nervous and respectful joking—another sign, we think, of their centrality. Students responded to Paul Bashford's announcement of his "different step" on baptism with a good deal of jittery banter about what is and is not Reformed. Graduates of a particular Christian college long associated with the seminary are described as "Reformed hit men." One of the Covenant House women gave BW a copy of a lampoon that had been circulating among students. (Sharing this satirical sheet, said the student, made her anxious. She feared she might somehow "get into trouble" for letting an outsider see it.) Beneath a picture of some faculty that had headed an advertisement for the school in various Christian publications, some students had affixed the following paragraph:

> What we can offer you at Evangelical: Professors fully committed to the inerrancy of Scripture and only occasionally committed to their own inerrancy; class registration and library privileges [at other seminaries in the area] at no additional charge (which is helpful since you will have had to mortgage your grandmother to come to Evangelical). Some facts about our faculty: Divinity degrees from Reformed Episcopal, Reformed Princeton, Reformed Dallas, Reformed Westminster, and Reformed Fuller; Doctorates from universities with names you can't even pronounce so you know they're good; Teaching experience in six seminaries and seven colleges (it's tough to get tenure these days).

Though the pivotal message at Evangelical Seminary is somewhat different from the representation of the school in publicity intended for a wider audience, the central dominant view is never contradicted in public settings and is often acknowledged. The dean, speaking at a celebration of the success of a seminary-sponsored off-campus program of a rather different flavor, says, perhaps for the benefit of faculty and trustees present, that the new effort is a combination of "solid, Reformed Presbyterian stuff mixed up with charismatic energy." Responding to a student who asks him why words and images have to be in conflict, Reg O'Neil, the visiting professor, told one hundred students who had come to hear him speak: "Here, in a Reformed and Protestant and biblical seminary, the world is arrayed against you and on the side of the aesthetic and the liturgical. Therefore we have to be iconoclasts. We cannot reconcile word and image short of the Lord's coming, or we will set up new graven images." The primacy of verbal expression and the inadequacies of pictures are major themes of the dominant message at Evangelical.

The dominant message entails certain ways of acting as well as thinking. "I can not only learn from them academically," says one student of admired faculty members, but "also from the whole life aspect." The "whole life aspect" of the dominant culture, which we will illustrate fully when we describe in the next chapter how the process of forming students works, includes reserved manners, relatively formal dress, dry humor, minimal decoration, traditional religious art and music, traditional art generally, strictly regular church attendance, lifelong marriages, children (often many of them, and sometimes schooled at home), and restrained styles of prayer and other religious expression. All these features bespeak the unvarying theme of the dominant message: The studious, Bible-centered Christian life, from which the inestimable reward and satisfaction of glorifying God is to be gained, is very hard work.

Finally, the status of the central message is signaled in the absence of open contradiction. A number of students and a few faculty at Evangelical are not hesitant to say that their views do not fit the Reformed profile. Some also object openly to some features of the "cognitive" approach, especially what they take to be its neglect of practical problems and its insistence that all theological teaching proceed by rational argument. But the core of the Reformed ideology—that God's plan for the world is inscribed without error in the original autographs of Scripture, and that intense and careful study of the somewhat corrupt version available to us can uncover a great part of that covenantal plan—is never challenged. Even self-proclaimed "heretics" like Pentecostal student Trent Lee see their view that the Holy Spirit continues to reveal God's plan in the present day as additive: Scripture is still inerrantly true and has priority. Likewise, students and faculty who think that "experiential" learning methods may be legitimate would not suggest that they replace "cognitive" ones. In fact, alternatives to the cognitive are usually presented as accommodations to individual limitations, as when Lois Boucher argues with Pamela that "the average Joe congregation member, the average me, for Pete's sake," cannot endure "hours and hours of lecture."

One core element of the central message may not be questioned in any form:

the inerrancy of Scripture. When a visiting lecturer who is held in high esteem by many faculty members says in a private meeting with faculty that he is "not a fan of inerrancy. . . . If I say I believe in it, I have to accept a great deal that other people mean by it," the faculty members challenge him with considerable passion. The guest says that he would prefer to say, "The Bible is true." The Evangelical Seminary faculty will have none of this. One counters with real vehemence: "You cannot throw out the concept because the word is misused."

Certain behavioral taboos are just as strong. Though, as we shall show, the educational process permits and at times encourages variations on approved ideas and patterns of behavior, there are clear limits. Avant-garde art (especially anything irreverent or scatological), angry or emotional interpersonal exchanges, extremely expressive religious behavior (for instance, speaking in tongues—that is, in incomprehensible syllables dictated by the Holy Spirit), and approval for sexual activity outside of marriage are never publicly displayed at Evangelical Seminary.

At Mainline Seminary the dominant message is introduced early and then regularly restated and reinforced. The message is that religious institutions should embody justice for all people and seek to transform human structures so that they are just and inclusive. "Justice for all people," says Trudi Darsa, is the one concept "everyone would affirm." She continues: "Put in theological categories, all persons are children of God and should have equal access to . . . housing, food, and the basic needs of life." Glen Fisher describes Mainline as concerned with "transformation of human social relationships in institutions." God's reign in the world would be evident if institutions—religious and otherwise—ceased granting privilege to some groups while oppressing others. The concern for justice leads to the considerable attention Mainline gives to two forms of injustice: racism and sexism. These kinds of injustice are overcome as people of all races and gender are included and given commensurate power in human institutions. Inclusiveness is the means by which institutions implement justice, and the resulting diversity is evidence that unjust aspects of the institution are being transformed.

Though "justice" is the central theological virtue at Mainline, daily life is focused on diversity and inclusiveness and the ongoing struggle to grant equal attention and power to diverse groups. In many ways, this effort, both at the seminary and in other institutions, is a political activity. Ben Somers thinks that Mainline presents students with many messages but that students would likely conclude by the end of their seminary careers at Mainline that the "gospel is political, not simply religious." Near the conclusion of her student tenure, Susan Arch reflects this view: "I am committed to peace and justice. . . . The social action task in the world is to heal the world though peace and justice." The dominant message is justice, but the dominant expressions of that message at Mainline are diversity and inclusiveness, reflected in language and activities.

Language, as Mainline student's manual states, "reflects, reinforces and creates reality." "Inclusive" language is a major emphasis of the dean's address to students in orientation: "Generous language . . . includes everyone, excludes no one." The dean also emphasizes the school's official policy about language from the student handbook. Inclusive language is the focus of campuswide debate during the second year, when retiring professor William Abraham Newman requests that the chapel choir sing a hymn he has written that contains male pronouns for God. Contra Newman, most people at Mainline believe that the pervasive use of inclusive language is evidence that a human institution is being transformed by the justice of God.

Exclusive language is often cited as a "taboo" in student interviews. The matter is so serious, in fact, that humor related to the topic of language is approached hesitantly. When a guest lecturer comments jokingly about the exclusive language for God in a closing hymn, the comment is met by an uncomfortable silence. Only after she remarks, "Won't these women ever be satisfied?" and laughs does the tension subside. Clearly, too, it matters who is the author of joking remarks. Women can make light of their own exclusion; African-Americans are free—to some extent—to joke about the terms of their marginalization (they can also admonish whites to "get some color"); but no one may make light of another's exclusion, and at Mainline, the burden of this prohibition falls most heavily on white males because they represent the one group that has least been excluded.

Language expectations are not the only way in which Mainline promotes its central message. The message about inclusiveness is evident in the way groups are formed and community life is ordered. Mainline faculty, administration, and students are vitally concerned about the representation of gender, racial, and ethnic groups in all community ceremonies (graduation, annual alumni gatherings, dedications of buildings), rituals (worship, religious holiday, inaugurations, memorial services), official publications (catalog pictures, the mission statement, the student handbook), and the composition of faculty, administrative committees, and other formal groups (the Community Committee, search committees, ad hoc groups). Mainline's course offerings and reading lists also reflect the emphasis on inclusion of various social groups. Inclusiveness at Mainline is construed to extend beyond the gender and racial/ethnic varieties. Diversity of denominations, inclusion of the physically handicapped, and, to a lesser extent, acknowledgment and inclusion of gays and lesbians are also valorized.

Social diversity is heavily promoted at Mainline. We came to call the promotion of diversity "matrix pluralism" because every cell created by crosscutting groups (African-American men, Hispanic women) must be filled. Any community rite, group, or policy that excludes the available variety at Mainline is open to challenge. A worship service focusing on African-Americans or Koreans, for example, must also include whites—although in less numerous and visible roles. Students worry that a dialogue group on racism is "mostly white," an informal discussion group "mostly male," a women's Bible study "all white," and the Association for Black Seminarians "all black." Members of a denomination with small representation among Mainline students raised concern when a discussion paper on new forms of field instruction felt "too denominational." Adequate diversity is recognized in its presence as well as its absence: many community events—especially worship services—are remarkable for the variety of their participants.

That Mainline is not as racially plural as it might be is cause for public lament. Faculty discuss the need for recruiting more Hispanic students. A gift of a Native American liturgical vestment to the departing academic dean occasions the admission that there are no Native American students at Mainline. Justice requires active promotion of the interests and perspectives of excluded groups, not just their presence and acknowledgment through care about language. The theology of liberation given prominence at Mainline posits a "preferential option for the poor," the view that God favors with special insight and other privileges those who have been unjustly deprived of their share of the world's goods. Because those who have been disadvantaged and deprived understand God's purposes with special clarity, Mainline emphasizes the necessity of openness to minority groups and willingness to make change on their behalf. Hence, the planning committee for the Asian issues retreat is restructured; the offending paintings in the "Risk and Integrity" exhibition are removed; and affirmative action policies are administratively enforced. Even with these efforts, however, members of the many minority groups are frustrated at how little the school and the denomination to which it is related actually succeed at including them and taking their views seriously.

Not surprisingly, given the pressures for change and the tensions built into Mainline's dominant message, "struggle" is a prominent motif of life at Mainline Seminary. Individuals struggle with the views, with unpleasant revelations about themselves, and with ideas about God, the world, and the church that challenge some they have previously held. Tommy Reiss muses, "I mean every day, every week I struggle to see God from the perspective of other people. . . . I mean it has been a growth experience. Not unlike the rack. I have been stretched." Just before graduation Boyd Arthur talks about his experience of Mainline as the first place where "people were pointing their fingers at me, about my prejudice."

The struggle is especially intense because the emphasis in Mainline's dominant message is on behavior and attitudes more than assent to doctrinal affirmations. It is not enough to *think* that justice is at the heart of God's will for the human family; one must deal justly with others. It is not enough for persons to *affirm* that racism or sexism is sinful; they must purge their patterns of speech and behavior of racism and sexism and figure out how to accomplish the same effect in the congregations and other groups they will eventually lead.

The difficulty of making institutions just is illustrated for students by the seminary's own struggles. When a new seminary finance director, for example, sends a memo to students describing a policy that will not permit them to enroll in classes until they have satisfied delinquent tuition bills for courses they have already taken, students complain to DA that the seminary advocates the interests of the poor but treats its own poorest members unfairly. Tensions built into Mainline's central message also contribute to the sense that "the struggle" is strenuous and difficult. Mainline values the uniqueness of each of its subgroups, including its right to remain somewhat separate in order to enhance its identity and power in the seminary community, but the seminary as a whole understands itself as a just community only to the extent that these groups are included as active participants on an equal footing. Such inclusiveness and equal regard are difficult to develop without some common views, but so much emphasis on group identity makes it difficult for common agreements to develop. A faculty member, commenting on the lack of progress in the faculty's effort to revise the seminary's mission statement, noted that "our attempts to write a mission statement last year suggest that we do best at identifying the *functional* character of our common work, and less well when we try to articulate *substantive* theological principles or impulses."

Different as they are in content, however, the central messages of Evangelical and Mainline function similarly. They project the most prominent intentions of the institution. They propound ideas and arguments that justify those intentions. They create a special argot that infiltrates serious discussion and casual conversation. They provide a map of the dominant culture's contours and boundaries, including its places of honor and forbidden territories. In all these ways, the central message of each school anchors the institution and provides a starting point and touchstone for its educational endeavors.

Variations

In both institutions, substantial variations on the themes of the dominant message are present. The central message in both institutions is central not only because, as we have tried to show, it has high status and the power to shape discourse but also because it occupies a mediating position among these variations. Some of the variations are looser versions of the dominant message that accommodate views held outside the institution. In both schools, one substantial variation is a stricter, purer, more orthodox version of the claims that the central message makes.

Thus the definition suggested by Professor Roy Parks of the sort of Reformed thought and outlook that is central at Evangelical is apt: "mild generic Calvinism." To liberal Protestants and indeed to many evangelicals, the Calvinist views that dominate the culture of Evangelical appear highly orthodox; but those perspectives *are* mild compared with the pristine and rigid Calvinism proclaimed by a small group of faculty and loyal student followers. Dubbed the hyper-Calvinists, hyper-Presbyterians, or Truly Reformed (sometimes shortened to "the TRs), these evangelicals insist that not only the structure of divine/human relationships but also the form of the church is dictated by Scripture. The approved form, they claim, is presbyterian—that is, governed by a body of ministers and elders who make decisions about doctrine and admissions to the ministry and who have supervisory control over individual congregations. The Truly Reformed also hang back from expressions of enthusiasm for missions, evangelism and other activities intended to foster conversions, because high Calvinism holds that God has already decided ("predestined") who will and will not be saved. And on *adiaphora*—matters that the dominant perspective has designated as open for legitimate disagreement—they take the most conservative positions. For instance, they strongly oppose the ordination of women as preaching ministers or as lay "ruling elders" in churches, and they make no concessions to either the theology or the expressive style of piety of charismatic evangelicals, who claim that they gain spiritual power and insight from searing encounters with the Spirit of God.

The counterweight to the purist Reformed perspectives is found in its most complete form outside the school, in its supporting constituencies. The segment of evangelicalism that sends students and financial contributions to Evangelical Seminary does want the authority of the Bible and basic Christian doctrines upheld, but it also incorporates ideas and practices that are anathema to the Truly Reformed. Its organizational structure is loose and informal. The tight denominational order that the TRs insist upon is not much in evidence. Many of the evangelical congregations that are linked to the school are independent (nondenominational), some loosely connected to each other by movement-style networks. Parachurch nonprofit organizations with missional or charitable purposes (for instance, campus ministry, abortion alternatives, and food and orphanage programs overseas) recruit many of Evangelical's students into the ministry and offer them positions when they graduate. These entrepreneurial churches and organizations, along with Christian businesses, political groups, and media ministries, all vie for membership and financial support. In this open market atmosphere, neither strict doctrinal orthodoxy nor the sober, reflective style of piety favored by the hyper-Calvinists find many takers. Sentimental art, music, and preaching, aggressive approaches to proselytizing, theological innovation, anti-intellectualism, and charismatic practices such as healing and casting out demons—all of which are rejected in the pure version of the Reformed vision—are widespread.

The dominant message at Evangelical Seminary comes down in between these two. Its position on forms of the church lines up with its emphasis on discipline and order, but it admits different kinds of order. Hence, spokespersons for the dominant view express special approval of local churches, which can set standards for admitting and disciplining members, and they voice suspicion of large parachurch organizations because they do not have such mechanisms. They do not, however, disapprove other systems—presbyterian or even episcopal—that have some system of discipline built in. In effect, they put the weight of the central message behind the legitimacy of diverse views about acceptable forms of the church.

Similarly, they enforce a policy of tolerating diverse strong opinions about the ordination of women. (The only positions that are ruled out on this question are those that insist that their view be adopted by all.) The dominant view also makes a place for missions and evangelism—activities that originated on the Arminian and revivalist side of Protestantism, which the Calvinists traditionally have opposed. "If Evangelical ever dips its flag on its commitment to missions," says Andrew Watson, a spokesperson for the dominant message, "we will have no right to exist." Roy Parks argues, contra his Truly Reformed colleagues and their fixed views of predestination, that human efforts to bring the gospel to others do count for something: "I want to make more room for Arminianism. They have some claim to the truth as well." More tentatively, the dominant believers permit some charismatically tinged activity, such as student vespers and the officially sanctioned student-led Monday worship in the seminary chapel. As Neal Huchett reported, the dominant view is warily noncommittal about Pentecostal theology: "Some are for it, and others against it," Roy Parks wrote in response to Neal's question about the school's position of the baptism of the Spirit, a Pentecostal teaching. In short, the message at Evangelical neither ratifies nor rejects the ideas and ethos of popular evangelicalism. The goal, at least the dominant one, is to send out leaders who can bring order and theological depth to evangelical institu-

tions without completely smothering the emotionalism and organizational loose-
ness that seem to make it vital.

Mainline's dominant message also comes down in between two poles. It advocates measures that would be judged radical by most members of mainline
churches, including its own denomination: aggressively to bear witness to justice
by assuring inclusiveness of race, gender, class, and sexual orientation at every
level of school and church life, and then to honor the resulting pluralism by finding patterns to affirm the different views and values these groups bring. Mainline
tries to shape its students so that they will lead the congregations they will serve
to incorporate this vision of justice and inclusiveness.

This view is moderate compared with the more austere and rigorous vision of a
smaller group of faculty. This group, comprised of persons who would classify
themselves as "feminist" and "liberationist," are pessimistic about the church's
capacity, as Susan Johnson puts it, "to headlight any visionary change in society."
Existing structures, including the school's sponsoring denomination, are perceived
as incapable of transforming corrupt social structures. Johnson takes this view:
"The latest sociological evidence about church people being more racist and . . .
sexist and more conservative than people who don't go to church doesn't give me
a lot of hope."

For this group of purists, Mainline's teaching should reflect an unremitting commitment to "liberation, social justice, and witness to justice." Such a commitment
is implicitly anti-institutional, because human structures have, over time, institutionalized the injustices these faculty want overthrown. The larger and more bu-
reaucratic the institutional structure, the less able it is to function in ways that
transform injustice. Johnson says, "I know [changes in the parish] can be made,
but I just haven't seen much of it. . . . I have a stronger faith in individuals and
groups within the church than the denomination itself." Thus, the purist group at
Mainline differentiates itself from the dominant message not so much in content—
both lay stress on social justice—but in a deep pessimism about the capacity of
the institutional church to be an agent of transformation to this goal. The purists
think that if the dominant goal at Mainline is taken seriously, the development of
new religious structures will be required. Johnson distrusts local churches but has
more hope for "base communities and WomanChurch [radical forms of Christian
worshiping communities developed, respectively, in South American countries and
by North American feminists] and, in some ways, the seminary." Cynthia Binder
says that one of her educational goals is "to prepare students never to be comfortable in the church." The purist faction understands that the seminary is educating
people to serve congregations but worries that in the end, the congregations will
neither be transformed nor become the agents of transformation social structures
need.

In order to be effective agents for justice, students must confront their own
deeply ingrained social attitudes: racism, sexism, classism, and homophobia. Betty
Trotter comments, "It would be wise to have more variety in what issues we deal
with . . . but racism is alive and well. Sexism is alive and well. *Backlash* is a
best-seller. We are going to have to keep [focusing on racism and sexism]." Main-

line's efforts to address these issues created by these concerns must give special attention to the experiences of particular groups, especially those that have been excluded from centers of power. Rick Santos thinks that reformist efforts that do not attend to "the privileged position as well as the epistemological privilege of the poor in the faith tradition" will not be successful. This sense of "epistemological privilege" extends to other groups who have been oppressed, and this more radical version of the Mainline dominant message argues for necessity of accepting one's own particularity and then hearing, learning from, and respecting the particularities of others—especially those who have been victims of cultural oppression.

The tension between the purist view at Mainline and the perspectives and values that have most influence in its supporting denomination is almost as great as the one between strict Calvinism and popular evangelicalism. Mainline's denomination honors inclusiveness as a principle and tries to effect it. But nowhere in the agencies and structures of the church, except perhaps in caucuses of groups seeking a more powerful role in denominational life, is the cause of pluralism pursued with the passion it is at Mainline Seminary, especially by the feminists and liberationists.[4] Denominations and their constituent congregations predictably have other dominant values, such as effectiveness in attracting members and financial support. Also predictably, the denomination is oriented to building up the denomination, and congregations to establishing themselves firmly in their local settings. Both assume that the organizational structures of church life are essentially sound. The feminist and liberationist purists at Mainline have concluded that these structures are fundamentally flawed, and they are pessimistic about the prospects of their being fixed.

The dominant message at Mainline combines elements from both positions. Inclusiveness is pivotal; it is not, as denominational practice and congregational ideology would suggest, simply one good value among many. An organization that excludes some groups as part of a larger social pattern of denying them justice and equal respect cannot do the work of God until that basic sinful pattern is corrected. But—liberationists to the contrary—the pattern can be corrected. Though drenched in sinfulness, the structures of the churches can be redeemed and renewed, and that indeed is the goal of the school: to shape students who are loyal to the church but fully aware of its deep flaws and who will work hard to change it in the next generation.

Glen Fisher, after long years of service at Mainline, reflects this dominant view: "To me, looking over the years, and knowing the history of the school, . . . this has always been a seminary that has been up to its eyebrows in the local congregation and that has always been fundamental in what we were teaching and the way we taught it." Another long-term professor, reflecting on the educational goal at Mainline, says "our primary vocation is equipping people for pastoral ministry. But equipping for pastoral ministry not in the sense of just simply being clinicians and technicians but equipping them, hopefully, that they can think critically about what it is they are doing as a pastoral minister, sociologically and theologically, think critically about the institutional church." Matthew Lincoln wants graduates who can "be both positively and responsibly committed to the institutional church," but when the need arises, "can transcend the institutional church and give some kind of prophetic critique of that institutional church." The dominant message at Mainline is more critical of the institutional church than the church would probably like, and more confident that the church can respond to its criticisms than the purist voices in the seminary think possible.

The dominant messages at both Evangelical and Mainline thus attempt to mediate between views outside the school and positions inside it that directly challenge outside views. Both seminaries also offer a further set of variations, some (though not all) of which are further efforts to accommodate perspectives in the religious culture that supports the school.

At Evangelical, for instance, there are numerous "less orthodox" variations. None is a well-formed party of opinion, but they can be roughly clustered into groups labeled progressive, inclusive, Pentecostal, practical, and denominational. As we will illustrate later in this chapter, some of these variant messages are closely related, but in each case there is at least a skeletal goal and cluster of supporting views, values, and sometimes other cultural habits.

- The progressive variation propounded by two or three faculty (at least one of whom almost never wears the faculty uniform of tie and jacket) seeks to mold students who will include in the discipline they bring to their leadership of evangelical institutions a special emphasis on (what the progressives argue is) the traditional evangelical commitment to social reform and social justice.
- The inclusive view, promoted by a few faculty and a number of administrators, changes the emphasis rather than the elements of the dominant view: The rough-and-tumble of contemporary evangelicalism—including its revivalist methods, charismatic energy, women's and ethnic caucuses, and even fundamentalists—should be welcomed warmly (rather than warily accommodated) as a source of strength and renewal for the Christian world and the school.
- The Pentecostal message, hammered out by a handful of faculty members and student leaders who more often develop their "message" individually than as a group, uses the style of rational argument favored by the dominant school culture to contend that Reformed rigor and Pentecostal "distinctives" (such as baptism of the Spirit) are not at odds.
- The practical message, promoted by a fairly large party of faculty who teach ministry subjects joined by administrators, tries to put both "training" programs for specialized ministries (with children and young people, for instance) and the varied "experiential" teaching methods in a better light than the dominant perspective, with its strong "cognitive" and intellectual bias, casts on them. Not everyone can be a church leader of scholarly temper, the spokespersons for the practical message maintain. The Christian world also needs skilled workers who can do special jobs and who are also "solid," if not deeply learned, on biblical and theological matters; it is the school's job to produce such persons, along with others who have more thorough theological preparation. Those who take this position observe the faculty/administrative dress code, but they often use relaxed, conversational methods of teaching—sometimes punctuated with films and field trips—that fall well outside the boundaries of pedagogical methods (lecture, line-by-line or word-by-word examination of texts) approved by dominant norms.
- Finally, a few, mostly older faculty and administrators argue repeatedly that the school's job of raising theological standards in the Christian world is best accomplished if students (and faculty members) choose a denomination and stick to it, a stance that varies

significantly from the dominant message that the local congregation is the form of the church that really matters.

Mainline's alternative messages are found in a loose association of faculty and students rather than in separable groups. The theme that draws this association together is theological tradition. A number of faculty members, including some like Matthew Lincoln who also contribute to the students' understanding of the dominant message, affirm justice and inclusion but do not want them to be defined as the exclusive center of what Mainline is about. They want the center to be identified as explicitly and traditionally religious—"the historic[al] faith," according to some, or "the catholic tradition," or "the christological position." Such religious stances do not exclude justice—all would affirm that they entail and even require it—but nevertheless, the variant faculty, to various degrees, worry that Mainline's unrelenting attention to inclusiveness and justice crowds out other centrally important theological virtues. For some, this is a very serious flaw in the seminary. Beth Dickerson was a student at Mainline and has returned to teach there. She recalls that "when I first came here I would say the unifying voice . . . [was] spoken in a Barthian accent. . . . [W]e were getting the residue of the tail end of neo-orthodoxy as it would get played out in the liberal Protestant setting. So there was a kind of christological center . . . and now that christological center is under attack in a variety of ways." She then cites feminists, others who want interreligious dialogue, and still others concerned primarily with cultural issues as the voices that are replacing the earlier neo-orthodox liberal theology.

Another, more subtle variation places value on Mainline as an institution that is part of a system of denominational organizations. Supporting the work of the denomination, training its leaders, contributing to its theological discourse, being sensitive to the denomination's critique of the seminary—these are all important activities for Mainline. This view is somewhat more pragmatic and less fraught with ideational and theological significance than others, but it is the strongly held position of some faculty, administrators, and students. Its proponents are not uncritical of the denomination, but they think that it is necessary to acknowledge that, as one administrator put it, "we are paid by those congregations and . . . they really are our responsibility."

In summary, on the spectrum of views and messages, the variant messages in both schools sit between the central, dominant message of the school and the views and values that have the most influence in the school's supporting constituency. The variations, however, are not uniform. They too are arrayed along a spectrum—some generally closer to the dominant message (justice/inclusivism at Mainline, "generic Calvinism" at Evangelical) and some closer to the edge of what is admissible into the school's culture (Pentecostalism, progressivism at Evangelical; evangelicalism, post-Christian perspectives at Mainline). Similarly, the faculty and administrators who voice and act out variant positions may locate themselves close to the center, varying central norms of thought and behavior in only one way, or very close to the edge—even over it, as we shall illustrate in the next chapter. Most of the positions at the outer edge of the spectrum, however, are occupied not by scattered faculty members and administrators with variant views but a huge phalanx of persons who, at least in their first encounters with the school and its culture, pose a direct challenge to its central message and patterns of life. Making up that phalanx are the seminary's students.

Students: A Different World

Both schools that we studied are fairly large in seminary terms, and their students do not all, of course, fit a uniform profile. But certain ideas, attitudes, and habits in each institution cluster as "the student culture." In both cases, these student cultures closely incorporate many views and practices of religious communities outside the school that the school's central message opposes.

Students arriving at Mainline are notable for their diversity in age, marital status, education, racial/ethnic heritage, theological position, and prior vocational experience. The racial and ethnic distribution of the 1989 entering class matches the United States population: about 80 percent white, 15 percent black, and 3 percent Asian. Students' economic and educational backgrounds are diverse; the largest group is middle-class, but some have been lower-middle-class or poor, and a handful have been upper-middle-class. They hold undergraduate degrees from liberal arts colleges, state universities, community colleges, historically black colleges and universities, and elite, selective colleges.

The average age of the entering class at Mainline in 1989 is thirty-eight. Only a handful of entering students are younger than twenty-five, recent college graduates, and typically single—Jenny Sherrod is an example of this small group. Students like Arlene Jervis, Tommy Reiss, Boyd Arthur, and Judy Ponder, in their midtwenties to midthirties, make up one-third of the class. The largest age group in the 1989 entering class is older—midthirties to midforties—and includes students like Sharon Paige, Daniella Byrd, and Mitch Tabor. Most are married or have been; about a third are remarried or divorced. Another one-quarter of the class is older than forty-five. Students in all these groups, including the youngest, have worked before coming to seminary, many for substantial periods of time and some in several different jobs or careers. The variety of prior positions is great—teaching, health care, journalism, computer programming. Service industry and "helping" professional or semiprofessional positions are most common, but the entering class also includes homemakers and industrial shopworkers.

The range of religious affiliations and theological views is considerable. Over half of the entering students are affiliated with Mainline's sponsoring denomination, and another quarter are from other mainline denominations. Much smaller numbers belong to black Protestant groups, conservative evangelical denominations, the Roman Catholic Church, or Eastern Orthodox bodies.

There are clear divisions on theological matters. Tommy Reiss remembers that "somebody observed to me when I got here that they thought the faculty is much more middle-of-the-road than the student body. The students are on one extreme much more conservative than the faculty, and on the other extreme much more liberal. I think that's very true." Interviews with Mainline students support this view. For instance, conservative Evan Shanks says that he is "going to be more in love with the Bible than most of the professors." Other students make it clear that they see themselves as located at the school's radical edge. Many fewer, to begin with, describe themselves as in the middle, though eventually a number report that they gravitate to that position.

Regardless of their place on the theological spectrum, however, most Mainline students, when they talk about their calling to ordained ministry, invoke the theme of service. A middle-aged African-American woman says it most directly: "I just felt a real call to be in service, serving God's people." This call to service, which includes meeting people's physical as well as religious needs, is clearly influenced by a background of lay activity in predominantly mainline churches. Peter Tomas is the son of a minister active in civil rights; Jim McClaren was a political activist himself "when I was younger" and talks about the importance for him of the denomination's stress on both personal and "social" holiness. Candice Brown credits her involvement on the deacon board of her interdenominational college church and subsequent work with refugees with moving her toward seminary. Doreen Clark "worked [in the church she joined after her husband's death] with lower-income people having problems primarily in housing and employment and food and clothes. . . . And I found that to be very rewarding." Only a minority of students were social activists before seminary, but almost all have liberal or moderate views on political and economic issues (although some are quite conservative on social issues such as homosexuality). They want seminary to give them resources for leading churches that honor God not only by worship but also by making the world a better place to live. They enter seminary with a sense that this is feasible because most have been part of congregations that accomplish this with some measure of effectiveness.

In addition to this service orientation, most students bring to seminary a history of personal struggle. A number have lived through difficult personal relationships with or deaths of family members; some have been ill or incapacitated themselves; many have faced at least one vocational crisis in the midst of which the call to ministry, first heard early in life, became stronger. Several describe the ultimate decision to "accept" the ministerial call as giving up a struggle against God: "I can't fight this anymore," says one; "It was like, 'Okay Lord, I give up,' " says another. For yet another group, economic difficulty and the disruption of changing career or family location fairly late in life make coming to seminary a wrenching experience.

Students arrive, then, from their quite diverse backgrounds, marked in two ways by the culture of the mainline Protestant congregations to which most have belonged: They know that modern life, including religious life, is tough. But they also have confidence that churches can make it better and that the school that most of them have sacrificed a good deal to attend will be able to give them what they need in order to serve in churches that serve their members and other people.

Evangelical students also display a considerable variety of backgrounds. One segment comes from what the school views as its traditional source for students: the central institutions of conservative Protestantism. These students (Ron Biddle, Laura Storey, Brenda Moore, and Sharon Madden, for example) are generally younger than others, coming to seminary either directly from college or with at most two or three years intervening. Most have grown up in "intact" middle-class families, some quite wealthy, that belong to churches of conservative denominations or to evangelical congregations of mainline denominations. A high proportion attended conservative Christian colleges (a few such colleges with long-standing Reformed ties send groups of students each year to Evangelical) or selective colleges and universities in the South. Many have some personal tie to the school: previous contact with a faculty member, a pastor who attended, or a college professor who strongly recommended Evangelical for its theological position and academic reputation. Another group, at least as large by our count and, according to administrators we interviewed, considerably larger than the other and growing, is made up of students whose "Christian" experience and identity is fairly recent. These students' early experiences vary. Some are middle-class, but many others come from working-class backgrounds. Some were raised as Roman Catholics (Cole Silas, Neal Huchett, Marilyn Flexner) and a few in Protestant families whose church membership was perfunctory (Amy Huchett). Many, like Amos Wayland, had no early religious training. The majority attended public or regional private colleges. In many cases, students' first "Christian" encounters were initiated by a fellow student who belonged to an evangelical campus group: Young Life in high school, Campus Crusade for Christ, Fellowship of Christian Athletes, Navigators, or InterVarsity Christian Fellowship in college. Often these campus organizations are students' primary experience of a religious community before they get to seminary; in some cases, the student group is the *only* previous religious experience. Other students who were converted as adolescents or young adults join local churches after college—indeed, for some, a church visited as an adult becomes the site of their initial conversion. But rarely do any of those who did not grow up in evangelical churches form ties to a denomination or even to a broader tradition—Baptist, dispensationalist, or Holiness, for instance. More commonly, they switch churches and traditions rather often, as they move from place to place, become disillusioned with their present congregation, or simply are invited to attend elsewhere by friends in the various evangelical organizations that many of them join. Many students in this segment choose Evangelical Seminary by chance or because they live in the surrounding region.

Though administrators told us that students who grew up in Christian families and those with less settled religious histories tend to function in seminary life as different types, we were impressed by how little difference religious background makes. Student friendship groups form along various natural lines—social class, dorm assignments—without regard to prior religious experience. The tight knot of Covenant House women, for instance, were united by both the accident of their housing arrangements and their middle- and upper-middle-class backgrounds. The differences in religious training were great: Laura, Brenda, and Sharon were born into conservative Protestant homes; Lois, Anne, and Janette were children of tepid or lapsed mainline Protestants and "became Christians" (student language for "became evangelicals") in high school or college; and Paula came from an ultra-conservative sect. But they immediately began to pray together, to testify to each other, to plan joint contributions to worship services with other students, and to share the intimate details of their spiritual lives.

What makes this possible is the fact that virtually all students who arrive at Evangelical have had a heavy dose of evangelical youth culture. Much more than any Sunday school training or college instruction in religion, youth activities, sometimes run by local churches but more often sponsored by the large organizations listed earlier, shape their religious beliefs, tastes, and practices. Thus despite the wide range of ages, prior experiences, and socioeconomic backgrounds in the student body, a shared culture emerges, drawing heavily on the ideas and patterns of activity the students learned in their youth organizations.

The core of the students' religious culture is a relationship, a deeply personal and emotional one, between the individual student and God. The relationship dates from a moment or process variously described as turning to, coming to know, loving, accepting, having, or knowing Jesus Christ; or letting Jesus Christ "into my heart [or life]." A great deal of students' time and energy seems to be oriented toward sustaining the power of this experience. The specific activity that accomplishes this best is worship, which in the students' view is "freer . . . and music with words that are something you can identify with."

The music of choice is the praise chorus; praise choruses are simple songs with a few words and predictable, singable tunes almost always accompanied by guitar, sometimes by drums and keyboards as well. Often the words will be projected on overhead slides if the technology is at hand, though the words are so easy and the basic choruses so well known that the overheads are probably unnecessary much of the time.[5] At the opening fish fry during the first year of our study, the new students gathered after eating lobster and corn on the hillside in front of the administration building. There, without benefit of song sheets or overhead slides, they sang praise choruses until it became too dark and cold to continue. Most of the students had never met before that night: They arrived at the school with praise chorus culture already ingrained. Though the songs are simple and repetitive, they seem to generate emotion. Some close their eyes tight as they sing. The leader modulates between loud and soft and sometimes injects sob-like sounds into his voice (leaders are almost always male students). On occasion, individual students also perform pop Christian songs found on professional recordings. Typically these are in the mode of love songs, like the ballad "I Wonder, Would I Know You Now?" that Ruthie sang in chapel before Paul Bashford preached.

Emotional singing of both the praise and professional kinds bleeds into emotional prayer, most of it addressed to God as Father.[6] Much of the prayer is exclamations: "Father, we just thank you and pray to you . . . ," uttered in urgent, fervent tones.[7] Impromptu services may end with a few more choruses after prayer. Planned ones almost always include a testimony as well, an account of how God has intervened in the speaker's life. Even planned worship, however, has an informal air. As Sam Carlson notes with asperity, informality is rife in student culture. Students wear "shorts and even baseball caps that they do not take off" in chapel, because they are "not church people . . . ; they come from these parachurch organizations." As in much of the wider evangelical world, religious activity is no longer a dress-up occasion.

Around worship like this and the personal relationship to God that it fuels revolve ideas that—like the elements of student worship—have their roots in popular evangelical culture. The deity the students talk about is highly responsive to their fervent communications with him. Though student prayers during their own services rarely take the form of explicit requests, many positive turns of events are interpreted retrospectively as the Lord's "leading" or as direct responses to prayers. God, in the students' view, is rather spontaneous, very much mixed up in cosmic decision making about how things will go each day. Some students are convinced that unseen powers are engaged in a constant, titanic battle that their prayers can affect. "I'm no fanatic," says Heidi Elkins, "but there are demons everywhere, even here." Heidi, an older commuter student who is peripheral to student social life, views the chain of events, including the failure of her husband's business, that led her to seminary as "the Lord parting the waters." But even sophisticated students like Anne Norton, who "hates [popular] Christian music" and other elements of the student culture, believes that prayer may change the course of world events. When the Persian Gulf War breaks out, she "feels like a failure" because she has been praying for peace. Louise Mason, a graduate student and firm advocate for women's ordination, "asked the Lord" for a computer. She got it: A staff member at the school sold her one at a reduced rate, and she chalked that up as answered prayer. Amanda Sunderbloom, a liberal student who feels so "out of place" at Evangelical that she finally transfers to another seminary, reports that she has "these deep personal experiences of God. I pray every day. I have prayer lists. I have had certain amazing experiences." One, she reports, was a gift of money at exactly the time she needed dental work; "I took that as a sign that God knows that I am doing my best for him." Signs are common occurrences. Albert Carr, who leaves Evangelical because it is not Reformed enough, pursues his courtship of Anne Norton after challenging God to give him a sign. (The sign—Anne showing up at the library—comes, and the courtship proceeds). Laura, moderate in every way, concludes that the fact that she and her mother have both been thinking she should go to seminary is a sign; on the strength of it, she decides to go. Students at every point on the theological spectrum feel the presence of a God who pays direct attention to the details of their everyday lives and who relates through interventions prompted by their requests.

Such a God contrasts rather sharply with the God projected by the central message of the school—a God whose consistent plan, written once in a single volume, does not change to accommodate any human desires; a God meant to be not entreated but better understood. God as seen in the student culture gives emotional and sometimes material rewards to those who accept him; God in the dominant view gives what is argued to be the greater but is also certainly the more remote satisfaction of apprehending God's glory. Christian life for the students has the flavor of romance; Christian life in the school's dominant view involves a great deal of tedious work. Even more than at Mainline, the contrast between the dominant and student cultures is great. In both settings, however, the contrast and the tensions it generates work to ultimately good effect: They create the dynamic educational processes that we now proceed to describe.

ELEVEN

The Process of Education and Formation

The educational processes in both schools we studied have the character of a contest. Students arrive imbued with the ideas, habits, and values of the very religious and social cultures that the school seeks to reshape. They encounter the school's dominant message and its variations, in explicit statements by pivotal figures, in the affect and behavior of those figures, and in the norms and activities of institutional life. They test the central message; they try it on; they resist and oppose it; they experiment with the variant possibilities. Both schools provide considerable freedom and opportunity for this struggle, and both also ratify what is usually the result: a compromise. Most students' views, values and, it appears, habits *are* reshaped by the ideas and behaviors the school promotes, but students do not entirely surrender the commitments, opinions, and tastes that they came with. Their goals, outlook, language, and manners when they leave are a melding—often painfully forged in intense engagements with each other and with those who represent the school—of what they brought with them and what the school has insistently set before them.

In this chapter we describe this process. In general outline, the process is the same at both sites. (The differences we did find are traceable, we think, to very different curriculum structures and student living arrangements at the two schools rather than to their "liberal" and "conservative" orientations.) As we describe it here, the process appears linear and orderly. In the total life of the schools, of course, it is not: All parts of the process are going on at the same time. But most students, both individuals and cohorts, experience a progression—from initial encounter to challenge and struggle to resolution. Our description here follows that progression. It focuses on what we see as the typical experiences. We also note the presence in both schools of a few students who never become engaged in the process and who, therefore, are not by our definition "educated" in the ways the schools intend, even though they may complete all the requirements for degrees.

Presentation and Re-presentation

The central message of the institution and its variants are repeatedly announced and embodied by key figures in the school. They are also enacted in an array of community practices.

For students entering Mainline Seminary, the school's message and character are presented first and most powerfully by Harriet Hercon. As academic dean, she dominates orientation with her insistence on language that "excludes no one" and her expansive gestures. She is the first to urge students to look critically at the church, the institution they are preparing to serve. Christianity—what the new students have come to seminary to "master," Hercon tells them—is perhaps not the institutional church, as they might have thought: "It's forgiveness, love, acceptance across cultures." As teacher of the Ministry and Mission course that all students take during their first year, Hercon provides the recipe for Christian theology: "There's always room for one more theologian. . . . It's like making a cake: you need lots of different ingredients, and so it is with theologies and theologians; they are made up of a lot of different elements of experience." In her teaching, she demonstrates her belief that differences amount to "rich diversity around a common theme" by watching closely for students' puzzled looks and teasing out the questions of those who are confused or uncomfortable. She tries to point students beyond themselves, to align them with the school's view that the church exists not for itself but for those who have been deprived of what they need: "Everything you learn here is for someone else." When she leaves, a fellow faculty member points out how she glues the pieces of the school's message together: Her unflaggingly loyalty "to Christ and Christ's church and this institution" is "remarkable," but all in service of "building a kingdom in a world in need of hope."

Though no one else presents Mainline's core message and values as effectively as Hercon, a number of other faculty members reinforce and amplify the views she so energetically promotes. During a second-year course, after Hercon has left the campus (and, says Tommy Reiss, a certain "vibrancy" goes with her), Marvin Miles reminds those assembled to see him inaugurated as professor that "the unity of humanity is not in sameness but relationship." He ends his sermon with a rhetorical jolt of the sort Hercon favored: "Thanks be to the God who scatters!" Trudi Darsa does the same, in her memo that the new dean commends as a "contribution" to the debate set off by Professor Newman's noninclusive hymn choice: "God/ess bless!" she writes. Cliff Mims reminds students that inclusiveness and respect for others' choices must extend not only to the racial and gender groups that Mainline regularly seeks to "include" but also to the conservative opponents of inclusiveness. No one, he says, should be called a fundamentalist unless they choose the title.

Other faculty members take up Hercon's role of modeling the school's ideals. Both young Mileses do this. Marvin gives a powerful demonstration, after Lu's suicide, of the conviction so central at Mainline that religious faith is directly relevant to human pain and suffering: "[He read] from the Bible with such passion and hurt, you felt he was one with what he was saying. And he was," says a student for whom the moment was the most memorable seminary experience. Mary's dramatic demonstration of gratitude for her husband's decision to share a teaching position and child-rearing responsibilities enacts for students the kind of relationship that diversity and justice require. "I want to thank Marvin personally," she says at their joint inauguration. "In this patriarchical world, Marvin had everything to lose and I had everything to gain by the arrangement," she continues, and she walks over to kiss and embrace him, setting off a standing ovation.

There are other faculty models as well. "They model what they teach," says Evan Shanks. Self-knowledge and authenticity are an important feature of the Mainline argument—purging oneself of biased and selfish attitudes requires first of all acknowledging that one has them—so faculty demonstrations of integrity carry an important educational message. For many students David Parsons embodies that quality better than any other figure at the school. Janet Cable, frightened by his "anger," wanted to drop his course at first, but persuaded by the registrar, she persevered. She was glad she did: "Something happened to both of us. . . . He must have such a love for theology. . . . He kind of like dances with it . . . so that you feel him as well as hear him. . . . He made light bulbs go on in my head." Tommy Reiss says that Parson's "gentleness" and "pain" were "very opening to me." "You know," he tells an interviewer, "[Parsons] has just jumped on my soul and shaken it and stomped on it, and it has been a very emotional ride."

Rituals and informal activities also instruct: The photographic grid, with the different ages, sexes, races, and nationalities of the students so clearly the point, has become the icon for Mainline Seminary over the two decades it has appeared repeatedly in publicity materials. Candidates for the Community Committee are identified on the official slate by sex and race. Issues retreats sponsored by the school take up in succession the interests of groups Mainline most assiduously includes: in 1990, Asian-American issues; in 1991, abuse of women (and others); in 1992, racism. Graduation each year is a carefully planned display of how much variety Mainline encompasses. The president describes the graduating class by its characteristics; Scripture is read in English, Korean, Xhosa, Chinese, and Mano, and signed for the deaf as well; a psalm is sung in Jewish cantorial style. Less officially, the needs of groups for recognition and fair treatment are regularly met. The newly renovated classroom building's desks do not accommodate "larger" students comfortably, so long tables with straight-backed chairs are added to the lecture hall.

Students also learn from the statements and manners of important figures that variations of the central message are permissible. The purist faculty members, like Johnson and Binder, repeatedly express pessimism about established church structures. In this, David Parsons, a "central" figure in other respects, joins them. "How do we bring up issues [like racism] and serve in the local church?" a student asks him. "I don't know how to respond," says Parsons. "[Which is] one reason I am not in the local church. No need for both of us to be miserable."

At Evangelical, several faculty members share the job of stating the central commitments of the institution and demonstrating the attitudes and manners that comport with those commitments. Evangelical's message is two-sided, and Roy

Parks presents one side, its critical views of popular evangelicalism. True evangelicalism is "biblical and God-centered"; it "[replicates] the habits of thought found in Scripture" and is best expressed in expository preaching. Modernity and the temptation to pander to people with modern sensibilities have eroded evangelicalism; despite the "fierce guard" of the inerrancy doctrine posted at the front door, human-centered, "selfist" modern ideas have come in the back way.

Reg O'Neil, on campus as a visiting instructor while we were doing our study, fills out many of Parks's favorite dicta in clever and memorable ways. He rattles students with deftly worded jibes at things they have been taught to respect. Evangelicals "can be as moronic as anyone around," he says. The situation is the result of revivals, which by most accounts were the fountainhead of American evangelicalism but which, in the coolly critical view of O'Neil (and Parks), caused "the meltdown of truth into feeling, theology into experience," and, O'Neil later adds, words into images. Feeling, experience, and images now dominate in the evangelical world, and the central message of Evangelical Seminary, as sternly but entertainingly proclaimed by Parks, O'Neil, and the faculty and students who agree with them, is that this state of affairs is a disaster.

Parks and O'Neil are the most articulate spokespersons for the dominant view of things at Evangelical. Parks in particular produces much of the theory and rationale for the importance of "mild generic Calvinism" on the contemporary academic scene. His faculty colleagues take his views *very* seriously. Almost all show up at the biblical-theological forum he organizes once he opens it to everyone. (When the group had a limited membership, the excluded faculty, well aware that this was a power center, petitioned for admission.) Some aspects of Parks's behavior as well as his ideas also have influence. Students are aware, for instance, that he left the Baptist congregation he attended when the new pastor's theology did not measure up and joined a Congregational one. The fact that such a powerful figure has no strong ties to a denomination confirms students' own casual attitudes toward denominations. Parks's and O'Neil's frequent acidic comments about parachurch movements and mission organizations that students *do* have loyalties to give students pause. In general, though, Parks's and O'Neil's influence is on what students think. They are not looked to as models of the kind of people students might like to become.

The figures students want to emulate, to live like, are Jerome Allen and especially Paul Bashford. Bashford and Allen broadcast and embody the other, positive side of Evangelical's message. In numerous ways they tell and show students that the kind of Reformed Christianity that the school promotes is strenuous but also that the hard work is profoundly satisfying. Allen, the taskmaster, concludes an hour in which he has driven students through intricate analysis of a Bible passage with a gush of enthusiasm for the sort of faith this difficult work can produce: "glory . . . blessedness. Do you praise God? Does it come from your heart, like cheering a team, like enjoying a sunset?" Paul Bashford, also famous for requiring hard work ("he digs a prodding stick into your side . . .—I think he's an incredible educator"), stresses another benefit: the ultimate security that the orthodoxy outlined in the Bible affords. *"The issue is right doctrine about God,"* he declares. "If we preach wrong, your faith is futile, and the end is the grave." He testifies to the painfulness, the "cost," of taking his independent stand against infant baptism but also to the deep satisfaction he has found in ordering his views and actions to what he is sure are the dictates of Scripture. Students get the point. Zak Korkas, who insists he has not "become anyone's clone," likes the "work ethic," being "stretched" in "painful" ways. "I'm learning," he says. He is seeking not "some great grandeur of a spiritual high" but the deeper satisfactions of solid biblical knowledge that he can take to "a world that is fallen." Students get the point not only from what Bashford and Allen tell them but from the "whole life aspect," how they conduct themselves at every point that the students can observe.

Other faculty teach other features of the central message by precept and example. Andrew Watson's parental manner, emphasis on disciplined living, and insistence on formal dress and organ music in all the worship services at which he presides all bespeak the restrained and respectful postures that match the sober and studious ideas and attitudes of the school's kind of Reformed Protestantism. Charles Oliver, pastor of nearby Whitley Church (which many students attend) as well as full-time professor of Bible, gives a vivid demonstration of how a skillful minister who is steeped in "mild generic Calvinism" can transform the prayer concerns of ordinary evangelicals—most of whom ask God for special immediate favors—into orthodox intercessions. A congregant wants a cure for an aunt with leukemia. Oliver, clearly unwilling to bend the core Calvinist view that God will exercise his will in accord with the covenantal plan he has announced in Scripture, prays that the relative be given "a sample of the healing that awaits us all." Sharp Dunlap stares uninterruptedly at the floor during a student-led chapel dominated by praise choruses and testimonies. Key faculty openly disagree about women's ordination; a light-hearted poster, that shows Bashford floating in an inner tube announces his presentation on believers' baptism. Both of these demonstrations of openness to difference signal to students that it is safe to entertain diverse opinions on these matters.

Other faculty present the variations on the central message and its concomitant style. Michael Tucker—brilliant, intensely scholastic, always ready with careful rational arguments for his strong and inflexible views—instantiates the Truly Reformed position. He teaches that those with authority should exercise it, and he regularly does so himself—or tries to. Certain that changing the pronouns in Bible translations to make them gender-inclusive is wrong, he proposes to end debate on the matter. The feelings of his faculty colleagues must give way to what he is sure is right reason. Presbyterial forms of church government, he announces to students, are the only ones that give authority its proper scope. He teaches that those who know the truth should teach it to those who are unsure; in line with that view, he writes essays for his congregation to study on issues such as the frequency of communion service, on which he thinks their views are wrong. Other faculty, though personally alarmed by the theology and behavior of charismatic students, who believe that the Holy Spirit confers "gifts" on them directly, are careful not to offend the significant number of such students by saying that they are wrong. Michael Tucker says so very publicly. Tucker's toughness never flags. Reporting his gratitude for the great kindness of the members of his congregation during the terminal illness of his baby daughter, he is nevertheless careful to make the exactly correct theological point: "No flower arrangement, no card, no casserole, no kind work can comfort the parent of a terminally ill child as can belief in the gospel." He is grateful for prayers as well but is compelled to point out that "we can never calculate the exact effect of such prayer."

Michael Tucker's purist position is much tighter and more rigid than the central one. Other alternatives are considerably looser. The two faculty members who teach missions, both of whom belong to Reformed denominations and congregations, are more fervently evangelical and less doctrinally focused than the central group. Missions is a core theme of the central message but is the one that fits least comfortably with the others. Classic Reformed theology emphasizes that God, not human beings, makes the decision about who will be saved. From that perspective it is not clear how fruitful it is for people to bring the gospel to others. Perhaps for that reason, missions is officially ratified but pushed somewhat to the side. From that position, Joel Cotton, the senior professor, projects a warm piety and zeal for saving souls that gratify students who find the dominant tone of the school too cool. (One student reports the "weird but nice" experience of a casual meeting on the stairs with Cotton, during which he interrupted the conversation eight times for prayer.) His junior colleague, Jesse Redlin, has a relaxed manner that sets him off from other faculty: He wears open collared, pastel-colored shirts from the southeast Asian countries where he served as a missionary; he performs in silly skits in public and encourages students to call him by his first name. He also teaches anthropological theory so that students can express the Christian message in terms that those in other cultures can grasp. The central faculty, grounded in their convictions that biblical truth is different (and sometimes divergent) from the "facts" of natural and social life and that such truth must not be diluted or relativized in any way, are wary.

They are even warier of the most progressive member of the faculty, Robert Harlan. Harlan never openly contradicts the central message—that truth is derived from inerrant Scripture, that hard intellectual work is required to discover it, that verbal expressions convey truth in ways nonverbal images cannot, and that congregations are superior forms of the church to denominations and parachurch movements. He does, however, diplomatically suggest that other things are also important and true. Practical experience should play a role in preparing people for "holistic" ministry, he says, along with rational, "cognitive" forms of inquiry. Harlan teaches a course on evangelism and mass media—a major villain, in the dominant view at Evangelical. He makes the daring suggestion to an interviewer (but not in the public debate) that a required course in evangelism (like missions, an awkward theme in a Reformed seminary) might be substituted for one of the several now required in Bible. He tells students that allegiance to denominations, even mainline ones like his own, is important, and he occasionally works for parachurch organizations. His beard and casual preppy clothes mark him as different from other faculty. Central faculty figures steer clear of him. Parks opposes him at every turn. Many students like him, but some—especially the Truly Reformed—think he has pushed the boundaries of solid biblical and Reformed teaching too far out.

Other perspectives are more haphazardly represented. There is a handful of Pentecostal and charismatic faculty members. Probably because everyone is aware of the historical Reformed hostility to these theological positions and styles of religious practice, none of these professors push the position very hard, but none hide it either. The most persistent and deliberate effort to make Pentecostal students feel welcome is exerted by a non-Pentecostal. Bruce Grantler, a quiet historian who once served as dean and is widely trusted despite his refusal to line up with the central figures (or anyone else) on most issues, adds a course in the history of the Pentecostal movement to the curriculum and regularly makes other "inclusive" gestures to students whose theology and piety are not of the approved kind.

The senior administration represents another loosely organized alternative view. Again, none of its members contradict the proponents of the central message, and the president in particular makes frequent if brief references to the importance of "classical" learning. Two key administrators—Sharp Dunlap, the dean of students, and chaplain Andrew Watson—are proponents of the "classical" view themselves. The others—the president, the dean, and their senior colleagues—portray themselves as realists obliged to soften the central position for pragmatic reasons. They emphasize the right of women to study for ordained ministry more forcefully than most other male leaders in the school, for instance, because a significant number of women students and potential students want to be ordained. They engineer the addition of programs with reduced academic requirements and increased "practical" emphases to raise enrollment. These administrators say that conviction as well as necessity leads them to these positions. The dean, a controversial figure among both faculty and students, jumps into the "and your daughters" controversy with verve, on the side of women's ordination. Sam Carlson, the powerful admissions director and "enrollment manager," takes a dim view of some of the militantly "cognitive" faculty. In the students' view, administrators represent a diluted version of the school's identity. No administrator is held in the esteem that Bashford and Allen attract. Most administrators, in fact, are referred to by their first or last names in student conversations, whereas most faculty are called "Dr." or "Professor" even out of their hearing. Carlson is invariably called "Sam" to his face.

Struggle

The students' arrival at Mainline and Evangelical seminaries creates a perceptible clash, as the institutions' most powerful voices and most vivid exemplary figures call into question the norms and practices of the religious communities that have hitherto shaped students' basic assumptions and beliefs. In both institutions the students recognize almost immediately that they face fundamental challenges, and they organize numerous formal and ad hoc mechanisms for dealing with the tension between the assumptions and habits they brought with them and those that the school is pressing on them. The dynamic at both sites is the same: School culture confronts student culture, and students improvise structures in which they can work together to shape a response. Both schools provide time, space, freedom, and approval for such activity. In both institutions, the process is a strenuous, absorbing, and frequently painful one for students.

Each institution's specific pattern of challenge and response, however, is distinctive. At Mainline Seminary, the pattern has a chronological structure, which appears to be the result of a curriculum that encourages students to complete several common courses that are taught only once each academic year. The attempt to move students through the three-year program in a sort of cohort does not entirely succeed: Only about 10 percent of students entering in 1989 actually graduated in 1992 (1989 entering class data, 1992 Graduation Ceremony Program). But the students who are enrolled full-time, and especially those who live on campus, are exposed to so many of the same courses and events during their first three years, and these students see so much of each other that their year-by-year responses to Mainline's messages and values progress along the same lines. This group of highly involved students tends to set the tone and create the structures for others to participate in the process.

On the surface, Mainline's dominant institutional view and the precommitments that students bring with them have a certain consonance: Both are oriented toward leadership in the church; both project a view of the church as responsible for human betterment as well as (indeed, as part of) religious faithfulness. But students come quickly to understand that their assumptions about "service" and the school's message about "justice" are very different. The first signal for most that there is a deep gap between their views and the school's is the language and pedagogical style of the Mission and Ministry course that Harriet Hercon and David Parsons teach together in the first semester. The students, who are well acquainted with churches that offer social as well as religious services and who therefore assume that learning to forge that connection as leaders will not be too difficult, are shown and told that their instructors think that it will be very difficult indeed.

The difficulty is demonstrated first by the ways that Hercon and Parsons talk. The students' convictions about the feasibility of "service" are based on experience, not intellectual or ideological justification; the teachers' case for justice, however, is set forth first as highly abstract propositions. Such language makes one student "feel like an idiot." Tommy Reiss calls the course "seven weeks of disconcerting hell." Doreen Clark says that the "foreign terms" made her feel "lost; I felt stupid." Faculty like Marvin Miles then introduce other difficulties. To students who come from churches that pay very little attention to the historical intricacies of the Bible, he makes clear that the famous battle of Jericho probably never happened and that he prefers that conclusion because the story presents God as a conquering warrior, which in Miles's view is not an attribute of God. "I'm not going to preach that [that the walls of Jericho really didn't fall]," says one student to a neighbor at the end of class.

The instructors' teaching style in the Mission and Ministry course is even more challenging than their discourse. As Hercon did with her questions about the film *The Mission* during orientation, they appear to push groups of students to confront each other, stating their views and interests even if others find them upsetting. Hercon reads a black female student's poem that "praised black and condemned white," a student reports, to which white students reacted with "stone cold silence." Parsons's teaching, too, has a challenging edge. When students complain about their problems understanding him (but not Hercon), the question of his style becomes entwined with the controversy about racism, because Parsons is black.

The point of these provocations, Hercon and Parsons explain, is not to produce antagonism per se but to show students how hard it is to accommodate the rights and needs of others to the extent that justice demands. Including others—*really* including others—is not as easy as the success of parish "outreach" programs to new groups might lead one to believe. One cannot, in fact, be genuinely inclusive, and therefore adequately just, without facing squarely one's deeply ingrained disinclination to do so. At Mainline, that disinclination is usually identified by the phrase "sexism, racism, and classism" (sometimes "homophobia" or "homophobism" is added). Eradicating those attitudes and tendencies is certain to be very hard and very painful for each person—and even harder and more painful for groups like denominations and local churches in which the students will spend the rest of their lives. The deep discomforts created by the confrontations in Ministry and Mission are a first taste of what it will be like—and, Hercon and Parsons emphasize, what it should be like.

Pain and struggle is the principal motif of students' memories of their first year. "My brain hurts, and sometimes it just whirls around, because what I know is truth and is seen to be as truth suddenly isn't truth for somebody else," says Tommy Reiss. "If it wasn't a struggle, it wouldn't be worth it," Judy Ponder recognizes early on. Students did not expect life at seminary to be easy, especially economically, and it is not: Many shop, cook, and eat together to hold down costs, and they skip meals, shop at thrift stores, and borrow money to stay in school. But none of them seem to have expected it to be wrenching in the ways it becomes almost immediately. Many viewed their struggle to "accept their call" as the pivotal one for ministry. The realization that more and deeper personal changes may be required is hard to take. Students do pay attention to the message, though. Some of them start to practice the confrontative style for themselves, speaking for their affinity group in ways that make other students uncomfortable and (unless they are white males) challenging the legitimacy of other groups' view of them. Other students try but are intimidated by the sharp responses of other groups: "I feel that I can't say anything right anymore," says a white woman student whose suggestion that Jesus may have been middle-class provokes a hailstorm of objections. Almost all examine their attitudes and motives regularly, hoping to discover and change the deep flaws (racism, sexism . . .) that might lead them to exclude others or deny them equity, even in subtle ways.

To find resources for all these activities—issuing challenges, protecting themselves from challenge, and especially making themselves better, more open people—students have recourse to groups. At first the groups are mostly those that the school organized before they arrived. In the early months of the first year, the *MTS Journal* is filled with announcements of Mainline's standard groups: chapel choir, the Community Committee, the Social Action Committee, the Spiritual Life Committee, the Association of Black Seminarians, and the Korean Student Association. But soon the school itself and its official structures are viewed more as the problem than as the solution. Leticia Payne, a member of two minority groups (Roman Catholics and African-Americans), complains that the administration has overlooked the interests of the official organization of another (the Asian-American group): "They claim to be so inclusive around here but they really are not." Criticism of the school for not meeting the criteria it establishes escalates, along with students' sense of personal responsibilities for each others' and the world's problems. Both reach a kind of peak at the time of Lu's suicide, when several students say that they think that if Mainline were "really a community," Lu would not have killed herself.

During the first year, to provide more satisfactory settings than the official clubs to deal with these pressures, students begin to form their own groups—often informal or ad hoc: the women's Bible study in Barlowe Hall; impromptu "prayer meetings" in a prayer room; and communal meals several nights a week in Barlowe Hall. They sit together in affinity groups in class—African-Americans in one corner, commuters in their business suits near the door, Barlowe Hall residents in the center. Students find comfort and support in their groups. They also find them constricting. They complain of feeling "boxed in"—by their racial, gender, age, and other identity groups, by the structured curriculum, by large classes, by economic constraints.

The group-forming process does not, however, abate in the second year; it gains momentum. New groups proliferate by ideology, leisure and ministry interests, and sexual orientation. There is the Women's Covenant Group (the transformed and formalized version of the informal women's Bible study), the Mainline Karate Association, the Mainline Craft Club, two feminist-womanist reading groups meeting on different days, a folk choir, a newly reactivated Mainline Evangelical Association, a lectionary study group, the Arts Committee, a group for "lesbian, gay, and bisexual concerns," a dialogue on racism, the Mainline Youth Workers Association, and the Mainline Community Drama Guild.

Crosscutting these and other activity and political groups is a set of larger and looser groups that are formed by common background, interests, and circumstances. Like most campus groups, they grow out of a complex web of relationships among on-campus students (a little over a third of the class members reside on campus at least a couple of nights a week), who draw in some commuter students (another third), and then involve only minimally the remainder of students who come to the campus for classes. The larger affiliation groups are less likely to be drawn into conflict with each other than the smaller, named groups, though some highly polemical coalitions and associations grow out of them. There are four such groups:

1. Conservative and older student pastors like Evan Shanks and Janet Cable. They live on campus for a couple of nights a week, belong to chapel choir and go to chapel faithfully, and find more to like and less to criticize in structures and program of Mainline Seminary than most other students (Evan Shanks says: "And when my professor says something that I can use in my sermon, I say, 'Wow, I can't wait to get that written down.' Isn't that great? And when you go to chapel and you hear something: 'Oh, what a great illustration! I will use it next Sunday.'"). They are offended by the radical criticisms of theological tradition and the church that Mainline permits and that the purist faculty members encourage, such as the lecture in which Sarah Kent argued that the Crucifixion was a case of divine child abuse.

2. Younger and more liberal student pastors, like James Englehardt, Susan Arch, and Tommy Reiss, who have many contacts with students outside the student pastor track, like Jenny Sherrod, Arlene Jervis, and Mitch Tabor. They are vocal about social justice issues (and focus on these issues in their churches) but are also very attuned to politics in their denomination. They use most of their nights at the seminary as a kind of escape or respite and go to restaurants or each other's rooms late at night and "talk about everything." They are active with groups like the Spiritual Life Committee, the Social Action Committee and, along with the other pastor track students, the campus choirs.

3. Younger, mostly single students who live and work on campus. They are key leaders on the Community Committee during the first and second years and chair groups such as the Social Action Committee and the group that supports gay students. This circle of students, which includes Jenny Sherrod, Judy Ponder, and Terrence Nunnally as well as Arlene Jervis and Sharon Paige, organizes many of the other groups—the international seminar, for instance, and the feminist-womanist and Marxist reading groups. They contribute frequently to the *MTS Journal* and they have many lines out to other groups: They sing in the choir with the student pastors and talk often and intensely with the black students. Members of this group who live on campus are likely to have rooms and/or doors decorated with "statement art" on issues of feminism, homophobism, capitalism, and so on.

4. The black students, such as Doreen Clark, Daniella Byrd, and Mitch Tabor. They are all active in the Association of Black Seminarians (Mitch, in fact, is president during his second year); they are leaders in several key campus controversies and frequent contributors to the *MTS Journal* on racism issues. Like the student pastors, they sing, especially in the gospel choir. They socialize together and tend to sit together in the back of the refectory "near the kitchen," a habit Doreen Clark traces to black culture, in which the kitchen "is a comfortable spot for us."

Mainline's different kinds of groups serve different functions. The affiliation groups are of longer duration and offer protection and support amid the often tumultuous political events at Mainline. As communities of friends that eat, party, and constantly talk together, they provide intimate settings in which students can work out their position in relation to Mainline's unrelenting challenge to students and the churches and society beyond them to be inclusive and stand for justice. Protection and intimacy are especially important as students "work it out," because the process is so personal: They are asked to replace or reshape some of their deepest tendencies and beliefs, thoroughly to refit themselves for the rigors for ministries of justice and inclusiveness. The more public groups—both formal organizations and more temporary gatherings and coalitions—provide more such protection, but their principal function is to give students a chance to try on the dominant posture of the school. In groups, or speaking for or representing them, they become agents of inclusiveness, insisting on their own and advocating others'.

So in the second year, students look for groups where they can "be heard." Some students find themselves aligned with several. The black students, operating out of both their informal network and their established organization, protest the art exhibit of black figures in the strongest terms. According to Doreen Clark, who led another protest effort in the first year, when the black group was still forming, the pictures "showed black people in a very depraved state." The younger, on-campus students produce a send-up of the abstract sculpture show. A quickly organized group produces "diversity ribbons" to protest the singing of Newman's hymn, with its "exclusive" male pronouns and metaphors for God. Prompted by Sarah Kent's rejection of the orthodox Christian doctrine of the Atonement, the head of the Evangelical Association and the straight gatekeeper for the homosexual students' group engage in an extraordinarily sophisticated debate in the *MTS Journal* about whose conception of God is more expansive. Sometimes, however, the parade of groups generates more noise than insight. In rapid succession, students write to the *Journal* denouncing racism against blacks at the seminary; then the exclusion of Asians and Asian-Americans; then the use of the words "deaf," "dumb," and "blind" in one of the racism letters because they are demeaning to those with different "physical capabilities"; and finally the "ageism" of a letter about the quality of Mainline's diverse (and older) student body. The last letter in the series, from a "low-income, single parent," reports that the writer, who fits into none of the previous categories, feels that the protests exclude her and her interests.

By the end of the second year, the constant self-assertion of groups and the pressure to include, acknowledge, and not offend all of them begins to wear on the students. Even Arlene Jervis, an activist when she came to seminary, is tired "of all the divisions and all of the camps." Some of the more conservative student pastors, picking up on the rhetoric that other groups regularly use, decide behind the scenes that they are "marginalized" but unlikely to be able to claim that status because they are white men with traditional views. By almost tacit agreement, they begin to "duck and cover," concealing their true reactions and opinions in order not to antagonize any group of their fellow students. This less-than-fully-candid approach is possible because the older student pastor group has subdivided into smaller, closer subgroups that can be depended on to keep each other's confidences.

Some of the students' responses to their own weariness are highly positive. Not all the older student pastors go into hiding. For confirmation and support, they do gravitate to the theologically traditional faculty, especially Matthew Lincoln, but some use that and other resources to try to make sense of the views that other faculty and administrators press in their direction (one describes the year as a time of a "challenge of faith . . . without a loss of faith"). Arlene Jervis spends more time in the church where she works and less in political organizing at the seminary. And James Englehardt and Mitch Tabor organize the deeply moving joint worship service for their two churches, black and white, and declare together that "the Blood of Jesus Christ which flows in each one of our veins is the love that conquers all . . . racism . . . prejudice . . . hate."

In the third year (not the last for most students, but the end is in view), slow progress is made toward resolutions of the cultural clash that dominated the first year and the struggles among groups that occupied the second. Some themes struck in earlier years continue to develop. Criticism of institutions for their failures to incorporate inclusive and just practices increases. The focus this year is not the seminary itself but the churches and the denomination. These are, of course, the target in the school's dominant critical message. The students, most of whose experiences in churches have been positive, have taken a long time to apply their early critique of themselves and the school to church institutions, but now they do. "We [in our denomination] say we don't exclude," says the student panelist on apartheid, "but we do." An older student, the editor of the "Evangelical Corner" in the *Journal,* draws a picture during the racism retreat of a fence dividing a white person and a black person. The fence, he tells the group, is the church. For some students, another pattern from the previous year hangs on. Like the "duck and cover" group of the second year, a few stay out of the fray, honoring the letter of inclusiveness, which requires them to keep their negative opinions about others to themselves, rather than the spirit, which demands openness and the personal catharsis of owning up to their prejudices. Terrence Nunnally calls this position "peace-agree"; a student who holds it suggests that Mainline add "Thou shalt not offend" as an Eleventh Commandment.

Many more students, however, take the more difficult path of confronting the full force of Mainline's message, including the austere purist version of it, and making up their own minds about what parts of it they will and will not adopt. By the sixth semester, a large number acknowledge the major and positive influence on them of David Parsons, whose direct statements about race and doubts about whether church structures can be reformed place him at least partly in the purist camp. Even more line up with Harriet Hercon, who left after this group's first year but remains the symbol of what the school cares about most: She stood for "the already and the not yet," a group of women students remembers. Then they puzzle out for themselves how traditional theological terms might be used in Hercon's approach: The Second Coming is not just a future event but also "the Kingdom of God" that is already partly present on earth. Arlene says that she does not think the clouds will open up, but "brokenness is going to be healed . . . and we'll really see God in each other."

Students' higher level of comfort with Mainline's messages and norms is evident in the freedom they feel in the third year to make mild jokes about them. The women who have been talking earnestly about Harriet Hercon and the Second Coming make light of their gender group's approach to the retreat they are headed to: "We have already discussed this. . . . Everybody is going to be menstrual. . . . Don't forget your Tampax." Mitch Tabor goes even further: In an article in the *Journal,* he suggests that "pursuit of [skin] color" is an "inalienable right" and urges legislation to make "out-of-season 'sun-tanning' a secured benefit of each health plan."

The student-led worship service on the morning of graduation represents a more serious resolution of the tensions. Almost everything about it suggests that the organizers—members of the core group of on-campus students who have been leaders from the beginning—have developed great confidence about displaying and promoting "diversity." The length and complex iconography of the printed program, the many pieces and styles of the service, including a skit with an actor in a bathrobe, the multiple sermons ("meditations"), and especially what the students say ("I came with one idea of God but now God has opened my eyes. . . . The Lord stayed the same, but everything looks different to me now"; "Woe is me. . . . Lord, I am a racist. Lord, I am a bigot. Lord, I am a man") testify that these students have "heard" what Mainline teaches. Their allegiance to churches and their parishioners is still present—the purists have not prevailed on that point—but the pivotal verb has changed. There is no mention of "serving" institutions; this group will go out and "prophesy" to them.

It must be emphasized that Mainline has not coerced students to take this view. The frequency and passion with which "diversity" and "justice" are preached are matched with a firm commitment to give students a great deal of freedom in most sectors of the institution's life. This is certainly the case in the classroom. Harriet Hercon sets a pattern in first-semester Mission and Ministry sessions: Many "lectures" in this school are in fact guided discussions that take shape as much from the students' questions and comments as from the instructor's advance plan. Though students remember the class (vividly) as the setting for difficult confrontations with each other and with strange language and ideas that they did not understand at the time, they also report that it was "a safe place" to let all of that [anger, pain] out." Others teach nondirectively too. One student remembers that Mary Miles "participated with us in deciding, but she didn't direct," and she probably wanted the class "to go in different directions." Some teachers invite great playfulness. Roland Pritchard places no limits on how much students can ham it up in their Old Testament and the Arts presentations. (Evangelical Seminary also—rarely—invites students to use the arts in their work, but only in a nonrequired subject, evangelism. No member of the Bible department at Evangelical would use music, art, or drama in the classroom.)

There is even more freedom outside the classroom. The school makes it simple and easy not only to start a new organization but also to get institutional funds for it: All the organizer has to do is submit a paragraph-long request to the Community Committee. Control of both the committee and the *MTS Journal* changes, in the second year, from the "whole community" (students, faculty, staff) to students alone. No institutional barriers or objections are raised to this student initiative. Protests of various kinds are routine and genially greeted. Often faculty members join them. The most dramatic demonstration of administrative openness is President Jack's quick decision to overrule his own subordinates and invite the students to leave their parody art exhibit in place. He goes further, in fact: He calls attention to it by impaneling a "jury" to select some of the send-up sculptures for awards. Mainline's pivotal leaders want its students to buy into its core views and values, but they also seem to be convinced that real ownership of those views and values is likely to occur only if students are given the freedom to leave them as well as take them.

Evangelical Seminary students are drawn to the school because it appears from a distance to be "solid," to offer sound views about the Bible (inerrant ones) and dependable methods for learning the Bible's precepts for Christian life. The affinity is roughly parallel to Mainline's students' assuming before they enroll that the school's emphasis on "justice" is the same as theirs on "service," though Evangelical students often are seeking a "solid" teaching not because they have experienced it in evangelical organizations (Mainline students know what service is because they have done it) but because the rough-and-tumble culture of popular evangelicalism is not solid enough. As we noted earlier, many of Evangelical's students have floated from church to church. Some of these departures are responses to church conflicts or malfeasance on the part of the pastor. In other cases, the students leave churches because they have been drawn into, or out of, one of the submovements in the evangelical world—the charismatic movement, or dispensational fundamentalism. Some students have never had a long-term alliance with a church; their principal point of attachment to evangelicalism is a parachurch organization. Most have been evangelicals long enough to see numerous evangelical churches, service organizations, and businesses disappear while others are created overnight and grow rapidly. A "solid" seminary that has been around for a century (a long time in the organizational world of contemporary evangelicalism) promises to provide the sort of anchor that many of them feel they need.

The students at Evangelical, like those at Mainline, learn right away that the school's view of things is in fact very different from their own. During orientation and in almost every class, the themes of discipline, restrained behavior, the uniformity of God's plan for the world in all times and places, the primacy of reason over feeling, and especially the necessity of hard work are hammered over and over. The Bible, students are told, if mined studiously, will prove the rightness of these values and postures. The message comes as a shock to many of the students, for whom the Bible has seemed readily accessible and has functioned primarily as a vast treasury of phrases to be set to praise music and as a biography of their romantic hero—Jesus Christ. The style of piety that the seminary's exemplars— Andrew Watson and the most admired young faculty members—repeatedly demonstrate is just as foreign to many new students as is the view of the Bible. A right relationship with God, these figures stress, requires suppressing one's selfish desires and strong human emotions (sometimes including intense religious feelings) in order to come to terms with God's will, which is nothing like ours, unlikely to conform to what we think we want, but much better for us than we can even imagine. In sharp contrast, some students have been immersed in a piety tuned exactly to their immediate feelings and needs. Several came to seminary because they were given personal signs: For Amos Wayland it was a radio announcement, for Laura a coincidence of telephone calls. Most believe that God gives what good Christians ask him for. Tastes in worship show the most dramatic difference between the school's dispositions and that of the students. For the core faculty members and almost all their "variant colleagues," the central event in worship should be an orthodox sermon on a biblical text, to which theologically correct prayers and dignified hymns can be added. Students arrive averse to "hearing another lecture" in chapel or church and accustomed to filling the interval of worship with fervent testimonies and religious love songs.

The clash between these cultures sets off a process like the one at Mainline Seminary, but there are several significant differences. First, though students at Evangelical begin to notice almost immediately the messages the seminary broadcasts to them and begin to try on those ideas and attitudes for themselves, they also maintain the very different cultural attitudes and practices that they brought with them far longer and more openly than do the students at Mainline. One reason for this difference may be that popular evangelical culture is "stronger" than its mainline Protestant counterpart: It has more distinctive language, patterns of behavior, symbols, and artifacts. The religious culture of the students who enter Mainline consists mostly of general ideas and attitudes. The Evangelical students have practices—manners, prayers forms, approved dress styles, and a vast inventory of songs—as well as a network of organizations with which many are still in touch. They hold onto all these features of their preseminary religious life far longer than the Mainline students continue to talk uncritically of "service" and congregational life.

A second difference is that the cultural clash at Evangelical is highly intellectual. Though Evangelical's dominant message contains very specific behavioral norms (assiduous work habits, formal dress, reserved manners, marriage, large families schooled in "Christian" settings), they receive far less emphasis than correct doctrine. The message's major criticism of present-day evangelical life is that it is hostile to the "cognitive" or "evangelical mind": O'Neil cites "the meltdown of truth into feeling, theology into experience, Calvinism into Arminianism" in explaining to students where American evangelicalism went fatally off the track. Bashford, a hero for many students, tells them that once he had reasoned his way to what he was sure were correct views about baptism, he acted on his beliefs even though he alienated some members of his family by doing so. Mainline Seminary presses its students to "work it out" in a painful process of personal transformation. Evangelical Seminary, with equal force and for many students just as much personal cost, tries to "get things straight"—that is, to change their minds.[1]

A third difference is that the basic structure of challenge and response at Evangelical is not chronological in the same sense that it is at Mainline. Though the diachronic pattern observed at Mainline (clash, struggle and contests, resolution) seems to obtain for *individual* students at Evangelical, it does not structure the experience of classes or groups. The reason for this is clear: Evangelical students do not move through its programs in cohorts. The order of courses is dictated mostly by convenience (for many students, even "full-time" students, it is fitted around almost full-time work schedules). Some institutional events do affect everybody (Kirt Holman's suicide attempt, the "and your daughters" controversy). But students encounter the school from such different angles, meet its key figures in so many different orders, and lead such different lives while enrolled that even demographic twins (for instance, two "spiffy" women in the inner Covenant House circle) are likely to react to the same event at the seminary in different ways.

Formal and informal student groups are very important at Evangelical, as they are at Mainline, but they play different roles in Evangelical's individualized educational structures. Both affinity groups (the Covenant House women, the charismatic single men) and formal organizations (a literary group, the Mission Fellowship) function as banks of like-minded persons from which conversation partners can be selected for the all-important process of "getting things straight." Most of the contests between school and student culture at Evangelical are worked out between two persons, in very small groups, or by individuals participating in public controversies on their own, without claiming the backing of larger groups. Contention among groups, which Mainline's pluriform culture seems to encourage, does not occur at Evangelical, where so much emphasis is placed on finding in Scripture, and conforming one's life to, a single correct set of orthodox beliefs and practices.

The cultural contest at Evangelical appears to be structured not by a schedule, as at Mainline, but by a sort of map. Students become deeply engaged in making sense of Evangelical's cultural messages and trying to reconcile them with their established beliefs and preferences by attempting that in several different settings. Those who avoid some of the settings do not get as deeply engaged.

The classroom is one of the settings. Most class time at Evangelical is taken up with instructors' prepared lectures, but the condensed question-and-answer sessions at the end of lecture hours are the focus of most student attention. The exchange with O'Neil runs the gamut of dynamics. First the comments are conventional: The students try to defend evangelicalism from the outside criticisms of it that O'Neil has had them read ("Wills seems unaware that not all evangelicals read the Bible ahistorically"). Then, when O'Neil pulls the rug out from under them by agreeing with the critics, the students try that tack. Then O'Neil switches position again. The students are getting tired: one complains quietly to another of "intellectual gridlock. . . . Every time I try to think my way through these things, every way is wrong." Finally, several decide to say what they think. One accuses O'Neil of fear of the mass media (he becomes defensive: "I have produced [television] documentaries. . . . How many have you produced?"). Later he apologizes. The students continue to argue with him. At the end of the hour, their opposition subsides, and his tone becomes conciliatory.

This pattern of exchange is typical. Evangelical's most influential professors, passionate in their devotion to the set of correct ideas they call "truth," go out on limbs. Some, like Allen, do it by pouring out prodigious amounts of energy and pushing students toward exhaustion. Bashford uses candid self-disclosure, an unusual and thus very noticeable tactic, given Evangelical's buttoned-down etiquette. But many others use methods like O'Neil's. Davis Saddler—in a statement that many evangelicals as well as liberals would judge uncivil—declares that John Cobb, who is viewed by many as an exemplary Christian as well as theological scholar, is "not a Christian." When Angie Harlan defends Cobb, Saddler accuses her of "fuzz[ing] out." She announces her distress at "the charge of being a fluff ball." Saddler apologizes for what he said, and he describes Cobb as "a wonderful person [who] serves the church unstintingly." But he also restates his case in strong terms: "His theology is dead wrong . . . disastrous for New Testament evangelism . . . . I just want to leave you with the joy of . . . biblical theology in the Scriptures. I do not have a great deal of time left, and that is where I want to spend my time. I take my stand on the Word."

Very likely, O'Neil, Saddler, and others do not plan to lose emotional control in class exchanges, attacking other scholars and students so sharply for holding views that oppose their own. Repeatedly, however, they permit themselves to take that step. They do apologize for offending, but they do not give substantive ground. What students seem to learn from repeated exchanges like this is that correct ideas, including their own, are more important than good feelings. That is, of course, one of the main points of Evangelical's dominant message.

With growing confidence, students demonstrate their mastery of no-holds-barred arguments in favor of truth. In class, Pamela Willis takes on James Cone, a nationally known African-American theologian, with a tenacity that matches O'Neil's and Saddler's. "Didn't Jesus die for all of us?" she asks after he says that Jesus died for black people and others "who are dying now." Cone laughs at her and accuses her of mouthing Roy Parks's views. She is not deterred. She will not grant his point and, having made the call, decides that Cone is guilty of the anti-intellectualism of which he accused her.

Students learn these procedures of digging for "the truth" and standing for it without compromise in class, but they practice them most often in a second kind of setting, the extracurricular activities of the school. Evangelical's list of school-sponsored events, organizations, and publications is much shorter than Mainline's, but the amount of theological energy expended in these activities is, if anything, greater. Paul Bashford's views on baptism, for instance, are presented in a special forum. Scores of students crowd into the event, and emotions—Bashford's and others—run high. He makes his declaration of willingness to upset his family by refusing to baptize his children as infants. William Emmett, one of the Truly Reformed students, argues with Bashford vehemently when Bashford says that he would rebaptize those whose infant baptism does not show "the fruits of the Spirit." Later, William Emmett worries that his passionate outburst may have violated another Evangelical norm—respect for teachers. But he is even more worried by the possibility that "my way of doing things may not be the right way." The exchange has not yet changed his mind, but it has made him consider—as Mainline's dominant culture seeks to do—that truth may matter more than nice manners, and perhaps more even than the kind of Presbyterian hyperorthodoxy that Emmett brought with him to seminary.

The Iron Sharpens Iron bulletin board offers similar opportunities for students to try out their capacities for finding true views and applying them in actual cases. Because the targets here are each other rather than faculty members or outside authority figures, the exchanges are faster and more furious. Rick Harvey writes a review of the Robert Mapplethorpe photo exhibit in the student publication. The review suggests that the exhibit may have some positive values. He is attacked from almost all sides on the Iron Sharpens Iron board. Ultraconservative Cary Draper accuses Rick of "discredit[ing] himself and . . . [bringing] shame and disgrace to the entire [Evangelical Seminary] community" by failing to acknowledge that "it is the Word of God *alone* which sanctifies and saves." Blair Jones, usually Rick's ally, also accuses Rick of "compromising Truth." Only Helen Pericone defends Rick's views, questioning the vehemence of the reactions to Rick and the attacks on his character. Brendon Martin joins her in chiding fellow students for condemning Rick personally. The student who posted a Bible verse that seemed to be aimed at Rick apologizes, but no one apologizes for or takes back their strong statements of opinion.

The student publication, with its annually changing names and editors, invites fuller and somewhat more temperate exchanges. The debate over the appropriateness of the "and your daughters" cartoon poster begins with "Point/Counterpoint" articles by Cary Draper and Blair Jones in *Didache II*. Their debate pushes beyond the obvious issues raised by the poster—Should women be ordained? Is it appropriate for one side in that debate to make fun of the other?—to a question that is a central focus of Mainline's dominant message: How do we know the truth? Words—of the Bible, of expository preaching of it, and of theological propositions derived from it—are the *only* medium that will "communicate truth," says Cary, taking a position akin to but more extreme than the dominant view in the faculty. Truth can also be apprehended by "discernment . . . beyond words," argues Blair, quoting the Bible ("because of practice have their senses trained to discern good and evil . . ."). When the debate hits the Iron Sharpens Iron board, it loses subtlety and gains an edge. Dean Diersen posts a testy notice accusing the students of lacking humor; students pin up sarcastic replies. Sarah Trumbell uses the phrase "masculine pride." Cary Draper (who accused Rick Harvey of disgracing the seminary over the Mapplethorpe exhibit) chides her for "point[ing] fingers and cast[-ing] insults." Someone mentions "lesbians" in a notice posted on the board; Sarah objects. Then, as seems to be standard, there are apologies and calls for "charity," but there is no granting of substantive points to the other side.

In a third kind of setting, "getting things straight" is practiced with less antagonism and edge. Out of public view and hearing—in dorm rooms, the library lounge, and the cafeteria, and on the many jobs in the school that students do for pay—there are discussions and debates that are just as serious and energetic as the ones in class and extracurricular settings, but much more exploratory and tentative. In the print shop, Ron Biddle and other students talk about theology while they are "folding stuff." The students who take studying "probably a little too seriously" do the same in the library. Such discussions can heat up. For a while, Lois Boucher and Pamela Willis are not sure whether their friendship will survive their different views about what teaching methods can convey the truth. Pamela opposes "sharing feelings." Lois insists that ordinary folk, herself included, cannot always live up to Evangelical's high "cognitive" didactic standard. Sometimes these more intimate exchanges are between equals: Students who respect each other's abilities work out together what it would mean to take seriously what key figures like Parks, Bashford, and Watson are urging them to accept. At other points, students push their version of the truth onto others, using some of the forceful tactics that faculty use with them. Anne Norton labels Sarah Trumbell's ideas about Kirt Holman's suicide attempt ("Kirt's problem was that he did not have enough faith") "stupid" and "fundamentalist." In this case, Sarah backs down, or rather disowns an idea that she quickly credits to "others."

Each of these three settings—the classroom, structured extracurricular activity, and small groups and pairs of friends—provides different resources for "getting things straight." Classes present examples of acceptable patterns of reasoning and of how to balance "truth" and other people's feelings. Non-class activities give students the opportunity to initiate the kind of exchanges that they have seen their instructors provoke and to figure out the implications of "the message" in a wide variety of specific cases. (The number of students who are highly visible in the school's extracurricular life is small, as the repetition of certain names suggests. Participation is not, however, limited to those who write articles and Iron Sharpens Iron postings. Almost every student who is present on the campus for substantial periods becomes involved the controversies. At almost no time of day, for instance, is there not at least one reader standing in front of the Iron Sharpens Iron board, and often there are several students engaged in discussion. And attendance at special events like the Bashford baptism talk is high.) In more intimate settings, the polemical stakes are lower, and students admit to confusion about some features of the message and dubiety about others. All three steps—learning to seek "the truth" from example, trying out the process, and hammering out an honest personal response to views and values the school presents—seem to be ingredients of a satisfying educational experience at Evangelical.

As we noted before, much of the time devoted to "getting things straight" at Evangelical is spent debating ideas. Other features of the culture are also tested, however. The practice that students most quickly adopt from the school culture is hard scholastic work. Because so much reading and writing is assigned, they have very little choice but to put in long hours, but many also buy into the high value placed on such activity—the belief that the truth of the Bible can be obtained only by conscientious study. Some do complain that their personal and spiritual lives are being damaged by the amount of homework, and others, like Lois, object to not the amount but the kind of study required. Most, however, buy the attitude, new to many of them, that faithful Christian life is hard work, and reorganize their patterns of daily life accordingly.

Students find it harder to accept another feature of the school's central view: that Christian life is usually not, and perhaps should not be, much fun. They are used to emotionally satisfying pious acts, and they do not give those up quickly. In tiny prayer sessions among friends, at the Mission Fellowship, at vespers and student-led service once a week in chapel, they continue to pray "just prayers"— to thank God for very specific special favors and to sing praise choruses. At the same time, they try out the school's approved style of worship. Most attend faculty-led chapel on occasion, a very few regularly. As the years pass, more and more take a public role in a faculty-led service, writing a theologically refined prayer for the occasion (rather than offering a spontaneous "just prayer"), or putting on a suit to read from the Bible. Other slow changes are evident too. Many give up the more extreme forms of youth group dress (though not Elvin Weyl, who continues to wear surfing clothes in midwinter and at chapel as long as he is enrolled); and as they approach graduation, they appear more often dressed like faculty members, usually because they have to deliver a sermon in class, go to a church internship position later in the day, or appear for a job interview.

Again, however, it must be emphasized that the passionate fervor with which ideas and values—especially the dominant ones—are promoted at the schools in this study does not amount to coercion. This is as true for Evangelical as for Mainline. Even though Evangelical's dominant culture does not valorize diversity of views or "liberation" of individuals and groups, central figures regularly demonstrate a commitment to letting students make up their own minds. Jerome Allen is very certain that Scripture interpreted properly (and he is the school's expert on scriptural interpretation) precludes the ordination of women, but he gives Paula Fleming an A on a paper that takes the opposite position. Andrew Nagel steps in at the end of the tense Saddler/Angie Harlan exchange to, in effect, give her permission to continue to hold her own views in the face of Saddler's "stand on the Word." "You're young," he says (a reference to Saddler's statement that he does not "have much time left"). "You can speculate." Students respond to the offer of freedom to form their own views. Zak Korkas, who appropriates for himself about as much of the dominant Evangelical message as any student, nevertheless declares with pride that he is "no [faculty member's] clone." Many other students congratulate themselves for having their own convictions and being able to defend them. They seem to have heard the message behind the message of "mild generic Calvinism": Truth and the ability to back it up with biblical authority and rational arguments matter more than anything.

Resolutions

In both institutions, students who have sufficient exposure to the central message and manners seem to be changed by them by the end of the third year. Very few students adopt the whole dominant message and all associated habits and values. Even fewer reject it entirely. Most make a substantial part of it their own, without entirely surrendering the goals, ideas, attitudes, and preferences that they brought to seminary with them.

Many students arrive at Mainline theologically and politically more conservative than most of the faculty, and much more favorably disposed to congregations and denominations. Therefore, it is not surprising that during their time in seminary the views of the majority become more progressive, especially in relation to the themes—inclusion of diverse groups, sensitivity to their feelings and views, and access to power for them—that the school constantly amplifies. The students' assessment of the importance and potential of churches is not greatly diminished, though most become convinced that refitting churches for adequate "service," now routinely redefined in terms of inclusion and justice, is going to be a harder job than they once thought.

Evan Shanks, for instance, from the Deep South and one of the more conservative students in the student pastor track, talks, as might be expected, of his "love" of "outstanding people" like Tory Campbell, one of the faculty members closest to his appreciative views of denominational and theological tradition. He also admits, however, that although he might have been "happier" at a more conservative seminary, where he would have had more conservative friends, he would not have "grown" as much at such a school, where "they tell you what is right to believe. . . . And you don't have to fight with them as much. And I guess I have learned to appreciate a little bit of diversity at Mainline and how God's grace can work in that diversity." Most important for him, he reports, has been his roommate, James Englehardt, who is the member of the student pastor group "furthest apart" from him theologically: "I usually find reality somewhere in between the way he perceives what is going on and the way I perceive what is going on." Evan is not anxious about how the new ideas and position he has developed at Mainline will fit into the "conservative . . . , more evangelical" churches he will serve. He is convinced that with respect to the Bible, "you can be critical [as he learned at

Mainline] and still love it." He thinks that he can change the views on women's issues at the kinds of churches he will pastor: "just a little bit of education . . . two sermons to bring them around." That might even be the case, he thinks, on openness to homosexuals, an issue that he thinks Mainline doesn't handle well either: "They [the churches] finding grace in the diversity, I think they could listen to that and say, 'Hey, wow, that's neat.' "

Other self-styled conservative students make similar reports. They accept the school's message about diversity and its insistence on considerate postures toward people who are greatly different as critically important. They realize that their churches have not yet made this step. They know that it is their job, and a difficult one, to "prophesy to the institution." But they think they can do it. Jim McClaren, a shy rural pastor, sums it up this way: "My foundations are still my foundations, but I have added a couple of new rooms onto the building." Mitch Tabor, an African-American student with a conservative background, says much the same thing. He labels himself "more liberal" than when he came to seminary, by which he means "more apt to listen to others."

Mitch, who joined James Englehardt in organizing the extraordinary joint worship service of their black and white congregations—a live demonstration of some of the consequences of "listening to others"—strikes another theme that is common in students' reviews of their time at Mainline: the discovery of "theology."

"The whole idea of theology," says Mitch, "was not even in my vocabulary." In contrast to Evangelical, where "theology" is synonymous with "truth" and most often means a set of firm doctrinal propositions supported by elaborate rational arguments about the meaning of the Bible, "theology" for Mitch and others at Mainline is the process of finding verbal expression for "something that you knew in your heart all along." "The curriculum required me to wrestle with theological issues," says Peter Tomas, "and I think I have not so much changed my mind, but . . . my thinking has kind of reordered."

The decision about which concepts, stances, and "theological" approaches taught at Mainline to incorporate and which to reject is less easily resolved for some students than for those just described. Janet Cable, who like those students is fairly conservative and a student pastor, knows that with her rocky marital history and the resistance she has encountered as a woman in ministry, she is a good candidate for feminism. However, she cannot take that step. She will not be "a doormat," but she does continue to hold onto the notion that so many students cherished when they entered but have since questioned—"serving": "I believe that we're called to be servants." She refuses to "start with" the "identification with the poor and needy" that is the basis for liberation theology, because her starting point is "Jesus Christ." But she adds that he was "a man for others"; she learns at Mainline to take a special pride in the interracial congregation where she is assigned to be minister; and she is the student who, after trying to transfer out of David Parsons's class because she did not like his "anger" in class, decided to stay and later found that "love for theology poured out of him, and . . . he made light bulbs go on in my head."

Students who, like James Englehardt, find themselves on the liberal side of the student spectrum at the beginning are sometimes pulled "leftward" (his term) by the purist faculty. James says he learned from Rick Santos that Jesus "came out of a people who were oppressed and abused . . . , is the liberator of the op-pressed[,] . . . [and therefore] theology is just really down and dirty with the people." He entertains some of the purist pessimism about local churches. Of the rather affluent one where he currently works, he says at one point, "You know, I have come to the conclusion that these people don't have the foggiest idea what it means to be a church. To them it's really a social club . . . and they want to keep it going because it's always been there." But James does not pull away from that church. Instead, he and Mitch organize their interracial service. In his sermon at that service, he declares that "as long as there are churches like [Mitch's black church] and [James's white church], there is hope."

Other very liberal students adjust in the other direction. Arlene Jervis came with some experience of "radical" social activism. She retains most of her activist commitments but adds to them new interests in spiritual matters and worship; she finds that she can approve of the fact that the church where she serves as a student assistant is "doing mostly inward, nurturing things." In fact, she finds that those "nurturing things" meet some of her personal needs. In the end, she says, she "looks more realistically at issues. How do they apply to lay people in my church? . . . I haven't changed much. I was already left of center. If anything, I've moved more to the center because that's where most of the lay people are."

Whatever their starting points, most students end up, like Arlene, creating a mixture of ideas and attitudes from Mainline's dominant culture and the others that have influenced them. Boyd Arthur, a musician and commuter student with a Southern Baptist background against which he has reacted in a liberal direction, accepts substantial parts of Mainline's message. He decides that he should move his family out of their affluent white suburb, a view he ascribes to "being at Mainline, and being challenged to not be in sheltered environments." He is avid to serve in local churches (he is slowly putting himself through seminary over a long stretch of years because most of the full-time jobs are for ordained people), but as a result of his encounter with liberation theology, he now understands that he may have to "stand up" to influential figures ("the biggest giver of the church") over important issues. Even so, he complains at length about the humorlessness of the purists and becomes known for interrupting solemn class discussion about inclusiveness and justice with "jokes" that stretch the boundaries of what is ac-ceptable in Mainline's dominant culture.

Tommy Reiss, who considers himself one of Mainline's really conservative stu-dents in the third year as well as the first, nevertheless has heard Mainline's domi-nant message and made a place for it in his thinking and behavior: "Every day, every week I struggle to see God from the perspective of other people. . . . I have heard their issues. I am in no way black. I am in no way female. I am in no way physically challenged. But I have been with people who are, and I am chal-lenged by the reality of their experience to include that in my theology and in my ecclesiology and in my existential being." He is glad that he has learned terms with which to express his traditional theological views. Some of those views have been called into question ("I used to know the Bible before I got here"), and Tommy is comfortable with the possibility that not all the questions can be answered immediately. At the same time, he worries that all the questioning makes room for "heresy"; it makes him "want to scream" to realize that some of his doctrinally shaky classmates are "headed for pulpits." He rejects the notion, which Harriet Hercon introduced from the "process" school of theology, that human beings are "partners with God in creation" ("We are not partners . . . , we are stewards . . . , just a little bit lower than the angels"). He agonizes about whether he "should make myself available to be a scapegoat for their [his black brothers' and sisters'] anger," and he does not feel that he has the capacity to be as fully "inclusive" as the school is pushing him to be.[2] As Tommy himself notes, the evangelical congregations where he is likely to minister will have a pastor with very different views and goals than they would have if Tommy had gone to Evangelical Seminary—the other school he strongly considered attending.

Evangelical's students also mix and match pieces of the school's forceful message and of the perspectives and preferences that they brought with them from the wider evangelical culture. On very public occasions, they sound almost exactly like the strongest voices in the school—for example, Jeffrey Barber in his graduation speech. Jeff, the student association president, grew up Pentecostal but is now a member of a Reformed denomination and husband of a graduate of Grove City College—a Christian college whose alumni are known on campus for their conservative, usually Reformed theology. He has become a model Evangelical student; at graduation he denounces seminaries that do not require thorough study of the Bible in the original languages: "Shame on us if the world is more studious and industrious than those committed to the gospel. How can such a precious message be handled with mediocrity? The Christian minister must be a diligent student. . . . God has called us to a ministry of the Word." At a subsequent graduation, there is more such accurate quotation of the school's self-understanding: "We need vision for effective ministry. . . . Without tools and lenses, we would spend our strength. With them, we can build. We have learned about God, his glory, but also the Bible, church, and world. The faculty have been like so many optometrists."

Out of the spotlight, however, it is clear that students do select among the school's favorite themes, modify them and, to a lesser extent, dissent from them. Jeffrey Barber himself has some "variant" views. He identifies himself as a disciple of Roy Parks, Reg O'Neil, and the Truly Reformed professor Michael Tucker, but he also expresses open admiration for a professor from another seminary who went on the trip to India with him—a theologian whose views are so radical that Barber's Evangelical faculty heroes would certainly judge them to be heretical or non-Christian. He also looks for strategies to convince his academically talented wife to modify her highly traditional conviction that she must be a full-time homemaker until her husband is established and her children are grown up.

Similarly, Ron Biddle, who describes himself as a "fish *in* water" at Evangelical, and who wants to be a "doctor of Christian faith" so that people will be "convicted by the truth," takes a position on denominations that differs from that of his mentors. Raised in the mainline Presbyterian Church (U.S.A.), he is determined to stay in it. He has not been convinced by the dominant approach to church life at Evangelical, which is that Christians committed to the truth should join congregations committed to true teachings rather than align themselves with denominations that may include persons and churches with heterodox or heretical views. "I am committed to [the PCUSA]," says Ron. "It's a wonderful denomination, and I think that its heritage is just something that can't be left to dissolve in the rot of society. I think it needs to be upheld." Zak Korkas is another example of the student who conforms to Evangelical's dominant view and values in many respects but cuts his own pattern in others. He belongs to an independent church ("I've not been geared to be a denominational person"); he buys into the hard work ethic ("I've been refined . . . through the pain of writing papers and learning languages. I had to take the hardest classes"); he shares the "mild generic Calvinists'" skepticism about hard-sell evangelism. He does not, however, accept the picture of gender relations that the core faculty projects—men in positions of social and Christian leadership and women, especially once they marry, in supportive domestic and educational roles: "I mean, men should be teaching kids in Sunday school, elementary school kids, and they're not. . . . I think it would free women up to seek out what they might be more called to do in ministries."

By the end of his time at the school, Neal Huchett, who came to Evangelical from the other side (Pentecostal and Arminian) of the evangelical tracks, has "become a Calvinist, meaning that I believe . . . in God's choosing, over and against free will, and God's ordaining of all things." He now understands ministry very much in Evangelical's dominant mode, as "helping those who are under preaching to incorporate the Word into their lives and to . . . help them incorporate the change that may bring about," a major move away from the Pentecostal idea that Spirit enters people directly, unmediated by words. He also embraces "hard work" with great enthusiasm ("probably a little too seriously . . . a little crazy"). At the same time, though, he remains Pentecostal and is critical of Calvinists who do not have a "vibrant, living relationship with Christ," and he claims to have gained "confidence in my own theology, so that I don't look at the professors . . . and say, 'Wow!' as much as I say, 'Well, I think my theology is a little better than yours.'"

Cole Silas and his charismatic friends create a similar cocktail of Evangelical's stance and their own. Cole takes a theological position "somewhere in between" Calvinist and Arminian. He holds fast to his popular evangelical tastes, especially in music. He is part of the small group of students who almost always go to chapel, and he uses his regular attendance as leverage to convince Andrew Watson to approve a weekly student-led service dominated by the praise music that he and many other students continue to like. A student in one of the "practical" master's programs (youth ministry), he does not spend a lot of time in "different debates that go on," but he acknowledges their importance: "I think we can learn from those as well." Though Cole's charismatic views and tastes are distinctive—a small minority of Evangelical students are explicitly charismatic—in many ways he is typical of the much larger group of students who come to Evangelical seeking "practical tools" for use in their ministries but who leave with a revised view of what they need: not only practical guidance, but also academic techniques for studiously mining the Bible and discovering its truth.

Evangelical's women students also construct positions that are mixtures of those they already held and others the school has urged them to consider. Brenda Moore, who followed Paul Bashford from the college where he first taught to Evangelical, associates herself with almost all of his views and with the conservative option on women's roles. She opposes the ordination of women and hangs out with other Covenant House women who share that view: "It's not that I would not speak to someone who believes in the ordination of women, but those of us who are more conservative and traditional are more comfortable together." In fact, she speaks to a wide range of other students. She attends events of the local evangelical feminist organization, and she listens seriously to their arguments: "Maybe our biblical idea of the family isn't so biblical after all," she muses after a presentation on justice in domestic settings. Brenda finally does not change her own opinion about ordination, but she does accept Evangelical's dictum that women's ordination is a topic on which orthodox Christians can disagree. Sharon Madden, unusual among the traditional women because she is enrolled in the M.Div. (preordination) program rather than the master's program most of them take to prepare for teaching, also moderates her opposition on women's ordination. Reflecting on the offenses of the minister who harassed her during her internship, she says she "would rather have [feminist] Mary Chang in the pulpit, never mind what her gender is." She decides against ordination for herself, but for new reasons: She agrees with Roy Parks that the "professionalization" of the ministry has hurt the churches. Paula Fleming, standing firmly on the other side of the ordination issue, also does not change her position. She persists in her Arminianism and in her practice of "prayer warfare" against demonic forces, neither of which gets much support at Evangelical. What she does learn and adopt from the patterns that Evangelical promotes is the style of argument. She gives reasons for her variant, even deviant, positions in the closely argued style that Parks, Bashford, and Allen esteem so highly. Allen acknowledges her success with the A he awards her paper in favor of women's ordination.

Pamela Willis and Anne Norton put together some of the most subtle combinations. Pamela has unbounded admiration for Roy Parks and agrees with him about almost everything. She befriends the traditional Covenant House women and conservative student association leaders like Jeffrey Barber and Kimberly Oliver. She refuses, however, to adopt the dress and manner that Evangelical projects as ideal for Christian women. During her time at seminary, her clothes become even more self-consciously stylish, her interests in high-brow secular culture more intense, her references to after-hours drinking more open, and her challenging class discussion style more blunt and challenging. She professes to have little interest in marriage and children. Her blunt, sophisticated style is a jarring contrast to the pastel, rather passive femininity of most Evangelical women. Anne Norton adopts that standard feminine style almost militantly, buying flower-sprigged jumpers and theorizing at great length about "submission." Yet she too cuts her own pattern. She talks casually and unjudgmentally about facts of secular life that most Evangelical students automatically profess to be horrified by, such as premarital sex, homosexuality, and religious pluralism. She takes the lead in urging her fellow students, most of whom (like most of the faculty) pay little attention to world events unless they have religious implications, to get involved in learning (and praying) about current affairs.

Not all Evangelical students work out these creatively mixed positions. A significant number do not have access to the resources for doing so. Some do not spend enough time at the school to hear the dominant message and to see it enacted. Others are physically present but so deeply troubled that they do not really take in what is going on around them. A small group of nonwhite and non-Anglo students (but not all of them) do not feel comfortable in the mainstream of the school's culture and therefore do not buy into it. Kate Prater falls at least partly into this category. Even though she has been associated with the school for a long time as employee and student, and even though students like Lois Boucher go to her for spiritual direction, she holds herself mostly apart from its values and concerns. She hides her charismatic leanings even from the faculty members she is close to. She "believes in what the seminary does," but she thinks it harbors "racist attitudes . . . out of ignorance, not intentionally," a view that only a few administrators who themselves do not share the school's dominant perspective would agree with. Kate traces her decision to engage in ministry with women to her childhood and notes that she was already doing it when she came. Despite her extensive exposure to the school, she accommodates very few of its emphases.

Much more typical of students who do not seem to be significantly affected by their experiences at Evangelical are Marilyn Flexner and Kenneth Schlitz. During much of the time they are enrolled, they are physically distant from the seminary. During her first year, Marilyn is lonely and homesick and commutes on weekends to her home in the next state; she leaves after the first year for an internship far from the campus; when she returns in the third year she lives off-campus. Though much happier, she does not become involved in friendship networks or in the flow of controversies and other events at the school. Like Kate, she plans to do work after seminary (with troubled children) that she was already doing before she entered. She is satisfied with the educational part of her seminary experience (she admits that she has formed few personal ties), but she does not seem even to have noticed the salient ideas, prevailing attitudes, or behavioral norms of Evangelical's culture, much less adopted them.

Evangelical Seminary has even less impact on Kenneth Schlitz. He commutes a long distance to campus and only makes the trip one day a week. He will take four years to complete the two-year program in youth ministry. Meanwhile, he works part-time in a church and as an undertaker. He mistakenly picked Evangelical because he thought he could get a "practical" education without too much of the theology he had been "overloaded" with in college. The value system of Evangelical has not rubbed off on him at all. He says his Bible courses have been a waste of time—a heretical statement in the context of Evangelical's house orthodoxy, where academic study of the Bible in particular is tantamount to holy work. He holds membership in a Holiness denomination, a subsection of the Arminian camp, but seems not to be aware that Arminian positions are widely challenged at Evangelical. He says that he has made friends at the seminary, but when asked to identify them he cannot remember any of their last names.

Students like these who "don't get it"—most of whom, in fact, do not even know what it is the school wants them to get—are not numerous at Evangelical, but there are enough who have not really "been there," in one way or another, to cause concern. Administrators and faculty talk mostly about the troubled ones—those who are too distracted even to do their course work, much less pay attention to all the subtler ways that the school tries to teach them things. In fact, the number of those whom the school doesn't reach because its highly flexible course scheduling permits students to graduate without spending much time on campus is probably greater than those who are emotionally disturbed. No parallel group is evident at Mainline. There are of course students, like Lu, who are mentally ill and unable to function. The problem of part-time students who work off-campus seems to be largely solved, however, by Mainline's student pastor track, which uses a variety of means—a more tightly structured curriculum, weekly overnights on campus—to make sure that such students are really "at school" while they are also doing so many other things.

Similarities and Differences

As we have noted throughout this and the preceding chapter, the two schools we studied, though they differ in many respects, go about the business of educational formation in strikingly similar ways. Both have a pronounced central goal: the reform of the religious movement with which the school is allied. In both cases, the school presents to its students not only arguments for that reform but also examples of the conduct that will bring it about. Both schools also present variations on the goal—one more radically critical of, others more accommodating to, the outside religious culture the school aims to modify and improve. Students in both institutions come imbued with the views and attitudes of that culture and, from almost the moment they set foot in the school, become engrossed in a struggle between the school's message and the perspectives they bring with them.

By the time the students leave the schools, their views and some of their patterns of behavior have changed. A few have adopted the central message and its prescribed manners and attitudes; a very few have rejected them completely. Most have made their own mixture: some tenets, manners, and opinions that the school promotes and some from the religious culture in which they were immersed before they came to the school.

The only significant difference in the processes of educational formation in the two schools we studied was the prominence of a chronological sequence at Mainline—students seem to go through stages in their encounter with the school's culture; at Evangelical, where the curriculum is not sequenced and many students study part-time, stages were not evident. At Evangelical, the intensity with which students struggled to make sense of the school's culture seemed to be related to the number and variety of different settings in which they were involved (classes, formal extracurricular activities, friendships, and informal groups) rather than to length of time in the program.

We suspect, however, that the differences we observed have something to do with our limits as observers. Because there were so many students at Evangelical living in so many different places and studying in different patterns, we could not track steps in the progress of individual students with any precision. At Mainline, because there was so much group activity, we could not map very well the trajectories of different students, the variety of activities in which they were involved, and the effects of those involvements. If we could have observed the students more intensively, we think that we might have found that Evangelical students also go through "stages" and that the formation of Mainline students is related to the variety and number of school settings in which they are involved.

Our description of educational formation at these two schools does not amount to a theory. It does, however, draw on and contribute to theories of culture and socialization. In the next chapter, we explore the implications of our observations for several bodies of theory. In the final chapter, we suggest what the implications might be for the educational practices of theological and other schools.

TWELVE

Culture and Formation: Theoretical Perspectives

In the preceding chapters, we have presented our data and interpretation of the ways in which the two seminaries' cultures function in the formation of students. We turn now to the relationship of our interpretations to a larger body of theory that has informed our work and to which, we believe, our work contributes.

We did not begin this research with a full-blown theoretical framework. To be sure, we had ideas formed both by reading the theory and research of others and by considerable personal experience in theological schools. We resisted forming a formal theory or hypotheses in advance, however, but instead proceeded inductively, from the ground up, doing our ethnographic work, sharing our field notes, putting forward tentative hypotheses in memos and meetings, often noting the relationship of our hypotheses to other theory and research.[1] This literature includes perspectives on organizational cultures and the institutions that produce them; on adult socialization, especially socialization into the professions, and on the history and sociology of American religion. In settling on these bodies of theory as frameworks for organizing our research and interpretation, we recognize that we could have chosen other options. For example, we could have chosen to do an analysis of power and status relations in the two schools; we could have used social class or gender analysis to interpret the data; or we could have used one of several other forms of organizational analysis. All of these are legitimate and important ways of viewing organizational dynamics and their relationships to other aspects of society. We chose instead to follow out the themes that the schools themselves take into account: self-description, organization to accomplish mission, aims in the educational process, student contributions to the process, and how the dynamics of school culture and student culture play themselves out in socialization into various forms of Christian ministry. To these issues we now turn.

Organizational Culture

As we noted in the Introduction, culture has become a major lens or frame through which to understand organizations and their dynamics, including educational institutions.[2] It is not our purpose here to review this large body of literature. In the Introduction, however, we mentioned several studies that have applied what might be called a cultural frame to theological seminaries and their role in the formation of students for ministry. We will return to the findings of several of these studies later in our discussion of professional socialization. We want now to reflect on our own use of the culture concept as the organizing frame for our study and what we have learned from it.

Our interpretation of the cultures of our two schools was developed as we observed, listened, interacted with, and interviewed students, faculty members and administrators over the three years we were at the schools. As we reflected on these observations, experiences, and conversations, we came to define the seminaries' cultures as those shared symbolic forms—worldviews and beliefs, ritual practices, ceremonies, art and architecture, language, and patterns of everyday interaction—that give meaning and direction to the life of the schools and the people who participate in them. This understanding of culture has been much influenced by the perspectives of Clifford Geertz (1966, 1973) and Ann Swidler (1986).

Geertz defines culture as *publicly available* symbolic forms through which collectivities and individuals experience and express meaning. That is, culture is not simply subjective meanings held in the heads of individuals in contrast to organizational or social structural patterns. Culture exists publicly, between individuals, in symbolic forms that are observable and need not be inferred from individual's private mental states. Rather, these "webs of significance," which Geertz likens to the maze of wandering streets in an old city (in contrast to neatly ordered suburbs), must be captured in "thick description." This we have tried to do in our ethnographic chapters, followed, in Chapters 10 and 11, by an effort to interpret the patterns that we described in the ethnographies, showing how they are arranged structurally.

Extending Geertz's perspective, Swidler (1986:273) defines culture as consisting of "symbolic vehicles of meaning, including beliefs, ritual practices, art forms, and ceremonies, as well as informal cultural practices such as language, gossip, stories, and rituals of daily life." With Geertz, Swidler emphasizes that culture includes shared practices, rituals, ceremonies, and patterns of interaction as well as shared ideas. That is, culture is inextricably linked with social situations. Swidler also argues against interpreting cultures as ahistoric values or value orientations toward which actors orient their action, an emphasis that finds particular expression in the work of Talcott Parsons (e.g., Parsons 1951).[3] Instead, she interprets cultures as "tool kits" of symbols, stories, rituals, and worldviews whose causal significance resides not in defining "ends of action" but rather in providing the cultural components that people use to construct "strategies of action"—general ways of organizing action that enable one to reach life goals.

Although our interpretation of the cultures of the two schools does not contradict Swidler's emphasis on culture as a tool kit, we believe that schools, especially graduate schools such as those we have studied, emphasize *giving reasons* for beliefs and actions. Knowing how to give reason for one's beliefs and actions may, of course, be thought of as a component of one's cultural tool kit, but it also implies that one is orienting action toward some normative goal: the reason for one's beliefs and actions. As we have proposed, each seminary articulates in its culture a normative goal. For Evangelical the goal is that of bringing religious discipline to Christian and social life and institutions according to God's plan as inscribed in the Bible. For Mainline Seminary, the goal is achieving inclusiveness and justice for all, both in the church and more generally in the world. In both instances, these are emphasized as broad normative goals toward which beliefs and practices should be oriented.[4] Such goals do not "cause" or determine beliefs or behavior, but they do provide desired directions toward which, from the school's perspective, students' and graduates' strategies of action should be constructed.

Geertz (1966) is helpful in this connection. He considers two ways that culture functions as a model: as a model "of" the way things are—an effort, for example, to state symbolically what "reality" is like so as to render it apprehensible; and as a model "for"—a set of instructions or a program by which one attempts to shape one's life. There is a sense in which the two schools' normative cultures function both as models "of" and as models "for." Each culture describes what, from the school's perspective, God's purposes for the world are—a model "of." Each also provides models "for"—a blueprint or tool kit for constructing one's life and ministry practices in harmony with those purposes. Models "of" function somewhat similarly to the way in which Swidler believes that ideologies function in what she calls "unsettled lives"—that is, periods of social transformation. As she writes (1986:278): "[I]deologies—explicit, articulated, highly organized meaning systems (both political and religious)—*establish* new styles or strategies of action. When people are learning new ways of organizing individual and collective action, practicing unfamiliar habits until they become familiar, then doctrine, symbol, and ritual directly shape action" (emphasis in the original).

These are unsettled times for participants in our two schools in at least a double sense: For most students, being in the school and encountering the school's powerful normative message involves learning many new ways of organizing both individual and collective action. What we called "getting things straight"—either as orthodoxy at Evangelical or orthopraxy at Mainline—involves learning and practicing unfamiliar habits of thinking and acting until they become familiar. Unsettledness also characterizes both evangelical and mainline Protestant Christian traditions—the ambient religious cultures of the two seminaries. Evangelicalism is generally acknowledged to be unstable, even chaotic, after a period of rapid growth; and mainline Protestantism is shaky, even panicky, after a quarter century of uninterrupted decline. The unsettledness of these broader religious traditions, combined with the rapid pace of social and cultural change, means that graduates will likely face challenges in their leadership roles for which there are no clearly delineated responses, no clear strategies of action—even for those who hold to an inerrant Scripture or a rigorous standard of inclusive justice. Thus, these powerful cultures to which the schools give expression aim at shaping the graduates' strategies of action, especially in contested areas, so that the strategies that are constructed are consistent with the culture's normative goal. Another way of saying this, commensurate both with Swidler's tool-kit imagery and the language we heard many times in our fieldwork, is that the schools aim to give the students tools for constructing their strategies of action in ministry. So the senior speaker at Evangelical's commencement can reflect on the "tools and lenses" he has gained— especially the tools of biblical languages and strategies of biblical interpretation— that will help him "build well" and "see well." Likewise, the graduating senior at Mainline feels strongly "that Mainline Seminary has given me the tools to work with and to work on my own faith." And he adds that he now has "a vision of ministry. . . . [T]he tools that have been in the box for the first four semesters [are] coming together."

As we have also tried to emphasize, the two cultures are not themselves unitary. While each states a normative goal at its center and supports that goal with various beliefs and practices, each also permits variations that can roughly be arranged on a continuum between pure opposition to and complete compromise with the external religious culture that the school addresses. Further, as we have seen, the students in each school form a student culture that draws not only on the dominant normative culture but also on the culture of other communities, especially religious communities, in which students participate outside of the school. This creates some of the contests that we have noted and leads to the formation of subcultures (Peterson 1965; Clark and Trow 1966) or student perspectives (Becker et al. 1961) which can either reinforce or subvert the school's normative agenda. The Covenant House women and the peer group of men of which Cole Silas was a member both partly reinforce Evangelical's normative culture but also filter it through experiences and perspectives that the women and men have brought from involvements outside the school. The different theological "camps" among faculty members and students—Truly Reformed, inclusivists, progressives, Pentecostals, denominationals—to some extent are subcultures within Evangelical. At Mainline, similar faculty and student variations exist, though around different cultural themes—for example, denominationalists and radical liberationists. The student pastors form a kind of subculture because of the curriculum track that they follow and because they live together during their time on campus each week. Minority students form another set of subcultural groups. Subcultures and extra-school environments are important for socialization, and we will return to them later. First, however, we want to raise the question of how these cultures (and subcultures) are produced and sustained over time.

Seminaries and the Production of Culture

Theological seminaries, like churches and like other schools, are institutions that are primarily engaged in producing and mediating particular cultures. Seminaries inherit, embody, transform, dramatize, and pass on particular traditions, beliefs, perspectives, ideas, and practices such as those we have examined. Indeed, many of the patterns of seminary life that we have observed at the two schools are representations of the cultures that have become institutionalized as part of each school's social fabric.

For cultural production and transmission to happen, seminaries require a variety of social resources, human and material. Human resources—faculty and students—are needed to produce and "consume" the culture. Human resources are also needed to administer and staff the organization and secure the necessary material resources to keep the organization running. Moreover, seminaries must develop patterns of internal organization and communication. Finally, they require sufficient legitimacy within their broader environment that enables them to sustain favorable relationships with important outside constituencies, draw resources from them, and have "outlets" for their particular "products." All of this is implied in naming them "institutions": They persist under changing circumstances and changing personnel, and they will continue producing and transmitting their particular cultural forms. Thinking about these institutional dimensions of seminaries and their cultures helps us to interpret some of the important differences and similarities that we have observed in the two schools.

As we have noted in previous chapters, the most casual observer visiting our two schools would have been struck by two things: on the one hand, striking differences, especially in the beliefs and ideology, symbols, ritual practices, and behavioral emphases of the two institutions; on the other, how much each school has in common with the other—common structures and processes. This seemingly paradoxical situation calls for explanation, and understanding seminaries as institutions helps. What are some of the major factors that account for the differences as well as the similarities in these schools and in the cultures that they produce?

In answer, we draw on several different sources. American religious history and the relation of our two seminaries to it provide a partial answer. We also draw on two theoretical perspectives from the social sciences: cultural production (e.g., Wuthnow 1994) and neoinstitutionalism (e.g., Powell and DiMaggio 1991).[5] The cultural production perspective emphasizes that cultures such as those that we have studied have not simply happened. They are, in considerable measure, the products of deliberate human activity over time. Neoinstitutionalists focus on the patterned and persisting character of organizations that make them institutions, but they pay special attention to an institution's relationship to its external environment. The environment is not only a source of the human and material resources that the institution needs for its functioning; it is also an important factor in shaping the institution's internal organizational and cultural patterns.

How, then, were the two very different cultures produced? And what accounts for the similarities we observed in spite of the differences?

History and Traditions

Each culture has been (and continues to be) produced as the school's leaders—successive cohorts of faculty members, administrators, and members of governing boards—have interacted with each other and with successive student cohorts. Over time, they have shaped their school's worldview and ethos. While both schools have antecedent institutions with which they claim some lineage, both in their current organizational embodiment are post–World War II institutions. Because of our intention to maintain their anonymity, we have chosen not to discuss the schools' recent histories or antecedents. We emphasize, however, the importance of institutional memory as one of the ingredients that shapes a school's culture, as Clark (1970, 1972) has shown by using the concept of an organization's saga—an institutionalized story that has evolved over time and recounts critical events and individuals in the institution's history. Clearly, both schools' present cultures are to some extent shaped by their institutional memories and the various individuals and groups that have formed those memories.

Besides their particular histories, each school's culture is also constructed from elements that faculty members, administrators, and students have drawn from various streams of the broader Christian heritage, from their particular interpretations of Scripture, and from various ecclesial and theological traditions. Each especially reflects important differences between Calvinists and the Arminian-revivalist tradition, differences that were especially prominent among Protestants in the eighteenth and nineteenth centuries. Strict Calvinists emphasize God's sovereignty and irresistible grace and play down revivalism. Arminians, who were early and strong supporters of evangelical revivalism, allow more room for the human will in accepting or resisting salvation. Both Calvinism and Arminianism have developed conservative and liberal forms in American religion. Evangelical Seminary's culture expresses conservative Calvinism, in both its Baptist and Presbyterian traditions. Mainline's culture, in contrast, is in the liberal Arminian heritage.

The two cultures are also inheritors of conflicts and movements that split Protestantism into conservative and liberal streams in the chaotic and expansive late nineteenth and early twentieth centuries. Partly the split came over the introduction of the historical-critical method for studying the Bible, a fruit of the Enlightenment and modernism (Hutchison 1992). Partly, too, it resulted from differing responses to urbanization and immigration. Whereas prior to the late nineteenth century, most Protestants would have referred to themselves as evangelicals, the term "evangelical" came to be the self-designation of theological and social conservatives who emphasized individual salvation, a personal moral life congruent with the ideals of the saved, and otherworldly rewards or punishment. Most would also have strongly resisted the use of higher criticism in interpreting the Bible. Liberal Protestants, in contrast, became this-worldly in orientation, holding that salvation applies to society as well as to individuals and emphasizing social as well as personal ethics. Also, they mostly accepted the use of historical-critical methods for biblical interpretation. Martin Marty (1976) refers to this split as creating two Protestant parties: "private" versus "public" Protestants.

The two-party split also spawned the fundamentalist/modernist controversies of the early twentieth century, with private Protestantism generally supporting fundamentalism, while public Protestantism was typically modernist in orientation. This controversy came to a head with the Scopes trial of 1925 in Dayton, Tennessee, over the teaching of evolution in the public schools. The trial resulted in a major public setback for fundamentalism (and the private Protestant or evangelical movement). Beginning in the 1940s, however, evangelicals, with varying degrees of fundamentalist influence, reemerged in what was called the "neoevangelical movement," of which Evangelical Seminary is a direct descendent.[6] Mainline Seminary, in contrast, reflects the legacy of public Protestantism, with both its social gospel and modernist impulses. Its culture also reflects more recent theological currents—for example, liberation theology, as expressed especially by African-American and feminist interpreters, and various postmodern theological emphases.

In an essay that draws on ethnographic data from our research at the two schools, Carroll and Marler (1995) examine ways in which the Evangelical and Mainline Seminary cultures reflect prominent themes in a more recent manifestation of the two-party split that, according to James Davison Hunter (1991), threatens to engulf American society in "culture war." As we noted in Chapter 10, we did not choose the two schools to represent extreme examples of the parties. Nonetheless, the two do divide along lines suggested by Hunter. Evangelical's culture expresses elements of what he calls "orthodoxy," with its commitment to an external, transcendent authority; the culture at Mainline reflects some elements of a "progressivist" perspective, one that privileges reason and experience over external, transcendent authority. Robert Wuthnow (1988), like Hunter, also sees a division that cuts across and is restructuring the older symbolic boundaries that have defined denominational differences in American religion. The current differences have their roots in many of the earlier developments in American religion that we have noted.[7] Whereas previously the "parties" tended to fall along denominational lines, Wuthnow argues that this is no longer the case—that many denominations, especially those that constitute Mainline Seminary's environment, experience the division as a "fault line" running through their middle. Moreover, such restructuring, in Wuthnow's view, has lessened the significance of denominations and heightened the importance of special purpose groups. These movements or organizations pursue particular, often single, agendas—for example, ethnic group concerns, feminist issues (especially for or against women's ordination), pro-choice versus pro-life attitudes, homosexual rights, family values, religion and public education, and varying concepts of mission and evangelism. As we have seen, the conflicts that such restructuring fosters in American society and religion find expression in the contests that occur within the cultures of the two schools. The Truly Reformed group at Evangelical Seminary and the liberationists at Mainline, respectively, are especially clear proponents of the two sides of the division. The centrists in each institution are less willing to take a hard line on some of the divisive issues and are more responsive to broader constituencies in their environments.

Although the characteristics of the two schools' normative cultures are illumined by the divisions described by Hunter and Wuthnow and by the earlier descriptions of a two-party division in Protestantism, we cannot accept metaphors of war or fissures and fault lines as adequate descriptions of what we found in the two schools. To be sure, there are representatives of both perspectives in the larger culture for whom the war metaphor clearly applies and who are willing to engage in extreme, even violent, activities to express their rage against the opposition. From the Weather Underground movement of the late 1960s to leaders of such disparate groups as the animal rights movement, the Christian Identity movement, and Operation Rescue of the 1990s, true believers willing to resort to strenuous or coercive measures can be found at both ends of the political spectrum. But that American culture generally, or Protestantism in particular, is divided into warring camps simply does not appear to be the case, and this goes for our two schools as well.

In the culture more generally, as Roof and McKinney (1987) show in their analysis of American religion, the situation is more aptly portrayed as a center with fringes than as bipolar. Indeed, Hunter (1991:43, 159) agrees that a majority of the public is not polarized between the two extremes. Some, as he recognizes, are thoughtfully bipartisan, and even more are ambivalent or apathetic. Analyses of survey data from the American public and from religious elites (Olson and Carroll 1992) show that this large middle is not likely to be easily mobilized by one extreme or the other. Our experiences in the two schools support this view. Only a few individuals at either institution are actively involved in efforts to mobilize others for either polar position. Even then, they seek to enlist others for involvement in nonviolent expressions of either of the positions.

Instead of conducting a war against secular humanists and liberals (on the part of Evangelical Seminary's faculty and students) or against fundamentalists and right-wing extremists (on the part of Mainline's faculty and students), much of the polemical effort in each institution is directed at other co-religionists. As we have shown, the keepers of the dominant message at Evangelical seem primarily concerned with the reform of evangelical culture. They seek to counter the "self movement" and the excesses of popular evangelicalism, with its romantic piety and often uncritical adulation of entrepreneurial religious leaders, and to bring it more in line with their Reformed theological emphasis on intellectual discipline and sober, reserved piety (Wheeler 1996). Their counterparts at Mainline are similarly concerned with correcting practices of their own and other mainline denominations and the institutions they have spawned, practices that block the realization of a just and inclusive church and society. The battle each fights is, therefore, not so much against the other Protestant side as against failures found within their own institutional and cultural contexts.

Adaptation to Particular Environments

As we noted, both the cultural production and neoinstitutionalist perspectives emphasize the importance of the external environment in shaping the institutional patterns, including the culture, of the two schools. The various theological and ecclesial streams, past and present, and their attendant emphases and conflicts are salient features of the environment in which the two seminaries exist and to which they are responding. Neither school, however, is responding to the whole of that larger environment. Each school's culture clearly reflects a selective adaptation (Wuthnow 1994:30–31) to this broader, diverse, and often conflicted environment. Each is selectively responding to different parts of that larger environment and to quite different constituencies.

For Mainline Seminary, the environment is first of all its sponsoring denomination and secondarily mainline Protestantism. As a nondenominational school, Evangelical Seminary has no single denomination to which it must be accountable.

Instead, its relevant environment is evangelical Protestantism, especially those denominations, institutions, and movements that are identified with the Reformed or Calvinist tradition and neoevangelicalism. These environments of the two schools are substantially different. To be sure, there is some overlap. Mainline draws some evangelical students from its own and other denominations, including some evangelical ones. It also experiences pressures from the evangelical or "orthodox" party in its sponsoring denomination. Evangelical likewise draws a number of its students from mainline denominations, primarily students who are evangelical in orientation. But for the most part, the two schools are selectively adapting to substantially different environments, environments whose constituencies overlap in only limited ways.[8]

As we noted in the preceding section, each school is concerned with the reform of its respective primary environment. The primary target of Evangelical Seminary's reforming efforts is evangelical culture and institutions, while Mainline Seminary's normative agenda focuses on reforming both the society and the church, especially its own denomination. Their reform agendas vary, therefore, because the environments at which they are aimed are not the same. There is a fit between each school's normative agenda and the way the school "reads" its environment. In this way, selective adaptation helps to shape the culture that is produced in the schools.

There is more: While each school aims at reforming its particular environment, each is also dependent on its environment for needed resources, especially for students and financial support, but also for congregations and other agencies that will employ its graduates. Each is in competition with other theological schools for these same resources. These competitive pressures also push for a "fit" between the cultural perspectives the school produces and the primary environment it aims to address. Such adaptation does not imply sinister compromises of normative ideals, as faculty and students at the schools sometimes accuse their administrators of making. Sellouts do happen, but adaptation is often a more natural, even unconscious, process that occurs as the schools engage in exchanges with their respective environments. As Wuthnow (1994: 31) points out, "Some organizations that might have a particularly 'true' or 'powerful' conception of the sacred [or "normative agenda," in our case] will nevertheless fail to survive against the competition of other organizations that simply fit in better with their cultural surroundings." We suspect that if the views of the Truly Reformed contingent at Evangelical or the strong liberationists at Mainline were to dominate their respective institutions more completely than they do, the two seminaries would have great difficulty surviving against their competition.

Institutional Isomorphism

The history and traditions that have helped to shape each school and the selective adaptation of each to a particular environment help to account for many of the differences in the cultures of the two schools. What, however, accounts for their similarities?

Neoinstitutional theorists Paul DiMaggio and Walter Powell (1983) use the concept of "institutional isomorphism" to indicate the ways in which organizations of a particular kind—organizations that share a common organizational field—come to resemble each other in form or substance even when they differ significantly in their normative agendas. Theological seminaries constitute a common organizational field that, in turn, participates more broadly in the organizational field of higher education, especially professional education. DiMaggio and Powell argue that as organizations sharing an organizational field cope with uncertainties in their environment, they become more and more alike. "Isomorphism," they argue, "is a constraining process that forces one unit in a population to resemble other units that face the same set of environmental conditions" (DiMaggio and Powell 1983:149). Partly this is a result of competition. A theological seminary cannot be too different from other seminaries and hope to compete for the resources that it needs to survive. More than competition, however, is at stake. Being like other seminaries is a mark of legitimacy within one's organizational field, an important factor for survival,[9] but at times unrelated to competitive fears or to a concern with improving performance (Meyer and Rowan 1977).

In the case of the two seminaries, one primary external pressure comes from regional and national accrediting agencies, especially the Association of Theological Schools, that set standards to which member schools must conform if their degree programs are to be viewed as legitimate. Many (though not all) denominations, for example, require graduation from an accredited theological school as prerequisite for ordination. Such pressures may be experienced as coercive since accreditation is at stake. But because they are defined as appropriate by members of the association, they are also often experienced as normative—what a "good seminary" ought to be like. Denominations are a second source of external pressure for common standards—especially, for Mainline, its sponsoring denomination. Evangelical Seminary, although nondenominational by charter, also is not free from denominational requirements that graduates must meet if they are to be employable in particular denominations—for example, courses in a particular denomination's history, theology, and polity. In addition to these accreditation and denominational requirements, there are also what DiMaggio and Powell call "mimetic" pressures: attempts to make one's institution like those that one believes are the most successful. Often these are other theological seminaries, but they may also include other professional schools and other institutions of higher education.

For these reasons our two schools have come to share a number of similar formal characteristics in spite of the sharp differences in the content of their normative cultures. While we called attention to some of these similarities in the first chapter, we repeat them here to emphasize the effects of pressures toward isomorphism: Each has somewhat similar governance structures and administrative offices; each has faculty with similar faculty rank structures; the faculty and students in each operate with relatively similar rules governing behavior and interaction; each school follows a curriculum structure that has some formal similarities; each organizes its degree programs according to a common set of standards; and each, within the constraints of its normative culture, emphasizes the norm of freedom of inquiry. These are some of the ways in which each school, in short, is recognizable as a theological seminary. While these seem such taken-for-granted characteristics that they hardly need mentioning, they nevertheless point to the schools' *institutionalized* character and to constraints from their institutional field to be isomorphic with other organizations sharing the field. We expect that these institutional similarities also help to shape the production of culture in the two schools by setting some limits on how widely either culture can vary while retaining its legitimacy as a theological seminary. While some of these formal characteristics and rules are deeply held and strongly upheld—for example, the norm of freedom of inquiry[10]—others are somewhat loosely coupled with day-to-day practices in the schools. Some serve a ceremonial purpose (Meyer and Rowan 1977), not mere window dressing but rituals that legitimate and validate the schools in the eyes of others in the broader institutional field. Thus, the schools can appear similar in many ceremonial characteristics common to their institutional field while giving expression internally to quite distinct cultures and practices. As Meyer and Rowan (1977) note, accrediting agencies, boards of trustees, and other outside constituents such as denominations often "accept ceremonially at face value the credentials, ambiguous goals, and categorical evaluations that are characteristic of ceremonial organizations."

In addition to the formal characteristics and norms that the two schools share, what is even more striking to us are the similarities that we found in the structural elements that constitute the two cultures (Chapter 10) and in the process of cultural formation that occurs in each (Chapter 11). These similarities are present in each despite the considerable differences in cultural content. This leads us to believe that our findings are generalizable both to other theological institutions and to a larger body of institutions of higher education. We explore implications for other schools in the next chapter.

Specialization and Culture

Cultural production also occurs through specialization, a process that is the opposite of isomorphism. Through specializing, a seminary develops a distinctive niche within its environment (Wuthnow 1994:32). This can affect the production of its culture.

We have already alluded to one form of specialization. Each school has tried to position itself in a relatively distinctive way within its particular religious and/or denominational environment. While evangelical culture broadly is the principal environment toward which Evangelical Seminary aims its programs, it seeks especially to distinguish itself as standing within Reformed orthodoxy. It also eschews hard-core and dispensationalist fundamentalism while holding to a high view of an inerrant Scripture. This distinguishes it from other competitors for evangelical loyalty, whether schools that are narrowly fundamentalist, Arminian, or Pentecostal in orientation or other schools in the Reformed tradition that are more relaxed on the issue of inerrancy. Evangelical Seminary does not turn away students who represent these other strands of American evangelicalism. Those who enroll, however, do so with the knowledge that they will encounter the particular expression of Reformed tradition that Evangelical represents. Similarly, though perhaps less obviously, Mainline Seminary occupies a particular niche within its broader denominational and mainline Protestant environment. Its strong emphasis on honoring diversity of gender and ethnic culture within a framework of an inclusive Christianity sets it off to a considerable degree from other schools within its denomination and from a number of other mainline seminaries. Students who enroll at Mainline know, or soon learn, that they will be pressed to understand theology and ministry in relation to their own and others' ethnic or gender identities and to find ways of incorporating this diversity within their understanding of an inclusive church. Even when they do not fully accept this position, they learn, as one student said, to "duck and cover" in order to live within the culture. By taking these particular stances, the two schools define their particular niches within the broader spectrum of their respective religious and ecclesial environments and shape their cultures accordingly.

Another kind of specialization involves program diversification in order to serve or attract particular constituencies and expand the resource base of the schools. Barbara Wheeler (1993:91–94) discusses a variety of such educational innovations in theological education: degree specialization, part-time programs, satellite centers and extension programs that reduce travel or residency requirements, and electronic transmission of some instructional materials.[11] Mainline Seminary, for example, developed its student pastor track to allow students who serve as pastors to spend more time in their parish settings. While this was in part a response to denominational pressures, it also filled a niche that other competitors were not filling. Evangelical Seminary also has specialized in order to attract new students. During the course of our fieldwork, the school introduced several two-year Master of Arts programs in functional areas of ministry—for example, youth ministry, counseling, and world missions and evangelism. This was done to draw students who do not wish to pursue the Master of Divinity degree, which takes longer, has more stringent requirements, and leads to ordination. Candidates for these new degrees are not interested in the pastorate or in ordination.

Program specialization has consequences for cultural production and transmission. Mainline's specialization concentrates a student pastor's time in a three-day week on campus and creates a separate, intensive engagement with the curriculum and with other student pastors; it also sharply limits opportunity for interaction with other students who are not in the special track. Further, it restricts the student pastor's participation in other aspects of the school's life and culture. In effect, it produces a somewhat separate, "student pastor" subculture. Evangelical's specialized M.A. programs appear to be successful in attracting new students. Some faculty members complain, however, that the students attracted by the special programs are much more diverse than was previously the case and that this is affecting the character of the school. Following distinctive program tracks also reduces the number of shared experiences (including shared requirements) that students have and changes the sequential process of socialization in which all or most participate. Thus, while various forms of specialization are often salutary in providing new opportunities for students to pursue a theological education and also in increasing student enrollment, such programs are not neutral when it comes to cultural production or the formation process.

Culture and the Formation of Students

Earlier in this chapter we spoke of the culture of each school as having two consequences: each culture gives expression to a normative goal that aims at shaping
the way students understand themselves and frame issues of ministry practice, and
each provides a cultural tool kit (to use Swidler's imagery) of knowledge, practices, and skills that students use to construct strategies of action for the various
problems and issues that will confront them as pastors or in other forms of ministry. In the previous two chapters we gave our analysis of the characteristics of the
culture of each school and the processes by which the culture is presented, represented, and responded to by students. In their encounters and interactions with the
school's culture, students are, in varying degrees, influenced and molded by the
culture, even as, in varying degrees, they affect the school's culture.

These considerations relate to a broader body of literature on the role of professional schools in socializing their students into particular professions (e.g., Merton
et al. 1957; Lortie 1959; Becker et al. 1961; Brim and Wheeler 1966; Coxon 1965;
Kadushin 1969; Olesen and Whittaker 1970; Carroll 1970; Bucher and Stelling
1977; Simpson 1979; and Kleinman 1984).[12] Among these interpreters of socialization there are important disagreements about the nature and outcomes of the
process. While it is beyond our purposes to review these perspectives (and arguments), it will help to locate our own contribution to the topic by brief reference
to several major lines of divergence.

In her work on the socialization of nursing students, Ida Harper Simpson
(1979:3–5) helpfully characterizes two of the important conflicting perspectives as
actually complementary. She uses two studies of medical education to provide the
contrasts. On the one hand, Merton et al., *The Student-Physician* (1957), may be
taken as representative of what Simpson calls the *induction* approach. In contrast,
Becker and his colleagues' *Boys in White* (1961) is representative of what Simpson
calls the *reaction* approach.[13] The induction approach assumes that there is a relatively clearly defined professional role—in Merton's case, that of physician—into
which students are being inducted as a consequence of their professional schooling. During medical school the student "develops his professional self, with its
characteristic values, attitudes, knowledge, and skills, fusing these into a more or
less consistent set of dispositions which govern his behavior in a wide variety of
professional (and extra professional) situations" (Merton et al. 1957:287). Thus, in
the induction approach, the study of professional socialization focuses on how
students learn and internalize the professional role. Reaction studies also focus on
students, but not as persons acquiring a professional role with its attendant values
and attitudes. Rather, such studies look at how students encounter various aspects
of the school and at the "identities and the commitments that sustain them during
their professional education and motivate them to complete it and go into professional practice" (Simpson 1979:4). Becker and his colleagues, who also studied
medical students, do not question that students learn particular attitudes and behaviors as well as requisite knowledge and skills. They question, however, whether
attitudes and behaviors learned as a student "will have an effect on the student's
behavior in the distant future" (Becker et al. 1961:240). More important in de-

termining future attitudes and behaviors are the characteristics of the contexts in which physicians or other professionals practice and the particular situations that they face.[14] Although this issue and others that also separate the two perspectives are substantial, the perspectives nevertheless, as Simpson (1979:4–5) suggests, complement each other in important ways: "The main variables studied by both are essential aspects of socialization . . . and their respective contributions [to understanding occupational socialization] need to be recognized and brought together."

Our own study, like Simpson's, reflects elements of both approaches. Each school assumes that most of its students will be entering some professional role associated with the church's ministry. This is clearer at Mainline Seminary, where most students are preparing for ordained ministry, usually as pastors of a local church in the sponsoring denomination. At Evangelical, although many students will become pastors of congregations, many others (if not a majority) will serve in specialized ministries, often in various parachurch organizations. Thus, the occupational roles that Evangelical's students enter are much more diverse, making socialization theory that emphasizes induction into a role less applicable. Both schools, nevertheless, are concerned that students have the opportunity to gain the knowledge and skills necessary for performing the particular roles in which they will engage. Each is especially concerned that students develop, at the heart of their cultural tool kit, a normative perspective or framework by which they are able to give reason for their decisions and behaviors in situations of ministry practice. Thus, the presentation and representation of each school's normative goal aim at forming in their students such a perspective, consistent with the normative goal, that will guide their response in the diverse situations that they will encounter in their ministries.

In attending to these processes by which students prepare for future roles, our study incorporates some of the key elements of an induction approach to socialization into the ministry; however, we did not attempt to spell out in advance dependent variables that we could measure as outcomes of induction into the professional role. We chose not to do so because of our desire to describe and understand, with as few preconceived notions as possible, the role that culture plays in the educational process. Thus, while we cannot say with much precision how well each school succeeds in producing certain specific socialization outcomes—for example, knowledge, skills, or attitudes—we have been able to say a lot about the role that culture plays in forming students. To put it differently, although we have not neglected either "inputs" or "outputs" pertaining to induction into ministerial roles, our major interest has been in opening up the "black box" and highlighting the characteristics of the culture of the two schools and the way that it works as a transformative agent.

In this regard, we have been especially influenced by Berger and Luckmann's (1966) important work on the sociology of knowledge and their discussion of ways in which definitions of reality (such as those embodied in the cultural messages of the two schools) are maintained. Such definitions are always subject to challenge and revision by alternative definitions, especially in a culturally pluralistic society. Even when the definitions are institutionalized ("sedimented") in language and codified in scripture and tradition, such definitions are not immune from threat. They must be nurtured and sustained. This is what the two schools are essentially about, and we have tried to show how the totality of the school experience functions in socializing students into the schools' definitions of reality and in sustaining those definitions. It is not just in the classrooms that students are socialized. The total experience of each school's culture teaches and reinforces the school's normative message as well as offering knowledge and skills needed for the practice of ministry. Thus, each school, taken in toto as a culture, functions in the manner of what Berger and Luckmann (1966:154–63) call a "plausibility structure." Such structures allow for face-to-face interaction and conversation with others who hold (or are reaching for) similar definitions of reality. Not all interaction and conversation need to explicitly address the school's definition of reality. Simply interacting with others who, one assumes, share one's convictions is important for sustaining one's belief that this is the way things are. Because we were outsiders, students were sometimes anxious about where we stood on issues. Did we share their convictions, or did we differ? As much as possible, we sought to avoid giving answers.

Students engage explicitly in sustained, often heated conversations and contests over their own sense of what is real and true, as we have already noted. In and out of the classroom, students at Evangelical work at "getting things straight." Students at Mainline are less inclined to argue over doctrines and ideas, but they too are deeply concerned with getting things straight—or, better, "doing things right"—in terms of interpersonal and intergroup relationships and ecclesial practices. Both implicitly and explicitly, their conversations reinforce the definition of reality that each school takes to be normative.

Berger and Luckmann's perspective, of course, is applicable not only to induction approaches but equally to Simpson's category of reaction approaches. We have also been interested in how students encounter the culture of the two schools and their responses to it. Much of what we described in the ethnographic chapters has to do with how students respond to and negotiate the schools' cultures. Furthermore, in agreement with Olesen and Whittaker (1970), we have emphasized the reciprocities and exchanges that occur in the interaction of students, faculty, and staff, who together shape the character of the socialization experience. Although we have used the term "formation" to describe the influence of the school's culture on students, we do not believe that students become mere clones of the culture or of particular faculty members. (Some, perhaps, do, but they are the exceptions.) Not only do the students encounter variations in the core message among faculty and other authority figures within the schools, but as we have shown, they are also encouraged according to the norm of free inquiry to think for themselves and develop, within limits, their own perspectives.[15] As we noted, student subcultures and peer or friendship groups form. They are based variously on such things as living arrangements, shared interests, social class, gender, or ethnicity, and they play an important role in the way that the students come to accept—or to question—the school's normative message or one of its variations. So, too, do the cultures in which students are involved outside the school, especially the congregations and parachurch groups in which they participate. As is true for the two schools, students also selectively adapt to the school's overall culture as they negotiate with it and ally themselves with one variation or another. They also become to some degree isomorphic as they conform to the overall cultural patterns and expectations of the school, especially the normative core, and with particular beliefs, values, and practices that are expected of those who participate in the school. Even when they do not fully agree, students learn to "duck and cover" rather than to openly challenge the norms. And students also "specialize": That is, they become different from others in the culture as they find their particular niche—for example, as future pastors, youth ministers, pastoral counselors, scholars, and missionaries.[16] Finally, as we have emphasized, some students are very little impacted by the schools' cultures. They simply are so little involved in significant encounters with the culture, especially outside the classroom, that they miss immersion in the rich symbolic, ritual, and conversational life that takes place in chapel, hallways, dorm rooms, dining halls, or student hangouts. One must "be there" to be formed in any significant way by the culture. In sum, students play an active rather than simply a reactive role in their socialization, even when they choose not to "be there." This is to argue, as Olesen and Whittaker (1970:207–9) do, for "an intersubjective view of persons in professional socialization as persons engaged in conscious choice-making and intentional behaviours directed to and with others, living, dead or fictional with whom they are implicated."

Of the various studies of professional socialization, especially of clergy, the one most closely resembling our own is that by Sherryl Kleinman (1984) of a mainline Protestant seminary. Although she was concerned (as we have been) only with seminarians during their seminary experience, Kleinman offers an interesting twist on the induction/reaction approaches. From participant observation in the school, she argues that its dominant ethos (its "normative message," in our terms) formed the students in such a way that it had the effect of *deprofessionalizing* them; that is, it undercut traditional expectations that clergy should speak and act authoritatively in their institutionalized role as God's representatives. The school's culture emphasized instead that the basis of the clergy role is in being an authentic person, one's "real self," in interpersonal relationships with laity, who with the clergy are "equals before God." Ministering, in this view, is "a matter of being a helpful, caring person" (Kleinman 1984:25). Use of specialized religious language and, especially, intellectualizing one's faith were discouraged. After an initial experience of "reality shock" over the redefinition of religion and the clergy role, students tended to accept the school's perspective, rejecting traditional expectations. In various experiences in which they interacted as aspiring clergy with laity, however, students found that laity often resisted the redefinition, looking instead for more traditional, authoritative clergy professionals. The dilemma was especially acute for women students, who, while valuing the school's perspective, nevertheless feared that parishioners would resist such an approach: "To act mainly in personal and egalitarian ways is to act 'feminine' and hence to indicate further to parishioners that they are not 'real' ministers (i.e., authority figures)" (Kleinman 1984:93). As a result, Kleinman (1984:101) concludes, students, especially women, were left without "a clear and coherent image of the profession as a distinctive and special occupation."

Unfortunately, our research, like Kleinman's, sheds little light on the lasting effects of professional education, since neither study followed students beyond graduation. On the basis of accumulated evidence and experience, we would maintain that the powerful normative message that each culture presents does in fact shape the perspectives that many (not all) of their graduates subsequently bring to their professional practice, for good or for ill. How (and where) graduates engage in ministry practice will vary in the degree to which the school's version of the normative view is supported. In some cases these settings will be in harmony with the normative view, albeit often in a less pristine form. At other times, however, as Kleinman's students discovered, the constraints of the practice situation will necessitate adaptations of and compromises with the normative message that one has learned from the school's culture. It will be difficult for a graduate of Mainline Seminary fully to honor the school's commitment to diversity and inclusiveness in most of the congregations that he or she may serve as pastor. As we commented above (Chapter 10), the majority of mainline Protestant congregations are notably homogeneous, and many of these congregations will resist efforts to make them more diverse. Likewise, the graduate of Evangelical Seminary who finds herself or himself on the staff of a teeming megachurch or leading a parachurch organization such as Young Life may find that those settings partake strongly of popular evangelical culture of the sort we described in Chapter 3. As such, they may present a considerable challenge to the highly cognitive, disciplined approach to faith and ministry that the school's culture privileges. So for both Mainline and Evangelical graduates some compromises and adaptations may be necessary. Some may "go native" and become acculturated to their new environment. Experience and limited observation of graduates of the two schools lead us to believe, however, that students who were deeply exposed to their seminary's culture will persist in trying to frame issues and make responses consistent with the normative orientation that the seminary experience helped to shape. The proponents of the reaction approach are probably correct in saying that the characteristics of the settings in which professionals practice have a powerful constraining effect on professional responses, yet we would not discount the lasting impact, for good or for ill, of normative perspectives internalized in the professional school experience.[17]

In any case, no professional school, including the two that we studied, can prepare students for all contingencies that they will face in their future practice. At best, they aim at shaping a normative orientation in their students and providing them with the tools they can use to construct appropriate responses to new or unanticipated challenges. They can also foster the understanding that professional socialization does not end with graduation but continues both in formal opportunities for continuing professional education and especially in the day-to-day learning that comes through reflection in and on one's practice as a professional (Schön 1983).

Summary of the Theory

To sum up, we state here the main points of our theoretical perspective, calling attention both to concepts and propositions that have helped us interpret what we have found.

1. A seminary's culture consists of those shared (publicly available) symbolic forms—worldviews, beliefs, ritual practices, ceremonies, art and architecture, language, and patterns of everyday interaction—that give meaning and direction to the life of the schools and the people who participate in them.

2. A seminary's culture is constructed or produced (a) by the interaction over time of successive cohorts of faculty, students, and others in the school, by their engagement with each other and with various streams of the Christian heritage; (b) through selective adaptation to particular aspects of the broader environment of which it is a part and with which it engages in exchanges of resources and "products"; (c) through pressures toward isomorphism with other organizations in its organizational field (other seminaries and other educational institutions) that arise out of the need to compete for scarce resources or to appear legitimate to important constituencies; and (d) through efforts at creating a distinctive niche within one's environment.

3. The culture that is produced has both a normative core—a stated aim of shaping student's capacities to accomplish certain ends and of forming their views and opinions in favor of some objectives and against others—and a range of permissible variations on either side of the normative core.

4. Students are formed by the seminary's culture as they interact with it and with others in the seminary context, which functions as a plausibility structure for nurturing and sustaining the culture's shared meanings and symbols.

5. Students (as well as faculty and staff) are not clones of the culture; instead, they negotiate with it, contest aspects of it, and use it as a tool kit for constructing perspectives that are in varying degrees of agreement or disagreement with the normative core of the culture.

6. Students' personal and social characteristics and their involvements outside the seminary context are important influences on the way that students negotiate the seminary's culture. They may reinforce or undermine its formative impact.

7. The impact of the seminary's culture on a student is in large measure a function of the extent of the student's exposure to it. One must be there to be formed by it.

THIRTEEN

Culture and Educational Practice: A Concluding Unscientific Postscript

After completing the fieldwork for this project, we made several presentations of our findings to scholarly meetings and groups of theological educators, including the faculty of one of the institutions we studied. At all these gatherings, we were asked to suggest what educators can and should do differently in light of our conclusions.

We are hesitant to make definitive recommendations for educational practice. We have rather confidently suggested that the patterns we identified in our ethnographic data (patterns that, as we have shown in the foregoing chapters, are remarkably similar in the two very different institutions in which we conducted our research) would emerge from the studies of the culture of many if not all schools. We have commented on large bodies of theory. We take these bold steps, based on studies of just two cases, because we know that our contributions to and comments on theory will be balanced by a great deal of research and comment by others. It seems to us unwise, however, to proceed from research like ours directly to suggestions for practice. The actual practices of education are deeply embedded in the local history, culture, and present circumstances of particular schools. Strategies for improvement and change that work in one place may fail disastrously in others. Studies like ours, intensive but limited in scope and number of sites, do not yield the kind of conclusions that can be "implemented" in the varied settings of actual schools with any confidence that the intervention will be appropriate or salutary.

The most responsible response to the question posed to us is, we think, to list several considerations that educators should take into account as they shape the programs and policies of their institutions. These considerations are quite general, which is fitting given the great variety of specific problems and issues that particular institutions face that we cannot possibly address from the limited base of our research. At the same time, these considerations reflect strong convictions about education that we have formed or had reinforced in the course of our research. There are three items on our list, and in all three cases our perspective pulls against some strong contemporary educational tides. Therefore, though we cannot produce firm recommendations, educational designs, or rules for educational practice, we hope that our general views will receive a serious reading from those who do.

1. *The culture of educational institutions plays a powerful role in how students are actually shaped, but institutional culture is not easily changed or manipulated.* We think we have shown, at least in two specific cases, that the culture that develops over time in a school—its core of normative habits and values and its range of permissible variations of thought and behavior—has a profound effect on its students as they encounter the school's culture and engage in the contests that result from different views, attitudes, and habits that they bring with them into the school. Typically, schools that, because of internal dissatisfaction or public pressure, decide to change their educational "product" attempt to do this by revising the formal pattern of studies, the curriculum. Our study suggests that curriculum change alone will not produce changes in what students believe, in how they act, and perhaps even in what content they have appropriated at sufficient depth to make a long-term difference in their capacities and aptitudes. These are shaped, we have concluded, by formal "symbolic vehicles of meaning" (Swidler 1986:273) and informal cultural practices.

Can culture, the network of local symbolic vehicles and practices, be changed? Educational research has, historically, been consumed by the effort to identify what is educationally effective and how effective agents can be employed most productively in various educational settings. Educators who want to do their jobs well pay attention to research that analyzes educational events, isolates the variables of influence, parses out the variance associated with each of the variables, and recombines them in different settings to enhance educational effectiveness. It is very tempting to react to findings like ours, which identify culture as an "effective agent," by asking how it can be reformed or redeployed to achieve more satisfactory results.

Culture does, of course, change. If we were to return to the schools we studied now, three years after our field research was completed, we would find some differences: subtle changes in the central normative message, a somewhat different array of variations on it, new symbols and terms in the "dialect" of the institutions, and perhaps some changes in manners, traffic patterns, and behavioral rules. (Leaders of both institutions have read our ethnographic portraits and have told us that although they recognize their schools in what we have written, the institutional cultures are not now exactly as they were then.)

Our understanding of how culture is produced makes us cautious, however, about suggesting that changes in institutional culture are easy to bring about deliberately. Local cultures are woven out of numerous strands of human and material resources, many of them donated to or forced on a local community by the larger ambient culture. Decisions made within local communities do play a part in shaping local culture, but frequently institutional ethos and other features of culture are affected as much by decisions that did not have culture shaping as their goal as by those that did. In any case, the extent of possible change is limited by the materials at hand. The decision makers in a school cannot simply take counsel and determine what sort of culture the institution will have. This is not welcome news for contemporary educators preoccupied with the "outcomes" of education. Not only are the sort of "outcomes" that school culture influences difficult to measure; culture is also not the kind of "input" that can be quickly and easily manipulated to produce a different result.

At the same time, our conviction that culture is a *publicly available* set of signs and practices keeps us from arguing that because "nothing can be done" about culture, a school can simply ignore the one that has grown slowly over time in its particular plot. Institutional culture is not readily recast or changed, but it can be recognized as an active element in the educational process. We think it is important for those who set the policies and design the programs of schools to try to figure out the lineaments of their school's own culture. As is widely recognized, this is not easy to do. It was because of the well-known difficulty of recognizing the features of a familiar religious and educational culture that the four of us "crossed over" into ones quite different from our own to conduct this study.

Still, given the power of culture—patterned signs and practices the institution does not deliberately design—to augment or undercut the effects of the formal educational activities it does devise, culture should not be overlooked. The people who run schools and conduct their programs should listen intently to and look hard at themselves: What views of the world are explicitly or subtly announced and endorsed? What ideas and statements of norms and values go unchallenged? What patterns of behavior are required? Which are forbidden? Whatever the formal authority structure, who really has power and authority? Once the outlines of an institution's norms, views, and practices have been uncovered, some assessment of their impact is usually possible. If the evaluation is negative, transformation of cultural norms and habits may not be possible, but sometimes destructive aspects of culture can be minimized by determined common effort. Positive features and values can be reinforced by ritual and ceremony.

We observed creative and corrective educational uses of features of culture in the two schools we studied. Although few of our informants could have provided the sort of comprehensive description of their institution's culture that we as outsiders pieced together over three years (though most recognized the one we provided), most had figured out the culture's main outlines, and those in positions to exercise leadership often used what they knew about the local culture as they led. Andrew Watson, the stately chaplain of Evangelical Seminary, invited the students to bring their contemporary worship and prayer style into the formal worship program and, in so doing, tamed it somewhat—one of the major goals of the school. President Stewart's legitimizing of the students' parody art show demonstrated that one could espouse pluralism and group identity without necessarily taking oneself too seriously. He demonstrated, in effect, that the school's high ideal of inclusiveness can be livable. We conclude from these and many other examples that schools should at least informally study themselves, map their own cultures, point up their good features, and minimize harmful ones, all the while remembering that culture develops and changes slowly and cannot be immediately fixed or transformed.

2. *Faculty dominate the students' experience of their school.* The greatest sur-

prise of this study to those of us who conducted it, all of us teachers or administrators in universities or seminaries, is how different the school looks to students than it does to us. To a faculty member, the institution's senior administrators and sometimes board of governors represent its character and intentions in most explicit form. Especially in larger institutions, faculty members feel that they have very little power. Important decisions affecting educational policy and the tone and flavor of life in the school are made, they think, by those more prominent in the educational hierarchy. Administrators and others who play governing roles usually accept this view of themselves: that as decision makers and public spokespersons, they have the greatest impact on how external publics perceive and experience the school.

From spending almost all of our time with students, we learned that for them this is not the case. For them, the school and its culture are best and most completely represented by the faculty. Students certainly know who the designated leaders of the institution are, and they are aware of the messages these leaders send. They encounter these leaders less frequently than they encounter faculty members, however, and they often do so in more formal settings that do not encourage give-and-take interaction. Where administrators do have such interaction—for example, when they also engage in the teaching role, as did Dean Harriett Hercon at Mainline—students take administrators' precepts and examples very seriously.

Faculty members do not comprise the whole of the institutional culture that students come to know. As we have shown, other students are a significant part of it. Space arrangements, aesthetics, and long-standing rituals and traditions—all of whose authorship or origins are obscure to students—are important too. Faculty members do, however, dominate the students' experience of the school. Students hear faculty statements about what is true and important far more often than any other messages; they regularly observe how faculty members conduct themselves; they have far more exchanges with faculty members—from which they learn what kind of arguments carry weight, which views gain respect, and what manners are acceptable—than they do with any other representatives of the school. Because of the amount, regularity, and intensity of contact between faculty and students, students frequently become fascinated with faculty members, seeking and trading information about their teachers' life outside the school. They learn from this information too, from what one of the students at Evangelical Seminary called "the whole life aspect" of faculty members, how the ideas and world views the school emphasizes are lived out. Faculty members, simply by being who they are as well as by doing the things they are paid to do, are the primary purveyors to students of institutional culture, with all its formative power.

This does not mean that faculty are the primary manufacturers of a school's culture. As we have noted several times, the raw materials from which any particular local culture is forged come from many sources. The background, training, current interests, and behavior patterns of the faculty are some of the elements that make up the culture, but there are many more. Decisions made by the "official" decision makers, those in executive and governing roles, have a great deal to do with how the components of culture, including the faculty, are combined with each other. As administrators and those to whom they report choose how to represent the school to outside audiences in mission statements and published materials; as they hire employees and make budgets; as they form alliances with other institutions, especially the agencies that regulate and accredit schools; as they erect buildings, furnish them, and landscape their grounds; and as they adopt and enforce rules of behavior and formal requirements for completion of courses of study, they play substantial if often unwitting roles as producers of the school's culture.

At Mainline Seminary, for instance, the senior administrators' decision to join with others—including some of their own faculty and "prophetic" voices in the seminary's sponsoring denomination—in emphasizing racial and cultural inclusiveness led both to the appointment of faculty members who endorsed this commitment and were racially diverse and to the recruitment of students from constituencies that represented diversity. At Evangelical, the decision by administrators to make women welcome in all the programs of the school, including those that prepare students for ordination, seemed to us to regulate the tone and status of the position held by several key faculty members: that the Bible does not permit women to be ordained or to instruct men about religious matters. Women's ordination became a matter about which Reformed, orthodox Christians at Evangelical Seminary may disagree. Most other planks in the theological platforms of these same key faculty members were, by contrast, essential tenets of the institution's central message.

Faculty members do not make the culture of the institution, but they are so important as announcers, enactors, and embodiments of the normative views and values of the institutions that we think the most direct way to modify school culture is to appoint different kinds of faculty. The changes that we observed in the cultural climate of our two schools during the interval of our study and since are mostly traceable to changes in faculty personnel. Some such changes occur by happenstance: for example, another institution succeeds in luring away a faculty member who has been a central figure (as Harriet Hercon was lured away from Mainline), or a new faculty member brings some surprise elements (Wilson Jeffers, the professor of preaching hired by Evangelical was not as fully committed to expository preaching, an important form for those who set the normative agenda at Evangelical, as his faculty colleagues assumed he would be). Others are planned effects. For example, faculty members who don't fit into the culture sometimes choose to leave for more compatible institutions, are not renewed, or are encouraged to go elsewhere (several members of the ministry department, which had low status in Evangelical Seminary's dominant culture, left in the two years after our study was completed). Or new appointments are made that, by either keeping the faculty profile the same or varying it, will affect the culture of the school for many years to come. Often this choice is determined by the outcome of power struggles between faculty and administration or within the faculty.

We think it is a mistake to give in to the present-day tendency to think of faculty members as laborers whose activities can be regulated by administrative managers to make changes in the products of education. Faculty members are powerful agents in the educational process, not functionaries. Their roles are complex and multifaceted: their ingrained patterns of speech and movement, long-established attitudes toward others and feelings about themselves, and deeply rooted convictions and commitments have at least as much to do with what students take away from the school as any syllabuses and lecture notes. Thus, it is very hard for them to change—at their own initiative and much less at the direction of others—the many dimensions of themselves that have effects on students. Those who think that educational change can be engineered by redesigning programs and ordering those who teach them to make changes in content and style do not understand the depth, subtlety, pervasiveness, and scope of the roles that faculty members play in students' educational experiences.

3. *Formative education requires prolonged and intensive exposure to an educational institution.* The clear lesson of our study is that the schools in which we conducted our research had significant formative effects on students who spent time in them and became engaged in school life. Students who were marginal to the life of the school or who were not exposed to it for very long may have absorbed certain academic "contents," but they were likely to leave with their preexisting views, values, and patterns of acting unchanged.

Two factors seem to affect how much formative power the school's culture has on the students. One is the duration of the experience. The influence of educational culture appears to increase with the length of time the student spends in it. It takes time for students to apprehend the institution's strongly recommended claims and patterns of action and more time to resolve the tension between those norms and the ones the students brought with them. The process we have described is a long one. First, students are exposed to the dominant message and its variants, each in explicit and enacted forms, which requires forming relationships with exemplary figures (especially faculty members), participating in school rituals, and learning the local dialect. Then they grapple with each other in attempts to clarify their own views and preferences and influence those of others. Finally, they try on new approaches and positions, often blends of the school's and their previous views, in settings beyond the school.

All these activities are hard to compress into short periods. The lengths and patterns of time required were especially evident at Mainline, where students traveled more or less in a cohort through the program. It took a year for students to comprehend the full significance of the central cultural message and its variations. It took another year to discover and experiment with the patterns of thought and action prescribed by the culture's central message, and still another year to adapt it to personal aptitudes and future work responsibilities.

The other significant factor in a student's exposure to institutional culture is the intensity of involvement. Students who become intensely engaged in a variety of activities seem to get the cultural message sooner and to grapple with it more seriously than those who restrict their involvement to taking the academic courses needed for the degree. Intense involvement does not necessarily require a long record of formally recognized extracurricular activities. Traditional student activities—at Evangelical Seminary, those organized by the student association—are one route to deep involvement. Jeffrey Barber, who became president of the association; Pamela Willis, who served as social director; and Anne Norton, who organized the current affairs program, all became deeply enmeshed in the school and its culture by accepting student offices. Other means, however, often serve just as effectively. Neal Huchett, for instance, became part of a group of studious students for whom the library functioned, as he put it, as a sort of spiritual center. Coming from a background (Pentecostalism) very different from the theological traditions and present-day culture of Evangelical Seminary, he nevertheless got the school's message quickly and used the close and intense relationships of the group of students who stayed in the library to hammer out for himself ways to live with Reformed views in a Pentecostal church. Friendship networks that grew out of first-year living arrangements functioned similarly for many other students.

We concluded that both the duration of exposure to the school and the intensity of engagement in more than one kind of activity in it are critically important for formation. The two factors have a complex relationship. To a certain point, length of exposure promotes intensity: The longer one stays around, the more opportunities for engagement—and the more various opportunities—one encounters. Eventually, however, duration diminishes intensity: If one stretches a course of study out over too long a period, one's academic work and other features of the school in which one studies demand only a small part of one's attention. Therefore, enrollment in programs intended to form students' capacities should, we think, keep them in school long enough, but not too long, for intensity of involvement to be sustained and significant formation to occur. How long that should be in particular cases depends on the program, the students, and the kind of formation envisioned.

All three factors just discussed—the difficulty of creating and changing culture, the prominence of faculty in students' educational experience, and the importance of significantly long, intense, and various experiences in conjunction with formal education programs—make us anxious about several directions in contemporary North American higher education. We have mentioned two: a preoccupation with outcomes and a tendency to view faculty as manageable labor. Both are linked to a larger development: All kinds of institutions, not just the seminaries we studied, are struggling with costs. States have cut money to publicly supported institutions, and even the most elite private universities seem to have difficulty raising sufficient funds to keep salaries competitive and facilities repaired.

One response to the crisis has been decentralization—the creation of small educational extension centers that offer instruction to students who live nearby and commute to class. In the past decade, theological schools have followed the lead of colleges and some professional schools (business schools in particular) in creating extension sites and centers for their programs. Some seminaries have spread their programs across the region in which they are located. Others have reached great distances, sometimes across the continent, to offer educational programs that have their particular theological stripe and religious fervor.

A second development has been efforts to reduce the cost of education to students by changing the pace of programs. In some fields, accelerated programs have been introduced in recognition of the fact that the longer a program takes, the higher the cost to the student in lost earnings. Accelerated programs have not caught on in theological education, but shorter programs have become prevalent.

Most institutions now offer two-year master's degrees in theology. Many of these programs attract new student constituencies, especially persons who intend to return to "secular" occupations, but the degrees are also increasingly used as a shorter route to vocational goals, including doctoral study and, in some cases, ordained ministry, for which a three- or four-year degree was the usual track in the past.

The other notable change of pace has been the trend to part-time study. More and more students in undergraduate and professional programs work virtually full-time while enrolled for degrees, spreading their studies out over a number of years. Seminaries have generally followed this trend; only a handful now require students to enroll full-time.

Simultaneously, higher education and theological education find themselves on the leading edge of rapidly shifting information technology that promises to make more information available at less cost than has been possible before. Developing technologies will, some claim, make it possible for schools to shift away from campus space into "virtual" space, which is cheaper to reach and to occupy. Optimistic prophets paint pictures of a populist educational utopia: more education brought to more people by highly efficient and minimally expensive means.

The problems of higher education institution will be solved, some say, by all these promising new forms of educational delivery. We do not doubt the feasibility of extension education, accelerated and shorter programs, part-time study, and the spreading of information by technological means. All these developments are well under way. Based on what we have learned in this research, however, we worry about what may be lost in too rapid or complete a shift to new forms.

Extension education, which moves one element of the school—the teacher—to a site convenient for the students, limits the range and variety of contacts students have with the institution's culture. Those who design extension programs do try to build in some devices for contact among students beyond class sessions, but given what we have seen of the complexity of culture and the difficulty of creating and changing it, we wonder whether programs that offer such limited opportunities for encounter with teachers, students, and institutional ethos will have the formative power of those that envelop the student with an array of experiences. Similarly, shortening or accelerating programs seems to us likely to limit the depth and amount of educational formation that occurs. Part-time study, especially if accompanied by full-time work, may make it difficult for the student to focus on both formal learning and all the unprogrammed opportunities that school life provides. We also have doubts about "virtual" education. We are not opposed to technology; however, teaching and learning by computer and various video technologies cannot, we believe, duplicate the intense and various experiences available to a student who physically attends a school. In summary, few of the new forms and technologies seem to us to deliver the full benefits of actually being there, on location at school, in its buildings, with its various populations, for long enough periods of time to learn what the school has to teach: the ways of life and worldviews as well as information and technical skills. We do not think that residential education is the only acceptable option. If those devising new forms were to find ways to duplicate or improve on the processes that we have mapped that are a function of being on site, our concerns would dissipate.

How important this is, whether "being there" is worth the undeniably high costs, depends on what a society (or a segment of it) hopes that education will accomplish. We have no doubt that the religious communities served by the two institutions we studied require the costly formative kind of education. The situations of the two communities are very different, but as we noted in the previous chapter, each in its way faces a social crisis, profoundly unsettled conditions. These crises cannot, we think, be resolved without formidably well prepared leaders.

Mainline Protestantism's crisis has been widely publicized. In recent decades, the mainline denominations, including the one with which Mainline Seminary is aligned, have lost millions of members and much of their former power to dominate social, cultural, business, and political life in the United States (Roof and McKinney 1987; Wuthnow 1988). Once confident, even arrogant, in their conduct of the ecclesiastical business and the prominent roles they played throughout society, mainline Protestants have become querulous and fearful as a result of their recent displacement. Advisers offer a wide range of measures to reverse mainline decline. Some suggest a return to traditional practices and standards of belief. Others urge the mainline to imitate the firm teaching, religious fervor, and skillful niche marketing of the new, more conservative churches that seem to be growing. A smaller number of counselors, mostly insiders, suggest that the mainline churches just hold on until the tide turns and conditions become more favorable for their sort of religious faith and practice.

Evangelical Protestants face a different set of problems. Evangelical Protestantism has undergone a recent resurgence. This development was as little expected by the evangelical leaders who laboriously built their movement earlier in this century as mainline decline was by the mainline leaders who had been enjoying a boom period after World War II. Evangelical leaders and institutions have responded to the new interest in enthusiastic and conservative religion by building: by expanding existing institutions and creating an amazing number and variety of new ones. The challenge facing all these expanded and new institutions—congregations (some of them enormously large), schools at all levels, mission agencies, religious businesses, even new denominations—is to convert the exhilaration that led to their founding and rapid growth into steady support for their continued existence. Again, there is much conflicting advice for how to bring this about. Some argue that a fervent revivalistic spirit is the very nature of evangelical religion: Evangelical institutions can only maintain themselves, say these advisers, by keeping the revival going. Others (including the faculty of Evangelical Seminary) worry that the movement is burning itself out by lack of organizational discipline and imperiling its future and its integrity by not enforcing rigorous standards of doctrine and taste.[1]

These religious crises and equally serious ones facing other religious groups in this country[2] have tripped off a vigorous debate about what kind of education is required for religious leaders. One group of eminent theologians has argued that theological education has to become more powerfully formative. In a series of books advocating change in theological education, they have reintroduced ancient terms for and concepts of education, such as *paideia,* the Greek notion of education as a process of inculcating virtues, and *habitus,* the medieval concept of a deep disposition rooted in wisdom about God.[3] In speeches and articles rather than books, many seminary administrators have argued against the theologians on grounds on of feasibility: They are determined to solve the pressing financial problems of theological schools and students by using some of the new forms of educational delivery described above (Perez 1995). Less vociferous but much more powerful than either set of advocates are the majority of theological educators who by their actions appear to favor the status quo: theological education that mostly limits its activities to critical academic study (formation being the business of the churches) in traditional classroom formats.

From the vantage point of our study, none of the parties in the current debate seems to us to be entirely right. We find ourselves in substantial agreement with those who want to strengthen theological education along the lines of *paideia.* As we have already said, religious communities in unsettled times do not know which strategies for action they should employ. Deciding what needs to be accomplished in particular settings—making hard choices among competing goods and then knowing how to pursue the chosen ends—requires leaders who have something more than the technical skill to put impersonally acquired information to good use. Such leaders need well-formed and deeply formed capacities. This is what prolonged and intense exposure to the culture of a school, and especially to the persons who are bearers of that culture, accomplishes: the shaping of capacities— the developing of the convictions and habits as well as analytical abilities and ideas that are required to act wisely and effectively.

We have already laid out our differences with the advocates of new delivery systems. We are afraid that the new formats make it less rather than more likely that students' minds, characters, attitudes, and commitments will be profoundly shaped by their educational experience. We also agree with the *paideia*-minded critics that traditional theological education places too little explicit emphasis on forming views and capacities. We have, however, a somewhat more cheerful perspective than most of those critics. After all, we studied two institutions selected in part because they were identified to us as typical of schools in their tradition. We found a lot of formation going on in both places. Certainly schools and teachers could become more aware of the patterns in which their students are being formed; certainly they could more energetically resist some of the pressures on contemporary education that corrode formative education. Still, significant numbers of students do get a formative education as we and the critics would define it. Present-day theological education may be imperiled by academic stuffiness and the lure of cheaper, novel formats, but our research suggests that it is not entirely ineffective in its present form. If the will can be found to remake it as *paideia* for religious leaders facing formidably difficult conditions, there is a solid base on which to build.

Similar questions face education generally. What needs to be accomplished? Does the acquisition of large amounts of information and narrow specialized skills answer the most pressing social needs? We think that the question deserves wide debate. For more than a decade, a utilitarian view of education, including higher education, has dominated. Educational activity is justified to the extent that it can be shown to produce economic benefits commensurate with its costs. In this view there is very little room for the kinds of education that prepare people to evaluate social goals, including the goal of economic progress and gain, or to conduct activities (such as many forms of art) that have limited economic benefit. The result is more dissemination of information but less perspective, more technological expertise but less guidance about what social goals technological expertise should serve.

In our judgment, the crises confronting the whole society are at least as serious as those facing the churches. These are unsettled times generally. Virtues, character, constructive values, wisdom, judgment, productive habits—citizens need these just as much as religious leaders do. If this is the case, how can higher education provide what the society most needs? Is the fashionable cost-benefit approach to education the most fruitful one? If a capacity to contribute to the common good and responsible citizenship are what is needed, then society will have to acknowledge the kind of education that nurtures such learning: the importance of face-to-face educational communities in the process of formation, and the pivotal role of teachers. Hostility toward education—the widespread tendency to blame it for consuming too many resources without curing society's ills—needs to give way to efforts to befriend schools and especially to invest heavily in those that offer students the opportunity to be formed in a culture as well as to benefit from excellent formal instruction. Such investment does require money. But even more, schools need care, attention, and supportive scrutiny, a critical kind of attention that goads them to do a really good job.

Even without making formal recommendations, we have pushed our findings from a limited study of just two cases rather far. We are convinced, however, that schools in this society—not just the seminaries we studied—already accomplish more than is generally recognized, even by them. They shape the character of the nation by the intended and unintended ways in which they shape the characters of their students. Powerful educational cultures, often unacknowledged, play a very big part in the formation of students' characters and capacities. The processes by which they do this need to be better understood. This and similar studies are only a start. Even before that understanding is complete, however, the role of schools as centers where commitment and the capacity to act on it can be formed must be affirmed. The future of not only ministry but also many other critical social enterprises is at stake.

Notes

INTRODUCTION

1. The Doctor of Ministry degree is a postgraduate professional degree for practicing clergy who have already earned the first theological degree, the Master of Divinity degree, which most denominations require for ordained ministers.

2. Other ethnographic studies of religious schools—in this case fundamentalist Christian high schools rather than theological seminaries—include those by Alan Peshkin (1986) and Melinda Bollar Wagner (1990).

3. At Evangelical, the researchers moved between various guest rooms in dorms for single students and in married student housing. At Mainline, the researchers stayed in rooms in single student housing for two years of the study and in married student housing during the final year.

4. We used the database program askSam for data storage and retrieval. While not always as user-friendly as we might have preferred, the program allows storage of freeform text and easy and quick searches of multiple files of data for either precoded key words or strings of text within the files. It proved an invaluable aid for sharing large amounts of data among the research teams and for data analysis.

5. An exception in the use of names is with public figures who visited the schools during our research. We did not believe it necessary to disguise their names.

6. The ATS allows for schools of other religious traditions to be members. Rabbinical schools, for example, have been members in the past. At present, none are.

7. These figures are taken from the *Factbook on Theological Education, 1993–94* (Pittsburgh: Association of Theological Education, 1994).

8. Some of the schools that we have classified as primarily oriented to mainline or evangelical Protestantism are non- or interdenominational schools; others are affiliated with a denomination. We have ignored these affiliation distinctions here in favor of classifying them by their predominant religious orientation.

9. Data for gender and minority characteristics of faculty members come from an unpublished study of seminary characteristics by the Auburn Center for Theological Education Research.

CHAPTER TWO

1. The catalog and other publications of ETS contain both a statement on women at the seminary ("[T]he seminary is committed to the full inclusion of women. . .") and a policy on harassment with procedures for appeal.

CHAPTER THREE

1. This witness was given in early 1991, at a time when the course of political events in the Baltic states was unclear, and it reflects the past experience of the speaker.

CHAPTER FOUR

1. Sylvester Barnes, professor of the Old Testament, holds quite orthodox views that some students consider old-fashioned.

CHAPTER NINE

1. Many African-American students at MTS prefer to retain traditional masculine references to God.

CHAPTER TEN

1. Several received the doctorate from Princeton Seminary, located near but not formally affiliated with such a university.

2. In Chapter 12, we relate our findings about the larger religious cultures in which our two schools are set to current sociological discussions about religious divisions and "culture wars."

3. The term refers to an academic style that features the use of precise rational arguments; to the conviction that religious truth can be adequately conveyed in verbal forms and may be obscured by nonverbal images; and to teaching areas in the curriculum—the "academic" fields of Bible and theology especially—where a scholastic style of teaching and argument is regnant, as they are not in the ministry field. George Marsden and others argue that the stream of evangelicalism that has these features is rooted in a philosophical movement, Scottish Common Sense Realism (George Marsden, *Fundamentalism and American Culture: The Shaping of Twentieth-Century Evangelicalism, 1870–1925* [New York: Oxford University Press, 1980], 10–118). At Evangelical Seminary, "experiential" is the contrast term for "cognitive," and experiential views and activities are identified with the ministry teaching field.

4. Some of the denomination's other seminaries are also known for their emphasis on liberation theology and social activism.

5. A formula that has made the rounds among evangelicals too old to appreciate praise choruses defines them as "four words, three notes, two hours."

6. Interestingly, though students almost always describe their relationship to God as a relationship to Jesus Christ, we recorded relatively few instances of Jesus Christ addressed

or even mentioned, by name, in spontaneous student prayer. Virtually all the prayers are addressed to "the Lord." That, of course, could refer to God or to Jesus.

7. We labeled this distinctive style of prayer "just prayer" because of the number of times the word "just" is typically used in a single prayer ("Heavenly Father, we just thank you because you are just the same wonderful . . ."). We later discovered that other observers of evangelical religious practices use the same term.

CHAPTER ELEVEN

1. The fact that the dominant culture at Evangelical lays such heavy emphasis on what students think rather than what they do may be another reason that they continue to "practice" popular evangelicalism—testimony meetings, praise singing, favor-asking prayer—even while their minds are being substantially changed about matters of belief.

2. Tommy Reiss is not alone in reporting that he has not satisfactorily resolved the question of how black and white people should relate to each other. Boyd Arthur and many other white students ask themselves whether inclusiveness requires intimate friendships (which many black students reject). White students say they have heard that black students like Mitch Tabor who reach out to them are criticized by other black students for doing so. Race is both the most powerful and the touchiest issue at Mainline Seminary.

CHAPTER TWELVE

1. This process reflects the method of grounded theory construction as described by Glaser and Strauss (1967) and Strauss (1987).

2. For a review essay summarizing the uses of the culture concept in organizational analyses generally, see Smircich (1983). Ouichi and Wilkins (1985) and Kuh and Whitt (1988) review uses of the concept in educational organizations. More recently, Bolman and Deal (1991) have contrasted the cultural frame with three other frames for analyzing organizations: structural, human relations, and political. For more general theories of culture by anthropologists see the review essay by Keesing (1974).

3. Robert Wuthnow (1992:40–44) points out that Geertz's discussion of religion as a cultural system (Geertz 1966) has been interpreted differently by sociologists and anthropologists. Sociologists have tended to interpret Geertz (who was a student of Talcott Parsons) within a Parsonian framework, emphasizing the subjective elements of culture (values, goals, or value orientations that define desired end-states of individual action). Anthropologists, however, have interpreted Geertz as moving away from Parsons by emphasizing a strong connection between culture and practice—the lived realities in which symbols come alive and which can be observed in social relations. Wuthnow believes that Geertz's perspective does privilege culture's individual connection, emphasizing culture as a subjective phenomenon; however, Geertz's emphasis on the *public* construction, apprehension, and utilization of symbolic forms seems to us equally clear (cf. Geertz 1966). Swidler, especially, has followed this latter direction.

4. In her study of Midwestern Seminary, Kleinman (1984) points to egalitarianism and community as characteristic of the normative culture (our term) of the school.

5. Wuthnow (1994) joins the cultural production and neoinstitutionalist perspectives to interpret what he calls the "production of the sacred" that occurs in various types of religious organizations and practices. We acknowledge a special debt to his work.

6. "Neoevangelicalism" is a designation for those evangelicals who reacted against strict

fundamentalists. Mostly reflecting the Calvinist or Reformed tradition, neoevangelicals sought to preserve the essentials of that tradition, including biblical inerrancy. They distanced themselves, however, from fundamentalist extremes. Billy Graham was a leader in the development of neoevangelicalism, as were Harold Lindsell, Harold J. Ockenga, and Carl F. S. Henry. They and other movement leaders developed a number of important evangelical institutions, including several seminaries and the influential evangelical journal *Christianity Today.* Various parachurch groups, such as InterVarsity Christian Fellowship, were also products of the neoevangelical movement. George Marsden (1987) refers to these institutions and networks as forming a "transdenominational" movement.

Evangelicalism is a very large and mixed phenomenon, and mapping it has become a major occupation among evangelical scholars, as, for example, Dayton and Johnston (1991). In addition to hard-core fundamentalists and "mildly" fundamentalist neoevangelicals, contemporary evangelicalism includes various groups of Pentecostals and those who stand in the Holiness tradition. Pentecostals to some extent and Holiness groups in particular represent the conservative side of the Arminian movement, while United Methodists, for example, represent its more liberal side. Other evangelical groups include various conservative Presbyterian bodies, Anabaptist groups, Campbellites, and dispensationalists.

7. For a fuller discussion of the theological antecedents of the theological and moral visions of the two schools, see Carroll and Marler 1995.

8. In their analysis of the culture wars thesis in relation to the two schools, Carroll and Marler (1995) argue that this lack of overlap is one of the factors that reduces open conflict between representatives of the two cultures. Many of the battles are fought within each culture, not between the two.

9. Both of these factors help to explain the demise of important experiments in theological education such as Inter/Met, an effort to establish a nonresidential, nontraditional seminary, based on an action-reflection educational model, which located the core educational experience within congregations and involved laity, clergy, and academics as faculty. Inter/Met was unable to compete for the resources it needed to survive or to gain legitimacy within its organizational field. See Hahn 1977 for a description and assessments of Inter/Met.

10. Freedom of inquiry, within limits, is particularly important in relation to the socialization of students, as we will note later in this chapter.

11. In her essay, Wheeler discusses both the positive and negative consequences of these various forms of specialization (see pp. 94–96).

12. For whatever reasons, studies of professional socialization, especially popular in the 1960s and 1970s, have attracted only limited attention in recent years. Among the exceptions are Kleinman (1984) and Schön (1987).

13. Even the titles of the two books reflect their contrasting perspectives.

14. For similar arguments about the importance of the structure of professional practice rather than values and attitudes internalized during professional education, see Carlin 1966; Friedson 1970; and Bucher and Stelling 1977). In somewhat similar fashion, neoinstitutionalists also reject socialization approaches in favor of cognitive models that emphasize the constraints of institutionalized schema, scripts, and categories on individual behavior (DiMaggio and Powell 1991:15).

15. In this regard, the two seminaries are what Etzioni (1976) calls "normative" rather than "coercive" organizations; that is, compliance is not coerced but rests on internalization of directives that are viewed as legitimate. There is also a "utilitarian" dimension (Etzioni's third type) to compliance. Grades and certification for future professional roles are also involved.

16. Recalling our discussion of variations among faculty at the two schools, we note that

faculty also selectively adapt to the overall culture, are isomorphic with it in its key elements, and find their own niches within the overall cultural configuration. Students are not the only ones who negotiate with the dominant culture.

17. In partial support of this hunch is Carroll's (1970) survey of a large sample of practicing clergy who had graduated from seminary between five and fifteen years previously. He found that his respondents' basic theological and ethical perspectives as well as their orientations to ordained ministry could be attributed in part to the effects of the "social climate" of the seminary that they attended. (By "social climate" he meant something similar to what we mean here by a seminary's "normative message").

CHAPTER THIRTEEN

1. See, for example, Wells 1993, 1994, and Noll 1994.

2. We have described the conditions internal to the religious communities that support the two seminaries we studied. Roman Catholicism, Judaism, and recently arrived religious groups in the United States face equally strenuous challenges. And all these groups face a common set of "external" challenges, such as rapidly increasing cultural and ethnic pluralism and changes in the age structure of the population (a change reflected in the fact that theological students in the last decade have been much older than theological students have ever been before).

3. See, for example, Farley 1983, 1989; Hough and Cobb 1985; Wood 1985; Mudflower Collective 1985; Browning 1991; Kelsey 1992, 1993; Chopp 1995.

References

Balmer, Randall. 1989. *Mine Eyes Have Seen the Glory.* New York: Oxford University Press.

Becker, Howard S., Blanche Geer, Everett C. Hughes, and Anselm Strauss. 1961. *Boys in White.* Chicago: University of Chicago Press.

Berger, Peter L., and Thomas Luckmann. 1966. *The Social Construction of Reality.* Garden City, N.Y.: 1991. Doubleday.

Bolman, Lee G., and Terrence E. Deal. 1991. *Reframing Organizations.* San Francisco: Jossey-Bass.

Brim, Orville G., and Stanton Wheeler, eds. 1966. *Socialization after Childhood.* New York: Wiley.

Browning, Don S. 1991. *A Fundamental Practical Theology.* Minneapolis: Fortress Press.

Bucher, Rue, and Joan G. Stelling. 1977. *Becoming Professional.* Beverly Hills, Calif.: Sage Publications.

Carlin, Jerome P. 1966. *Lawyers' Ethics: A Study of the New York City Bar.* New York: Russell Sage Foundation.

Carroll, Jackson W. 1970. "Seminaries and Seminarians: A Study of the Professional Socialization of Protestant Clergymen." Ph.D. diss., Princeton Theological Seminary.

Carroll, Jackson W., and Penny Long Marler. 1995. "Culture Wars?: Insights from the Ethnographies of Two Protestant Seminaries." *Sociology of Religion* 56, no. 1: 1–20.

Carroll, Jackson W., and Barbara G. Wheeler. 1987. *Report of a National Study of Doctor of Ministry Programs.* Hartford, Conn.: Hartford Seminary.

Chopp, Rebecca. 1995. *Saving Work: Feminist Practices in Theological Education.* Louisville: Westminster/John Knox.

Clark, Burton. 1970. *The Distinctive College: Reed, Antioch, and Swarthmore.* Chicago: Aldine Publishing Co.

———. 1972. "The Organizational Saga in Higher Education." *Administrative Science Quarterly* 17, no. 2: 178–84.

Clark, Burton, and Martin Trow. 1966. "The Organizational Context." In *College Peer Groups,* edited by Theodore M. Newcomb and Everett K. Wilson, 17–65. Chicago: Aldine Publishing Co.

Coxon, Anthony P. M. 1965. "A Sociological Study of the Social Recruitment, Selection and Professional Socialization of Anglican Ordinands." Ph.D. Diss., University of Leeds.

Dayton, Donald W., and Robert H. Johnston, eds. 1991. *The Variety of American Evangelism.* Knoxville: University of Tennessee Press.

DiMaggio, Paul J., and Walter W. Powell. 1983. "The Iron Cage Revisited: Institutional Isomorphism and Collective Rationality in Organizational Fields." *American Sociological Review* 48 (April): 147–60.

———. 1991. "Introduction." In *The New Institutionalism in Organizational Analysis,* edited by Walter W. Powell and Paul J. DiMaggio, 1–38. Chicago: University of Chicago Press.

Etzioni, Amitai. 1976. *A Comparative Analysis of Complex Organizations.* Revised and enlarged edition. New York: Free Press.

Farley, Edward. 1983. *Theologia: The Fragmentation and Unity of Theological Education.* Philadelphia: Fortress Press.

———. 1989. *The Fragility of Knowledge.* Philadelphia: Fortress Press.

Friedson, Eliot. 1970. *The Profession of Medicine.* New York: Dodd, Mead.

Geertz, Clifford. 1966. "Religion as a Cultural System." In *Anthropological Approaches to the Study of Religion,* edited by Michael Banton, 1–46. London: Tavistock.

———. 1973. *The Interpretation of Cultures.* New York: Basic Books.

Glaser, Barney, and Anselm Strauss. 1967. *The Discovery of Grounded Theory.* Chicago: Aldine Publishing Co.

Goldman, Ari. 1991. *The Search for God at Harvard.* New York: Random House.

Hahn, Celia A., ed. 1977. *Inter/Met: Bold Experiment in Theological Education.* Washington: Alban Institute.

Handy, Robert T. 1987. *A History of Union Theological Seminary in New York.* New York: Columbia University Press.

Hendrickson, Paul. 1983. *Seminary: A Search.* New York: Summit Books.

Hopewell, James F. 1987. *Congregation: Stories and Structure.* Philadelphia: Fortress Press.

Hough, Joseph C., and John B. Cobb. 1985. *Christian Identity and Theological Education.* Atlanta: Scholars Press.

Hunter, James Davison. 1991. *Culture Wars: The Struggle to Define America.* New York: Basic Books.

Hutchison, William R. 1992. *The Modernist Impulse in American Protestantism.* Durham: Duke University Press.

Kadushin, Charles. 1969. "The Professional Self-Concept of Music Students." *American Journal of Sociology* 75 (November): 389–404.

Keesing, Roger M. 1974. "Theories of Culture." *Annual Review of Anthropology* 3:73–97.

Kelsey, David H. 1992. *To Understand God Truly: What's Theological about Theological Education.* Louisville: Westminster/John Knox Press.

———. 1993. *Between Athens and Jerusalem: The Theological Education Debate.* Grand Rapids, Mich.: Eerdmans.

Kleinman, Sherryl. 1984. *Equals before God: Seminarians as Humanistic Professionals.* Chicago: University of Chicago Press.

Kuh, George D., and Elizabeth J. Whitt. 1988. *The Invisible Tapestry: Culture in American Colleges and Universities.* ASHE-ERIC Higher Education Report No. 1. Washington: Association for the Study of Higher Education.

Lortie, Dan C. 1959. "Laymen to Lawmen: Law School, Careers, and Professional Socialization." *Harvard Educational Review* 29 (Fall): 363–67.

Marsden, George. 1984. "The Evangelical Denomination." In *Evangelicalism and Modern America,* edited by George Marsden, vii–xvi. Grand Rapids, Mich.: Eerdmans.

———. 1987. *Reforming Fundamentalism: Fuller Seminary and the New Evangelicalism.* Grand Rapids, Mich.: Eerdmans.

Marty, Martin E. 1976. *Righteous Empire: The Protestant Experience in America.* New York: Dial Press.

Merton, Robert K., George Reader M.D., and Patricia L. Kendall, eds. 1957. *The Student-Physician.* Cambridge: Harvard University Press.

Meyer, John W., and Bryan Rowan. 1977. "Institutionalized Organizations: Formal Structure as Myth and Ceremony." *American Journal of Sociology* 83, no. 2: 240–363.

Mudflower Collective. 1985. *God's Fierce Whimsy, Christian Feminism and Theological Education.* New York: Pilgrim Press.

Noll, Mark A. 1994. *The Scandal of the Evangelical Mind.* Grand Rapids, Mich.: Eerdmans, InterVarsity Press.

Olesen, Virginia, and Elvi W. Whittaker. 1970. "Critical Notes on Sociological Studies of Professional Socialization." Translated by England Cambridge. In *Professions and Professionalization,* edited by J. A. Jackson, 181–221. Cambridge: Cambridge University Press.

Olson, Daniel V. A., and Jackson W. Carroll. 1992. "Religiously Based Politics: Religious Elites and the Public." *Social Forces* 70 (March): 765–86.

Ouichi, William G., and Alan L. Wilkins. 1985. "Organizational Culture." *Annual Review of Sociology* 11:457–83.

Parsons, Talcott. 1951. *The Social System.* New York: Free Press.

Perez, Lynn. 1995. "The Decentralization of Theological Education." *Seminary Development News* 9, no. 2 (October): 1–3.

Peshkin, Alan. 1986. *God's Choice: The Total World of a Fundamentalist Christian School.* Chicago: University of Chicago Press.

Peterson, Richard. 1965. "On a Typology of College Students." In *Research Bulletin.* Princeton: Educational Testing Service.

Powell, Walter W., and Paul J. DiMaggio, eds. 1991. *The New Institutionalism in Organizational Analysis.* Chicago: University of Chicago Press.

Roof, Wade Clark, and William McKinney. 1987. *American Mainline Religion.* New Brunswick, N.J.: Rutgers University Press.

Schön, Donald. 1983. *The Reflective Practitioner.* New York: Basic Books.

———. 1987. *Educating the Reflective Practitioner.* San Francisco: Jossey-Bass.

Simpson, Ida Harper. 1979. *From Student to Nurse.* New York: Cambridge University Press.

Smircich, Linda. 1983. "Concepts of Organizational Culture and Organizational Analysis." *Administrative Science Quarterly* 28:339–58.

Strauss, Anselm. 1987. *Qualitative Analysis for Social Scientists.* New York: Cambridge University Press.

Swidler, Anne. 1986. "Culture in Action: Symbols and Strategies." *American Sociological Review* 51:273–86.

Wagner, Melinda Bollar. 1990. *God's Schools: Choice or Compromise.* New Brunswick, N.J.: Rutgers University Press.

Wells, David F. 1993. *No Place for Truth.* Grand Rapids, Mich.: Eerdmans.

———. 1994. *God in the Wasteland.* Grand Rapids, Mich.: Eerdmans, InterVarsity Press.

Wheeler, Barbara G. 1996. "You Who Were Far Off: Religious Divisions and the Role of Religious Research." *Review of Religious Research* 37, no. 4 (June): 289–301.

———. 1993. "Critical Junctures: Theological Education Confronts Its Futures." *Annals of the American Academy of Political and Social Science* 527 (May): 84–96.

Wilkes, Paul. 1990. "The Hands That Hold," *Atlantic Monthly,* December, 59–88.

Wood, Charles M. 1985. *Vision and Discernment: An Orientation in Theological Study.* Atlanta: Scholars Press.

Wuthnow, Robert. 1988. *The Restructuring of American Religion.* Princeton: Princeton University Press.

———. 1992. *Rediscovering the Sacred.* Grand Rapids, Mich.: Eerdmans.

———. 1994. *Producing the Sacred.* Urbana: University of Illinois Press.

Index